Between the Mountains and the Sea

Dun Laoghaire-Rathdown County

PETER PEARSON

Peter Pearson is a painter by profession, but has had a lifelong interest in the protection and enhancement of historic buildings. A graduate in art history from Trinity College Dublin, he is author of a variety of architectural publications, including *Dun Laoghaire/Kingstown* (1981) and An Taisce publications such as *Restoring Your Old Building* (1984) and *Temple Bar, Saving the Area* (1985). He is co-author of *The Royal St George Yacht Club* (1987) and *The Forty Foot* (1995), and contributor to *The Book of Dun Laoghaire, The Book of Bray* (1987), *Gaskin's Irish Varieties, Dun Laoghaire Guide* (1978), *Department of the Environment Conservation Guidelines* (1996), *History of Dublin Hotels* and *History of Bewley's.*

He has been chairperson of the Drimnagh Castle conservation project since 1986, a founder member of the Dublin Civic Trust, a member of the board of directors of the Irish Architectural Archive and a member of the Heritage Council since 1996.

Between the Mountains and the Sea

Dun Laoghaire-Rathdown County

PETER PEARSON

With photographs from the author's collection
and specially-commissioned photographs
by Robert Vance

THE O'BRIEN PRESS
DUBLIN

First published 1998 by The O'Brien Press Ltd.
20 Victoria Road, Rathgar, Dublin 6, Ireland.
Tel. +353 1 4923333 Fax. +353 1 4922777
e-mail: books@obrien.ie
website: http://www.obrien.ie

ISBN 0-86278-582-0

British Library Cataloguing-in-publication Data
Pearson, Peter, 1955-
Between the mountains and the sea : Dun Laoghaire/Rathdown County
1.Architecture - Ireland - Dublin 2.Dublin (Ireland) - Social conditions
I.Title
941.8'35

1 2 3 4 5 6 7 8 9 10
98 99 00 01 02 03 04 05 06

Typesetting, layout, editing, design: The O'Brien Press Ltd.
Index: Muire Spring
Maps: Design Image
Jacket illustrations – Front: A nineteenth-century view of Killiney Bay by Patrick Duffy
courtesy Gorry Gallery. Bellevue, Blackrock by Robert Vance. Front flap: Dun Laoghaire
about 1940 Gillman collection
Endpapers – Front: From Harvey's panoramic view of County Dublin, c. 1850
Back: The departure of Queen Victoria from Kingstown Harbour, 1849
Printing: MPG Books

The O'Brien Press receives
assistsance from

The Arts Council
An Chomhairle Ealaíon

Published in association with
Dun Laoghaire-Rathdown County Council

Contents

To Phil

Acknowledgements

I would like to pay special tribute to Mr Daniel Gillman of Bray, a sprightly nonogenarian and longtime resident of the Dun Laoghaire area, who made available his outstanding collection of photographs, prints, maps and pictures, together with his great knowledge of houses, family history and past events.

I would also like to remember Kathleen Turner, Paddy Gallagher, William Stuart, Mariga Guinness and Matt Byrne, all of whom greatly loved their country's heritage.

Work began on this book in 1987, and many people have helped since that time. If I have omitted anybody from the following list it is not by intent, but only because so much time has passed! The book is dedicated to Phil Stewart, who for a long time, along with our sons Adam and Jerome, has lived with the writing, maps, pictures and visits to places and buildings. Many other people have contributed in many different ways – some provided information about places or people while others lent photographs.

I would like to thank the O'Brien Press, especially Michael O'Brien, Íde ní Laoghaire and Ivan O'Brien, for taking on the job of publishing the book within a very short space of time. Thanks also to Lynn, Aoife, Muire, Eoin, Dolores and all the staff, who have made a great contribution. I would especially like to thank Donal Marren, former Cathaoirleach of Dun Laoghaire-Rathdown County, the Irish Georgian Society and the School of Irish Studies for their generous support and help. Particular thanks must go to Robert Vance for touring around every part of the Dun Laoghaire-Rathdown County to take photographs for the book, also to Mark Boland and Terry McDonagh for additional photographs of Blackrock and Dalkey, and John Stafford for a picture of Longford Terrace. A special acknowledgement is due to Kevin B. Nowlan for reading and commenting on the text at the early stages.

I would like to thank the staff at the National Library, especially the director Brendan O'Donoghue, Matthew of the conservation department, Elizabeth Kirwan and Gerry Kavanagh, and the curator of manuscripts Noel Kissane; thanks also all the staff in the Dun Laoghaire, Blackrock, Stillorgan, Dalkey, Deansgrange, Dundrum and Glencullen public libraries. Thank you to the staff and photographer at the national archives; Siobhán and all the staff at the Royal Irish Academy: Dorothy Kelly, Siobhán D'Oir and all the staff at the Royal Society of Antiquaries of Ireland; David Griffin and the staff of the Irish Architectural Archive; the staff at the Bord Fáilte photo library; Andrew Bonar Law for the use of Saunder's sketches; Colin Scudds for information about Corrig Castle; Mrs Barbara Clark for slides of Shanganagh Castle; Neville Figgis for the book about Stillorgan; Robin Goodbody for sharing his wide knowledge of local history; Colin Houlihan for his auction brochures and newspaper cuttings; Arnold Horner of the Department of Geography, UCD, for advice about maps; John O'Sullivan for useful photocopies about Dun Laoghaire; the Murphys, late of Danesmote; Philip and Patsy Harvey; Michael McGovern for his photo of 'the big tree'; Mr Dennis Kelleher of Shanganagh Castle. Thanks to the secretary of Leopardstown Park Hospital, Noreen Quinn of Riversdale, Brother Jarlath of the Order of St John of God, Mr Rawson of Kill Abbey, Sister Brigid Clare of Dunardagh, Sr Catherine Leonard of St Raphaela's, Fr Farragher of Blackrock College, Sr Power of Mount Anville, Mr Corrigan of Wyckham, the Christian Brothers, Sr Joseph of Lourdes Hospital, the Walkers of Fernhill, the Embassy of The Netherlands, the British Embassy, the sisters of the Cluny Convent, Brother Gregory of St Benildus and Sr Veronica of Kilmacud House.

I would also like to thank the following for their co-operation and help, including the many owners who allowed their buildings to be inspected and photographed: Angela Alexander, Anne Brady, James Adam & Son, Bruce Arnold, Brigid Aylmer, Robbie Brennan, Mary Bryan, Edith Byrne, Mr and Mrs Carroll, Alison Carter, Hugh and Maureen Charlton, Mark Cochrane, Dr Maurice Craig, Fergus D'Arcy, Sylvia Dockeray, John Doyle of H. J.

Byrne in Bray, Dr G. D. Doyle, the staff of the European Foundation (Loughlinstown), Anna and Tony Farmar, Alexis Fitzgerald, Christopher Fettes (St Columba's College), Desmond Fitzgerald the Knight of Glin, Finnegan Menton, Orla Gallagher, Teresa and James Gorry of the Gorry Gallery, Dublin, Father Elton Griffin (of the Carmelite Friars), Dr John de Courcy Ireland, Fred Hamond, Mrs Heatley, James Howley, Paddy Healy, Billy Hodnett, Rob Kyle, the Kelly's of Rosefield, Mr and Mrs F. Jackson, Mr Noel Judd, Niall Higgins, Sara Kenny of Hamilton Osborne King, Mr and Mrs Law, Deirdre Kelly, Mr Gerry Kinsella, the Kylemore Clinic, Michael Lynch of Fingal County Parks Department, Cormac Louth, Ken and Cynthia McLenaghan, Mrs McCormack, Pat McAfee, Mrs Vicky Mason, Stella Mew, Caroline and Barney Mullins, the Marist Fathers at Casino, Mary McGrath, the McKenna family, Philip McNamara, the O'Connell FitzSimon family, Hugh O'Connor, Freddie O'Dwyer, Gerard O'Kelly, Mr Terry O'Malley, Lindis Page for her help with typing, Mr Con Power, Mrs Lucy O'Kelly, Carl and Leonora O'Sullivan, the Earl of Pembroke, Leslie Roberts, David and Veronica Rowe, John and Jane Ryan, Nick and Georgina Roche, Fergus and Kathleen Rowan, the Order of St John of God in Stillorgan, Fr Mitchell of St Columba's Church in Ballybrack, the staff at St Michael's House (Prospect Hall), Paddy Shaffrey, Ruth Sheehy, Mr Bob Smith, Pia Bang Stokes, Leo Swan, the late Mr and Mrs Tomkins, UCD's buildings office and the faculties of architecture and law, Geoffrey and Michael Willis, Jeremy Williams, Geraldine Walsh and Mrs Anne Wilson.

Picture Credits

Illustrations from author's collection: pages 3, 4, 8, 9, 23 (bottom), 26 (all), 27, 28, 30 (both), 33 (top), 35 (both), 37 (both), 38 (all), 39, 40, 41 (both), 42(both), 43, 45, 47 (top), 49, 50, 51, 53, 55, 56, 57 (all), 59, 60, 61, 62 (top & centre), 63 (top), 66 (top), 68 (all), 69 (all), 70, 71(bottom), 72, 73 (both), 74 (bottom), 75, 79, 80, 81 (both), 82 (top), 83 (both), 84, 87, 90 (top), 91 (both), 95, 96 (bottom), 98, 100 (all), 101, 103, 104 (top pair), 106 (top), 108 (all), 110 (top), 112, 113 (all), 115 (both), 116, 117, 118, 119, 123, 124 (bottom), 127, 128, 129, 130, 131, 137 (all), 138 (both), 139 (top), 141 (top), 142 (top pair), 143 (bottom), 144 (both), 145, 147 (both), 149, 150, 152 (both), 153 (all), 154, 158 (both), 159 (both), 161 (all), 162 (all), 163 (bottom), 164 (bottom pair), 165 (top), 166 (bottom), 167 (bottom), 168 (bottom), 169, 170 (both), 171 (top), 173, 174 (both), 176 (top pair), 177, 179 (both), 180 (bottom), 182 (both), 183 (both), 184 (both), 185 (all), 186 (both), 188 (both), 189 (top), 190 (bottom pair), 191 (top pair), 192 (bottom), 193 (both), 194 (both), 195 (both), 196 (both), 197 (bottom left), 198 (bottom), 199, 200 (both), 201 (top & bottom), 202 (all), 203 (both), 204 (all), 205 (both), 206, 208 (bottom), 209 (all), 210, 215 (both), 216 (both), 217 (both), 218 (both), 219 (both), 220 (top), 221 (bottom), 222 (both), 223, 224 (both), 226, 227, 228 (both), 230 (bottom), 231 (both), 232, 233, 234 (bottom), 235, 236 (top), 237 (bottom), 239 (bottom), 240, 241 (top), 242, 244 (bottom), 245 (all), 246 (top pair), 247 (all), 248 (top pair), 250, 254 (top), 255 (bottom & centre), 256 (bottom), 258 (bottom), 260 (bottom), 261 (bottom), 262 (top), 264 (centre), 266 (bottom), 271 (top), 273, 274, 275 (top), 276 (both), 277 (both), 278 (both), 279 (both), 281 (both), 283, 284 (bottom), 285 (bottom), 286, 287, 291 (bottom), 293 (top pair), 294 (both), 295 (top), 297 (bottom), 299 (bottom), 301 (top pair), 306 (both), 307 (both), 308 (bottom), 309 (bottom), 310 (bottom), 311 (both), 313 (bottom pair), 315 (bottom), 316 (bottom), 318 (top), 319 (both), 322 (top), 323, 325 (bottom), 326, 327 (bottom), 329, 330, 331 (both), 332 (top), 333 (bottom), 334 (all), 335, 336 (both), 338 (centre), 339 (bottom), 340 (top), 341 (bottom), 343 (both), 346 (both), 347, 348 (both), 349 (top), 352 (all), 353 (top pair), 354, 357 (bottom), 358 (bottom), 360 (all), 361 (both), 362 (top)

New photographs by Robert Vance: pages 28 (top), 36 (both), 44, 46, 58 (bottom), 59 (top), 61 (bottom), 62 (bottom), 65, 70 (bottom pair), 71 (top), 75 (bottom), 76 (bottom), 77, 78, 85, 92 (top), 96 (top), 102 (top), 135 (bottom), 176 (bottom), 187, 197 (bottom right), 207 (bottom), 230 (top), 238 (top), 239 (top), 251, 254 (bottom), 256 (top), 259 (bottom), 260 (top), 261 (top), 264 (top), 265, 268, 270 (bottom), 272, 285 (top), 292 (both), 293 (bottom), 295 (bottom), 296 (bottom), 298 (bottom), 299 (top), 302 (bottom), 303 (both), 308 (top), 309 (top), 310 (top), 312, 313 (top), 314 (top), 320 (bottom pair), 321, 324 (bottom), 325 (top), 337 (both), 338 (top & bottom), 344(bottom), 345, 350 (both), 351 (top left), 353 (bottom)

Illustrations from the collection of Daniel Gillman: pages 1, 2, 11 (bottom), 24, 29 (top), 47 (bottom), 48 (bottom), 49 (bottom), 54, 58 (top), 63 (centre), 67, 89 (bottom), 90 (bottom), 93 (top pair), 94 (bottom), 97, 99 (bottom), 102 (bottom), 105 (both), 106 (bottom), 107 (all), 109, 110 (bottom), 114, 120 (bottom), 121 (both), 122 (top), 125, 139 (bottom), 140 (top pair), 141 (bottom), 146, 148, 156, 165 (bottom), 172, 189 (bottom), 192 (top), 229, 236 (bottom pair), 246 (bottom), 248 (bottom), 252 (top), 262 (bottom), 269, 271 (bottom), 280 (top left), 284 (top), 300, 302 (top), 304, 315 (top), 316 (top), 31 7(top), 328 (both), 339 (top), 341 (top), 344 (top), 349 (bottom), 355 (top), 358 (top)

James Adam & Son: page 314 (bottom); F. E. Ball: pages 64 (bottom), 327 (top), 355 (bottom); Mark Boland: pages 94 (top), 201 (top left), 207 (top), 234 (top), 241 (bottom), 243 (both); Andrew Bonar-Law: pages 20, 45 (top), 318 (bottom), 324 (top); Edith Byrne: page 190 (top); Christies: page 298 (top); Mrs. Barbara Clark: pages 31 (top), 32 (all), 33 (bottom); Miss Deane-Oliver: page 25; Hugh Doran: page 359 (both); The Earl of Pembroke: page 213 (top); Finnegan Menton: pages 175, 197 (top); The Fitzwilliam Museum, Cambridge: pages 211 (bottom), 212 (both), 213 (bottom); Robin Goodbody: page 317 (bottom); David Griffin: page 253; Guinness Ireland Group: pages 180 (top), 320 (top); *Porter's Directory*: pages 155, 22, 23 (top); Hamilton Osborne King: pages 21 (top), 333 (top); Bill Hodnett: pages 220 (bottom), 221 (top pair); The Irish Architectural Archive: pages 29 (bottom), 74 (top), 140 (bottom pair), 142 (bottom), 357 (both), 362 (bottom pair); The *Irish Press*: pages 208 (top), 257, 297; Paul Kerrigan: page 124 (top); Terry MacDonagh: pages 86, 88 (bottom), 89 (top pair), 104 (bottom); Michael McGovern: page 52 (bottom); The National Archives: pages 211 (top), 214 (both), 244 (top), 252 (bottom), 258 (top), 266 (top), 322 (bottom), 351 (top & bottom); The National Gallery of Ireland: page 340 (bottom); The National Library of Ireland: pages 21, 31 (bottom), 60 (bottom), 64 (top), 66 (bottom), 67 (bottom), 76 (top), 99 (top), 112 (bottom), 132, 135 (top), 143 (top), 151, 157 (both), 160 (both), 164 (top), 167, 171 (bottom), 178, 181, 198 (top), 225, 237 (top), 238 (bottom), 249, 270 (top), 275 (bottom), 296 (top), 332 (bottom), 342 (top); The O'Brien Press: pages 255 (top), 342 (bottom); The Ordnance Survey of Ireland: pages 27 (top), 52 (top), 92 (bottom), 280 (centre), 288 (top); Derek Pearson: page 166 (top); Con Power/Fergus D'Arcy: page 280 (top & bottom); *The Irish Builder*: pages 134, 288 (bottom); Leslie Roberts: page 259 (top); Manning Robertson: pages 93 (bottom), 168 (top); The Royal Society of Antiquaries of Ireland: page 63 (bottom); Hazel Smith: pages 263 (both), 267; John Stafford: page 191 (bottom); Glascott Symes: pages 289, 290, 291 (top); W. F. Wakeman: pages 56 (top), 84 (bottom), 120, 301 (bottom)

Introduction
The County and Its History

The history of the area described in this book is very closely bound up with the story of Dublin itself. Many of the inhabitants of the houses described were successful merchants and business people, noted artists, or were involved with the politics of the day, either for or against the establishment. In politics, people like Lord Edward Fitzgerald, Robert Emmet, Lord Fitzgibbon and Michael Davitt come to mind, while writers such as George Bernard Shaw and Samuel Beckett, as well as the painter William Orpen could be mentioned.

Much of the wealth which enabled these houses to be built was generated in Dublin, and their owners commuted to and from the city. Fortunes were made in coal, shipping, wine and spirits, tanning and leather, and even in such unlikely enterprises as manufacturing buttons or pins! Great Victorian entrepreneurs like William Dargan spent much time in their Dublin offices, but lived outside the city. The people who lived in the lesser houses of the county often worked in the capital or found employment in the local big houses, institutions or businesses.

The entire county of Dublin consists of a large area on the east coast of Ireland which stretches some forty miles from north to south and runs inland for about twenty miles. Its shape is irregular and it is bordered on the east by the Irish Sea, with Dublin Bay and the capital at its centre. To the south lie the Dublin mountains and County Wicklow, while from the west the river Liffey flows in from the plains of County Kildare.

County Dublin is now sub-divided into three new regions: Fingal County to the north, South County to the south-west, and Dun Laoghaire-Rathdown County to the south east.

The subject of this book is the Dun Laoghaire-Rathdown County, an area which falls between the Dublin mountains and the sea. Merrion strand at Booterstown and the river Dodder at Milltown form part of the western boundary of this administrative district, while the town of Bray lies just beyond its most southerly limits.

This area was described in 1846 by the *Parliamentary Gazetteer of Ireland* as 'a Maritime Barony – it contains the beautiful and

brilliant sweep of coast from Blackrock round by Dalkey and Killiney to Bray ... The other parts of the Barony consist, in a general view, of rich champaign ground, and are very profusely powdered with mansions and villas and embellished with wood, shrubbery, lawn and garden.'

Once a completely rural area, its green fields have been steadily disappearing over the past thirty-five years under an advancing tide of new roads, houses and other developments. Dublin is a thriving and busy metropolis, and the Dun Laoghaire-Rathdown County is now probably the wealthiest and most prosperous district of Dublin, if not of the whole country.

Visitors who have been away from Dublin for more than ten years find it hard to believe that Ireland has changed so much, and can scarcely recognise Dublin city and its surroundings. The built-up patchwork which now makes up the greater Dublin area is changing by the day, with ever-increasing speed. Now, in the last decades of the twentieth century, we are witnessing the greatest and fastest period of change that has ever affected the county during its long history. A great many of the old buildings and houses described in this book have disappeared and have been replaced with new buildings. However, much still remains despite the constant pressure to re-develop and to build on every available piece of land.

The County of Dublin has existed as an administrative district since Norman times. A county belonged to the king and was an area for which he delegated power to a local lord. The Normans created counties throughout Ireland, giving control to a local lord or count, who in turn appointed a sheriff to police his lands. It is said that King John was the first monarch to formalise the establishment of counties of Ireland in general and of County Dublin in particular.

It would appear that this process evolved gradually and was only completed in 1605 when County Wicklow was created by

carving a piece out of what had once been a much larger County Dublin. During the sixteenth century County Dublin stretched from Arklow to Skerries and was, in theory, under the control of the king. In reality, much of this mountainous territory in the southern half was in fact dominated by the O'Tooles and the O'Byrnes, and the inhabitants of County Dublin protected themselves by erecting a defensive ditch – The Pale. Church lands were excluded from the control of the county and these were usually marked by the presence of a stone cross. Several of these crosses survive, such as those at Tully, Rathmichael, Kilgobbin and Jamestown. It is said that the barony of Uppercross, which takes in much of the lands to the west of the river Dodder, was named after such 'cross' lands.

The barony of Rathdown extended south of the river Dodder all the way into County Wicklow. Half of this barony now lies in County Wicklow while the other 'half barony of Rathdown', which lay in County Dublin until 1993, now constitutes the Dun Laoghaire-Rathdown County. The boundaries of County Dublin have never remained absolute and certain areas have been swapped in the interests of better administration – for example, until the recent reorganisation of the county Rathfarnham and Howth lay under the control of Dublin Corporation which made little geographical sense.

Dublin city, with its own corporation, has always remained independent of the administration of the county. During the nineteenth century a number of local urban district councils were established, including Blackrock, Killiney, Dalkey and Kingstown. The Kingstown Town Commissioners were set up in 1834, and were later renamed the Kingstown Urban District Council, which in turn became Dun Laoghaire Corporation in 1920. The Blackrock Town Commissioners came into existence in 1860, and built a town hall some five years later. The township of Killiney, Ballybrack and Loughlinstown was formed in 1866, and the Dalkey Town Commissioners were established during the 1860s and acquired a town hall in 1868.

The Local Government Act of 1898 meant that the general electorate could vote in local elections as previously only ratepayers were eligible. This still excluded women, unless they had a college qualification.

The power of the County Council in its first twenty-five years of existence was limited, and it was only in 1930, under the Local Government Act that the responsibilities of the old urban district councils, rural district councils and the former Rathdown Board of Guardians were all brought together. The Rathdown Board of Guardians was responsible for running the workhouse at Loughlinstown.

After 1930 the new Dublin County Council became responsible for a wide range of services including refuse disposal, water supply, drainage, housing, roads, libraries and parks. The science of 'planning', which is a twentieth-century practice aimed at directing and controlling the development of an area, was added to the council's duties, and this has become a complicated study in its own right.

The first meeting of the new Dublin County Council was held in Kilmainham courthouse in 1898, but in 1900 Number 11 Parnell Square was acquired as a headquarters. Between the years 1941-8, the County Council was dissolved and a commissioner was appointed to run its affairs. During this period a coat of arms was created for the County Council by the Genealogical Office. The coat of arms bears a raven standing on a hurdle, which represents the raven of Fingal standing on the hurdle ford of Dublin (Báile Átha Cliath). In 1991 a new Local Government Act created the opportunity to divide the unwieldy county council area from a single entity into three separate areas each with its own administration. This resulted in the counties of Fingal, South Dublin and Dun Laoghaire-Rathdown.

The Borough of Dun Laoghaire was established by the Local Government Act of 1930 and matters of policy concerning the administration and development of the area were decided by the elected council. Dun Laoghaire Corporation was dissolved in

1994 and was amalgamated with part of the old Dublin County Council to become a new body – Dun Laoghaire-Rathdown County County. Dun Laoghaire town hall was chosen as its headquarters, and following the addition of a major new building it has become the County Hall. The old corporation, during its sixty-four years in existence, was administered by a borough manager who also acted as town clerk. Among the many responsibilities of the corporation since the 1930s has been the provision of water, sewage and drainage, maintenance of public health, bathing establishments, weights and measures and shop inspections, municipal parks, rubbish collection, road maintenance, public lighting, cleansing, fire brigade and ambulance, town planning, housing, allotments, public open spaces/parks, public libraries and vocational education. Water was supplied to the area from Dublin Corporation's Vartry water scheme, although some of the old urban district councils had earlier constructed their own reservoirs, such as the one at Killiney Hill.

Prior to 1893, all sewage was discharged untreated into the sea at various points along the coast. Three years later sewers were laid in Blackrock and Dun Laoghaire which intercepted all the various schemes and brought the sewage to a central tank where it was pumped through a three-quarter-mile long pipe, out into the sea. The Public Health Department was a combined function of the Dublin County Council and Dun Laoghaire Corporation and concerned itself with such things as insanitary dwellings, child welfare and dairies. For example, in 1936 there were forty-nine cow keepers and eighty-seven 'purveyors of milk' within the

Dun Laoghaire borough area. The corporation provided a considerable area of land mainly at Booterstown slobs and Castlepark Road for allotments, and many of those who availed of these were unemployed. The average size of an allotment was one-ninth of an acre, and 'each man received £2 worth of seeds, free implements and some loads of manure' (*Dun Laoghaire, Its History, Scenery and Development*, Manning Robertson, 1936). The curiously-named activity known as 'road scavenging', which involved clearing and sweeping the roads, was carried out by direct labour, while the construction and maintenance of roads was mostly done by contract.

Dun Laoghaire Corporation possessed a refuse destructor since the 1890s in which rubbish was burned, but by 1930 dumping was carried out at the Rock Road to reclaim land for Blackrock Park and in certain disused quarries. Compared with today, the quantity of household waste and rubbish generated was slight. Now, having exhausted all the landfill sites where millions of tons of unsorted rubbish was dumped, a new initiative has come from all the local authorities in the Dublin area with the principal emphasis on sorting and recycling all kinds of waste.

The Kingstown Urban District Council and later Dun Laoghaire Corporation erected a very substantial number of local authority houses over the last century. Between 1888, when the first of the municipal housing schemes was undertaken, at Victoria Buildings in Blackrock, and 1936, over 1500 houses and flats were erected by the local authority to accommodate the homeless and the less well-off. In 1936 a large house-building scheme of 146 houses was begun at Monkstown Farm. Dublin County Council also constructed many stone-built cottages and other houses during the same period.

In 1936 there were sixty-eight acres of public open space in the Borough of Dun Laoghaire, including Blackrock Park, Marine Gardens, the People's Park, the Salthill Gardens, Sandycove Gardens, Coliemore Park, Sorrento Park, Vico Road and Killiney Hill. Later, Dalkey Hill and quarry were purchased to enlarge the Killiney Hill Park. For many years Dun Laoghaire Corporation provided public baths with excellent facilities at Blackrock and Dun Laoghaire.

*   *   *

The scope of this account of the Dun Laoghaire-Rathdown County is mainly concentrated on the visible and tangible remains of its history, namely the built environment. The architectural heritage of any suburb of a great city will always be vulnerable, and is likely to be the first casualty of 'progress'. Unfortunately, the protection of historic buildings in Ireland has been weak, and the listing of houses and buildings of

architectural significance has only ever happened in a random way. Even an important building such as Rathfarnam Castle came close to having a housing estate built on its doorstep. Others were less fortunate, like Frescati in Blackrock, which was demolished after a ten-year conservation battle. If we had Frescati today, a house whose great depth of historical association with Lord Edward Fitzgerald, one of the leaders of the 1798 rebellion, which is so well documented, would we not treasure it as a national monument?

However, during the last ten years there has been a considerable change in Ireland in people's attitude towards the architectural heritage. A value has been put on significant old buildings, and in many cases on other structures such as cottages and humble stone buildings. People now see the worth of stone walls and will sometimes fight to protect this kind of craftsmanship in their area.

More than anything else it has been the houses, both large and small, and usually standing in their own grounds, whose numbers have been most decimated. At least a hundred important old houses have been demolished in the former County Dublin since the 1960s and many more have also disappeared. An old house, whether standing on half an acre or on fifteen acres, presented an opportunity for development, and generally speaking the house was regarded as a nuisance, and would eventually be demolished.

Many of those which have survived did so because their role was changed from family residence to institutional uses whether religious, educational or hospital. Where there was once a scene of great opulence and grandeur, with gardens and farms run on model lines, there was now a new purpose, often providing a place of refuge for the sick, the blind or the mentally disturbed.

Other interesting ventures are also taking place, for instance in the Dun Laoghaire-Rathdown County three major projects are underway which will provide new attractions and places of interest for the public. Cabinteely House, with its restored walled garden, will be opened as a museum of carriages and vintage cars, while the gardens at Old Connaught are being carefully restored by Emplagri, a charitable trust. The Overend's house at Dundrum has also been left in trust to the nation, and will be opened to the public as a model organic farm.

The building of new roads, especially of dual carriageways like the Shankill bypass or the Blackrock bypass, has radically changed the appearance of familiar places throughout the Dun Laoghaire-Rathdown area. Though there are obviously many benefits in terms of traffic management in a city where over a million people live, and though such roads may seem so convenient to many motorists, the scale and extent of the engineering works

has also created great losses in the natural and historic environment. The proposed South-Eastern motorway which will link up with the Southern Cross Road, will have the most profound effect on the Rathmichael, Carrickmines, Kilgobbin, Sandyford and Rathfarnam areas. For instance, it will mean that most of the Rathmichael and Cherrywood Glen district will be subject to huge earthworks and changes in the landscape, and later, when it is complete, areas will be divided in two and residents will always hear the rumble of traffic, even at a considerable distance.

Such roads have encouraged us to speed past in our cars, oblivious to the character and identity of an area, and making it impossible for us to notice important features like an old tree, a Victorian postbox or a milestone. The cry of progress has always be the loudest, often without consideration for the historical context of where we live or for the longterm view. Open space, groups of trees and hedgerows have been relentlessly diminished, so that the concept of any kind of 'green belt' is very hard to realise.

Here and there we find gaps in the patchwork of development, like the Liffey valley, Santry woods and the lands at Loughlinstown. But how long can such areas last without some special protection?

Back in the late 1930s it was proposed that Dublin should have a green belt surrounding it to preserve the countryside around the city for the benefit of its inhabitants. It was suggested that an absolute limit should be created, beyond which no further building would be permitted. Strict controls of this kind have been implemented in other countries.

One of the most ironic results of the impersonal suburbia which much of County Dublin has become is the mania for nostalgia. The widespread loss of identity and history has led to an often superficial interest in the past and a taste for pseudo-

historical styles, whether in the guise of neo-Georgian housing estates, Tudor-style townhouses, or fake Victorian shopfronts. There are also many examples of 'olde worlde' pubs, (some thatched) crammed with old books and faked-up memorabilia in the area.

While the demand for so called ' period' houses is always on the increase, much that is genuinely old and of historical worth continues to be lost. There are virtually no genuine thatched cottages left in the county, yet some of the highest prices ever paid in this country have been given for old properties which are described in this book.

It is my hope that this publication may help in the rediscovery of the identity of Dun Laoghaire-Rathdown County; it will record what has been lost and make the case for protecting what is worthwhile in what is left. As G. O. Simms wrote in his portrait of Tullow parish: 'There is a tradition to be traced and appreciated in every locality. Pride of place is a legitimate indulgence.' He went on: 'Prisoners of history are those who know little of the culture and civilisation in the background of their neighbourhood – if it is unwise to forget our history, it is important also to understand it, by searching for all kinds of information, gleaned from tombstone or register, or by word of mouth.'

A study such as this must be subjective and selective, as the sheer size of the area under consideration is so great, its history so varied, and its architecture so full of interest. The book is laid out area by area, and the built heritage of each district is examined accordingly; thus the focus may be on the remains of a medieval castle, a Victorian house or a twentieth-century church. In each section there will be a description of the area and an overview of its historical development. An attempt will be made to place the various buildings in their chronological context.

The study of Ordnance Survey maps has played a vital part in piecing together the historical jigsaw. The Ordnance Survey was established in 1824, originally to provide accurate military intelligence and to present a correct assessment of the extent of property holdings, for taxation purposes. Its work coincided with the period when the population of Ireland was at its greatest, and so the first maps, which are of a very high quality, provide a valuable record of the settlement of both urban and rural areas. The Ordnance Survey was also responsible for arriving at definitive or 'official' names for places where there had sometimes been doubt.

Naturally, a book such as this must pay tribute to previous publications which covered the same ground, amongst which authors John Archer, Francis Elrington Ball, John D'Alton, Samuel Lewis and Weston St John Joyce must be mentioned.

The research for this book comes from many sources. It has drawn on many printed references, many excellent local histories

and maps, early pictures, drawings and photographs. In some cases original documents such as leases or account books have provided valuable information, but a great deal has been learned from actual visits to almost all of the buildings which are mentioned. Careful examination of buildings and places has provided fresh information about their history and date. Personal recollections and word-of-mouth stories have also been very useful. Newspaper articles, especially from the last thirty years, are sometimes the only record of recent events in local history.

In writing about the county, it seemed reasonable to begin at Shankill in the south, on the borders of County Wicklow, where we also examine the history of Rathmichael and Loughlinstown. We then follow the varied coastline through Killiney and Ballybrack, past Dalkey Island and into Dublin Bay. From Dalkey we move to Sandycove, Glenageary and Deansgrange. Next comes Dun Laoghaire and Monkstown, then Blackrock, Mount Merrion and Booterstown. Stillorgan leads us into Kilmacud, Leopardstown, Foxrock, Carrickmines and Cabinteely. We look then at the area around Kilternan and the foothills of the Dublin mountains. Lastly, the book examines the regions of Dundrum, Windy Arbour, Roebuck and Clonskeagh, and finishes with Churchtown and part of Rathfarnham.

On this journey, we will discover a county full of variety. It includes what is probably the finest artificial harbour in Ireland at Dun Laoghaire, and three large parks formed out of the demesnes of Cabinteely, Killiney and Marlay, with large tracts of unspoilt mountain landscape and several beaches which are all accessible to the public.

There are some very historic houses and castles in the area and a good number of interesting churches. Many of the Victorian terraced houses of County Dublin are now listed buildings and are well cared for. The industrial heritage has fared less well, and there are few enough mills or forges left. But in this district we have inherited the first railway line in Ireland and a fine collection of railway stations, bridges and viaducts. The county at present has one motorway, which will eventually be connected by means of the South-Eastern and Southern Cross routes to the M50 and to all the main roads which radiate out from Dublin.

Dun Laoghaire-Rathdown County is part of the great hinterland of Dublin city and owes its origin to that city. Many would consider the county to be as much part of Dublin as O'Connell Street or St Stephen's Green. The county is undoubtedly a suburb, with its many residential areas, but it is also the playground and garden of the capital.

CHAPTER 1

Shankill

Shankill Castle

The name Shankill, meaning 'old church' from *sean chill*, applies to a large area stretching from the sea to Carrickgolligan, which was once called Shankill Mountain. Shankill Castle stands below this hill on Ferndale Road, which joins Loughlinstown with the village of Old Connaught.

The ruined castle has a large vaulted undercroft from which a wide and lurching spiral staircase ascends to a roofless space above. This large chamber, with its two mullioned windows, was once the hall of the castle, and though at present full of vegetation, its current owner hopes eventually to re-roof it. Shankill Castle is, apart from the church ruins at Rathmichael, one of the earliest surviving structures in the area.

Shankill Castle, 1797, sketch by James Saunders

A sketch of 1797 by James Saunders of Trinity College Dublin (sketchbook in private collection) shows the roofed castle, with its attached house which was a typical dwelling from about 1740 with a central gable and small porch. There was a small, oval, attic window in the gable, a feature of such early houses. The house was considerably altered in the early nineteenth century when Tudor-style windows were inserted and extra gables were added. The sketch also shows a collection of thatched farm buildings in the vicinity of the castle and a dovecote attached to the castle wall.

Shankill Castle is said to have been built in the fifteenth century by the Lawless family, who were of Norman origin and had previously lived at Shanganagh Castle. The property later passed by marriage to a member of another Norman family, Robert Barnewall of Drimnagh Castle.

In the fields behind the castle are a group of modern houses, conspicuously situated on the sloping hillside.

Shanganagh Castle

John Taylor's map of 1814 shows the three surviving medieval castles of the district: Shankill, Shanganagh and Puck's. However, two other early castles, which had existed at Loughlinstown and Old Connaught, had by this time either disappeared or been replaced.

Shanganagh Castle, now in ruins, occupies one of the oldest inhabited sites in the area. In 1654 it was described as having two orchards, a garden, a grove of ash trees set for ornament and a mill. The thatched

castle was burnt down in 1783 and was then used as a barn – the memory of this function survives today in the name of a nearby house 'Barn Close', one of a pair of late Georgian-style houses.

The mills continued in use and were probably rebuilt during the eighteenth century, along with a millhouse and a kiln. The millhouse survives and vestiges of the former mill race can still be seen. A map of the Roberts estate of 1826 shows all of these buildings as well as the nearby Abingdon House, which is depicted as a typical two-storey, eighteenth-century farmhouse.

Watercolour by William Westall, 1810, showing the intact ruin of Shanganagh Castle with Killiney, as yet undeveloped, in the background

Shankill – the Village

Shankill, now by-passed by the N11 motorway since 1991, lay on the route of every traveller to the south. It was a small village on the main coach road to Bray, Wicklow and beyond. Even in the eighteenth century there were frequent complaints about the condition of the road. The diary of Judge Day of Loughlinstown House, written in the early nineteenth century, describes the breakdown of carriages on the main road outside his gates as well as various accidents.

In 1818 'the abstract of presentments at Michaelmas term', part of the official parish records, informs us that John Farran and David Towson were paid £2 11s 4d for making a curb to the footpath along the mail-coach road at Shankill.

Not surprisingly, coach-building and forging became important trades in the area and in 1911 *Porter's Post Office Guide and Directory* carried two advertisements from coach-building firms: De Arcy of Loughlinstown and Murphy of Shankill. They were advertised as builders of dog carts, governess and outside cars, vans and lorries of all descriptions!

Nearby, horses were shod and other repairs made at J. J. Doyle's

Roberts estate map from c. 1826, showing Shanganagh Castle and village, with mills, barns and cottages clustered around the castle

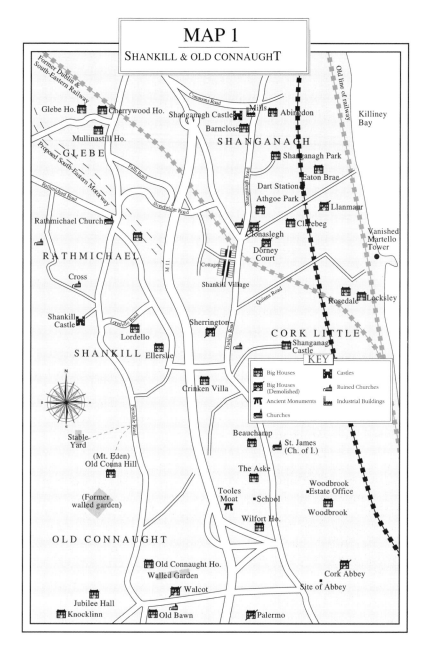

MAP 1
SHANKILL & OLD CONNAUGHT

Doyle's Forge won many prizes
for skilled work as farriers

forge which was established in the early 1800s and was once attached to a Victorian house with a pretty garden in front. No trace of these activities remains in Shankill today, which is a pity as the village was once famous for the manufacture of horse shoes. Shoeing horses was Doyle's main business, and they were kept very busy with all the horses belonging to the gentry, the workhouse and a local bakery.

A ledger from the 1920 period gives a good picture of the work of the forge at that time. Among their many clients in 1924 we find Lieutenant Colonel Erck, whose nearby house, Sherrington, will be discussed shortly. Doyle's charged Colonel Erck 4/- for making hold fasts for the gutters, 2/- for repairs to a potato digger and £2 for cutting oats.

Other clients included Wentworth Allen of Shanganagh Castle, Captain Riall of Old Connaught and Sir Stanley Cochrane of Woodbrook. Apart from shoeing horses, Doyle's were much in demand for erecting fences. Hundreds of yards of barbed-wire fencing were put up at Barrington Jellet's orchard at Clonard in Dundrum and a new boundary fence was erected for Charles T. Wallis of Dorney Court. Wallis was a general carrier and forwarding agent to the railway companies with offices at 33 Bachelor's Walk. Work for the Leopardstown racecourse included shoeing farm horses and fixing a meadow mower.

The Rathdown Board of Guardians were also important customers, and work varied from ploughing for turnips to mowing a meadow and grubbing early potatoes. There was also a steady flow of repairs to be done, and unusual tasks such as making alterations to a motor ambulance in 1925.

Kennedy's bakery in Cabinteely maintained a fleet of horse-drawn delivery vans, and their horses (up to twelve at any time) needed constant attention as they were shod about once a month.

JOHN MURPHY,
COACH BUILDER.

Dog Carts, Governess and Outside Cars, Vans and Lorries of all Descriptions,

Made of The Very Best Seasoned Material by Experienced Workmen AT POPULAR PRICES.

SHANKHILL, Co. DUBLIN.

As this advertisement from 1911 shows, making and repairing carts and farm machinery generated much work in villages such as Shankill until as recently as the 1940s

The New Village

The present village of Shankill is not of ancient origin. Its real beginnings date back to an event in the 1860s when the local landlord, Sir Charles Domvile, evicted his tenants from his lands nearby.

Domvile, who was descended from an Anglo-Norman family which had settled in Ireland in the early seventeenth century, owned the lands of Loughlinstown and much of Old Shankill. Old Shankill consisted of a group of cabins and cottages located on the slopes of Carrickgolligan, more commonly known in the area as Cattegollager. There is an extraordinary story about Domvile, whose once highly influential family at one time also owned much land in Templeogue and Santry. It is said that Domvile had arranged a sort of horticultural competition for his tenants and on discovering that some of them who lived in Old Shankill had won the prize for the largest cabbages and the finest vegetables, he decided to increase their rents! The rent increases were not paid, and this led to a bitter struggle and, ultimately, to the tenants' eviction.

The evicted tenants were given land by a charitable and generous neighbour, Mr Tilly of Chantilly. This land, still called Tillystown, lies in a hollow behind the shops of the present Shankill village. Curiously, the Ordnance Survey map of 1912 refers to Shankill village as Chantilly.

Cabins were set up there and in 1910 some of these cabins were replaced when thirty-six well-built granite cottages were built here by the local authority. Two years later a Carnegie library was also built here. Like other Carnegie libraries in County Dublin, it was well built and has an impressive entrance in cut stone, a red tiled roof, a cupola and weather vane. The library has had many different uses including that of a court house, and even a temporary church.

For many years Shankill village did not present its best face and was a straggling collection of poor shopfronts, derelict sites and advertising hoardings. This was partly due to the unfortunate fact that the main

Ruin of cottage on the slopes of Cattegollager

The Martello tower near Bray. There were once four Martello towers on the coast at Killiney Bay, two of which fell into the sea due to erosion of the cliffs.

Dublin to Wexford road pounded through the narrow village and created noise, dust and dirt. The building of the new motorway may have sliced the area in two, but it has certainly given Shankill a new lease of life. New lighting and paving, financed by a European Union-funded improvement scheme, has greatly improved its appearance. Its shops now stretch from near the old railway bridge towards the top of Quinn's Road, and since the completion of the bypass many of them have been improved and various derelict sites have been built upon. Probably the most interesting village building was the Shanganagh Lounge, once the Shanganagh Hotel, which has now been completely replaced by a new, old-style pub. An ancient inn called the Nages Head appears to have existed on this site in 1757. Ten years ago this lounge still had a Victorian appearance with evidence of a closed-up former shopfront. There was an original nineteenth-century oil-lamp bracket hanging from the front wall, a reminder of old coaching days.

Towards Bray, the former Garda station occupied one of a pair of old gabled houses which may once have belonged to the demesne of Shanganagh Castle. There is a small oval panel in the façade of each house, both of which are marked on the first Ordnance Survey map of 1837. In the early 1900s these barracks were manned by the R.I.C. (Royal Irish Constabulary), with a sargeant and four constables.

St Anne's Church, situated at the intersection of the old road to Loughlinstown and the road to Ballybrack, was built in the 1930s on a site donated by the Field family (noted victuallers in County Dublin) of Shanganagh Park house. The modern Hiberno-Romanesque church was dedicated in 1936. Before St Anne's was built, local people had to make the journey to churches at Little Bray, Ballybrack or Cabinteely.

Shankill was once served by two railway lines, the Dublin and South Eastern Railway (better known as the Harcourt Street line; it was closed down in 1958) which took an inland route to the city, and the main line from Dun Laoghaire, which follows the coast and is now serviced by the DART (Dublin Area Rapid Transport). Though the present DART station at Rathsallagh, a new housing estate at Shankill, serves the area quite efficiently, many regret the short-sighted closure of the Harcourt Street line, especially as the suburbs have continued to expand and the number of cars continues to increase.

The railway to Bray, which passed through Dun Laoghaire, was opened in 1854 and was extended to Wicklow in the following year. Almost simultaneously, the Harcourt Street line was opened and it quickly gained the reputation of being the main route for Wicklow and Wexford, whereas the present DART route, now the only line to Bray, was seen as the branch line, serving the mail boats at the harbour.

Coastal erosion near Shankill has always caused many problems and in 1915 the track of the present DART line was moved inland. Several relics of the earlier line exist and can be seen near the shore, for instance at the bottom of Quinn's Road the old embankment and part of a stone bridge survive.

Shankill station, which served the Harcourt Street line, was converted into offices after the line's closure in the 1960s, and the special siding for the Ballycorus lead works can still be seen at these offices. Indeed, the nearby road leading from Shankill to Rathmichael and on to Ballycorus was built to accommodate the carting of ore from the station to the smelting works. Close by is Rathmichael schoolhouse, which was built in 1892 and replaced the old national school in Loughlinstown.

Victorian Houses in Shankill

The arrival of the railway prompted developers to build houses for the new middle classes who wished to enjoy the healthy air of County Dublin, and be able to commute to the city. A proposal was made in 1860 to build sixteen terraced houses close to what is now called Falls Road, but, despite the proximity to the railway, the scheme never got off the ground.

Corbawn An interesting Edwardian house called Corbawn was built here for Thomas Falls, a solicitor, but it was demolished in 1988 by the County Council to make way for the new Shankill bypass.

Porter's Post Office Guide of 1911 describes Shankill as follows: 'a pleasant residential district, 10 miles from Dublin ... a favourite residence of the Irish judges and upper class of Dublin Society'. This was the social scene then, and had been all during the second half of the nineteenth century when so much house building took place in the area.

Rosedale and **Locksley** are twin houses, built in the early 1860s by a Dublin brewer and entrepreneur named Perry, from a family of brewers and solicitors who had settled in Blackrock, and they are typical of the period. They were erected on lands near the sea situated at the bottom of Quinn's Road. Both reflect the Victorian spirit in their solid construction, high spacious rooms, wide plaster cornices and large windows.

A feature of both houses is the attractive, double-entrance porch with their arched windows and elegant, scroll-shaped, cast-iron railings. Each has a low, pitched roof with projecting eaves and ironwork brackets. Even now in the 1990s, with Shankill so built up, these houses enjoy pastoral views over their walled gardens of the Sugar Loaf mountains and Bray Head.

Sherrington, a mid-eighteenth-century house which was demolished in 1978

Towards the sea, at a short distance from the houses, the waves relentlessly eat into the soft clay cliffs of Killiney beach. This coastal erosion caused the ancient village of Longnon, marked on John Speed's map of 1603 (the first printed map of the city of Dublin), to fall into the sea and much later two Martello towers and a limekiln suffered the same fate. The remains of this village are said to be visible offshore at exceptionally low tides, and seaweed-covered walls and masonry have been reported.

Sherrington was a small Georgian house of great character which was demolished in 1978. Originally redbrick, with a Venetian-style doorcase in cut granite, this two-storey house was

*Details from the ceilings in
Clontra, which were painted in
the 1860s by John Hungerford
Pollen, a contemporary of
William Morris*

*The magnificent greenhouse
at Clontra*

the home of the Erck family since 1878. It had previously belonged to a
Judge Martley. In more recent times the house served as an office for the
caravan park which still operates here.

Kathleen Turner, who recorded much of the local history of the area,
recalled visits to Sherrington where Miss Caroline Erck, then over ninety,
presided over tea parties. Indian and China tea would be offered and
everybody played lexicon. In summer, croquet would be played and
Miss Erck would stand over her guests to make sure they were playing
by the rules! She was very popular in Shankill and established a coal
fund to make sure those less well off had enough coal for the winter.

Her father, Colonel Wentworth Erck, was a keen astronomer and built
an observatory tower in the grounds of Sherrington. In 1959 two windows were erected to the memory of Colonel Erck in Rathmichael parish
church where he had been a dedicated parishioner.

Clontra One of the most unusual houses in the county is Clontra, which
is also situated at the bottom of Quinn's Road. A unique house, two storeys high, it was designed by architects Deane and Woodward in the
'Italian medieval revival' idiom and its atmosphere is decidedly continental, reminiscent of some of the smaller Venetian palaces. The whole
house, including servants' quarters, was impeccably constructed out of
the finest granite masonry. Clontra was built for the Right Hon. James
Lawson, who was the Attorney General around 1860. It is quite a small
house, with all the principal reception rooms located on the upper floor,
as was the tradition in medieval buildings. The bedrooms are on the
ground floor. As in Italian palaces and villas, the main entrance is
approached by a flight of steep, stone steps, which leads the visitor up to
the hall with an air of expectation and mystery. The shape and use of
each room is expressed in the external appearance of the house. The
dining room has an imposing Venetian Gothic window and sandstone
balcony. The gentle social activities of the drawing room are
hinted at by the richly embellished cut-stone work of the
Gothic window and by the wide bay window which once
allowed open views of the sea. The exposed open timber
structure of the dining- and drawing-room ceilings are
reflected outside by the prominent roofs and tall, granite chimney stacks.

But what is perhaps most spectacular are the painted decorations of these ceilings and murals. These decorations and
murals were carried out by the artist John Hungerford Pollen in
about 1862. The paintings include subjects such as spring and
autumn in the dining room, and a hunter being offered a
goblet of wine by his wife, a peasant woman about to kill a
chicken and a roof full of birds such as swallows in the drawing
room.

Pollen was friendly with William Morris, the Oxford artist
and idealist, who with John Ruskin established a new taste for
nature-based design and quality craftsmanship. Pollen, again
working with the architects Deane and Woodward, also decorated the picture gallery in Kilkenny Castle and much of the

interior of the University Church in St Stephen's Green.

The lawns at Clontra are spread about the house like a carpet running right up to the doors, and with the deeper green of the pine trees create a beautiful setting. The greenhouse is an unusual example of Gothic ironwork, and contains an orange tree, a peach tree and some vines.

Old Connaught Village

Old Connaught village, which according to Eugene Curry (in his notes for the Ordnance Survey 1837) is 'Sean Chonnach' meaning 'old inhabitants', was described in the civil survey of 1654 as having a castle which was valued at five pounds. It belonged to James Walsh 'an Irish papist' who owned five hundred acres of mostly arable land. Walsh occupied 'one castle thatcht – an orchard and a garden plott', all of which was valued at £20. It is said that the Walshes eventually disposed of their lands and emigrated to France.

Old Connaught is a small, pleasant village whose focus was once a grassy triangle which was the junction of four roads and was described by Samuel Lewis (whose *Topographical Dictionary of Ireland* was published in 1837) as having 'a flourishing plantation of horse chestnut trees in its centre'. The village has been turned into something of a quiet backwater by the construction of the new motorway and is no longer a short cut for motorists.

By the early nineteenth century most of the parish was owned by the Roberts family and the village had, as Lewis puts it, 'several neat cottages and the handsome residence of R. Morrison, Esquire, the architect'. Today's Old Connaught Avenue, though now partly consisting of a bridge over the dual carriageway, was described by John D'Alton (*The History of the County of Dublin*, 1838) as 'a straight and noble avenue, over hung with elms, beeches, sycamores and some fine walnut trees'.

Ordnance Survey map of Old Connaught village, 1912

Sir Richard Morrison, as we have already seen, was responsible for designing several houses in this district. His own house, Walcot, was located just opposite the ruins of Old Connaught Church, but unfortunately was destroyed by fire. A new, larger house of the same name was erected in the 1860s, and this was in use as a hotel until 1952.

Jubilee Hall It seems very likely that Morrison designed the alterations which were made to Jubilee Hall, an impressive Regency-style house which overlooks Old Connaught village, where the eighteenth-century houses of Old Bawn and Graigueconna are situated.

Jubilee Hall gives the impression of being a large castle, but it is in fact a modest-enough-sized house with many projections, turrets and castellations, all of which give the appearance of a rambling mansion. The house commands a magnificent view of Old Connaught Avenue, Killiney Bay and the town of Bray.

Jubilee Hall, which appears on a map of 1814, was enlarged and rebuilt in the Tudor-Gothic idiom. The hall and staircase have Gothic-style windows of cut granite, while elements of the earlier house may include the projecting bow with its wide, Georgian-style, Wyatt windows. The interior decoration is lavish, with Gothic plasterwork vaulting in the hall and upstairs corridor. There is much fine woodwork,

Georgian staircase at Old Bawn, Old Connaught village

Jubilee Hall has many charac-teristics of the architecture of Richard Morrison, with its bold geometry and fanciful, medieval Gothic towers

including a richly carved oak staircase and the panelled doors of the hall.

Old Connaught House, which is not to be confused with Old Conna, is a plain eighteenth-century building which was greatly altered in Victorian times. A grand, eight-columned, granite portico was added to the front of the house, and a conservatory built onto one end. Inside, some of the Georgian features remain, such as the delicate, late eighteenth-century plaster cornices which ornament the principal rooms. A beautiful, semi-circular plasterwork panel decorates the hallway. The original house was burnt down in 1776. In 1783 it was bought by the Right Rev. William Forgore, the Bishop of Limerick. Soon afterwards it became the property of the Plunkett family, who are said to have largely rebuilt it, making Old Connaught 'a centre of hospitality and of the highest and most cultured gatherings' of the day. For instance, they were visited by Sir Walter Scott in August 1825 and he stayed in the house. One of the family, who became a well-known and well-loved Archbishop of Dublin (his statue stands in Kildare Place), made further additions and improvements to the house and grounds. He added a large conservatory, which has now vanished. A billiard room was added and the park and gardens greatly enhanced.

Eighteenth-century plasterwork in the entrance hall of Old Connaught House

The Ordnance Survey map of 1912 shows an ice house and a gasometer which belonged to the house. During work on the construction of a new driveway in 1893, Archbishop Plunkett's workmen accidentally opened a Bronze Age burial mound which contained human bones, shells and various ornaments. The principal driveway leading from the Bray Road at Woodbrook was one of three driveways which led to the house, each of which had its own gatelodge. This driveway ran quite close to the burial mound which was known as Toole's Moat, a very sizeable archaeological site which would have been located just seawards of the new road. When excavated during the 1880s, it was discovered to be a natural hill or esker on which an earlier burial had been made. It was levelled during the 1960s to make way for playing fields at the new St Brendan's School. In a biography written in 1900, Archbishop Plunkett's dedication to his parkland is described: 'The Park, of which the most is made by skilful planting – an art in which Lord Plunkett took especial pleasure – and the ample lawns and gardens are objects so charming and interesting that no visitor to Bray should fail to ask permission to see them.'

While the house now lies vacant and uncared for, a large eighteenth-century walled garden laid out by Archbishop Plunkett close by is at present being fully restored and is partly used as an organic vegetable farm. Two ponds and a fountain, along with the original pathways, are being brought back to life.

Old Conna Somewhat confusingly, there are two houses called almost by the same name, Old Connaught, but the second and more modern one goes by the name of Old Conna.

Old Conna is perhaps the best-sited house in the district as it stands high on the slopes of Carrickgolligan and has fine panoramic views all around. It replaced an earlier eighteenth-century house called Mount Eden, the home of John Roberts, but no trace of it remains. However, a most attractive stable and farmyard does survive nearby as part of the eighteenth-century establishment. This includes several stables, a steward's house, an estate office and an octagonal granary.

The present Old Conna house was built in the early 1860s for Phinias Riall, whose coat of arms appears in the porch. During the 1950s Old Conna became a 'luxury hotel' and was well known as a retreat for

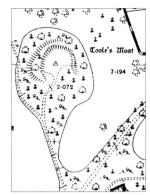

Toole's Moat once stood close to the line of the present N11 motorway

Bookplate from the library of Phinias Riall, who built Old Conna

The impressive garden frontage of Old Connaught House – the conservatory to the left has now gone

Old Conna House, one of the most extravagant Victorian houses built in the county, was erected about 1865

filmstars who were working at Ardmore studios in Bray. The hotel closed in 1963 and the house was bought twenty years later by Aravon, a preparatory school, which had been located in Bray since the 1890s.

The designs for the house, by the architects Lanyon, Lynn and Lanyon, were published in the *Dublin Builder* in 1865 and show an extravagant Tudor-Gothic mansion. The entire house was constructed in granite, with sandstone window mullions and door surrounds. A tower and copper flèche rises over a narrow butler's staircase, while the principal staircase is lit by a richly decorated, stained-glass window. The interior is elaborately decorated with Tudor-style fireplaces, oak panelling, and compartmented plaster ceilings, some of which have lattice-patterned designs.

The dining room at Old Conna

The gardens at Old Conna were once outstanding and boasted many unusual specimens of plants, shrubs and trees. All kinds of rare plants flourished in the Rialls' garden, and it was here that the first cordyline tree to be grown in Ireland was recorded. Old Conna also boasted excellent specimens of Californian redwoods, rhododendrons, azaleas, tree paeonies and magnolias.

The Shanganagh Estate

The Roberts family, who were of Welsh origin, acquired the lands called the Shanganagh estate in the early eighteenth century, and during the years 1750-65 Lewis Roberts won a Gold Medal from the Royal

Dublin Society (RDS) for having planted and maintained 38,000 trees here.

Later in the century a 'first rough drawing' of 1793 shows proposed new avenues, walks, and a new pond. A temple-like structure or summer house was to be built and much new tree planting carried out in the vicinity of Shanganagh Castle. It seems unlikely that all of these improvements were actually carried out, but we do know that Roberts laid out Corbawn Lane and planted many trees there some time before 1814.

In the early nineteenth century the estate belonged to John Roberts, and was very extensive. His lands swept from his home in Old Connaught down to Shanganagh Castle near the sea, and northwards towards the Loughlinstown river at Shanganagh bridge. From maps which survive in the National Library it can be seen that John Roberts also took a great interest in his property and was constantly improving it by laying out new paths and planting trees.

The present DART line runs beside one of these old avenues of trees which were shown on an estate map of 1826. This map shows the area of Corbawn Lane, Quinn's Road and Shankill with virtually no buildings at all.

John Roberts' house, which was called Mount Eden and later Old Conna, is shown on a map of 1810. The house was a rectangular eighteenth-century building with a bow end, but unfortunately nothing of it survives as it was completely rebuilt in 1868. The map shows a beautiful estate with a large walled garden, hundreds of trees and a substantial stableyard.

The Shanganagh and Old Connaught estates passed to the Riall family through the marriage of John Roberts' daughter, Anne, to Charles Riall in 1801. These estates produced a large income throughout the nineteenth century. For instance, William Hopper of Shanganagh House paid a half-yearly rent of £191. John Quin of Bray paid £145 12s 6d per half year for his lands in Shankill, including the site of the present Aubrey House and lands at Quinn's Road. General Sir George Cockburn of Shanganagh Castle paid a half-yearly rent of £1715 10s 2d

These were among the larger rents paid to the Riall estates; others came from properties such as Jubilee Hall, Palermo (now demolished), Thornhill (now St Gerard's School), Valombrosa, Wilfort and The Aske, houses in Old Connaught village, a forge, all

One of the many plaster copies of classical sculpture in Shanganagh Castle

Loughlinstown Estate map, c. 1826. The Roberts family managed their lands with care and planted many avenues and belts of trees.

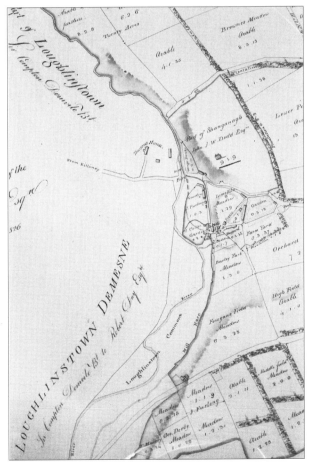

The picture gallery at Shanganagh Castle

Pillar commemorating the passing of the reform bills of 1832, which bears the inscription 'HUM BUG' (below)

of Shankill including Tillystown, Sherrington, Abingdon, Barn Close, and the mill at Shanganagh.

Seaview, or Knocklinn as it is now called, is yet another house with a fine panoramic view of the Irish Sea, Bray Head and the Little Sugar Loaf mountain. It is situated on the Ballyman Road, and has unfortunately deteriorated over the past twenty years to the point where it is now in the grip of dry rot. Though essentially Victorian in appearance, it is actually a much earlier house of the eighteenth century whose original cut-stone doorcase and beautiful fanlight remain intact.

Bay windows, two symmetrical wings and an elaborately decorated interior formed the principal alterations which were probably carried out in about 1860. The hall and staircase exhibit decorative plasterwork, including fluted over-doors which are characteristic of the 1790s.

The house was occupied in the late nineteenth century by D'Olier, a noted Dublin wine merchant, and not surprisingly it was equipped with a good brick-built wine cellar!

Shanganagh Castle (not to be confused with the medieval ruin) is one of the largest and most interesting houses of Shankill. It is a late eighteenth-century house which was largely remodelled into its present castellated form in 1818 by Sir George Cockburn. It is now used as an open prison, called Shanganagh Castle, by the Department of Justice and is well looked after. Cockburn was Shanganagh's most notable owner and had, it appears, led a very interesting life. During reconstruction work in 1959 a bottle containing a letter was found in a tower. In the letter, dated 1818, Cockburn tells us that he is making alterations to the house. The letter discusses the history of the area and the politics of the day, in particular the military exploits of Napoleon. Cockburn had first-hand experience of the Napoleonic wars, having been a general in the army which led him to travel widely in Europe.

Seaview, also known as Knocklinn, is an eighteenth-century house which was enlarged in the Victorian period

In the bottle letter he writes: 'As to modern times, I enclose a newspaper in this bottle, whether in a damp climate it will be preserved is more than I can tell. I shall probably be long dead and decomposed before this bottle is disturbed – but, like all things on earth, this tower and this bottle will come to their finale – also should this be preserved and after found, the reader may rely on its correctness.'

It was during Cockburn's stay in Italy and subsequent visits there that he acquired many fascinating treasures in the form of marble sculpture,

Shanganagh Castle, remodelled in 1818 by Sir George Cockburn, a collector of antiquities

Sculpture of grotesque warrior which once stood at Shanganagh

Pillar at Shanganagh estate

architectural fragments, pictures and statues. Cockburn was a close friend of Lord Cloncurry, who was also often in Italy buying antiquities and whom we shall meet when we come to discuss his home in Blackrock.

The survival of a unique collection of photographs of the house and its contents allows us to form an idea of the remarkable museum that Cockburn had created in Shanganagh Castle. Indeed, much of the castle was designed and built especially to accommodate his collection. Even today, with the contents gone, gracious plaster-casts of reclining female figures and Roman masks may still be seen in the hall. Niches were specially made to take a bust of a Roman emperor or an urn.

The catalogue of the auction held here in 1936 includes the entire collection and the finest of china, mirrors, clocks, furniture and other ornaments. The monumental room contained several 'stone sepulchral chests' or sarcophagi, busts of Socrates and Hercules and other carved stonework. The paintings included views of Dresden by Canaletto, portraits of George Cockburn and Mrs Catherine Riall, landscapes by William Ashford and Richard Moynan, classical subjects by Angelica Kaufmann, and a view of Shanganagh Castle by J. A. Daniel.

George Cockburn engaged Sir Richard Morrison, who in the early 1800s was a fashionable neo-classical architect, to remodel Shanganagh Castle. He enlarged the old, bow-ended, eighteenth-century house by fronting it with new rooms, all with projecting bows, and he added arched windows with stucco hood mouldings. A new 'medieval' roofline was created by the addition of various towers, battlemented parapets and turret-like chimneys. The interior is severe, but full of surprises. Early photographs show the hall with its Doric columns and sculpture-filled niches, and a chamber full of Roman antiquities which would have rivalled Soane Museum in London.

In the grounds, Cockburn erected two pillars and a grotesque statue of a warrior. One such pillar stood in front of the castle and bore an inscription stating: 'Erected in 1832 by General Sir George Cockburn G. C. M. to commemorate the Reform Bills passed this year' – but six years later he added: 'Alas to this date a hum bug!'

Cockburn, like many of his contemporaries, was a supporter of political reform, which would have meant greater democracy, less control over government by the aristocracy, a larger voting population and an end to many abuses of civil rights, such as those used against Catholics in Ireland until 1829.

Cockburn married a daughter of the Riall family of Clonmel, and by coincidence her brother had married a Roberts from Old Conna. In this way the Riall family inherited the Roberts estate which included all of Shanganagh, Old Connaught, parts of Shankill and Little Bray.

The main entrance to the castle was through a pair of tall, castellated, mock-Tudor gate piers, but these were demolished in 1979 and only one of the original pedestrian gates is left in position.

Crinken In the late eighteenth century George Cockburn's father, a Scotsman named Cockburn, had purchased about a hundred acres from the Roberts estate, to which he and his descendants continued to pay an

Crinken House, an early nineteenth-century villa, now used by the Order of St John of God

annual rent of about £170. A rent book of 1836 shows that he also made an annual payment of £48 for Crinken Villa. This may refer to a Tudor-style house on the Bray Road, now known as Crinken Cottage, or possibly the delightful villa called Crinken House, lately the home of the Packenham-Walsh family. Cockburn may have built this house for letting, a popular practice during the nineteenth century. However, Mrs Frances Seymour, in her book about Bray (*A Hundred Years of Bray and Its Neighbourhood, from 1770 to 1870*), says that Crinken House was built by a Mr White.

A neat, cut-stone portico graces the front entrance which leads the visitor into this miniature neo-classical villa at first-floor level. The interior decoration is delicate. The exquisite Regency-style windows were, until recently, a notable feature of the house, but unfortunately they have been replaced.

Crinken once enjoyed a tranquil, wooded setting, but this has dramatically changed since the construction of the new motorway, which now passes close to the house. Crinken is now part of the St John of God facility which is mostly accommodated in a new building which stands adjacent to the house.

Crinken Cottage is another very pretty house, situated directly on the Bray Road and also probably built by George Cockburn.

St James's Church The main road from Shankill to Bray is a picturesque survivor of pre motor-car days. The road is flanked by old stone walls and the tall, mature trees of the various houses. The effect is particularly striking at Crinken, where St James's Church is to be found set back from the road behind beautiful, Gothic-style, granite gate piers. The church, designed in the English Gothic style, is constructed entirely of granite, and was erected in 1840 at a cost of £2900. The site was

Ellerslie, Shankill

donated by the Magan family who lived nearby at Corke Farm. A generous donation of £2000 was made by Mrs Clarke (presumably of Dorney Court) towards the construction of the church, while other local patrons included Lord Plunkett of Old Connaught. Maps of the 1820s and earlier indicate the presence of a chapel at Crinken, very close to St James's, but this must have disappeared by the mid-nineteenth century.

The Orchard is a fine Edwardian redbrick house, built around 1911 by the Farran Darley family. Possibly designed by Richard Caulfield Orpen, it is typical of the period, with its asymmetrical façade, stone mullioned windows, oak doors and panelled study.

Ellerslie Whitewashed walls, over-hanging roofs and oriel windows, combined with climbing shrubs and ivy, make Ellerslie an unusual and picturesque house. A delightful one-storey drawing room, with Wyatt windows and an almost Japanese-looking curved roof, was added to the southern end of the house. These and other additions may have been the work of the architect Sir Richard Morrison, who was living in Old Connaught in about 1830. A long range of whitewashed stables and sheds, incorporating a dovecote, extend from the back of the house.

The Aske, Beauchamp and Wilfort

The Aske, a house which was originally called Oak Lawn, was built some time after 1832 on lands leased from Charles Toole of Wilfort. The name Aske appears to be a corruption of the word esker – a glacial deposit – and may be derived from the mound of the nearby 'Toole's Moat'. The name appears on a map of 1772, and describes a 32-acre lot which was adjoined by a small field called Sparrow's Nook. The Aske is typical of the much-favoured Gothic style of the early nineteenth century. Several architectural pattern books were published at this time which promoted this style where gables proliferate, and carved wooden bargeboards, pinnacles and tall chimneys abound.

The Aske is a most appealing non-basement house, designed and decorated in this idiom, and it has been carefully maintained in its original state. It is essentially a square house with treble gables on two fronts, all of which are ornamented with carved timber bargeboards. It has a very unusual cast-iron porch with Gothic pinnacles which was made in a Dublin foundry, and a long timber verandah which incorporates two bay windows. The whole effect, with the ornamental trellis work and Gothic pinnacles, is strikingly accentuated by the black and white painting scheme of the house. Internally, the Gothic features of the plasterwork and woodwork, combined with the latticed glazing and coloured glass panels, create a refined Regency-Gothic atmosphere.

A present-day view of The Aske

The Aske was advertised for sale in 1854 as containing 'a dining room, two drawing rooms, a breakfast parlour, seven bed chambers, besides servants' apartments with kitchen, butler's pantry, laundry, dairy, wine cellar, water closets and all convenient accommodation for the residence of a gentleman of station'.

The gate-lodge at The Aske is particularly worthy of attention as it is a delightful miniature of the main house with its oriel window and attractive bargeboards.

The Aske, a Tudor-style house erected during the 1830s

Cuilin, an attractive, Regency-style house, built about 1830

Above: Decorative door surround in Wilfort

Below: Wilfort House, built in the 1790s

The first owner of The Aske appears to have been a man named Garde. Later it was owned by the Verners of Corke Abbey, and then the Farran Darleys.

Beauchamp, also situated on the main Bray Road near Crinken and built about 1830, is a relatively compact house. It was much enlarged in the late nineteenth century by the addition of a pair of two-storey bays to the front and to the sides. The first inhabitant of Beauchamp was Sir Lovelace Stamer, a wine merchant.

Wilfort, now visible from the slip road to Bray, is an important house dating from the late eighteenth century. From the exterior, which consists of a plain, square Georgian house, there is little indication of the outstanding quality of the rooms inside. On entering, there is first an octagonal hall, and beyond, an oval staircase of great delicacy. The plasterwork is in the style of the Dublin stuccodores, George and Michael Stapleton, and is typical of the 1790s. The door surrounds have reeded mouldings with ornamental heads, medallions and swags, while the principal rooms have plastered niches and delicate cornices. The curved, panelled doors of the staircase give access to the various levels of the house. As early as 1814, its resident owner Charles Toole operated a nursery on the lands of Wilfort. The Tooles had a shop in Dublin and another nursery at Castlewood Avenue in Ranelagh.

Toole's Moat, which has already been mentioned, was the name given to a large mound which once stood between Wilfort and The Aske, very close to the line of the new motorway.

Cuilin, originally called Highnam Lodge, may have been built by Charles Toole, as the initials CMT can be seen on the front steps. Due to the construction of the N11 motorway, Cuilin is now situated at the bottom of a cul de sac on the Alley's River Road. It is an unspoilt example of its type, with bay windows all delicately glazed in the Tudor style.

Woodbrook, lying between the old Bray Road and the sea, is an impressive three-storey house facing west across an artificial lake towards the Wicklow mountains. A Georgian house which stood here in the early nineteenth century was doubled in size by Sir John Ribton, who added a new Italianate front and colonnaded wings. The new Victorian house, designed by George Papworth around 1840, featured an elaborate Ionic portico, ornately decorated pavilion wings, a pediment containing a coat of arms, and a cast-iron ballustrade at roof level.

The interior is of interest, containing an elaborate ballroom whose coved ceiling is decorated with *grisaille* (that is, monochrome) paintings, a pillared dining-room with murals by Zucharelli, and a library with oak panelling.

Woodbrook was owned by Sir John Ribton in 1850, and the house and contents were purchased by Henry Cochrane of Bray around 1880. Sir Henry, as he later became, made his fortune from the manufacture of mineral waters, sold under the brand name of Cantwell Cochrane.

Woodbrook, a Georgian house remodelled about 1840, now best known as the location of Woodbrook golf course

Sir Henry's son, Stanley Cochrane, inherited Woodbrook and the family fortune and developed a reputation for lavish entertainments, including hosting cricket teams at his private grounds.

A sports enthusiast, he also laid out a private golf course at Woodbrook. A golf club with a very prestigious membership was formed here in 1921 and today forms part of the Woodbrook golf course, of which fine views may be had from the DART trains. Stanley Cochrane was also very interested in music and he built a small opera house to which he brought many notable performers from abroad. The opera house survives along with its copper cupola and clock. A Regency-style steward's house and a stableyard can be seen on the avenue which leads to the present-day golf club.

Corke Abbey is certainly a name of great antiquity. A large house of that name once stood on the site of the present housing estate, and it in turn is believed to have been built on the site of an abbey. A holy well, possibly attached to that abbey, was noted by Eugene Curry in 1837, when he was making descriptive notes of the area for the Ordnance Survey (notebook in the Royal Irish Academy). He tells us that there was an old burial place to the side of Corke Abbey House and that headstones and bones were frequently dug up.

Corke Abbey was a large Victorian house, built in the Tudor style with wide-mullioned windows and prominent brick gables. But behind this façade there was clearly an eighteenth-century house, and various notices in the *Freeman's Journal* during the 1790s tell us that its owner, the Hon. Theophilus Jones, often entertained nobility and gentry, including the Lord Lieutenant and the Earl of Camden.

The house was owned by the Verner family for most of the nineteenth century, and it was probably Sir W. Verner who enlarged and rebuilt it and added a fine ballroom. It was sold to David Frame in 1920. He established the Solus factory on the site in 1935, and for many years it provided much employment in the Bray area and produced electric light bulbs, car lamps, drinking glasses and neon signs. Frame eventually demolished the house in the 1950s.

Corbawn Lane

Corbawn Lane was a straight, tree-lined road of great beauty, which ran directly down to the sea from Shankill. It is marked on Taylor's map of 1814 as a 'new road', and in 1818 it was described as Cauban Lane, but it was also sometimes called Roberts' Avenue, after John Roberts who laid it out. Corbawn Lane remained a beautiful avenue of mature beech trees until about thirty years ago when, with the arrival of a number of new developments, many of the fine trees were cut down. Further recent changes, including the provision of a roundabout, have detracted from its integrity as an avenue, but many of its fine trees are still there. Several significant houses have disappeared on Corbawn Lane.

Clonasleigh, a Victorian house from about 1840, was demolished to make way for a massive, low-rise shopping development, which, while it may serve its purpose, does little for the character of Shankill. Clonasleigh was the subject of a long planning battle on behalf of the Holohan family who wanted to develop a 'hypermarket' there as early as 1972.

Elsewhere on Corbawn Lane a particularly handsome house named Dorney Court was demolished in 1985 (and is now the site of Shankill Garda station) and in 1987 another Victorian residence called Llanmaur was also razed and its lovely gardens were bulldozed.

Dorney Court was originally called Clare Mount and was built by Thomas Clarke around 1832. It was elaborately extended in the 1880s,

Dorney Court, a fine Victorian house, which was demolished in 1984 and is now the site of Shankill Garda Station

An inlaid timber floor in the drawing room at Dorney Court

when a ballroom was added along with a richly carved stone porch and an unusual, Gothic-style, cast-iron balcony which ran right around the exterior of the house.

All this work, including beautiful gilt plaster cornices and an inlaid decorated floor, was almost certainly carried out by Charles T. Wallis, a Dublin carrier or agent for transport, whose descendants lived here until 1946. The drawing-room floor, inlaid with at least six different woods, was oval in shape and was enriched with a border of leaves. Dorney Court was a house of quality; even the shutter knobs were made of cut glass.

There was also a fine walled garden behind the house, and the whole demesne was surrounded with mature trees. The parkland had been carefully planted, especially that part where the Dublin, Wicklow and Wexford railway passed through. A granite-capped stone wall extends along from the railway bridge around to the entrance of Dorney Court, this having been done at the request of local residents to enhance the locality.

Decorative balcony at Dorney Court

The felling of many magnificent trees here in 1984 caused much controversy and underlined the lost opportunity for this land to have been acquired as a public park.

Instead, lands were bought near Crinken and a park and cemetery laid out there, stretching back towards the sea behind Shanganagh Castle. This small greenbelt is now the only piece of open land which will hopefully remain to prevent the eventual merging of Bray and

Llanmaur House, built in 1869, viewed from its once-magical walled garden

The demolition of Llanmaur House in 1987

Shankill. The cemetery covers fifty acres of land and was established by the board of the Dean's Grange cemetery in 1981.

Llanmaur was completed in 1869, a typical Victorian detached house, conservative in style but built to last. Its plasterwork was simple, with only the ceiling roses being ornate; the French-style mantelpieces were imposing but plain.

Originally built for a solicitor named Archibold Robinson, it was later owned by a Judge Gordon, whose gun of 1916 vintage was found behind the shutter panel during demolition! In 1929 it was purchased by Claude Wilson, whose daughter Mrs Kathleen Turner, author of *If You Seek Monuments*, lived here until her death in 1985. Kathleen Turner was a dedicated local historian. She had many extraordinary interests and talents, and created a magical walled garden where she cultivated an important collection of unusual plants. It was a most attractive garden

Shanganagh House, built around 1823 on the Roberts estate, now used by different community groups

with its alley of evergreens and its box hedges laid out in the geometric forms of a diamond, heart, club, spade, and circle.

In the 1930s she learned to fly, and acquired a licence. She also studied navigation and was an accomplished painter. It was sad, one day in 1987, to witness a bulldozer smash through the wall of the pretty, cobbled yard, breaking the granite wall and churning up the grass of the old lawns.

Eaton Brae, another fine Victorian house on Corbawn Lane, has survived, but most of its grounds have been built upon.

Shanganagh House/Park Further north and originally set in spacious parkland lies Shanganagh House, later called Shanganagh Park. It is said to have been built in 1823 and first belonged to William Hopper. During his ownership a stone coffin containing human bones was discovered on the lands.

Shanganagh later belonged to the Darcy family who were Dublin brewers, but they subsequently moved to Kilcroney, a magnificent cutstone house near Enniskerry. More recently, it was occupied by Patrick Field, who kept prize horses on the land. Field had very successfully managed racehorses at Glencairn for the famous Boss Croker of Tammany Hall in America. Field was wealthy in his own right, and owned much property in Ballybrack and Killiney.

In 1970 Dublin County Council served a compulsory purchase order on 112 acres of land at Shanganagh Park in order to provide housing and community facilities there. The old house has been kept as a community centre and the lands are now part of Rathsallagh housing estate.

CHAPTER 2

Rathmichael

This ancient cross stands on an old lane which leads to the ruin of Rathmichael Church. The cross may have symbolised entry onto Church property.

Rathmichael lies on elevated ground above Shankill, half-way between Loughlinstown and Old Connaught. Though still a very pleasant agricultural and residential district, it will shortly be divided in two by the Southern Cross motorway.

At the heart of Rathmichael is its ancient ruined church and round tower, situated inside the earlier structure of what must have once been one of the largest ringforts in Ireland – a symbol of the great importance of this place long ago. Rathmichael was one of the few places in County Dublin which had the right, since medieval times, to hold an annual fair. The fair, which in 1801 chiefly traded in horses, cattle and frize (frize was a type of cloth used in rough garments and cloaks), was held on 10 October.

The old church of Rathmichael, which has lain in ruins since the middle of the seventeenth century, captures the spirit of old County Dublin – a place of quiet, rural solitude with old walls and hedgerows, and narrow laneways. The early church appears to be of Norman date, and has an unusually long, narrow nave. The chancel arch collapsed in 1852. A fascinating collection of *leacs* or inscribed stone slabs can be seen at Rathmichael, and are evidence of human settlement and cultural achievement from some pre-Christian period. The stones are decorated with concentric circles, cup marks and herring-bone patterns and are similar to other *leacs* which survive in the graveyards at Dalkey, Tully, Killegar and Kill of the Grange.

The presence of a round tower suggests that Rathmichael was a place of considerable importance in Early Christian times. A narrow laneway, running between high ditches, connects the church with the Bride's Glen, where the original Rathmichael glebe (parish) house was situated. The house is still there, standing on a high ridge overlooking the glen and it is recorded as having been built in 1630. A glebe house and lands were granted to a clergyman as part of his salary, or a benefit-in-kind. With the demise of the church at Rathmichael in the seventeenth century, the glebe house was let out to tenants and the parish was united with that of Bray. In 1751 Cherrywood House became the new glebe house, and was owned by the parish until 1860. Mullinastill, another eighteenth-century house in the Bride's Glen, also served as the residence of the rector of Rathmichael during the nineteenth century. There was once a tuck mill at Mullinastill, and the old house may have been the residence of the local miller – a tuck mill, or fulling mill, was where woollen cloth was washed in the process of manufacture. Upstream at Heronford there was another old mill, used for grinding corn. Rathmichael was to remain part of the parish of Bray until 1872 when it was re-established as a parish in its own right.

The eighteenth-century parish had to deal with many of the day-to-day problems of the area and, in a way, fulfilled the role of the present-day local authority. It managed schools, provided for the poor, policed the district and was responsible for the upkeep of roads. It was the obligation of the poor to provide labour for such tasks, giving six days free of charge per year, while the gentry were expected to supply materials, horses and carts.

Puck's castle 200 years ago

The parish provided a school and schoolmaster's house in Loughlinstown, built in about 1830 on land donated by the Domvile family and run by the parish. The Silver Tassie pub is said to occupy part of the old school buildings.

The present Rathmichael Church of Ireland church was commissioned by the Domviles in 1860 and was designed by Benjamin Woodward. This architect, with his partner Thomas Deane, had designed and built many beautiful Gothic Revival buildings, but at Rathmichael he produced a nineteenth-century church in the Hiberno-Romanesque style. The result is very pleasing – an intimate, granite church which consisted of a rectangular nave with an apsidal chancel. To this simple geometry a neat, gabled porch with a Romanesque doorway and a further semi-circular vestry were added.

Puck's Castle, which stands above Rathmichael, is a small tower house which has been in ruins since the eighteenth century and now requires repair if it is to survive

The prominent roofs which project on corbels over the ashlar stone-work walls, and the small, round-headed windows, are suggestive of some of the early ruined churches of south County Dublin, such as Tully or Kill of the Grange. There are at least a dozen such ruined churches in the wider area south of Dun Laoghaire, and through this church at Rathmichael we can perhaps visualise how they might have looked in their heyday.

While it was customary for church patrons and gentry to reserve a private pew, the Domviles went a step further and provided themselves with high-backed chairs, screened off by red velvet curtains. One of Rathmichael's most dedicated rectors, the Rev. E. W. Burton, is commemorated by a fine high cross which stands in the grounds of the church and harmonises so well with its Romanesque architecture.

CHAPTER 3

Loughlinstown

The large tract of agricultural land which stretches from Loughlinstown to Lehaunstown, and which is bordered by the Bride's Glen and the fascinating ancient church of Tully, is about to be transformed from farmland into suburbia. Heavy earth-moving equipment has already moved mountains of earth which have been piled up around a new bridge which will cross the stream at Loughlinstown.

It is the loss of a wild and natural piece of countryside – on such a large scale, and so near to the densely built-up areas of Loughlinstown and Ballybrack – to more concrete and uniformity, which makes these works seem like an assault on the familiar rural landscape. The most significant historical loss is the obliteration of Beechgrove House, which once stood close to the main road, and was long ago a famous inn.

Beechgrove once stood close to Loughlinstown village, but no trace of the house now remains

Beechgrove The site of Beechgrove House is now buried under ten or fifteen feet of earth, but the house was actually demolished some twenty years ago. Nearby, the Glendruid stream is contained by stone walls and flows under a beautiful archway. At Loughlinstown this stream is joined by another which flows through the Bride's Glen under the impressive railway viaduct.

Beechgrove was a very appropriate name, as the rolling hills were until recently well stocked with mature beech trees. I estimated one tree, felled early in 1998, to be about two hundred years old.

The inn, of which the house was once a part, was called Owen Bray's

The impressive Loughlinstown viaduct which once carried trains from Bray to Harcourt Street station

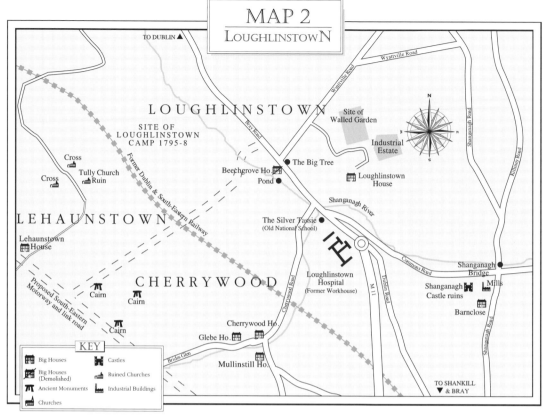

MAP 2
LOUGHLINSTOWN

TO DUBLIN ▲

L O U G H L I N S T O W N

SITE OF
LOUGHLINSTOWN
CAMP 1795-8

Site of
Walled Garden

Industrial
Estate

Cross
Tully Church
Cross   Ruin

The Big Tree
Beechgrove Ho
Pond   Loughlinstown
House

L E H A U N S T O W N

Shanaganh River

The Silver Tassie
(Old National School)

Lehaunstown
House

C H E R R Y W O O D

Cairn
Cairn

Loughlinstown
Hospital
(Former Workhouse)

Shanganah
Bridge

Shanganagh
Castle ruins   Mills

Barnclose

Cairn

Cherrywood Ho
Glebe Ho

Proposed South-Eastern
Motorway and link road

Mullinstill Ho.

Brides Glen

TO SHANKILL
▼ & BRAY

KEY

Big Houses		Castles	
Big Houses (Demolished)		Ruined Churches	
Ancient Monuments		Industrial Buildings	
Churches			

Inn, and during the eighteenth century it was a renowned hostelry and the meeting place for the famous Kilruddery hunt.

Already by 1817 a Miss Plumptree noted that the inn had been converted into a 'gentleman's seat', the quaint nineteenth-century term for a residence, and that its roadside frontage had now become the back of the house.

A small, stone-walled enclosure, perhaps once a small garden, lies upstream, but it will probably be soon swept away.

A watercolour sketch of Loughlinstown camp shows how well-established it had become by 1798. It was also the scene of much commercial and social activity

Loughlinstown House, viewed from the terraced gardens, now the site of the new office blocks of the European Foundation

The Loughlinstown Camp

During the turbulent period of the 1790s Ireland became the scene of mounting unrest. There was a real fear that a French invasion might take place along the coast near Dublin. Loughlinstown was chosen as a strategic location from which to guard the coastal approaches. Colonel George Napier, the British army officer-in-charge, was of the opinion that the high ground of Lehaunstown and Loughlinstown overlooking Killiney Bay would be the best place for a defence force, and accordingly a great military camp consisting of about four thousand soldiers was established here. The camp covered an area of one hundred and twenty acres at Loughlinstown and was set up in 1795. The following year the entire camp marched to Bantry Bay in the space of three days to prevent the French from landing there.

Various military manoeuvres were carried out in order to train the men and every Monday there was a large market held where country people came and sold their produce. A print in John Ferrar's *A View of Ancient and Modern Dublin* illustrates the camp with its rows of tents and wooden huts covering a huge area. There were special kitchens with stoves which could boil sixty kettles simultaneously.

Many entertainments, balls and military reviews were held and people flocked from all around. On one occasion *The Freeman's Journal* reported that the road to the camp was packed with the citizens of Dublin who 'trundled hither on coal porter's cars, half roasted with the heat of the day and half smothered in clouds of dust. Every vehicle from the Royal George to the dust cart was in motion on the Bray Road, and every hack horse, mule or ass, that could be procured for hire, joined the cavalcade.' A temporary ballroom was specially erected for dancing.

Major La Chaussée, a Frenchman in the English army, drew up a report on Killiney Bay and what should be done to defend it. Among many recommendations he suggested that batteries should be constructed along the coast, that guns should be set up near the cliffs, that

Duncan's map of 1821 shows the proximity of the Loughlinstown Camp to Killiney Bay, whose shores it was set up to defend in the event of a possible French attack

Loughlinstown House, viewed from the garden front, showing the oldest part of the house, with its brick window surrounds

hedges and ditches parallel to the shore should be destroyed and that the country houses should be fortified. Of course no invasion of Dublin ever took place and in the year following the rebellion of 1798, the camp was dismantled.

A plan by the United Irishmen to subvert the Catholic and pro-nationalist soldiers in the camp in order to raise a rebellion in Dublin, was foiled by a spy called Armstrong. He had attended meetings with the Sheares brothers who were the leaders of this plan to 'surprise and take the camp at Loughlinstown'. The Sheares were arrested and executed in July 1798 on the strength of Armstrong's evidence.

The renewed war between England and France which broke out in 1803 provoked the construction of the Martello towers all along the Dublin coastline. Seven towers were built in Killiney Bay alone, but these will be discussed later.

Loughlinstown House is hidden from general view as it is situated on a ridge above the main road. It is one of the oldest and largest surviving houses in the Dun Laoghaire-Rathdown County and is of considerable architectural interest. It is now occupied by the European Foundation, a research establishment, and is used as offices. Some years ago a large new office building was added to the east of the house. Loughlinstown House appears to have been built in two separate stages, the older and more attractive part now forming the back of the building. The front, with its high-ceilinged rooms and handsome staircase hall, dates from the latter half of the eighteenth century. The original front entrance, with its pretty, redbrick, Venetian doorway, rendered walls and central pediment, is suggestive of the early 1700s.

A long central corridor, paved with old flagstones, runs down the middle of the house, and off it there is a large, vaulted wine cellar.

The terraced gardens to the side of the house have been sacrificed to a new office building, but the rest of the grounds are well maintained. All of the original lands which once ran back to Ballybrack have been completely built up with houses, industrial development and schools since their purchase in 1976 by Dun Laoghaire Corporation. Here there was once a large enclosed garden, some woods, and two small lakes.

Loughlinstown is chiefly associated with the Domvile family who owned it for about three hundred years. Sir William Domvile was appointed Attorney General for Ireland in 1660 and his job was to settle all claims and disputes arising from the recent rebellion (of 1641). For his services, Domvile was given the castle, town and lands of Loughlinstown including 457 acres.

Sir William replaced the medieval castle of Loughlinstown with a new house and he lived there until his death in 1689. The seventeenth-century house is described in Francis Elrington Ball's *History of the County of Dublin* (Vol. I, 1902) as having a large hall, a great parlour, and a little parlour with tapestry hangings. It was richly furnished with chairs upholstered in 'Turkey-worked', expensive looking-glasses, and heavily embroidered curtains.

Sir William's son, also William Domvile, continued to live at Loughlinstown and he extended the family estates by renting Shankill Castle and lands from the Archbishops of Dublin for £75 per annum.

During the eighteenth century the Domviles chose to live at Santry Court in north County Dublin and left Loughlinstown unoccupied, which may explain why Mrs Delany, the noted eighteenth-century diarist who lived in Glasnevin, found the place to be 'old and ruinous' in 1752. But a particularly interesting toy has survived from the Domviles' time at Loughlinstown in the form of a large doll's house. The doll's house, which is now a big attraction at the National Museum in Collins' Barracks, was made for the Great Exhibition in London of 1851 and contains models of Chippendale, Adam and Hepplewhite furniture. It was made by the Cushendall Toy Company in County Antrim.

Loughlinstown was rented to Mr Justice Robert Day in 1796, and he remained there for the rest of his life. He died in 1841 at the age of ninety-six. Day was a very interesting figure and has left us many fascinating impressions of life at Loughlinstown through his diaries and notebooks (which may be inspected at the Royal Irish Academy). He entertained often and among his frequent guests were his neighbours General Cockburn of Shanganagh Castle, the Leesons of Ballyman, and Lord Plunkett of Old Connaught.

The staircase of Loughlinstown House, showing the Venetian window – this formed part of the mid-eighteenth-century additions to the house

His diary for March 1827 records: 'The Cockburns and the Leesons dine with us and pass an agreeable day.' On another occasion a party of guests staying at Loughlinstown go to see 'Lord Meath's new house' at Kilruddery, and on another day no less than five members of parliament were present for dinner, including Henry Grattan MP of Tinnehinch, and the Solicitor General Doherty MP.

Lord Valentine Lawless Cloncurry, an important collector of antiquities and a traveller, was a close friend of Robert Day. Like Cloncurry, Day travelled a lot and at the age of eighty-one he made a long European tour with his carriage and servants, passing through Paris and Geneva. In his notebook under the heading 'hints to travellers in Italy/necessary articles' Day includes a list of essentials: pistols, pocket knife and fork, ink powder and pens, court plaster [presumably a type of make-up for the face!], toothbrush and both wells of the carriage to be stocked with candles for the lamps. He also tells us that ten drops of essential oil of lavender, distributed through a bed, will banish bugs and fleas!

Carriages, of course, broke down quite frequently and accidents were not unusual. Robert Day records picking up Lord Plunkett and his sister, who lived at Old Connaught,

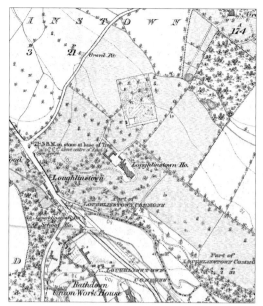

The 1843 Ordnance Survey map showing Loughlinstown House and demesne, with the workhouse or hospital to the south

and whose carriage had broken down on the road to Dublin. Day himself often went to Dublin, and sometimes stayed overnight in Morrison's Hotel in Dawson Street. In 1834, he notes returning from Dublin with a thirty-pound chest of tea from Twinings and 20lbs of coffee, both items of considerable value at that time.

One day there was a serious chimney fire in his office at Loughlinstown but it was put out by the 'neighbouring peasantry who in obedience to the summon of my labourer's bell gathered immediately'. Judge Day's establishment was run by 'seven labourers, one steward and gardener, two old women gate-keepers, one helper, four man-servants and five maid-servants. There were four or five milch cows, two plow bulls, several heifers and calves, and two stalled bullocks.'

The judge died in 1841 and was buried in the graveyard at Monkstown and a marble tablet was erected to his memory in Monkstown church.

Loughlinstown is now hardly recognisable as a village and is probably better known as one of the first stretches of dual carriageway to have been built in Ireland. However, before the construction of this massive road it consisted of a hamlet with several houses and cottages nestling close to the Loughlinstown river and was famous for its 'big tree'. This very old and large sycamore tree was surrounded by a circular granite seat and an old lamp-bracket was attached to its trunk. A famous County Dublin landmark, the tree was killed when trenches were cut for roadworks. This was not the first time that a roadway significantly altered Loughlinstown. In a drawing from 1835 by Charles Vallancey Pratt, it was shown as a quaint settlement of thatched cottages and trees. Pratt notes that 'the foreground of this sketch is now hardly to be recognised, the new line of the road from Loughlinstown to Bray in 1836-7 passing right through it'. After the building of this road there were houses on both sides, including a gate-lodge to Loughlinstown House, but these all disappeared with the building of the dual carriageway.

There was a forge in Loughlinstown which, early this century, carried the following advertisement: 'shoeing, general smith, agricultural engineer, maker and repairer of ploughs, harrows, gutters, gates, fences etc.' Today there is little business here as traffic flies by, but an enterprising individual has opened a shop selling the plastic hubcaps which are so often lost off modern cars!

Loughlinstown Commons embraced the fields on either side of the little river and extended east as far as Shanganagh Bridge. The Commons remained unaltered for a very long time – Mrs Delany, writing in 1752, noticed many 'cabbins' there, which were probably thatched, mud-walled structures, inhabited by the very poor. There are still a number of cottages on Commons Road, and there is one thatched cottage on the Bride's Glen Road. The mill race which once fed the corn

The 'big tree' at Loughlinstown

The dual carriageway at Loughlinstown Hospital

mill at Shanganagh ran through the Commons. Shanganagh Bridge, a delightful, small, cut-stone structure of three arches, was built in 1829. A worn plaque records the names of the overseers and the mason.

Loughlinstown Hospital The records of the Rathdown Board of Guardians make sad reading, as they tell of many lives spent in the Loughlinstown Workhouse. Now Loughlinstown Hospital, the building was opened as a workhouse in 1841 as part of the government's answer to poverty and destitution. At the time many workhouses were built around Ireland, mostly according to a standard plan. They were run in a very severe manner and were barely humane in their treatment of inmates.

Of the seven or eight hundred inmates who were housed in Loughlinstown in the late 1840s, many had simply been unemployed. Sometimes relief work, such as the repair of roads or walls, was arranged, but mostly the men swept around the buildings, worked the water pump and did horticultural work, while the women washed, sewed and ironed. In 1848 many of the inmates died from fever and the following year cholera struck the district.

The workhouse complex, built on an elevated site, occupied twenty-one acres and the buildings incorporated dormitories, workrooms, classrooms, a chapel and an infirmary for 'lunatic' patients.

Part of the original structure, including a square, stone-built water tower, were demolished during the construction of the dual carriageway, but the remaining workhouse buildings are now incorporated into the hospital.

CHAPTER 4

Killiney

Killiney is noted for its hills which command excellent views of Dublin Bay, the Irish Sea and the surrounding mountains. The obelisk on the summit of Killiney Hill is a conspicuous landmark of the area, and has been part of the scenery since the middle of the eighteenth century. It was this special scenic quality which in the nineteenth century first attracted developers to build houses in this area, giving it the distinctive residential character which it still retains. As we shall see, these hills and their slopes were almost devoid of any buildings during the eighteenth century, apart from the famous obelisk and the ancient ruined church. By 1839, when Samuel Lewis was compiling his *Topographical Dictionary of Ireland*, there were already many 'favourite places of residence, and several pretty villas and rustic cottages' in the area.

Killiney and Dalkey hills became fashionable places for Dublin's Victorian residents to picnic and take the air

Killiney extends over a large area stretching from the bay across by Ballybrack and west as far as Glenageary, while to the north it encompasses Killiney Hill itself and is bounded by Dalkey. By the middle of the

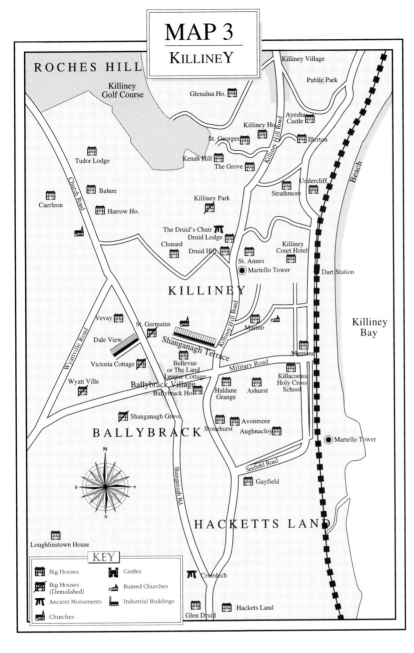

MAP 3
KILLINEY

ROCHES HILL

Killiney Golf Course

Killiney Village

Public Park

Glenalua Ho.

Ayesha Castle

Killiney Ho.

St. Georges

Illerton

Tudor Lodge

Kenah Hill

The Grove

Undercliff

Balure

Killiney Park

Strathmore

Caerleon

Harrow Ho.

The Druid's Chair

Druid Lodge

Clonard

Druid Hill

Killiney Court Hotel

St. Annes

Martello Tower

Dart Station

KILLINEY

Vevay

St. Germains

Marino

Killiney Bay

Dale View

Shanganagh Terrace

Victoria Cottage

Bellevue or The Land League Cottage

Mentone

Wyatt Ville

Military Road

Killacoona Holy Cross School

Ballybrack Village

Haldane Grange

Ashurst

Ballybrack Ho.

Shanganagh Grove

Stonehurst

Avonmore

BALLYBRACK

Aughnacloy

Martello Tower

Seafield Road

Gayfield

HACKETTS LAND

Loughlinstown House

KEY

Big Houses	Castles		Cromlech
Big Houses (Demolished)	Ruined Churches		
Ancient Monuments	Industrial Buildings		
Churches		Glen Druid	Hackets Land

The Druid's Chair, a curious monument which was probably reconstructed during the nineteenth century

nineteenth century Killiney was firmly established as one of Dublin's most favoured residential quarters and today this reputation remains unchanged as house prices become ever higher and ever more unreal.

It is a particularly attractive area, with its many trees, beautiful gardens and south-facing slopes which have the benefit of a sea view. There is also easy access to the beach. It is what estate agents like to call a 'mature' area, well furnished with large gardens, shrubs and trees, properties bounded by stone walls and with a wide variety of architectural styles. From Killiney village, the narrow Killiney Hill Road winds

A Gothic doorway at the ancient ruined church of Killiney

An Early Christian cross, bearing the image of a head, at Killiney Church

downhill towards Shanganagh, while to the east the DART station provides convenient access to trains bound for the city.

It is the western portion of Killiney which has changed most, where beyond Killiney golf course many new houses were built at Avondale, Ballinclea, Watson's and Ballybrack.

The Druid's Chair, which, though it looks like a prehistoric burial mound is considered by some to be a fake, is probably the oldest monument in Killiney. It was opened up during the eighteenth century when three stone cists were found there, and, in the fashion of the time, a grove of oak trees was planted. It is thought that some of the excavated stones were re-arranged to form the so-called Druid's Chair.

Charles Vallancey Pratt, a noted antiquarian, inspected the monument in the early nineteenth century and believed it to be genuine, and so it came to be marked on the early Ordnance Survey maps as a 'Pagan Temple'. Later historians such as William F. Wakeman, the antiquarian, condemned it as a forgery, nonetheless many houses in the immediate vicinity were taken with its romantic antiquity and were given such names as Mount Druid, Druid Hill, or Temple Hill.

The name Killiney is derived from the Irish, Cill Iníon Léinin, which translates as 'the church of the daughter of Lenin'. The ancient ruined church of Killiney is delightfully situated among trees on Marino Avenue and must originally have had an excellent view of the sea. As the roughly circular aspect of the site suggests, the church may have been erected inside a rath or older place of worship.

The church is dedicated to the daughters of Lenin, who are thought to have established a religious settlement here in the seventh century. The small-scale proportions of the sturdy church are pleasing to the eye. Its short nave and chancel are connected by a small, stone arch and appear to be of early Norman date. The church remained in use until the seventeenth century when it became a ruin. Among its many interesting features is the flat-headed entrance door with a carving of a Greek cross on its under-side.

Killiney Obelisk has been the subject of much attention since it was built in the 1740s. It was intended as the centrepiece of a great undertaking to plant and landscape the hill, which at first was called Obelisk Hill, and more recently has become known as Killiney Hill. The obelisk was the main attraction of the lands of Mount Malpas or Scalpwilliam in the eighteenth century and visitors were brought by coach, on horseback or walked to the summit to admire the view.

In early times this area was included in the lands of Rochestown and Dalkey Commons and belonged for many centuries to the Norman family of Talbot (the same Talbot of Malahide Castle) and through them the property passed eventually to Colonel John Malpas who, in the early eighteenth century, built a brick house for himself at Rochestown.

It was Malpas who erected the distinctive, cone-shaped obelisk on Killiney Hill, as a marble plaque on it records: 'last year being hard with the poor the walls around these hills and this etc. Erected by John Malpas June 1742'. This inscription is now very worn and hard to read – indeed, the obelisk itself is in need of general repair. Early engravings

show a flight of steps leading up to a viewing balcony, but these were later removed for safety reasons. The winter of 1741-2 was known as 'the hard frost' and was a time of much poverty and suffering among the poor. Malpas was one of several landowners who carried out building projects in order to provide some employment.

A smaller structure, sometimes called Boucher's obelisk, lies partly hidden among the trees and rocks and may be contemporary with its larger parent. The inscription 'Mount Malpas' is to be found above the door, and though this was an eighteenth-century name for the park, it is difficult to date this monument with any certainty.

Robert Warren, who owned the estate for much of the nineteenth century, repaired the obelisk in 1840, and it is also possible that he was responsible for building the miniature obelisk and so-called 'wishing stone' or pyramid, which stands nearby. Warren was addicted to building, developing and improving his estate, and as we shall see he did so with the best of design and materials. For instance, he erected the elegant, granite-built, gate-lodge tower at Killiney Hill Road, and placed an inscription on it to record the date of its completion – 1853. The tall, ball-capped gate piers which grace this entrance were also probably erected during the eighteenth century, although the present gates are smaller and of a later date. This entrance was somewhat altered about ten years ago, when the derelict tea rooms which adjoined the gate lodge were removed. Warren also built the magical cut-granite archway and gate-lodge which is such a feature of Killiney village. The gateway, which is part of a small house once called Camelot, is surmounted by a

This well-known print of Killiney Hill illustrates the dramatic location of the obelisk and part of the eighteenth-century deer park wall

Two inscribed plaques on Killiney Obelisk which record the year of its construction (top) and the year of its repair (bottom)

An oil painting of the Warren family viewing some of their property at Ayesha Castle

castellated rampart which connects with a large circular tower and smaller lookout.

A similar cut-stone, octagonal gate lodge with crenellated gate piers and battlemented walls, was built for Killiney Castle at the 'Dalkey' entrance and is still in use by the hotel.

In the park near the obelisk there are also a number of stone-built picnic tables which a nineteenth-century engraving shows in use, with a party of fashionably dressed Victorians enjoying an *al fresco* meal. Not far off in the woods are the remains of a pump house.

Killiney Castle In 1740 Colonel John Malpas built a house called Mount Malpas, now Killiney Castle, as a speculative development. Malpas must have let the castle in its early years, for in 1752 Falkiner's *Dublin Journal* carried the following advertisement: 'Roxborough, formerly called Mount Malpas, containing 150 acres of land enclosed by a stone wall and a new well-furnished house of six rooms and two large closets on a floor with offices.'

Killiney Castle today

Certainly, Thomas Sherrard's map of the Malpas estate, made in 1787, shows the castle to be a fairly modest house, with no elaborate gardens or plantations which would compare with Rochestown House, the principal Malpas residence.

Peter Wilson, writing about Dalkey in 1768, says that the new owner of Mount Malpas, the Right Hon. Henry, Lord Viscount Loftus of Ely, had made many improvements to the house and gardens. He comments on the magnificent view of the city, bay and harbour of Dublin, and describes the gardens as being 'enclosed with high stone walls, stocked with the best fruit trees, and such a collection of flowers as must captivate the most insensible eye'.

Loftus was obviously possessed of a passion for improvement and, like Malpas before him, he carried out other major works in the area, including the cutting of a new carriage road around Killiney Hill, blasting stones and bringing earth to cover the bare out-crops of rock, and planting the west side of the hill with various types of trees and shrubs. Wilson also says that Loftus intended to build a banqueting house in the woods, but never realised his plan because in the meantime he had inherited Rathfarnham Castle, where he directed all his energies.

Part of the entrance gates to Killiney Castle

In 1790 another important landowner, John Scott, Lord Clonmel, leased Killiney Hill with the intention of building a large house there. Clonmel already had a very elegant house at Neptune in Blackrock, but presumably because he was so wealthy and was hungry for new projects, he spent large sums of money on the creation of a deer park at Killiney and employed many men in making roads and building walls.

The castle, which is now the centrepiece of Fitzpatrick's Castle Hotel, does retain various features of the eighteenth-century structure, despite having been much altered since.

The original Mount Malpas was a seven-windowed, two-storey-over-basement, Georgian house. Sherrard's map shows the castle in this form. It must have been Robert Warren, the nineteenth-century owner of the Killiney estate, who, in 1840, was responsible for the addition of the mock medieval corner towers, turrets and battlements.

The Chippendall Higgin cross, which stands near the summit of Dalkey Hill

A later inhabitant named Thomas Chippendall Higgin, who bought the castle in 1872, added a half-octagonal castellated tower, cut-stone doorway and entrance porch to the front. The door-case with its carved plaque and swan-neck pediment is in the seventeenth-century style. Higgin had the unusual distinction of being buried on Dalkey Hill in 1906, where a broken cross bears the inscription: 'Dust thou art, to dust returneth, Was not spoken of the soul'.

Killiney Hill Park, or Victoria Park as it was called when first opened to the public in 1887, had been purchased by the Queen Victoria Memorial Association from Robert Warren Junior for £5000. It was opened by Prince Albert and has remained a public park ever since. Dun Laoghaire Corporation enlarged the park in the late 1930s by purchasing the rest of Dalkey Hill and the lands at Burmah Road, bringing the total area of the park up to two hundred acres. This included the huge area of Dalkey quarry where work first began in 1815 to extract stone for the construction of Dun Laoghaire harbour. The corporation also tried to buy Mount Eagle in order to extend the public park at the Vico Road, but they were outbid at auction by Con Smith, a private buyer. The Vico fields, the now-wild land above the railway at White Rock, had been bought by public subscription in 1926 to prevent any further building from taking place which might spoil its natural beauty – thus it is quite surprising to see large apartment developments now appearing in an area of such

The plaque at the entrance to Killiney Hill Park, which records its official opening in 1887 as Victoria Park

An ambitious proposal by Warren of the 1840s to develop the whole of Killiney Hill – fortunately it never came to fruition

high public amenity so close to the lands which the corporation had once tried to purchase to prevent such building.

The Vico Road did not exist until 1889 when it was officially opened to the public by the Lord Lieutenant. Up to then, the eastern side of Killiney Hill was all part of the Warren estate and completely private.

Robert Warren had facilitated the construction of the railway between Dalkey and Killiney by allowing it to traverse his property at the Vico fields. He was, no doubt, well compensated, but was also provided with a private halt (the remains of which can be seen) and a footbridge giving access to White Rock. A massive retaining wall was built at White Rock to carry the railway line above. An interesting detail connected with the sale of Warren's estate in 1872 was that the purchaser of the lot, which included part of Dalkey Commons, was entitled to gather seaweed from the shore below.

An ambitious plan to develop the entire Killiney Hill estate was drawn up for Warren by the architects Hoskin & Son around 1840 (the plans are in the National Library). The development proposal, which was to be called Queenstown, planned for terraces of very grand houses overlooking Killiney Bay and for other detached residences, and would have completely destroyed the deer park which had been so carefully created in the eighteenth century. Doubtless many of the proposed houses would have been elegantly designed and very well built, rather in the style of Sorrento Terrace, but we must be grateful that this scheme was never executed as we would not today have the great amenity which is Killiney Hill.

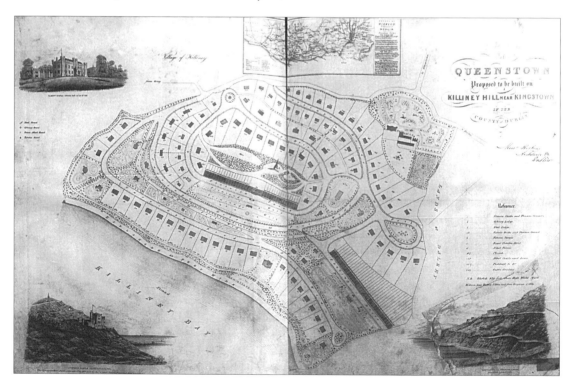

Ayesha Castle, the most dramatically-sited house in Killiney

The plans also illustrate Killiney Castle, Ayesha Castle and Mount Eagle in small vignettes. These houses were then called Albert Castle, Victoria Castle and Coburg Lodge, all so named in honour of the new British monarch and her consort. The family title of Queen Victoria's husband was 'Saxe Coburg'.

Victoria Castle, renamed **Ayesha Castle** in 1930, was one of Warren's projects which was successfully completed. A pseudo Norman castle, built of local Dalkey granite, it is dramatically situated on the side of Killiney Hill with excellent views towards Bray and the Wicklow mountains. Victoria Castle, with its impeccably cut stonework is essentially square in plan, with a large, half-octagonal, projecting block and a circular tower. It is approached from a terrace or forecourt and has rather severe, round-headed, narrow windows and a plain entrance door. The silhouette is very striking with its many crenellations and battlements.

Holy Trinity Church, built on a segment of the parkland on Robert Warren's Killiney Hill estate

A small Gothic summerhouse near Mount Eagle

The staircase at Mount Eagle

Bellevue Park, now the convent of the nuns of St. Joseph of Cluny

The architect may have been Sandham Symes, who is recorded as the designer of Mount Eagle, another Warren development.

Victoria Castle was occupied from 1880 until 1927 by the family of Clifford Lloyd, a solicitor. The Lloyd family were kin of Provost Lloyd of Trinity College Dublin. Then its interior was gutted by an accidental fire. It was bought by Sir Thomas Talbot Power, owner of Power's distillery, who used his considerable wealth to restore it to its present condition. Power, who had bought the ruin for £1800, created an impressive interior with an oak-panelled hall and dining room and a magnificent spiral staircase. He re-named the castle 'Ayesha' after a fictional goddess who rose from the flames in Ryder Haggard's book *She*. Ayesha Castle was sold in 1996 to the Irish singer Enya for over £2 million.

Mount Eagle, which has an equally remarkable location overlooking the sea, was designed by Sandham Symes and built in 1837. Sandham Symes was a nephew of Robert Warren and was commissioned by him to design many new buildings around Killiney Hill. A fine wooden model of the house, which has always remained on display at Mount Eagle, bears Symes's signature and illustrates the unusual Y plan of the house.

Like Ayesha, it is built completely in granite ashlar, in squared and jointed blocks of stone, and it also has a broad terrace which looks out over the Irish Sea.

Unlike Ayesha, it is designed in the neo-classical style and is decorated inside with plasterwork in the Greek Revival manner. It also has an attractive double staircase and is completely symmetrical in plan. The stables of Mount Eagle, which are also very well built and have cut-stone details, back onto the road.

Robert Warren also took a leading role in the building of Holy Trinity Church, as he gave the site for it and made a substantial donation towards its construction – there is a plaque to him in the church. It was completed in 1858 to Sandham Symes's designs. It was built in a simple Gothic idiom and has a quaint, octagonal belfry. There was a private gate from Killiney Castle into the grounds of the church for Warren, and an attractive Gothic entrance gate for the general public.

Bellevue Park On the west side of Killiney, looking back over Dublin Bay, is Bellevue Park, now occupied by the St Joseph of Cluny convent and school. Bellevue once controlled a large estate which extended as far as Glenageary, where at the top of Adelaide Road there was an entrance and gate-lodge to the house. This long avenue led to a small house which appears on a map of 1816 and which seems to have been rebuilt around 1830 for a banker named Alexander Boyle, of the Dublin firm Boyle, Low and Murray. It is a large, square house with a projecting Ionic portico. The most unusual feature of Bellevue is its circular hall, which carries a gallery or landing and a top-lit dome above. Six curved doors lead to the principal rooms and to the staircase, which itself is of note as it is a cantilevered stone structure of great elegance. The present convent chapel was built as a billiard room by the Anketell Jones family, who owned Bellevue until 1898. The room was designed in the lavish Italianate style of the 1890s. A large mantelpiece, which is an outstanding example of oak carving, is the centrepiece of a very elaborate

The magnificent carved oak mantelpiece of the billiard room, now the chapel, of Bellevue Park

A dance programme from Bellevue Park

decorative scheme of panelling and plasterwork. The two large bow windows of the drawing-room and dining-room offer fine views over Dublin Bay.

A sale notice of 1898 gives a full picture of the house and estate. The house was advertised as being a seven-minute walk from Glenageary railway station. The outbuildings comprised three coach houses, two stables and substantial farm buildings. There was a large barn with tyings for twenty cows, and a four-faced clock tower stood between the two yards. The walled garden stood on about one acre, and included a large fernery. Bellevue had two tennis courts in 1898, one grass and one surfaced in 'asphalte'.

During the ownership of the Blacker Douglas family, landed gentry from County Armagh who bought Bellevue in the early 1900s, the model farm and ninety-acre estate was kept up. Most of the curved, brick-lined walls of the enclosed gardens are still standing and were once entered by a carved granite doorcase which is still there but now blocked up, and which may have been the original entrance of an earlier Bellevue house.

In 1930 the house was owned by David Barry, who was chairman of B and I shipping company, and afterwards became the property of Patrick Belton TD. He sold Bellevue to the order of St Joseph of Cluny who established a school here. The rest of the lands were developed with houses.

Rochestown House, had it survived, would almost certainly have had the distinction of being the oldest house in Killiney. It stood almost exactly on the path of Avondale Road, not far from the present Killiney shopping centre, and is almost completely forgotten. The house was built close to the ruin of Rochestown Castle, a fragment of which was still standing in about 1900, and which was photographed by Thomas Mason for Ball's *A History of the County of Dublin*. The ivy-clad ruin was

The ruins of Rochestown Castle

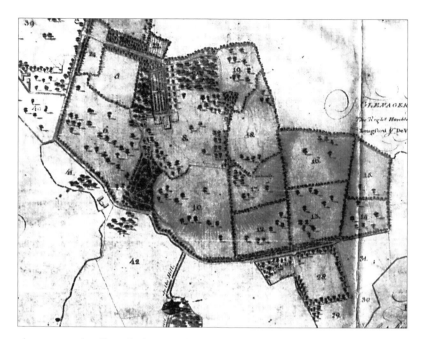

Sherrard's map (1787) of Rochestown demesne, showing the house (top left) surrounded by its formal gardens and woods (courtesy National Library)

Rochestown House as illustrated in Ball's History

shown on the first Ordnance Survey map as an 'ivy turret'. John Rocque's map of County Dublin, made in 1757, shows the house as the most significant residence in the area, with extensive outbuildings, a large walled garden and a well-wooded demesne.

Ball informs us that the mansion was built by John Malpas whose name, family arms and the date of 1750 appeared on a carved stone high up in the pediment of the house. This stone is said to have fallen during a storm, shortly before the house was demolished, but its whereabouts, if it survives, are unknown. The photograph of Rochestown published in Ball's *History* shows a gracious, mid-eighteenth-century, five-bay, three-storey house with tall Georgian windows. Ball says that the house had its own 'brewery, and a pigeon house, enclosed in a court yard, and close by there were gardens, pleasure grounds, orchards, and a bowling green'. Gaskin informs us that the nineteenth-century occupants of Rochestown, the O'Kellys, had the house furnished with many curiosities, including a portrait of Squire John Malpas and a large collection of Irish shells.

A beautiful map of the Malpas estate at Rochestown was made by Thomas Sherrard in 1787. This hand-coloured map, now in the National Library, illustrates the extent of the property, running from Kill of the Grange as far as Killiney Bay. It also gives an impression of how well-planted it all was, for all the roads are lined with trees on both sides. A large formal garden and a kitchen garden are shown close to the house, and a laneway, which now provides access to the golf club, is also marked.

The order of John Malpas's estates at Rochestown contrasts with the wilder appearance of the hills at Killiney, and this idea of the wild romantic landscape, where nature is organised by man but appears to flourish at will, must have appealed to Malpas and his eighteenth-century friends.

Today's Rochestown Avenue already existed at the time of Rocque and, as its name suggests, was laid out as part of a grand approach to the Malpas residence.

Flowergrove is an early house on Rochestown Avenue, which was part of the Malpas estate and still stands. It was built in about 1760, in the plain, Georgian style but with the most unusual feature of a slightly curving front wall. There were later additions, *circa* 1820, of two-storey wings, a new entrance to the side, and a ballroom to the rear. Flowergrove, with its white-painted cornice and eagle, is situated directly opposite Johnstown Road, and commands a fine view of the Dublin mountains.

Granitefield Another old house which appears on a map of 1816 is Granitefield. It stood almost opposite Flowergrove but was completely engulfed by the Victor Hotel, now re-named The Rochestown Lodge.

The rocky outcrop which is known as Roche's Hill was called Rochestown Hill in the eighteenth century. At this time it was used as a source of stone and evidence of quarrying can still be seen. There is a public right of way around Roche's Hill, passing through the golf links which occupy much of the western slopes, as far as the Ballybrack Road. Killiney Golf Club was established in 1903, and soon afterwards a most attractive timber pavilion was erected. This white-painted pavilion, which is still in use, is thought to have been purchased at an international exhibition in Dublin.

Flowergrove, built in about 1760 on the Rochestown estate

Roche's Hill was the subject of a notorious planning compensation case in 1986. An investment company had bought the hill in 1980 for £40,000, and almost immediately applied for planning permission to build houses there, even though it was zoned as amenity land. Being refused, they successfully won a compensation claim in the Supreme Court. This case and other similar cases shocked local residents and the general public.

However, Roche's Hill remains unspoilt, with its many granite outcrops, yellow gorse and lack of any trees, and gives an impression of what Killiney Hill might have looked like before it was planted in the eighteenth century.

Beechwood House, which had been built by 1787, stood on a narrow site at

Steam engines transported the inhabitants of Killiney to and from the city for almost a century

the bottom of Ballinclea Road. A five-windowed, two-storey-over-basement house, it appears to have been remodelled in Victorian times with the addition of mansard windows, a rendered façade and a decorative ironwork balcony. In more recent times a hotel operated here but the house was eventually demolished, though its handsome cut-stone, Georgian entrance gates still stand.

The lands of Ballinclea between Killiney Hill and Rochestown were not part of the Malpas estate.

Ballinclea House stood between Bellevue Park and Roche's Hill on the east side of Ballinclea Road, but was demolished during the 1950s. It was an attractive late-Georgian house, built about 1800, with double bows. These two-storey bows had gracious Wyatt windows which were ornamented with pediments, and there was a ballustraded parapet and a projecting porch with four pilasters. The house was built by the Talbot

A Lawrence photograph from around 1900 shows how few changes have occurred to the landscape near Killiney

family who were descendants of John Malpas and they lived here until the 1930s. Ballinclea had a noted collection of paintings which were transferred to the main Talbot residence, Malahide Castle, when the house was sold. It was approached by an avenue of walnut trees and once also had a fine wood of beech trees, which were known as Talbot Woods, but these were cut down in the 1940s during the Emergency. The original entrance gates may still be seen, and the most unusual stable buildings, which are laid out in the shape of a horseshoe, have been converted into houses.

Ballinclea House, which today gives its name to a residential area in Killiney

Victorian Killiney

The potential for building on the southern side of Roche's Hill was soon realised, and in the nineteenth century such houses as Glenalua Lodge and The Peak were built. The Peak is a two-storey, five-windowed Victorian house while Glenalua Lodge is a villa-type residence, with a Gothic-style porch. Since then many new houses and bungalows have been erected, taking full advantage of the wonderful sea and mountain views.

After the extension of the railway to Killiney during the 1850s, there was a rush to build houses which would have the advantage of these views and the convenience of easy access to Dublin city. Most of this development took place in the area extending south from Killiney village towards Ballybrack and the sea. More than forty substantial Victorian houses were erected here, an area which was quickly to become a coveted location in which to reside.

But some houses had been built before the arrival of the railway and Samuel Lewis, writing in 1839, lists eight new residences in Killiney, including Killiney Park, Saintbury, Killiney House, Marino, Martello Farm, Druid Cottage, Ballybrack Grove and Kilmarnock. Some of the earliest nineteenth-century houses in Killiney were villas, and Mount Malpas is a good example of this type.

Mount Malpas By Killiney standards Mount Malpas is a modest house, probably built around 1840, and stands near Mount Eagle, which as already mentioned has unrivalled views of the sea. It stands one-storey-over-basement and has a particularly colonial air about it, probably due to its first-floor ironwork verandah. The house made news in 1997 when it was sold for £2.3 million.

Killiney Park House (locally called The Park House) is one of the older houses in the area and was owned by an English family called Waterhouse, who themselves lived nearby at Claremount and Glenalna. They were silversmiths from Sheffield, and had a jewellery and silversmith business in Dame Street in Dublin. The family owned a considerable amount of land in Killiney, which they subsequently developed.

A map, dated 1767, of the lands of the Dean of Christchurch Cathedral, Dublin, showing the ancient ruined church

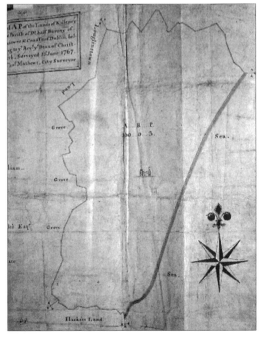

*Above: The entrance gate
to Druid Lodge
Right: Druid Hill*

*Typical Victorian plasterwork
detail from the drawing room at
Druid Hill*

Killiney Park House, a five-bay, two-storey, non-basement residence, was probably built about 1830. It had a hipped roof with over-hanging eaves. The house had two entrances, one from Killiney Avenue and one from Killiney Hill Road, and a walled garden of about half an acre. There is a small folly tower, built of granite, which stands on a former driveway to the east of the house. Following its sale in 1965, Killiney Park was demolished and a group of large, split-level houses was developed, now called Killiney Heath.

Nearby is Druid Hill and Druid Lodge, two houses which take their name from the adjacent monument, the Druid's Chair.

Druid Lodge was built in the 1830s but was greatly enlarged some thirty years later by the addition of a new block to the front. This extension, with its rendered walls, projecting pilastered porch and fine Victorian interiors, gave the house new views over Killiney Bay. The plasterwork cornices with their ivy leaf motif, the ceiling roses and the woodwork are all of great quality. In its grounds is a curious stone structure, known as the 'spite tower', which is said to have been built close to the neighbouring house in order to cause annoyance! This, however, is probably a myth as the tower was built long before any house appeared on the site of Druid Hill. It is more likely that the Victorian owners of Druid Lodge wished to have a better sea view, and some time in the 1850s they erected this fine castellated granite tower, with windows and a viewing platform.

Druid Hill was built around 1902, in the Tudor manner, with first-floor bay windows, gables, a red tiled roof and a white-painted cupola. In the wall, at the corner of Killiney Hill Road and Killiney Avenue, there is a Gothic arched doorway with the name 'Druid Hill' cut in stone above it.

The lands of Killiney belonged to the Church since medieval times. In 1842, the ground rents of Killiney, which originally belonged to the Dean of Christchurch, were 'sold' to various landlords such as the e familyDomviles, and later the Pim family; and the Church still demanded a tithe from the annual rent. The sale of the estate of George Cecil Pim in 1947 reveals that his family were the chief landlords for all of Killiney, from Seafield Road to Killiney village and from the beach to Shanganagh Terrace.

A map made for the Dean of Christchurch Cathedral in 1767, showing his lands which then stretched from Hackettsland to Roche's Hill, shows only one building, the ancient ruined church. A later survey of 1810 shows that the lands, then let to Compton Domvile of Loughlinstown, had been crossed by new roads which gave access to the Martello towers and batteries which had recently been erected. There were also two small houses on the Military Road, two near the ruined church, one which is possibly Dorset Lodge, and two others near Druid Lodge. There were two further cottages near Killiney village. There is little evidence that there were any houses of note built here before about 1830.

The first Ordnance Survey map of this area, published in 1843, marks Templeville, Glenfield, Killiney Lodge, Killiney House, Desmond, Percy Lodge and Dorset Lodge as the principal houses on Killiney Hill Road.

The so-called 'spy tower' at Druid Hill, which was erected to take advantage of the exceptional views

Killiney House is a neat, two-storey villa and is a contemporary of Percy Lodge. Both are typical of the 1830s with their two-storey, double-fronted arrangement. Both have bay windows and hipped roofs with projecting eaves.

Temple Ville, which stands just to the north of Druid Lodge, is one of Killiney's few Georgian-style houses, and is historically interesting for once having been used as a church. Indeed, a curious feature of its chimney stack is a small, arched opening which may once have housed a bell. Church services were held here until the opening of St

Temple Ville, one of the few houses of eighteenth-century origin in Killiney

Marino, an attractive Arts-and-Crafts-style house which was rebuilt in 1909

Matthias's Church, Ballybrack, in 1835. The house is a five-bay, two-storey, non-basement residence with dormer windows. The interior exhibits typical late-Georgian features such as a narrow cornice and six-panelled doors.

St Anne's is situated quite near the Martello tower and is a large Victorian house with terraced gardens. The house has many similarities with Druid Lodge, and it is possible that the same architect was involved. For example, both have the unusual feature of rounded corners, and a small gable in the centre of the façade. St Anne's was first owned in the 1860s by the Du Bedat family, who were noted stockbrokers in Dublin. Later inhabitants included Sir John Barrington, Lord Mayor of Dublin in 1865, and the writer Constantine Fitzgibbon.

Desmond was the original name of a house now called Padua, and though built during the 1830s, it was later enlarged by the addition of three-storey bay windows.

Marino Though this house is included among the early 1830 houses of Killiney, a plaque on the wall records the fact that it was largely rebuilt: 'this house was built by Lawrence A. Waldron 1909'. It is a large 'Arts and Crafts'-style house with wide-mullioned windows which have small, leaded panes of glass. It is roofed with small slates and has dormer windows. The entrance has elaborately carved brackets and is built in the form of a projecting bow.

In the garden there is an attractive octagonal gazebo with round-

Decorative cast-iron balustrade from the staircase at Montebello

No expense was spared in the building of Montebello, one of Killiney's finest Victorian houses in the Italian style

headed windows of coloured glass. It is now the residence of the Australian ambassador. The original house was occupied by a Joshua Cheator, or Chaytor, who owned a substantial amount of land in Killiney and built a number of Victorian houses including St Anne's, Buenavista, Abbeylands and Mentone. Cheator had previously lived at Purbeck Lodge in Monkstown where he had constructed four houses.

Many large detached houses of a purely Victorian type were constructed in Killiney in the second half of the nineteenth century, and good examples of these include Marathon, Lismellow, Fortlands, Cliff House and Montebello, all of which are to be found on Killiney Hill Road. Similar houses were built on Killiney Avenue, a new road of the 1850s which linked the residential area of Killiney with the church in Ballybrack. Such houses include Laragh, Clonard and Suquehanna.

The weathervane at Palermo bears the letter H from the Hone family, who built it

All of these large Victorian houses were built to reflect the status and position of the family that lived there. These houses required an imposing front, a grand hall and a well-furnished drawing room. A larger residence with a couple of acres needed a gate lodge and a winding avenue which brought the visitor to a broad gravel sweep in front of the hall door. Whether the architecture was Italianate or Gothic did not matter greatly. Many of the earlier houses were plain, so it was common for wealthy Victorian owners to add porticos, stucco enrichments, cornices and brackets. Often a billiard room would be added at the back of the house.

Montebello is a fine example of a mid-Victorian house, and was probably built for the Kirkwood family, who were landed gentry from County Roscommon. It was later occupied by A. E. Goodbody, solicitor, in the early 1920s. It was lavishly decorated with the best of joinery including Egypto-Greek style pillars and barley-sugar columns in the hall. A projecting semi-circular porch opens onto an elaborate flight of granite steps. The house, which has a noble aspect, is two-storeys-over-basement and has a pediment feature at parapet level. There is a small, octagonal summer house in the garden and, at the entrance to a winding avenue, a gate-lodge which bears a coat of arms depicting three scallop shells.

A granite pyramid, called the Dorset Monument, records the accidental death of the Duke of Dorset

Palermo An interesting feature of Palermo, another house on Killiney Hill Road, is a decorative ventilator and weather vane which stands on the pointed roof of a small outbuilding. There is an H cut into the metal of the weathervane which reminds us that this house and its twin, South Hill, were built by the Hone family, who had other property interests in Killiney and were related to the well-known Irish artist Nathaniel Hone.

Strathmore A large house called Strathmore was built for William Henry, a retired wine merchant, in about 1865. It was later the residence of Judge Bramley, from 1880 to the 1940s. Strathmore, now the Canadian Embassy, was considerably altered, and the entrance portico was moved to one end of the house rather than centred at the front.

The Hall A house now called The Hall, situated near the top of Strathmore Road, was once used as a schoolhouse by the Church of Ireland parishes of Killiney and Ballybrack. Its long, slated roof and

Court-na-Farraige, now the Killiney Court Hotel, was built in the 1860s

pointed ventilator make it a familiar landmark on Killiney Hill Road.

Killiney is today a place of old stone walls and narrow leafy roads which twist downwards towards the sea or wind upwards into the hills. Strathmore Road, Kilmore Avenue and St George's Avenue are some of these pleasant lanes, which are dotted with a wonderful variety of houses. Oakdene and Dorset Lodge are two very charming, rambling houses of a modest size, and which probably began as small houses but were frequently extended. Dorset Lodge, now called St Declan's, was named in memory of the fourth Duke of Dorset who was killed when he fell from his horse while hunting near here. The duke, who was a step-son of the Lord Lieutenant, was only twenty-two when the accident occurred in 1815, and it was decided to erect a monument in the form of a stone pyramid on the spot where he fell. This monument is now in the grounds of St Columba, a house near Ballybrack Catholic church.

In 1861 *The Dublin Builder* announced that the architects Deane and Woodward were designing 'six new dwelling houses for different parties, amongst whom is Mr Joseph Robinson, the eminent concert singer. The foundations have been laid out.' The six houses include Illerton, Alloa, Undercliff, Cliff House and Fernside.

Illerton, built in 1863 for William Bewley was a brick house of Gothic design, but was later rendered and considerably altered. The house was acquired by the Jameson family who changed the name to Alloa, after the Jameson family seat in Scotland. Hidden away at the bottom of a private avenue, was once the home of artist Flora Mitchell (widow of William Jameson), whose book *Vanishing Dublin* is now long out of print and is much treasured.

Fernside also exhibits various Gothic features such as the slated hall-door canopy and windows.

Undercliffe and **Cliff House** belong to a group of romantic architectural styles much loved in Killiney. Both houses, dating from the 1860s, have circular towers with conical roofs. Undercliff was designed by Benjamin Woodward and has an unusual L-shaped plan.

The Court Hotel, formerly a private house called Court-na-Farraige, also belongs to this group of fanciful, French chateau-inspired houses. It was designed in 1865, probably by the architect T. N. Deane for William Exham, and is ornamented with an extravagant series of stone-capped gables, and a conical tower, all elaborately surrounded by a now-vanished, two-storey verandah. A second conical tower was added in the 1970s when the hotel was extended.

Kenah Hill – the building of this large, Victorian mansion was partly responsible for the financial ruin of the Du Bedat family

One of the most elevated locations in Killiney is St George's Avenue, which was probably first developed in the 1880s when Kenah Hill was built by the Exham family.

Kenah Hill, originally called Frankfort, is perched at the top of the hill among Scots pine trees. It is a very large Italianate house with rendered walls and decorative mouldings around its windows and doors. The main elevation is six bays wide and two storeys high and there is a large, half-octagonal bow facing the garden front. The main entrance is articulated by fluted Ionic pilasters. The house has lately been completely renovated and separated from its rather attractive stableyard. The enclosed yard has a distinctive cupola with louvres and a copper dome. Kenah Hill, earlier called Stoneleigh, was the home of Francis or Frank Du Bedat. Du Bedat became President of the stock exchange in Dublin,

St George's, built in 1882, is richly decorated with stained-glass windows and Gothic Revival detail in wood and stone

*St. George Slays the Dragon –
carved detail from over the
entrance door of St. George's*

The Italianate tower at Mentone

but in 1890 he commited a major fraud with his investors' funds, a crime for which he was ultimately jailed, and the family name ruined. He died in Paris in the 1920s. George Bernard Shaw is said to have modelled his play *The Doctor's Dilemma* on the real-life character of Frank Du Bedat.

The writer Katherine Tynan, who lived there for a time, remarked that her grand piano looked like a postage stamp in the drawing room!

St George's was designed and built by George Ashlin, the noted architect. His wife was the granddaughter of Augustus Welby Pugin, a devoted admirer of the Gothic. It is no surprise that St George's, built in 1882, is something of a Victorian Gothic extravaganza, built in red brick with its steep and varied tiled roofs, conical tower, Gothic fireplaces and a small, panelled chapel. The walls were once decorated with William Morris wallpapers. There is still a remarkable collection of stained glass, executed by Edward Frampton, to be seen throughout the house. The windows represent the architect and his wife in prayer, as well as St George, St Dorothea and various subjects such as music, poetry, architecture and painting. There is also an excellent stone carving of St George and the dragon over the front door. The staircase landing is ornamented with corbels which are painted with coats of arms.

Ashlin also built Carrigrennane on the lands of St George's, as a residence for another member of the family. It is designed in the mock-Tudor style, in imitation of a timber-frame house, and its redbrick gate-lodge bears the date 1882.

The Grove, now a large nursing home, is also to be found in this vicinity. It is a very impressive, late Victorian house, with many gables and bay windows. An unusual arched ballustrade, made of terracotta, encloses the driveway in front of the house.

There are a number of interesting houses which date from the turn of the century and employ certain mock-Tudor features such as half- timbered gables, mullioned windows, and verandahs, usually in combination with redbrick. Such examples must include Namur, Aileen and Gaileen, all on Killiney Avenue.

The Military Road joins Ballybrack with the railway at Strand Road. It must once have served the Martello tower there and a battery which is now the site of Killiney railway station. Several very large houses were erected on the Military Road including Killacoona, Mentone, Ashhurst, Kilmarnock and Rathleigh.

Killacoona House is now incorporated into the Holy Child convent school, and, like The Grove and Carrigrennane, it was a large, redbrick, Tudor-style house, built facing south with views of Bray Head in the distance. The drawing room, now used as a library, is decorated with pilasters, carved in the Renaissance style, with masks and foliage. An earlier, smaller house, once called Martello Lodge and later renamed Little Anstice, was purchased by the nuns and now serves as a residence.

Mentone is another classic house of the Victorian period, having the usual ornate external treatment of stucco enrichments, lined walls, arched windows and a hipped roof with bracketed eaves. But Mentone can also boast an Italianate tower which is a landmark in the area.

Ashurst was built in 1861. *The Dublin Builder* informs us that 'a large mansion is being commenced under the directions of Messrs Lanyon, Lynn and Lanyon, architects, for the Hon. Judge Dobbs, and will cost some £4,000 or £5,000'. It remained in this family but was mostly let, until it was sold as a residence for the Archbishop of Dublin, John Charles McQuaid.

Ashurst, one of the largest houses in Killiney, built in 1861 for the Hon. Judge Dobbs

It is a very large, redbrick mansion, somewhat severe and institutional in character, though it is attractively set amidst mature trees and gardens. It was designed by W. H. Lynn in the Gothic manner, and makes clever use of yellow and slate-coloured brickwork. A tall, square tower which rises above the entrance, and once contained water tanks, was heightened by the Archbishop to create a viewing room. There is a well-built, granite gate-lodge on the Military Road.

The gate-lodge at Ashurst

Kilmarnock, which for many years was known as Haldene Grange, is yet another impressive house, situated originally on about nine acres. Dating from about 1830, the original house was greatly enlarged around 1860 by the Right Hon. David Fitzgerald, when a whole new series of spacious rooms and a grandiose Italianate façade to the front were added. The hipped roof with its bracketed eaves, projecting porch with its balcony, and all the stucco enrichments are typical of the work of architect Charles Geoghegan, who designed the additions.

Lion masks are a feature of the joints of the cast-iron gutters and also of the unusual railings which protect the area at the front of the house.

Kilmarnock belonged to the Talbot Crosby family of Ardfert Abbey, County Kerry, until the 1940s. More recently it was known as the Cenacle Retreat House, during which period a large residential block was built to the rear.

Unusual cast-iron sphinxes at Kilmarnock

Opposite page: The White Cottage, built as a summer house and tea rooms, is still a landmark on Killiney Beach

Two pairs of castellated, stone-built houses, including Vartry Lodge and Dunmara, were erected on the seashore at Killiney

One of many ornate garden buildings which are so much a feature of the houses in Killiney

Rathleigh Opposite Kilmarnock is Rathleigh, a plain, five-bay, two-storey house which, like its neighbour Salerno, appears on the first Ordnance Survey map of this area in 1840.

Stonehurst and **Avonmore** are approached from the bottom of Killiney Hill Road and Seafield Road respectively. Both are built of cut stone. Avonmore was designed by William Murray in a rather ecclesiastical Gothic style. Stonehurst, of similar appearance, is a many-gabled, steep-roofed house with timber bay windows. The wrought-iron gates and cut-stone gate piers, with their Gothic caps, are of outstanding quality.

The family of Field, who were originally wool merchants and butchers, came to own a substantial amount of land in Killiney. William Field, who was a grocer in Ballybrack, obviously enjoyed the pun on his name when he named Seafield Road, which he developed. Some of the houses which Field erected were given names such as Gay Field. William's Park, called after Field himself, was built close to the present Bayview estate. During the second half of the nineteenth century, Field acquired various leases of lands in Shanganagh and Killiney, which he either sub-let for building or developed himself. His interests included the ground rents from Druid Lodge, Druid Hill, Mount Druid (now Marathon), and other houses in that part of Killiney Hill Road. He also received

A modern view of Killiney, showing Ayesha Castle and Temple Hill in their well-wooded surroundings

rents from St Columba's Church in Ballybrack, and Beechlands, Eaton Brae and Glen Brae, which are all in Shankill.

A remarkable pair of semi-detached, stone-built houses are a conspicuous feature of Killiney beach. These houses, which include Vartry Lodge, Dunmara, Carraig-na-Mara and Supermare, are the work of architect George Wilkinson who designed many railway stations and workhouses. They are constructed in rustic granite block-work with battlemented towers and wings. With their stonework towers they are successful in creating a defensive appearance although inside they are typically Victorian in their comfort and decoration. These houses, and the Martello tower which has been converted to residential use, directly overlook the sand and shingle of the beach, at the point where the Loughlinstown river joins the sea. Wilkinson also designed Temple Hill for the Hone family, an impressive Victorian house with a fine temple in its grounds, currently owned by the singer Bono.

Killiney Beach has long served as a favourite bathing place and it is not surprising that Rocque's map of 1757 shows a bath-house somewhere near White Rock. The old tea rooms on the beach are a more modern relic of bathing and boating activities, and though the white-painted structure might look more at home in Greece, it was used up to the 1950s as a dance pavilion and tea rooms. It was also possible to hire rowing boats here at the White Cottage, as it is called locally.

There have been a number of serious pollution problems in Killiney Bay including an oil spill in 1979 and ongoing complaints about sewage. Dublin County Council spent about £5 million in 1981 to improve sewage treatment and to lay a mile-long pipe out into the sea. More recently, the situation has improved and Killiney beach has been awarded the European blue flag, to indicate a high state of cleanliness of the beach and its waters.

As already noted, Killiney's first railway station was built for the convenience of Robert Warren, almost above White Rock, and possibly in anticipation of his proposed Queenstown development. The station was not convenient to most of Killiney's new residents, and in 1859 a new one was opened on the site of an old battery or fort and a further station was built at Seafield Road. In 1882, these were abandoned and finally a new Killiney station, still in use, was opened.

The Killiney and Ballybrack Township was formed in 1866 and was responsible for the administration of local affairs. They had the power to levy rates and make improvements in the area. Their duties included the regulation of hackney cars, carriages and cabs, and in 1891 a booklet of bylaws was published for the drivers of these vehicles. There were four stands – one at the railway station, one at Military Road near Ballybrack House, one at Shanganagh Road near Firgrove and one at Killiney Avenue. It was laid down that the heads of the horses should face in a particular direction – for example, at Military Road they were to face the sea! Hackney cabs could carry only four adults and were obliged to use lamps at night. 'The driver shall wear decent apparel and be civil, and able to read and write, and shall not use any insulting, obscene, or profane language to any person or persons what so ever, nor smoke when employed', the rules dictated. There was also a full list of charges, for example from Ballybrack post office to any part of Dalkey would cost two shillings, while a trip to the railway station cost one shilling and six pence. Sightseeing trips could be arranged to places like Powerscourt Waterfall or Glendalough, but in these cases fares had to be agreed with the drivers.

This drinking trough for horses stands at the junction of Killiney Road and Ballinclea Road

Most houses in Killiney and Ballybrack had their own supply of water, usually drawn from wells located near the house. Though the Vartry water supply had been piped from County Wicklow to Dublin in 1868, Killiney remained without its own reservoir until the early 1890s. Shortly after the transfer of Killiney Hill Park to the Township commissioners in 1891, a reservoir was constructed, quite discreetly, into the side of the hill, just above Killiney village. A shelter was built above it, and was used, within living memory, for dancing on summer evenings.

Sir John Gray, who was chairman of the Dublin Water Commission, had bought up the surrounding lands at Roundwood to prevent their purchase by profit-making speculators, and he re-sold them to Dublin Corporation without profit. Gray was the proprietor of *The Freeman's Journal* and lived at Lower Strand Road in Killiney, where after his death his house was re-named Vartry Lodge.

CHAPTER 5

Ballybrack

Ballybrack is situated between Loughlinstown and Killiney, and its village, which emerged during the nineteenth century, is geographically very much part of Killiney. Socially, Ballybrack marks a sharp divide between the newer 'working-class' districts on the Loughlinstown side and the well-off residential areas of Killiney.

In 1816 there was no village here and the only significant road was the Military Road which connected the Martello tower at Killiney with the main road at Loughlinstown, where the great military camp had been located. Church Road, which would later link Rochestown Avenue to Ballybrack, was not yet laid out and only a few houses such as Carrickmoleen and Ballybrack Grove (later called Shanganagh Grove) are shown.

Map of Ballybrack, showing Kavanagh's Nursery, Madden's Cottages and Shanganagh Park House

As we have already seen, the Domvile family were enormously influential in these parts of south County Dublin as they were the ground landlords of the whole of Shankill, Loughlinstown, Kilbogget and Killiney. These lands, including all of modern Ballybrack and much of Killiney, were granted to the Domviles in 1663 by King Charles II. Thomas Sherrard's map (1787) of the Malpas estate confirms that Mrs Domvile was the current owner of these lands, and that they were still undeveloped.

In 1811 Sir Compton Domvile leased the Ballybrack lands to a pair of developers named Moore and Oxley. A cottage belonging to a Mr Moore, situated near Killiney village, is shown on a contemporary map. Together they leased 42 acres and 65 acres respectively, with the condition that they must build quality houses there. The lease contained the usual conditions prohibiting the making and burning of bricks and the building of mudwalled cabins with thatched roofs, but it also stipulated that they must plant ten three-year-old trees in place of any one tree cut down.

Domvile also donated a site for the new Protestant church at Ballybrack, St Matthias's, which, as already mentioned, was opened in 1835. The

Vevey House was among the first new houses to be built in Ballybrack in about 1830

church, funded by the Board of First Fruits, is typical of the period in its cruciform plan and plain appearance. It is of granite construction and has a square tower with narrow, Gothic openings and slender pinnacles. Once located in a quiet, tree-lined road, it now stands beside the dual carriageway leading to Loughlinstown.

The new road to Ballybrack was subsequently called Church Road, and, until recently, it remained largely unaltered since the middle of the nineteenth century. It has just been widened and completely reconstructed, with granite-faced walls on either side. Church Road was the site of the first new houses in Ballybrack, and these include Ballybrack Lodge, now Vevey House, Moore Field, Harrow House, and Balure. All are double-fronted houses, yet of modest size. Ballybrack House is similar in style, though a little larger. All of these are characteristic of the Regency period and range in date from the 1820s to the 1840s. Typical features include a fanlight over the hall door, bright rooms with wide Georgian-style windows, simple plasterwork cornices and marble mantelpieces with pillars. Moore Field is a single-storey-over-basement, villa-type house which is dated to 1824.

The first Ordnance Survey map gives us a good picture of the various other villas which were already built by 1840, and these include Wyattville, Ridge Hall, Firgrove, Rock Field, Sarah Villa, Victoria Lodge and Albany. Some of these, for instance St Germain's and Wyattville, have been demolished, and new developments have been squeezed in. At Firgrove the old house remains amid a development of 'town houses'. Victoria Lodge, a pretty, single-storey 'cottage orné' with decorative bargeboards, became the site of a new group of shops.

It was during the middle of the nineteenth

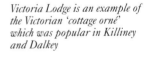

Victoria Lodge is an example of the Victorian 'cottage orné' which was popular in Killiney and Dalkey

Madden's Cottages

A map showing the Land League cottage in Ballybrack, home of Michael Davitt

century that Ballybrack village quickly established itself, with the arrival of various shops and a post office. Cottage-style houses were built on Mountain View Road and there was a growing community of gardeners, carpenters and house painters living here who found employment with the new wealthy residents of the area. Many of the labourers employed on the Domvile estate at Loughlinstown lived in Ballybrack.

The many gardens of Killiney and Ballybrack created a considerable demand for plants of all kinds, and there was a nursery in Ballybrack since the 1890s. The nursery, known as Kavanagh's, was located on the south-facing lands adjoining Victoria Lodge, and was depicted on a map of 1908 as having rows and rows of trees and shrubs. Its entrance was on Wyattville Road just beside the constabulary barracks – this barracks was attacked in 1922 and an attempt was made to burn it down.

More recently, Watson's nursery operated on the lands between Church Road and Cabinteely. Watson's, in business since the 1920s, specialised in fruit trees, shrubs and roses, and they also had a flower shop in Nassau Street. Following the sale of the nursery in the 1960s a large housing development was erected by Gallagher's, the builders.

Other groups of dwellings were built near Wyattville Road, including Madden's Cottages, Lynch's Cottages and Smith's Cottages. Most of these were replaced by Dun Laoghaire Corporation in 1956, when Dale View Park was constructed. An earlier terrace of eighteen semi-detached cottages called Dale View was built in the early 1900s.

Shanganagh Terrace was a fashionable Regency-style group of villas, constructed by a builder named Byrne, who himself lived at number eight. The terrace, which was begun in about 1845, was built close to Ballybrack village. It consists of about fifteen terraced houses, five of which are single-storey-over-basement. These five attractive houses have bracketed eaves, with a small gable over each front door, and most of them still have their original Regency-style windows.

Later developments on Church Road included such houses as Violet Hill, Larkfield, Tudor Lodge, and Caerleon. Tudor Lodge is a wide five-bay, treble-gabled house with delicate timber bargeboards, and was built about 1880.

Caerleon, a fine redbrick mansion set amid extensive gardens and mature trees, is today occupied by the Kylemore Clinic. It was built in the late 1880s for Frederick Trouton, a wine merchant. A most unusual feature is the arched corner loggia and terrace which form part of the house and give access to the gardens.

Evergreen is another distinctive house and stands on the corner of the Military Road and Killiney Hill Road. It is noteworthy for its unusual neo-classical frontage, with its single-storey wings, Wyatt windows, stucco embellishments and Ionic portico.

The Land League Cottage, originally named Eden Hill, but also called Ballybrack Cottage and more recently Roselawn, stood just behind the village, off the Military Road. It was named the 'Land League Cottage' when a gift of it was made to Michael Davitt, the labour leader, in recognition of his great efforts to help Irish tenant farmers. Like many other 'cottages' in the area, the front presents only a single storey while behind there is a large basement or garden level. Davitt lived there from 1888 until 1896, but whether he was the actual owner or not is not clear.

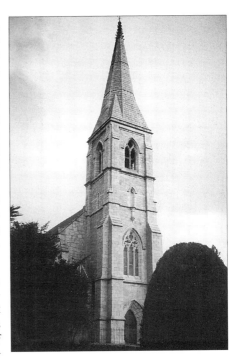

The Catholic church of Saints Alphonsus and Columba, Ballybrack

Another Killiney resident, John Blake Dillon, one of the leaders of the Young Ireland movement who was forced into exile, lived at Druid Lodge.

The Catholic church of Saints Alphonsus and Columba is a landmark which can be seen from all around. The church, built in the 1850s,

The parochial house, a fine cut-stone villa in the Gothic style

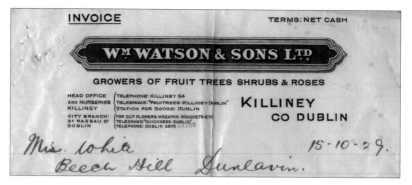

INVOICE   TERMS: NET CASH

Wᴹ WATSON & SONS Lᵀᴰ

GROWERS OF FRUIT TREES SHRUBS & ROSES

HEAD OFFICE   (TELEPHONE: KILLINEY 54
AND NURSERIES (TELEGRAMS: "FRUITREES-KILLINEY-DUBLIN"   **KILLINEY**
KILLINEY   (STATION FOR GOODS: DUBLIN
CITY BRANCH: (FOR CUT FLOWERS-WREATHS-BOUQUETS-ETC   **CO DUBLIN**
31 NASSAU ST   (TELEGRAMS: "QUICKNESS-DUBLIN"
DUBLIN   (TELEPHONE: DUBLIN 2572

Mrs. Cohia   15-10-2 9.
Beech Hill   Dunlavin.

stands on high ground just behind the village and is entirely constructed of granite. Its tall, Gothic spire was added in about 1870 and was the gift of Mrs Boland, of Boland's Bakery. The first parish priest was Fr John Harold who had promoted the building of the church, and he remained there until his death in 1868. A later incumbent here was Father James Healy of Little Bray, and there is a marble bust of him in the church.

The parochial house is an elegant and unusual cut-stone villa, quite similar to any other single-storey-over-basement house in the vicinity, except for its choice of Gothic detail. The use of granite for the walls and chimney stacks allows the house to sit comfortably with the nearby church, while all of its windows and doors are adapted to the Gothic form. The stone-built schoolhouse is also in harmony with the architecture of the church.

The cromlech at Ballybrack was sketched by Gabriel Beranger in the 1780s and was in much the same condition then as it is today, though its setting has changed since the development of many new houses in the vicinity during the 1980s. Some flints and a roughly made knife were found near it. Some 150 cromlechs have been recorded in Ireland, all burial tombs from the Neolithic period. Ballybrack cromlech is small in comparison to those at Brennanstown and Kilternan.

Nearby stood a villa-style house of Victorian date, which, taking its name from this ancient monument, was called Glen Druid. Having lain derelict in the early 1980s, all but its granite gate piers were demolished. Houses and a halting site for Travellers were constructed on the site.

The Ballybrack or Shanganagh cromlech, one of the smaller Neolithic tombs

Hackettsland owes its name to the fact that these low-lying lands belonged to a John Hackett in the fourteenth century. Little did he imagine that six hundred years later all of his fields would be built over with houses, or that the first proposal in 1972 to erect 174 houses here would be the subject of a prolonged planning wrangle.

CHAPTER 6

Dalkey

Dalkey, with its coastal roads, many sea views, and rocky bathing places, is imbued with a maritime quality. It has managed to retain its own special identity, one which is quite different to that of neighbouring Killiney or even Dun Laoghaire, and, though this is partly due to its position, it is mainly because its residents have, since the nineteenth century, so jealously fought to protect it.

Castle Street, with its two castles, church, shops and houses, still has the quality of a small town. Indeed, Dalkey has been designated a 'heritage town' and is included in a national list of some twenty such places. The title is aimed largely at promoting these towns as tourist venues, and it is unclear whether the designation should also mean that the historic fabric, such as old houses and shops, should be carefully conserved as a priority – too many old buildings in the country are crudely modernised with cement finishes and PVC windows. Dalkey has escaped from much

Victorian terrace in Dalkey with The Muglins in the background

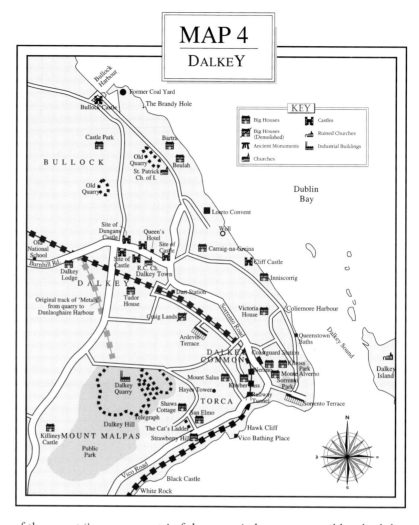

MAP 4
DALKEY

KEY

Big Houses   Castles

Big Houses (Demolished)   Ruined Churches

Ancient Monuments   Industrial Buildings

Churches

Bullock Harbour

Former Coal Yard

The Brandy Hole

Bullock Castle

Castle Park

Bartra

BULLOCK

Old Quarry

Beulah

St. Patrick Ch. of I.

Old Quarry

Dublin Bay

Loreto Convent

Site of Dungans Castle

Queen's Hotel

Well

Old National School

Burnhill Rd

Site of Castle

Carraig-na-Greina

Cliff Castle

Dalkey Lodge

Site of Castle

R.C. Ch. Dalkey Town

Inniscorrig

DALKEY

Dart Station

Original track of 'Metals' from quarry to Dunlaoghaire Harbour

Tudor House

Victoria House

Coliemore Harbour

Craig Lands

Sorrento Road

Queenstown Baths

Dalkey Sound

Ardevin Terrace

DALKEY COMMON

Coastguard Station

Dalkey Island

Nerano

Khoss Park

Mount Salus

Monte Alverno

Dalkey Quarry

Hayes Tower

Khyber Pass

Sorrento Park

Shaws Cottage

San Elmo

Railway Tunnel

Sorrento Terrace

TORCA

Telegraph

Dalkey Hill

The Cat's Ladder

Hawk Cliff

Killiney Castle

MOUNT MALPAS

Strawberry Hill

Vico Bathing Place

Public Park

Vico Road

Black Castle

White Rock

The Wexford train disappearing into a tunnel at Dalkey

of the worst 'improvements' of the twentieth century, and has had the benefit of being 'the last village' on the south shore of Dublin Bay, so that the need for greater or wider roads, which might pass through it, should never arise. Also, the district has been well served by the railway since 1844, and today's DART service continues to connect the inhabitants of Dalkey with the city.

The railway makes a very discreet appearance in Dalkey, passing through mostly in a cutting, then disappearing into a tunnel from which it emerges onto the dramatic coast of Killiney Bay. Most of this unique coastline remains unspoilt because the scope for development has always been limited by the presence of the sea on one side and Dalkey Hill, with its public park, on the other.

However, there has been consistent pressure to build apartment blocks and other houses on every available piece of land, sometimes to the detriment of the natural landscape and its comparatively unspoilt coastline. It could be argued that this process began when the first large houses and terraces were erected in the mid-nineteenth century, but at that time the scale and density of such projects was generally modest –

and the designs were usually ornamental! By comparison, today's developers are often greedy to pack in the greatest number of residential units, and there is often scant regard for the existing character of the place.

Yet, Dalkey has kept its particular charm. Without doubt, the presence of granite, which is to be found everywhere, contributes to this. Granite was used in the building of the ancient churches and castles, the Martello towers, the Loreto Convent, the harbours of Coliemore and Bullock, the nineteenth-century churches and many houses. It can also be seen in the footpaths, steps and window-sills in every part of Dalkey. But perhaps the most noticeable use of this fine stone is in the granite walls which form part of the network of small roads which abound in Dalkey.

One of the most colourful publications about Dalkey is James J. Gaskin's *Irish Varieties*, a book printed in 1869 at a time when Dalkey was undergoing great change after centuries of neglect. Gaskin had witnessed the Victorian transformation of Dalkey from an ancient village surrounded by fields into a town with its own administration and a coastline dotted with many fine residences. In the space of about thirty years, commencing in 1840, Dalkey saw rapid development. Houses and terraces sprang up here and there among the rocky terrain, and sites with a sea view were eagerly snapped up. Gaskin recorded all these happenings and included in his book as many printed references to Dalkey as he could find.

Dalkey, in comparison with Killiney, seems to have a greater diversity of house types. There are many more cottages, small villas and terraces, and the gardens are generally smaller.

Ancient Dalkey and Its Island

The name Dalkey means 'thorny island', and is derived either from the Norse 'Deilg-ei' or the Irish 'Deilg-inis'. It has been suggested that thorny island is most likely a reference to the shape of Dalkey Island, rather than a description of its vegetation. It is true that the island has the shape of a tapering thorn or dagger, and that it rises at the northern end of Dalkey Sound from small rocks and islands to a substantial height at its southern end. Legend has it that the Maiden Rock, at the northern extremity of Dalkey Sound, is so called because two 'maidens', who were perhaps gathering shellfish or seaweed, became stranded there and were drowned. Anyone who has ever handled a boat in the sound will agree that the current which accompanies the tide can be very powerful and should be treated with great respect.

An extraordinary plan for the area was proposed in the early 1800s, before Dun Laoghaire harbour was built, which would have involved closing, almost completely, the southern end of Dalkey Sound. The idea was to create a harbour by the construction of a breakwater

A chart by Alexander Nimmo, showing Dalkey Island, c. 1820

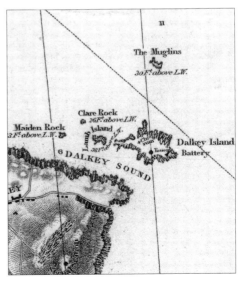

which would have originated at Sorrento Point. Fortunately, it was abandoned.

Dalkey Island guards the southern approaches to Dublin Bay, which, though considerably built up, it is still a very beautiful coastline. The island remains completely unspoilt and its resident goats and rabbits are left undisturbed except by visitors during the summer. At the back of the island, sitting among seagull nests, long grass and rocks, it is hard to believe that a capital city with over a million inhabitants lies just seven miles away.

St Begnet's Church The ruin of the ancient church of St Begnet on the island is in remarkably good condition and creates a bold profile with its two buttresses or antae, its square-headed, west-facing doorway and little belfry. During the construction of the Martello tower in the early 1800s, workmen used the church as a place of shelter and built a fireplace in its eastern gable.

A ship nearing The Muglins from John Roque's map of County Dublin, 1757

There is little doubt that Dalkey was a place of very early settlement, and archaeologists have found evidence of a promontary fort on Dalkey Island. Promontory forts are usually located on a headland, with sea on all sides but one, where a fortified ditch would be constructed. A similar fort existed on Lambay Island. A fascinating find of a stone axehead, possibly dating from 4000BC, was made in 1991, nearby in the sea near The Muglin's rock.

The Muglin's, a large barren rock to the north of Dalkey Island, which now carries a red-painted, cone-shaped lighthouse, was the scene of an unsavoury, eighteenth-century event. In 1766 *The Gentleman's Magazine* carried a report which related how the bodies of two pirates named McKinley and Zeckerman were hung in chains on The Muglin's for the murder of a Captain Glass and his family. The pirates had commandeered a ship, sailing from the Canary Islands to London, with a large

The ruined church of St Begnet, Dalkey Island

quantity of Spanish dollars, some jewels and other valuable cargoes, and proceeded towards Ireland having brutally murdered and thrown overboard its captain and crew. They were caught near Waterford and brought to Dublin where they were tried and hung. Their bodies were first hung on the South Wall at Dublin port, but, following complaints from the public, they were removed to The Muglin's!

Near the western shore, on Dalkey Island, is a fresh-water well, marked on some maps as 'the Scurvy well', and its waters are said to possess curative powers. The well was probably last used on a daily basis by the soldiers who occupied the Martello tower and battery during the nineteenth century.

Above left: The ruins of the fort or battery on Dalkey Island

Above right: Stonework showing the position of swivelling guns

Medieval Dalkey

The lands of Dalkey, Killiney and Shankill were granted to the Church in medieval times and the Archbishop of Dublin established a manor at Shankill in order to control these lands and collect dues from his tenants. In Dalkey, he had the right to collect a sort of tax which consisted of 'a prise of fish', and he could grant tenancies in the form of burgages. A burgage included a strip of land which could be cultivated, and many of them backed onto the town, where the tenant had the right to graze cattle or sheep on the common. It might also include an orchard or garden. In 1326 the archbishop granted thirty-nine burgages in Dalkey.

The king also held land in Dalkey, which in the thirteenth century he granted to Reginald Talbot in return for an annual rent of one goshawk! Such birds must once have been common around Dalkey, and it is interesting that the Hawk Cliff, near the Vico bathing place, was still to be found on nineteenth-century maps. However, Talbot found himself in trouble in 1369, when his goshawk was deemed to be 'un sound, un fit, and of no value – a fraud on the Court, and a grievous damage to the King' and he was fined!

Decorative cartouche from Thomas Reading's map, 1765

Rocque's map, 1757, shows that Dalkey had changed little since medieval times

A map of ancient Dalkey made in 1765 by Thomas Reading shows the position of Dalkey's medieval churches and the division of plots of land

There are two churches dedicated to St Begnet in Dalkey, one on the island and one in Castle Street in Dalkey village. The latter, which stands beside the Goat Castle, is attributed to the ninth century, with later alterations. In the graveyard there is a stone slab, inscribed with cup marks and concentric circles, one of the so-called Rathdown slabs (also at Rathmichael and Tully churches) and almost certainly of pre-Christian date. St Begnet is believed to have been a local saint of the seventh century, whose feast day is 12 November.

Dalkey was described in 1757 by John Rocque as 'Dalkey, 7 castles' and all writers describe it as a medieval town which once flourished as a seaport. Records show that large quantities of fish were caught off Dalkey and were exported to places such as Chester and Bristol. Charles V. Smith, in his excellent study, *Dalkey – Society and Economy in a Small Medieval Irish Town* (1996), revealed that few records survive to document the extent of Dalkey's trade or its status as a town. He concludes that its origins were based on agricultural and fishing activities, and that from the fourteenth century onwards it was favoured as a place in which vessels unloaded part of their cargo before attempting to sail up the shallow river Liffey to Dublin itself.

Until the completion of the South Wall in the 1760s at the mouth of the Liffey, and even after, Dublin port was notoriously difficult for ships to reach in safety. The combination of prevailing westerly winds, shallow waters and a sandbank which is still known as the bar, caused numerous shipwrecks. For this reason it suited many shipowners to unload some or all of their cargo at Dalkey.

While Dalkey is frequently described as a port, we do not know of the existence of any quays or jetties, nor is there any mention of dues being collected by customs. There may have been an early quay at Bullock, as Bullock Harbour was for centuries under the control of the Cistercian monks of St Mary's Abbey in the city, and it was they who built the castle here.

Though Dalkey was once noted for its seven castles, only two now remain. They were built, it would seem, in the fifteenth century as fortified houses for merchant families. The castles were used to store valuable merchandise such as wine, and also provided some protection for the town against possible attack by the 'wild Irish'! The surviving castles are attractive late-medieval structures, but have no very elaborate features such as carved chimney pieces or windows.

Charles Brooking's map of 1728 shows Dalkey's seven castles still intact, but forty years later Peter Wilson reported that most of the town walls and one castle had been destroyed, leaving only six. The

Ordnance Survey map of 1843 shows only five surviving castles. The ruins were obviously considered by some to be a convenient source of building stone, and Wolverton Castle, which stood near the corner of Dalkey Avenue, was reportedly demolished by William Porter in the 1840s to provide material for building Tudor House. Dungan's Castle stood opposite, almost at the corner of Ulverton Road, and belonged to a family of merchants who prospered here during the sixteenth century. The ruin of Archbold's Castle remains today as the most unaltered of the group, though its surroundings were paved in 1986 when the Corporation built townhouses nearby.

This early nineteenth-century engraving of Dalkey village shows three of its seven castles and the unquarried slopes of Dalkey Hill

The Goat Castle, which was converted into a town hall in 1868, belonged to the Cheevers family in the sixteenth century. The name Cheevers, which is of Norman origin, is derived from the word *chêvre*, meaning goat, the same animal being a feature of their coat of arms. During the late nineteenth century the principal chamber, upstairs, served the Dalkey town commissioners as their council chamber, while a 'modern' hall, added to the back of the castle, has seen much use by the community.

The Goat Castle, which became Dalkey Town Hall in 1869

An early nineteenth-century engraving of Dalkey shows the two castles, surrounded by some cottages and other ruins and, most interestingly, a pair of stocks. The stocks were located at the entrance to the present-day carpark, beside the church, and are a reminder of how law and order were kept in the town. As Dalkey was in Church hands, justice was administered in the Archbishop's court, presided over by his

The medieval origins of Dalkey can still be visualised here in its main street

seneschal. In the late sixteenth century Robert Barnewall of Shankill Castle was fined ten shillings by the court for not having a pair of stocks! Similarly, those accused of certain crimes could seek the refuge of the Church, as happened in the case of a man who stole an anchor in Dalkey and sought sanctuary in the church on Dalkey Island.

Dalkey was granted the right to hold a market in 1482, and it has been suggested that the market place may have been located at the wider part of the main street where Convent and Sorrento roads converge.

Dalkey Quarry

Rocque's map graphically illustrates the extremely rocky nature of the whole district of Dalkey. It was the presence of this rock so conveniently near the surface of the ground which led to many quarries being opened in both Dalkey and Bullock during the eighteenth century.

Granite, this durable and attractive stone, was much in demand for paving in Dublin and for the construction of the great South Wall at the entrance to the Liffey. The Ballast Board, who were charged with improving the port of Dublin, removed large quantities of granite from quarries here.

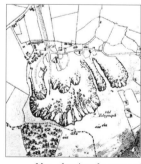

Map showing the extent of quarrying activities in Dalkey

The history of quarrying in Dalkey culminated in the opening of the massive quarries at Dalkey Hill in 1815, in order to provide stone for the building of Dun Laoghaire Harbour. Dalkey quarry, with its cathedral-like cliffs, represents an extraordinary change to the natural landscape, all wrought by human effort. It is almost impossible to imagine what this hill, once part of Dalkey Commons, might have looked like before quarrying began and it was cut away and removed.

The Commons covered two large tracts of land including the present quarry area to the south of the town and all of the land that lay between Dalkey Hill and Dalkey Sound. This included much of the Coliemore and Sorrento Road areas. A description by Peter Wilson of Dalkey in 1768 comments on the very rocky nature of the common but adds that it 'affords most excellent pasture for sheep'.

It is not generally known that there was once a cromlech on Dalkey Commons and that it was destroyed when quarrying began. Weston St John Joyce says it was removed when the Martello towers were being built. In 1780 Gabriel Beranger made a drawing of it and noted that it was called the Cloch Tobair Gailline, meaning 'the cromlech of the well of Gallion'. It consisted of a massive rock supported in the usual way by several smaller boulders.

It was Captain Toucher, who in the early years of the nineteenth century had campaigned vigorously for a new harbour at Dun Laoghaire, who got permission to open a quarry on part of Dalkey Commons for the sole purpose of constructing what was at first to be called 'an asylum harbour'. The asylum harbour would provide refuge for ships which were waiting to sail up the Liffey into Dublin. The need for such a

Above left: Dalkey quarry in a painting from the 1840s

Above right: Making hay in Dalkey, with the quarry machinery visible to the right – watercolour, c. 1835

Dalkey quarry around 1930, showing the windmill which stood on The Metals, and the track on which trucks conveyed stone to Dalkey harbour

A groove worn in the stone by the cables of the trucks from Dalkey quarry

harbour was made all the more urgent when two troop ships were wrecked in Dublin Bay in 1807 and some of the 380 victims were buried in St Begnet's graveyard in Dalkey village.

The construction of Dun Laoghaire Harbour was seen as a great humanitarian undertaking and was widely supported. At the height of this enormous engineering project, more than six hundred men were employed, many of them working in the quarries at Dalkey. Living conditions were poor and, while some managed to build cottages for themselves, others lived like squatters in cabins and tents on the land of the Commons.

It has been suggested that many of the numerous cottage-style houses which are to be found in Dalkey had their origins as quarrymen's cottages. It may well be that following the closure of the quarries the former stonemasons and quarrymen were happy to sell their holdings for a good price to the new middle-class residents.

By 1837 Samuel Lewis was able to comment: 'There are also numerous pleasant cottages, commanding fine views of the sea, which are let during the summer to respectable families.' Small, low-roofed cottages abound in and around Sorrento Road and Leslie Avenue, and these may indeed have once been the homes of quarrymen.

By far the most interesting surviving group is to be found at Ardbrugh Road where a picturesque cluster of cottages is located at the entrance to the main quarry, high up overlooking the bay. There were once as many as twenty small cottages here, approached by paths too narrow and twisty for any car to get in. Some of the smallest cottages have since been joined together or rebuilt.

The Dalkey Rifle Club, 1899

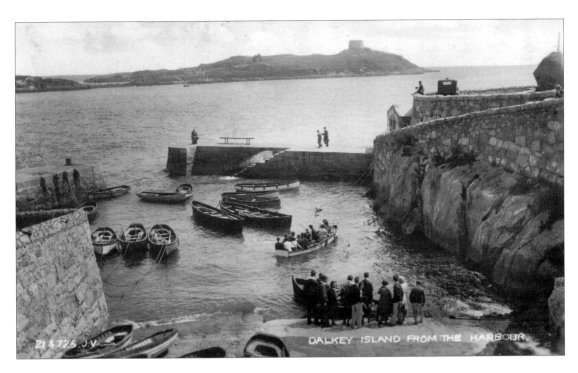

Eighteenth-century Dalkey

Coliemore Harbour, c. 1940 – it has changed little over the years

'Dalkey is the last village within the bay of Dublin. It is seven miles from the capital, and stands on the base of a high mountain. Though now a miserable village, it still exhibits proofs of its having been formerly a place of some importance.' These were the comments of a tourist named John James MacGregor, writing about Dalkey in 1821 in his book *The New Picture of Dublin*, and they were repeated by other writers in the eighteenth and early nineteenth centuries. There is considerable evidence to suggest that Dalkey was a prosperous small town in the fifteenth and sixteenth centuries, thriving as a shipping outpost of Dublin, but from that 'golden age' until the nineteenth century the castles were left to decay and the village lay neglected.

Rocque's map (1757) shows Dalkey as a place largely unchanged since late medieval times – a small village, clustered around a single main street, with one 'road' leading to the cove at Sorrento and another to connect Dalkey with the inlet or creek at Bullock. The bay at Sorrento provided some shelter from northerly and westerly winds, while Bullock offered protection from southerly winds. In favourable conditions, ships could anchor in Dalkey Sound and there was always a little inlet at Coliemore which would have served as a convenient landing place. The construction of Coliemore Harbour, with its two short piers, was begun in 1868, and the work was carried out by a local builder called John Cunningham.

Later maps by John Taylor, 1816, and a chart by Alexander Nimmo for the Commissioners of Irish Fisheries, 1823, agree with Rocque's layout of roads in Dalkey and show no path or road leading from the town directly to Coliemore.

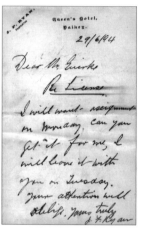

Top: The eighteenth-century
frontage of The Queen's Hotel
Above: Notepaper from the
hotel, 1894

John Rutty, writing in 1772, observed: 'Near Dalkey is a lead mine, where it is said that some hundreds of tons of ore have been raised. I got 42 grains of lead from 90 grains of ore, fluxed with equal parts of salt.'

All the earlier maps also indicate the location of the Dalkey lead mines at Sorrento Point and blocked-up passages and tunnels have been reported in this vicinity, particularly near Sorrento Terrace.

The King of Dalkey

In the late 1780s a satirical society was formed in a hostelry called The Palace, in what is now Dublin's Temple Bar area, and its president was elected with the grand title of 'King of Dalkey (island), Emperor of The Muglins, Prince of the Holy Island of Magee, and Elector of Lambay and Ireland's Eye, Defender of his own Faith and Respecter of all others, and Sovereign of the Most Illustrious Order of the Lobster and Periwinkle.'

Various proclamations of a political and satirical nature were issued and every summer, at least until 1797, a lavish ceremony took place on the island, including the coronation of the king! *The Dalkey Gazette* described the scene on 16 August 1796: 'On Sunday morning, at the dawn of day, his Majesty King Stephen came in a private coach to The Palace, attended by their graces ...' They set sail from Sir John Rogerson's quay. 'His Majesty's arrival [at Dalkey] was announced by firing of rockets, discharges of artillery and the most unbounded shouts of applause from the surrounding multitude ...'

The events of 1798 may have put a different colour on these ceremonies. Though they were an occasion for fun and entertainment, there was undoubtedly a serious element of political satire.

The Queen's Hotel

Dalkey village was a quiet place in the eighteenth century. A map of 1765 by Thomas Reading indicates a house and garden and two inns, The Red Crowe and The Sign of the Ship. The former is now known as The Queen's and was previously called The Queen's Royal Hotel. The Queen's Hotel is probably the oldest and most impressive house in Castle Street and though it may once have incorporated earlier structures, its three-storey elevation, squat windows and thick walls suggest a mid-eighteenth-century date. There is a handsome cut-stone doorcase similar to one in Dalkey Lodge. The Queen's is set back from the street and had its own large gardens to the rear. During the nineteenth century it changed hands frequently and in 1879 was bought by the Dublin Southern District Tramway Company for the purpose of acquiring part of the lands for their tram depot. It was then purchased in 1894 by Jeremiah Ryan for £710, as a going concern complete with furniture and billiard-room fittings. Things did not go well for Ryan, and when pressed for a cheque by his solicitor only two years later, he wrote: 'trade has been very bad since the roads were broken up'. This was probably referring to the ongoing work of laying water mains in Dalkey, which

Dalkey Lodge, the oldest house in the area

was then being connected to the Vartry water supply.

Barnhill Road, which joins Dalkey at its western end, was once the main road to Dublin and very likely takes its name from the presence long ago of a large barn, which might have served the tenants and farmers of Dalkey.

Dalkey Lodge, which is located on Barnhill Road, is the oldest surviving house in the area. It was described by Peter Wilson in 1768 as follows: 'On the west side of town stands Dalkey Lodge, a neat house belonging to a citizen.' Wilson is best known as the publisher of *Wilson's Almanack*, the comprehensive eighteenth-century directory which was brought out annually. On a wet day, having nothing better to do, Wilson wrote a short account of Dalkey as he saw it. He describes the excellent view from Dalkey Lodge, across Dublin Bay to 'the new light house and adjacent works, the Hill of Howth, skirted in summer with a mixture of delightful spots of corn and other grounds'.

The lodge is a large house, three storeys in height and five windows wide, with an attractive cut-stone doorcase of mid-eighteenth-century date. There are also a number of later additions to the side and to the back. In Victorian times the house was owned by Thomas Henry, who installed a sundial bearing the inscription 'Dalkey Lodge A D 1869'. A quarry which once adjoined the lodge has been filled in and there is now a small estate of houses here named Old Quarry.

As Barnhill Road was one of the principal roads into Dalkey, where better to locate the business of a farrier? The remains of an old forge can still be seen in the horseshoe-shaped entrance, now blocked up, at the

Statoil filling station on Barnhill Road. The garage behind was once an old schoolhouse.

Barnhill was another eighteenth-century house which stood near the present Saval Park Road. It was heavily Victorianised by the addition of bay windows two storeys in height, and a large Tudor-style porch. The hall was tiled and fitted out with mahogany panelling.

Nineteenth-century Dalkey – The Coastline

By the mid-1830s, when Samuel Lewis was compiling his *Topographical Dictionary of Ireland*, Dalkey was beginning to change. The construction of Dun Laoghaire Harbour, which continued from 1815 well into the 1840s, undoubtedly provided much employment in Dalkey Quarry, and boosted the whole economy of Dalkey. Lewis described the village as having 'a two penny post', a constabulary police station and a coast-guard station. He mentioned the Martello towers, the quarry, a national school and about six important houses, among which were the Rev. Hercules MacDonnell's Sorrento, Mr Brabazon's Charleville, Mrs Johnson's Barn Hill, Mr Armstrong's Braganza, Mrs O'Reilly's Shamrock Lodge and Mr Hank's Coliemore.

Within a few years the building of houses would begin apace. Dalkey was to follow the pattern which was being set all along the southern shore of Dublin Bay and in the coastal villages of County Dublin. The new middle classes, who had done well in the professions or in business, wanted to live 'rus-in-urbe', that is to say, they wanted country living with all the convenience of being in close proximity to the town and they would only travel to the city when necessary.

The decade of the 1840s was a period of intensive development in Dalkey. One of the first large buildings to appear was the Church of the Assumption which was built in 1840. This was followed by the Loreto Convent in 1842, and St Patrick's Church in 1843. The following year would see the arrival of the experimental Atmospheric Railway in Dalkey, and the first houses of Sorrento Terrace were erected in 1845.

One of the many nineteenth-century cottages in the Dalkey area

The Church of the Assumption was initially a plain, rectangular building with Gothic windows. Transepts and a square tower were added later, and there is a rather unusual fan-vaulted ceiling inside. It was built on a site donated to the parish by the Connolly family, who were bakers in Dalkey.

The Loreto Abbey, or convent, stands overlooking the sea on lands once owned by Charles Leslie of Carraig-na-Gréine, which we shall discuss shortly. The site, with its open aspect, is certainly a healthy one and can be both inspiring and bleak, especially in winter.

The convent is an imposing Tudor-style structure, cruciform in plan and built of local granite, with Gothic windows and narrow corner turrets.

The date 1842 is carved into a stone over the door, along with the crest of the order and the motto 'Maria Regina Angelorum' (Mary Queen of Angels). These substantial buildings were further added to in the nineteenth century as the school grew in size.

The spectacular setting of the Loreto Abbey, built in 1842

Other religious denominations were provided for in Dalkey, and in 1861 a Wesleyan Chapel, now converted into a private house, was also built. It was greatly supported by the wealthy McComas family who lived at Cliff Castle.

St Patrick's Church stands on a prominent site above Bullock Harbour. Plans for a new Protestant church in Dalkey were first mooted in 1836, and a site was offered near Bullock Castle by Alderman Arthur Perrin. The church was completed by 1843 to the designs of Jacob Owen, and has a cruciform plan with a somewhat squat, square tower. The church is characterised by its beautiful ashlar granite and long, narrow, Gothic windows. It was built on a site (leased for ten thousand years from the Earl of Carysfort) lying between an old quarry and the Ballast Office Road. The east window features elaborate tracery which incorporates the Star of David.

St Patrick's Church, built in 1843 – it exhibits outstanding granite stonework

Close by, at the entrance gates, stands an attractive granite-built sexton's house, constructed in 1868 to the design of the architect Edward Carson, whose family lived originally in Harcourt Street and later in Dalkey. His namesake and relation became the notable Unionist politician and leader. The Carsons had lived in Dalkey at Mount Alverno. The original designs show a pointed roof with decorative ironwork finials over the front door, but unfortunately this striking feature has disappeared.

The stone-carved Gaelic lettering on the entrance piers to Carraig-na-Gréine

The collossal Doric columns, each formed of a single stone, from the entrance to Carraig-na-Gréine

In 1870 Charles Leslie, a wealthy wholesale chemist, made a large donation to the parish for the purpose of building a school and meeting hall. More than a century later these buildings would be the setting of the first non-denominational primary school in Ireland, the Dalkey School Project, which had its origins here in 1978.

Carraig-na-Gréine, built by Charles Leslie around 1830, is a very striking, if severe, cut-stone house. This Doric-style villa was the height of fashion when it was built. It represented everything that was different from the equally popular 'Tudor style' of the period. This classical idiom, also used for the railway station and yacht clubs in Dun Laoghaire, belonged to the cult of the Greek revival. It stands one-storey-over-basement, with a central, recessed entrance flanked by Doric columns. The tall, granite columns are remarkable, as they are cut from single pieces of stone. Sadly, the house has lain derelict for the past few years, following its sale by the Loreto Sisters who had used it as a primary school. It was Leslie who constructed the tunnel, now unfortunately blocked up, near the shore at the bottom of his grounds in order to preserve a right-of-way to a well. Leslie had bought up several small holdings in the area in order to build his house, and had tried to cut off access to the Lady Well, as it was known. The tunnel meant that the public could still visit the well without having to cross Leslie's land – and, perhaps more importantly to Leslie, without being seen from the windows of his house!

There was once a fine walled garden and also a collection of unusually attractive coachhouses here, both of which were recently demolished in order to build sheltered housing for elderly people. The buildings were fronted by a long, symmetrical wall, articulated by granite niches, coigns and string-courses. Equally well built is the gate-lodge, with its arched windows and pedimented entrance. Like the main house, it is an outstanding example of finely jointed granite masonry. The entrance gates at Leslie Avenue are formed by five tapering granite piers and have an archway of wrought iron.

The now-demolished stables of Carraig-na-Gréine

Leslie Avenue is one of Dalkey's most charming narrow roads, and has some of the smallest surviving cottages in the area, including St Jude's and one called Tiny Cottage!

Among the principal houses built on Harbour Road after 1830 were Beulah, Bartra, Charleville and Glencairn, all situated near St Patrick's Church.

Charleville, with its gables and chimneys, is an L-shaped house with cut-stone, Tudor-style details. There is a small 'spy tower' in the corner of the gardens.

Glencairn, once called Dalkey House, was a large, square structure of Victorian date. It was demolished to make way for a development of redbrick apartments.

Coliemore Villas

Beulah is a compact, two-storey-over-basement house with prominent overhanging eaves. It was designed in the Regency style and has attractive bow-ended rooms. Standing as it does on a height in nearly three acres of grounds, it surveys all of the coast between Dalkey and Bullock.

A special feature of the larger Dalkey houses with a coastal frontage are the private jetties or boat harbours. Brennan's Folly – so named after Charles Brennan who lived there at the turn of the century and who may have built the 'harbour' – was the name given to such a harbour located among the rocks near Beulah.

Bartra, built about 1845, is a wide, Victorian-style house which stands on a terrace overlooking the sea near Bullock. Originally three windows wide, it was greatly enlarged by Judge John Monroe. It was also the home of the Booth family, who took a great interest in the affairs of Dalkey and put up money to assist the local Urban District Council in the purchase of Dalkey Island from the British War Office. The McCormick family, who operated coal boats out of Dun Laoghaire Harbour, were later inhabitants of Bartra. When sold in 1981, it stood on over five acres of lawns and gardens, and included the Martello tower, substantial stables and a gate-lodge.

The Shangri-La Hotel, which will be rememberred by many older residents, consisted of four terraced houses which backed onto the sea. The houses were built in the 1840s and were originally called Henrietta Place. Henrietta Place, with its three-storey-over-basement houses, was similar to the many terraces which were being built in Dun Laoghaire at that time, such as Charlemont Terrace on the seafront. They were in the late Georgian style and had typical pillared doorcases and fanlights. Tempe Terrace, on Coliemore Road, is in the same style, with slightly different decorative details, and was built by 1837. The hotel was demolished in 1979 as part of a big development scheme. The new apartments built here were called Pilot View and the first phase had been erected some years earlier on the site of a plain, villa-type house (built in the 1840s) which bore that name.

Top: The former Dalkey Island Hotel, which incorporates the original Coliemore Lodge

Above: Coliemore Lodge in the nineteenth century, showing its original porch which was later enlarged

Coliemore Lodge, Lota, Elsinore, Inniscorrig, Cliff Castle and Rarc an Ilan form an impressive group of Victorian marine residences which lie between Carraig-na-Gréine and Coliemore Harbour and which in 1834 were the scene of the most bizarre activities. The story revolves around a girl named Etty Scott, daughter of a Scotsman who had come to Ireland to supervise the granite-loaded trucks which ran from Dalkey quarry to Dun Laoghaire Harbour. Etty, described as a beautiful, romantic girl with fanciful ideas, dreamt that a massive hoard of gold lay buried under 'the long stone', a granite outcrop near Coliemore Road. Somehow she persuaded about thirty-six quarrymen and labourers to devote themselves completely for many weeks to the search for gold! Nothing was found, but years later some of Etty's followers who had built cabins nearby found financial reward by being able to sell their plots to the builders of the new houses such as Iniscorrig, Lota and Elsinore

Coliemore Lodge, which until recently was known as the Dalkey Island Hotel, was built about 1830 and at first was called Coliemore Cottage. It stood beside the quaint and tiny harbour which in 1837 was sufficiently developed to merit description on the Ordnance Survey map, but still had no piers. Whether the cottage was demolished or enlarged is difficult to say, but the house, which remains at the centre of the hotel, was a large, five-bay, two-storey-over-basement structure. The porch, of which the middle part is original, bears the monogram of the Weldon Moloney family, who once lived here. The once-beautiful gardens are at present used as a carpark and are completely covered in tarmac.

Rarc an Ilan F. Milo O'Flanagan, in his article about Old Dalkey (1941) comments that Rarc an Ilan was one of the first houses in the area to be given an Irish name, and that the newspapers of the day commented favourably on this new practice! The house was lived in, in 1847, by

Robert Cordner, a lace and trimming manufacturer of Parliament Street, Dublin.

Cliff Castle, which has also had a life as a hotel, is a large Victorian house, decked out as an extravagant, mock medieval castle, to the designs of architects McCurdy and Mitchell. The square house has three circular corner towers and all the usual Tudor trimmings, but the whole effect, with further stone-built towers and battlemented terraces, which lead down to a small harbour among the rocks, is impressive. Cliff Castle was occupied by a Henry Baldwin Q. C. in 1850, and became a hotel in 1920 when it is said to have been frequented by famous figures such as Arthur Griffith and Oliver St John Gogarty.

Inniscorrig was built in 1847 for Sir Dominic Corrigan, a noted physician. Corrigan, who originally lived at Merrion Square, took a keen interest in Dublin zoo and he built his own aquarium at Iniscorrig. He campaigned for the provision of the Vartry water supply and was critical of the poor-quality drinking water generally available, especially for the poor. He also pointed to the need for an adequate water supply for fire-fighting purposes. A Catholic and an MP from 1870 to 1874, he was highly successful and well respected. He is buried in St Andrew's Church, Westland Row.

Photographs of Iniscorrig taken in about 1870 show a gabled, square, stone-built house with prominent chimneys. Later, the house was almost doubled in size by the addition of a short tower, extra rooms and an enormous conservatory. Corrigan cannot have been an overly modest man, as over his hall door he placed a bust of himself! A visit of King Edward VII to Iniscorrig is commemorated by a crown and a star, set in pebbles on either side of the main door. A terrace, protected by a decorative cast-iron railing, looks down on the largest private harbour on the

Inniscorrig, originally built in 1847 for Sir Dominic Corrigan, an eminent physician and Catholic Member of Parliament from 1870 to 1874

Dalkey coastline. There was also a small crane and a flagstaff.

Victoria House   Martin Burke, the owner in 1850 of the Shelbourne Hotel in St Stephen's Green, built Victoria House. It stands overlooking Coliemore Harbour, and, like so many houses of the period, began modestly enough but was greatly enlarged in the late nineteenth century by the addition of a new front and a conical, capped tower. James Milo Burke, Burke's brother, lived at another Dalkey house called the Khyber Pass and later at Queenstown Castle. He, along with Provost MacDonnell of Sorrento Terrace, became very involved with the Dalkey Town Commissioners and was instrumental in organising the construction of the new piers at Coliemore Harbour which were completed by 1869.

Sea-bathing was becoming fashionable in the mid-nineteenth century, and Dalkey then had no less than two commercial baths, located on Dalkey Sound: the Queenstown baths, run by a Mrs McDonnell, and the Clifton baths run by a Mr Kavanagh. The public bathing places included the Vico, not marked on the 1867 Ordnance Survey map, which always rivalled the Forty Foot for the excellence of its bathing conditions and is still very popular.

Top: The now-vanished Scotch Rath

Above: The inscription and urn which until recently stood over the entrance to Scotch Rath

Queenstown Castle, which may have begun its life as Springfield Castle in 1837, was occupied in 1850 by Robert Smyth and had a small harbour.

Scotch Rath, later renamed Berwick House, is a large, bow-ended, late Victorian house which once overlooked Coliemore Harbour, and was built of red brick and granite. Over an entrance gate was an inscribed stone brought from Berwick House in Rathfarnham, a retreat house which moved here and led to the change of name. The house was demolished in recent times to make way for a block of apartments.

Nerano, high above Coliemore Harbour, is a local landmark because of the large statue of a sailor which stands on a rock in the terraced garden. The sailor, who surveys Dalkey Island, may have come from MacAnaspie Roman cement and stucco works in Pearse Street, Dublin. The MacAnaspies, who were one of the first residents of Nerano, were noted for their production of stucco eagles, urns and statues, which were often placed on buildings and in gardens. In any case, by 1863 the statue, which is accompanied by a capstan, an anchor and a seal, was lying on the ground and was restored by a new owner of Nerano, John Fleming. Nerano and Island View, both of which appear on the 1837 map, are plain houses of the late Georgian type which have been somewhat altered by later additions.

The stucco-modelled sailor at Nerano

Kilross stands above Nerano, and is said to have originated as a chapel, when a small oratory was constructed by a Franciscan in the 1830s and locals were permitted to attend mass there. A house was later added to the chapel.

The Coastguard Station Close by, on Beacon Hill, are the five houses of the Coastguard Station, which were built in the 1840s and once incorporated a look-out, a laundry and a well. A report on the coastguard service in 1824 recommended that an eight-person station be established here with a watch and a boathouse, and commented that Killiney Bay is much used by 'pilot boats who smuggle when the opportunity offers'!

An early photograph of Dalkey coastal houses, taken around 1870, showing Lota, Elsinore, Inniscorrig and Cliff Castle

Sorrento Terrace

The views from Sorrento Terrace and the Vico Road are unparalleled in County Dublin, stretching as they do across Killiney Bay to the wide sweep of Bray Head and the Wicklow Mountains. There is also a marvellous sense of space, with the great expanse of sea and sky which stretches out into the Irish Sea.

Members of the Dalkey coastguard at Beacon Hill, c. 1890

Original plans for the construction of twenty-two houses at Sorrento Terrace – they were never completed

Sorrento Terrace, consisting of eight Victorian houses, was probably the most daring building project to be carried out in the area. As already mentioned, a similar but far more ambitious plan for Killiney Hill, to have been called Queenstown, was proposed by Robert Warren of Killiney Castle in 1840, but it came to nothing. A surviving plan (in a lease of 1845) shows that Sorrento Terrace was planned to run to twenty-two houses. The land was owned and leased out for building by Hercules Henry Graves MacDonnell, a barrister, who stipulated that the sum of at least one thousand pounds sterling had to be expended on each house, which was designed in accordance with the working plans of architects Frederick Darley and Nathaniel Montgomery.

The residents were not permitted to 'alter the proportions, appearance or uniformity of Sorrento Terrace' by 'building, painting or omitting to paint'! The houses were erected by Edward Masterson – of George's Street, Kingstown – a local builder of high reputation. As an index of house prices, it is interesting to trace the fortunes of a property in Sorrento Terrace. One house, built for £1000 in 1845, was sold in 1925 for £650, and finally made £450,000 in 1990; what next? In 1998 Number One Sorrento Terrace, called Sorrento House, sold for an amazing £5.9m. This house, being the end house, was slightly larger than the others, and was first owned by Rev. Dr Hercules Henry Graves MacDonnell. It stood at the end of the terrace and its extensive grounds took in the whole of Sorrento Point. During the ownership of Sorrento House by Judge Thomas Overend in the early 1900s, regattas were held here by the Dalkey Amusements Committee. A flagstaff marked the starting line for the Dalkey regatta, while guests were entertained on the lawns of Sorrento House to the pleasant strains of band music.

Sorrento Terrace – the building of these houses was begun in 1845

The terrace shared a boat slip and bathing place and it was intended that there should be a common promenade along by the shore. A

pleasure garden for the benefit of the residents was planned for Sorrento Hill, now the public park. The Dalkey Amusements Committee was formed by a number of residents in order to arrange events and entertainments in the area and to manage Sorrento Park, which had been donated in 1894 by Dame Blanche MacDonnell. The park was open and free to the public all year round. The remains of a bandstand with its old gas lighting and seats can be seen there.

The Dalkey Regatta, which was a regular event in the 1890s

Programme from the Dalkey

Most houses built at this time were provided with a coachhouse and stables, but as there was no space for outbuildings at Sorrento Terrace some of the houses were given these facilities on Sorrento Road, at some distance away.

Tucked into the corner of the bay is Sorrento Cottage, which was built by 1837 as a single-storey villa, and was used by the MacDonnells. It was later enlarged by the addition of an extra storey.

Another prominent Dalkey resident was Alexander Conan, who was chairman of the Amusements Committee in 1899, and lived beside Sorrento Park in a house called Monte Alverno. A different house called Mount Alverno, built in the 1830s, was one of two properties which Conan amalgamated to create a single house, which he designed him-

Monte Alverno, rebuilt as a large, cut-stone house in the castellated baronial style

self. The result is a house in the style of a baronial castle, built in granite with wide bay windows, battlements, and a small, octagonal flag tower. There is also a square folly tower in the corner of the garden.

The Khyber Pass Hotel The imposing Khyber Pass Hotel once stood on a great height over the railway and commanded some of the best views of both Killiney and Dublin bays. It was demolished in December 1986, having stood derelict for nearly six years. As the fortunes of the hotel declined, blocks of apartments were built in the

Right: The Khyber Pass Hotel
Above: The mosaic floor at the entrance to the hotel
Below: Carved timber bracket from the entrance to the hotel

grounds against a background of considerable local opposition. The house, which bore the name Khyber Pass since the middle of the nineteenth century, was originally a handsome two-storey-over-basement building with an entrance facing Dalkey. It was built by James Milo Burke who lived there until about 1880, when he moved to Queenstown Castle, a house overlooking Dalkey Sound. It is said that Charles Stewart Parnell lived here for some time. The house was greatly enlarged, probably in the late nineteenth century, by the addition of a whole new front, consisting of two-storeyed bay windows and an elaborate canopied entrance with a mosaic floor. The entrance was placed at the Dalkey Hill side of the house. The exterior was treated in the Italianate manner with lined rendering and an attractive cornice.

Bryan Cooper, who was a staunch Unionist, lived for many years at the Khyber Pass. A member of the noted Sligo family of Markree Castle, he was born in Simla in India in 1884 and became a unionist MP for South County Dublin in 1910. He was one of the few politicians of his background to remain in politics in Ireland after 1920, and he was elected to the Dáil in 1923 as an Independent.

In 1946 the Coopers sold the house to a builder named M. P. Kennedy who had developed the lands of Granite Hall in Dun Laoghaire, and he established the Killiney Heights Hotel by converting the old house there.

The Vico Road

The Vico Road was originally a private track, inaccessible from Dalkey and closed to the public. As early as 1861 (according to *The Dublin Builder*) there were moves being made to continue this road around to Killiney, and pressure was being applied to Mr Warren, the owner of Killiney Hill, to remove a wall which was built across it. In 1889 the private rights were bought for the public by public subscription and a new road was made, which has allowed the public for over a century to enjoy the unsurpassable beauty of this area. In 1928 the land between Vico Road and the sea was put on the market. Local residents saw the opportunity to purchase the Vico fields and prevent further building there in order to preserve the open space and famous views for ever. Once again, the people of Dalkey and Killiney responded generously to a public appeal, and the lands were bought for £1500.

In her appeal to the public on that occasion, local resident and author Katherine Tynan described the Vico Road: 'Cliffs golden with gorse these days, and tremulous with bird-life and bird-song: the bay, sometimes blue as a sapphire, sometimes all a silvery fleece with some mysterious light from overhead: mountains of crystal and chalcedony! – It is God's gift to all of us. Let us hold it sacred!'

Strawberry Hill In 1967 the owners of Strawberry Hill were refused planning permission to demolish the house and erect an eighty-bedroomed hotel on the Vico Road. However, the Minister for Local

The area around the Vico Road looking surprisingly barren in the 1890s

Hayes's Tower, which was demolished in the late 1980s

Mount Henry – this Victorian print shows the newly-built house, with as yet no planting of trees or shrubs

Government overturned the decision and approved the plan. Fortunately, the hotel was never built.

Strawberry Hill was one of the first houses to be built on the Vico Road. It is a single-storey-over-basement, Italianate villa with a short tower. The house, possibly designed by Hoskin & Son as part of Warren's grand plan for Killiney Hill, was built around 1850 for a Mr Stevenson, who was general manager of the Alliance and Dublin Consumers' Gas Company. There is an attractive plasterwork panel on the front of the house. The house was used as a small hotel during the 1960s.

The Dublin Builder informs us that in 1861 a pair of houses was completed at Vico for Mr Henry Gonne and are probably the houses which stand below the road and directly above the railway at the Vico bathing place. They were designed by Mr Lyons and 'present gabled cantilevered roofs, with ornamental brackets, large bay windows, commanding magnificent views of the surrounding unsurpassedly beautiful scenery, and fitted throughout with storm shutters, essential during the winter months in this exposed situation'.

San Elmo, on the Vico Road, was built around 1870 by Henry Hayes, a wealthy tanner who had already built a fine house called Stratford in Rathgar. A large house with half-octagonal bows and a semi-circular porch, it stands high up overlooking Killiney Bay. In its extensive grounds Hayes built a square viewing tower for his daughter and it is said that a grand piano was housed in the uppermost room. Though not of any great architectural interest, this notable landmark was unfortunately struck by lightning and became dangerous in 1986. As Dun Laoghaire Corporation were unable to assist the owner in repairing Hayes's tower, as it was known, it was demolished.

GEORGE BERNARD SHAW'S FORMER HOME . . .
TORCA COTTAGE, DALKEY, Co. DUBLIN
Situate in a small exclusive residential area.   *Adjoins the National Trust.*

Torca Cottage.

The Lounge.

Overlooking Killiney Bay and Wicklow Mountains.

G.B.S. writing of Torca Cottage :—"*I lived on a hill top with the most beautiful view in the world. . . . I had only to open my eyes to see such pictures as no painter could make for me.*"

Large lounge, 3 bedrooms, modern kitchen with refrigerator, central heating, out-office, garage, garden.

This completely modernised charming old-world residence, with its intimate Shavian associations, is beautifully furnished with hand-made Irish Tudor furniture, valuable paintings, including one of G.B.S. 8 miles from Dublin City. All sporting facilities. The perfect retreat from the cares of the day.

This property may be purchased without 25% purchase tax by non-Irish nationals.
Full details from SWEENEY, M.I.A.A., Sole Agent, Dun Laoghaire, Ireland.   Tel. 86177 and 81333.

The name Torca appears on the first Ordnance Survey map of the area published in 1837 as 'Toyca', and a few cottages are shown in what was otherwise a completely wild part of Dalkey Commons. One of the first large houses to be built here was Mount Henry, situated at the very end of Torca Road near the famous Cat's Ladder, a pedestrian right-of-way to Vico. But perhaps Bernard Shaw's Torca Cottage is the best-known house in this quiet area. The cottage may have replaced one of the earlier quarrymen's cabins on the same site, for it is a well built structure, double-fronted with a high-ceilinged living room and three bedrooms inside. Shaw lived here from 1866 until 1874, and later wrote: 'I lived on a hill top with the most beautiful view in the world – I had only to open my eyes to see such pictures as no painter could make for me.'

A narrow track runs from Torca Road up above the quarries to the Old Telegraph, the old stone ruin on top of Dalkey Hill which is generally referred to as a 'castle'. This telegraph tower was built at the time of the Martello towers and was used for signalling or for sending messages by semaphore to ships of the navy and the other various military installations. The tower was built in 1807, and was restored and probably made more picturesque by Robert Warren, in the 1850s.

Between Dalkey Hill and the town lay the 'Glebe Lands' which once belonged to the Church and are now part of Ardeevin Road and Cunningham Road. A number of developments took place on Ardeevin and Knocknacree Roads in the late nineteenth century, including the building of Craiglands House and Ardeevin Terrace on the site of an old quarry.

Craiglands, demolished in 1986, was a large, bay-windowed Victorian house with an imposing front. It was ornamented with

An advertisement for the sale of George Bernard Shaw's home, Torca Cottage

A view of Dalkey from Killiney Hill

Ardeevin Terrace

cut-granite details, such as keystones in all windows, and a large, arched porch which was approached by a particularly long flight of granite steps.

A noted Dalkey builder named John Cunningham had commenced building houses on this side of the railway, on the old 'glebe lands', during the 1860s. He built four semi-detached houses, called Cunningham Terrace, and laid out a new road of the same name. Here, in the 1890s, he erected two outstanding houses, Harvieston and Santa Maria.

Harvieston, a large house in the Tudor fashion, was built for the Eason family, who were the owners and founders of the highly successful stores. They also ran a circulating library. It has an attractive corner tower with a slated, conical roof, while **Santa Maria** is a redbrick, bay-windowed house with Gothic features. Both command fine views of Dublin Bay.

Lios Mór, Knocknacree Road, is an unusual cut-stone, Edwardian house, with a beautiful timber verandah covered by an ornamental, tiled roof.

Mount Salus, a name suggestive of the healthy airs which were naturally to be found there, was a mid-nineteenth-century development which also included a variety of Victorian residences such as Monte Vista, Combre, and a pair of semi-detached houses actually called Mount Salus. The pair at Mount Salus were built around 1840 and have

Photo by William Lawrence of Dalkey, c. 1890, showing the many fields which still surrounded the town

Kent Terrace is a handsome, Tudor-style terrace of four houses, erected in the 1830s

many cut-granite features, including porticos, half-octagonal bow windows and a balustrade.

Tudor House was built around 1840 in a commanding position overlooking Dalkey town, and is an imposing five-bay house. It has a plain appearance in a Tudor style, with a painted, rendered front and three small gables. In the early 1900s Tudor House was used as a school where boys were prepared for entrance exams to 'Public schools and Osborne Naval College'. The fees were twenty guineas per term for boarders, one guinea per term for the laundress, three shillings for stationery and five shillings for games. Much of the grounds of Tudor House have recently been built upon, as have those of neighbouring St Joseph's, formerly called Bay View. Bay View is a modest 1830-type of house with an unusual first-floor balcony, while Melrose and Lynton, also close by, are bay-windowed houses of mid-nineteenth-century date.

Ceiling rose from Melrose

Kent Terrace, at the bottom of Barnhill Road, is a distinguished row of four Tudor-style, terraced houses, which were built by a Mr Frederick Porter, an architect, and his brother, William Porter, whose descendants are still resident in Dalkey. The houses were erected in the late 1830s and have pointed gables, wide Regency-type windows with drip labels and small, Gothic, glazed fanlights. Each of the hall doors is studded with iron nails in the medieval manner. A plaque on the last house bears the date 1839, and soon after this we find Frederick Porter resident in Number One Kent Terrace. It seems likely that Porter designed this terrace and Tudor House as well.

The Dalkey Town Commissioners was established in the mid-1860s and the Town Hall opened in 1868 in the old castle. The commissioners included various notable residents. Among the many issues which confronted them was that of health, and in the early years of this century there was always the threat of smallpox, which could be fatal. The

Victorian postmark from Dalkey

Dalkey Urban District Council, as it became in the late nineteenth century, endeavoured to provide proper sanitation for every dwelling in the district as there were many people living in most unhealthy conditions. The council prosecuted several landlords and owners of property for not erecting closets, privies, or ashpits.

There were many dairies in Dalkey at the turn of the century, and in 1903 the council prosecuted no less than five 'dairy men', three of whom were women, for having sold milk which was 'adulterated with ten parts of added water'!

The Railway

Following the successful completion of the first railway in Ireland in 1834, from Dublin to Kingstown (now Dun Laoghaire), plans were soon put forward to extend the line as far as Dalkey. Of course, there had been a small railway, with iron tracks, running between Dalkey Quarry and Dun Laoghaire Harbour, which had been used to transport granite. Part of this track, known locally as 'The Metals', still exists, but the bulk of it was sold by the Kingstown Harbour Commissioners for the purpose of constructing the 'Atmospheric Railway'.

This experimental railway was designed by Robert Mallet to run on the principle of suction or atmospheric pressure. It was a unique invention and attracted much interest.

A fixed engine, attached to a cylindrical pipe, drew the train along by means of a vacuum at speeds of up to 40mph. Near Barnhill Road there was an engine house, equipped with three Cornish boilers, and a tall chimney which was for many years a landmark in Dalkey. Similar projects had been tried, with limited success, in Paris and London. The service commenced in 1844 and lasted for ten years.

Plans for the railway were not without objectors, as some felt it would be noisy and disruptive, like Alderman Arthur Perrin who was a neighbour at Castle Park. In Dun Laoghaire, the new residents of the seafront terraces requested that the railway be kept out of sight and the company obliged by covering over much of the track in a deep cutting. They provided a terminus at Dalkey between Barnhill and Castle Park Roads.

The Dalkey Engine House, built in 1844, which powered the Atmospheric Railway

Engine house at Dalkey.

The old atmospheric line was eventually widened to two tracks, and the new conventional railway from Dun Laoghaire to Bray became fully operational by 1856. This involved building a new station at Dalkey and extensive tunnelling under Dalkey Commons and excavation of rock along the cliffs at the Vico fields. The station at Dalkey is an attractive single-storey building, with a central open loggia. It retains many of its original features such as its windows with their elegant Italianate architraves.

A network of horse-drawn tramlines was laid out in Dublin during the 1880s and Dalkey became the terminus for one of these lines. The tramyard, with its stone setts and wide tracks, may still be seen in Castle Street, and some of the tram sheds, where the trams were kept, survive. For many years, the most elaborately decorated and comfortably equipped tram in Ireland lay in the grounds of Wolverton House, where it was once used as a summer house and office. This lavishly furnished electric tram was used by the directors of the Dublin United Tramway Company to inspect their lines. It was fitted out in oak with Waterford glass lamps, velvet-covered seats, a cocktail cabinet, and had windows depicting scenic views of Dublin in coloured glass. Having been almost totally destroyed in 1984 by vandals who set it on fire, it is now being restored by members of the National Transport Museum in Howth.

Schoolboys at Castle Park at the end of term

Castle Park The Ordnance Survey map of 1867 gives us a very good picture of Victorian Dalkey. The fields between Dalkey and Sandycove were still relatively undeveloped and small quarries were dotted across the landscape. The most significant house was Castle Park, formerly known as Castle Perrin, whose lands extended from Dalkey to Sandycove and included the quarries behind Bullock Harbour. The first Ordnance Survey of this area from about twenty-five years earlier shows a very different landscape as Ulverton Road, Church Road and Carysfort Road did not exist. Ulverton Road was formed during the late 1840s when some new houses were built on it.

The original house at Castle Park was probably built in the 1820s, for it remains, with its late-Georgian windows, a recognisably earlier part of the larger house. By 1830 it was owned by Alderman Arthur Perrin, who lived in Bullock Castle and rented Castle Perrin to well-off members of the British administration in Dublin. It was Perrin who enlarged the house by building an imposing mock-Tudor mansion facing the sea, which is today the centrepiece of Castle Park School. A battlemented tower rises over the halldoor, and the whole effect, with its grey,

Ceiling rose from Castle Park

rendered walls, is rather sombre. A large hall with an arcade in the Tudor manner is the most striking internal feature of the house, but all of the rooms have elaborate plasterwork cornices and centrepieces.

In 1851, the Right Hon. John Richards, Third Baron of Her Majesty's Court of Exchequer, was in residence, and some twenty years later we find another legal personality, the Hon. James O'Brien, Second Justice in the Court of the Queen's Bench, renting Castle Park.

The school was established here in 1904 by W. P. Toone, and in its early years attracted many pupils from England and abroad. The school has been diligent in preserving the surrounding fifteen acres of fields and trees. Indeed, it is such an important area of open space that should the property ever come on the market the local authority should give serious consideration to its acquisition.

A fine walled garden lies behind the house and is still very well maintained. The base of a small, circular greenhouse, which originally had a rather elegant, onion-shaped dome, may still be seen in the garden. The rather grandiose, castellated, Norman-style entrance on Castle Park Road, with its archway and circular towers, incorporates a gate lodge which is of earlier date.

Bullock Castle, standing on high ground overlooking the harbour, was built by the Cistercian monks of St Mary's Abbey in order to protect their fisheries. They chose a commanding position and built a solid granite castle of modest size. It has stood the test of time, and is probably the best-preserved medieval structure of its kind in south County Dublin. Joyce says that the monks extracted an annual toll of about six hundred fish per boat from fishermen using the harbour.

The Tudor-style entrance hall of Castle Park

A spiral staircase leads from the ground floor, with its vaulted undercroft, to the main space or hall above. The castle was restored by the Carmelite Sisters for the Aged and Infirm, the current owners, during the 1960s and was for a while open to the public. The battlements and cap towers, or look-outs, are all in very good condition. A carved stone head may be seen on the southern corner of the Castle, beside the archway.

The Crown lands of Dalkey, including Bullock Castle, were bought in 1683 by Colonel Allen of Stillorgan, and by descent passed to the Carysfort estate.

Bullock Castle appears in many paintings and engravings of the eighteenth and early nineteenth century. As early as 1698 Francis Place depicted it, just prior to the erection of the adjoining house, but showing several thatched cottages in the vicinity. There was no harbour as we know it today and the grounds of the castle fell away to a steep and rocky shore. The creek at Bullock was, naturally, in continuous use since medieval times and in the eighteenth century there were many reports of confrontations between smugglers and the revenue officers.

Some time in the early 1700s a three-storey, gable-ended house was added to the north-east corner of the

castle. A fine sketch from 1813, by Charles Pratt, shows it with a project-ing porch and oval window in the attic pediment. A row of cottages backed onto the main road, and a defensive corner tower with an enclosing wall (or bawn) stood near the top of the castle steps.

In 1804 the house and lands of Bullock Castle were leased by the Carysfort estate to the Ballast Board for the purposes of quarrying. The board made improvements to both Bullock and Sandycove Harbours and used them to load granite for shipment across the bay to Dublin, where it was needed to repair the Great South Wall and build new quays in the port.

In 1817 a twenty-four-year-old man named William Hutchinson was appointed to supervise the quarrying and shipment of stone, to manage the lifeboat stationed at Sandycove, and to oversee the pilots at Bullock. He was paid £100 per annum and he had the use of Bullock Castle. Hutchinson was to become an important figure in the history of Dun Laoghaire Harbour where he was later made Harbour Master.

The eighteenth-century house was enlarged in Victorian times and a granite porch was also added where there was once an unusual letter-box in the form of a lion's mouth. In the years before its demolition during the 1980s, the appearance of this house was spoilt by the inser-tion of aluminium windows.

Bullock Castle, showing its adjoining early eighteenth-century house and bawn tower in the distance – engraving, published 1791

Aerial photograph of Bullock Harbour, showing the rocky nature of the coastline

The gardens of Bullock Castle once extended southwards to include all of the site now completely covered by the buildings of Our Lady's Manor. During the early 1960s the Carmelite Sisters for the Aged and Infirm, who are based in the USA, were invited to establish an institution in Ireland by Archbishop John Charles McQuaid. The new one-hundred-bed block was opened in 1965 and further large extensions have been carried out which unfortunately dominate the harbour. The latest building project beside the castle involved the demolition of its adjoining house.

Bullock Harbour

Before the construction of Ulverton Road, the route from Sandycove to Dalkey passed along by Bullock Castle, and down a steep hill, now known as Castle Steps, behind Our Lady's Manor, past a group of houses called Perrin's Cottages, and on to join the Ballast Office Road at Bullock. These four cottages were built by Arthur Perrin, for his employees at Bullock Castle and Castle Park, sometime before 1837. The Ballast Office Road was so called because that body was responsible for carting stone to Bullock Harbour for shipment across the bay to Dublin.

The Pilots' Cottages, which stood on the quayside, were solidly built. Only three now remain from an original ten which were built sometime after 1807 by the Ballast Office, at a cost of £10 each, to house pilots who

worked out of Bullock Harbour. The ten cottages, which were advertised for sale in 1866, had been built on lands leased from the Earl of
Carysfort. The pilots provided a valuable service to shipping in Dublin
Bay. Their job was to sail out in small pilot boats, often in treacherous
weather conditions, and guide ships safely up into the port of Dublin. In
1911 there was only one pilot listed as resident in the cottages, but at
Bullock Harbour there was also a fisherman, a lightship keeper, a
seaman, three gardeners and a yacht and boat builder named John
Atkinson. Atkinson built many of the yachts known as Dublin Bay 17
footers, a number of which still sail at Howth. The Ballast Office managed the affairs of Dublin Port and in the early 1800s took leases on land
at Bullock and Sandycove for the purpose of quarrying. Bullock Harbour is still under the control of the Dublin Port and Docks Board, which
is 'descended' from the original Ballast Board. Stone was carted down
the Ballast Office Road for shipment across the bay in small vessels
called lighters.

Stone has been extracted from many places at Bullock, including the
area at the back of the harbour where great rocks plunge into the sea
and quarry marks and holes are still to be seen. These rocks are reached
by a stone doorway which bears an inscription. There was once a tavern
at the bottom of Castle Steps known as Golden's Inn, which must have
been popular with the stone carriers and sailors alike. The cut-stone
quay on the castle side of the harbour was doubtless built by the Ballast
Office to facilitate this work. The harbour is mentioned by Captain
Bligh, of *The Mutiny on the Bounty* fame, in his report on Dublin Bay.
Bligh deserves to be better known for his excellent survey and chart of
Dublin Bay, which he made in 1800. Of Bullock, he wrote: 'This is a dry
harbour – It lies between Dalkey and Dunleary and has a quay on the
West side, to which small vessels come to load with stones.' He also
records the existence of the remains of an earlier wall or pier which once
gave Bullock Harbour some protection from northerly winds. Off the

The fine granite-built pier and quays at Bullock Harbour are now used chiefly for leisure purposes

Drawing by W. F. Wakeman showing cranes on the pier at Bullock, the coal yards and the Pilots' Cottages, c. 1888

entrance, which he says is bad, is a rock which can be seen at low water on spring tides, which he calls Old Bullock.

In the later nineteenth century the harbour was used by small coal-boats making deliveries to Downey's coalyard there. Heavy iron rings, which were once used for ropes to winch the boats into the harbour, may still be seen. The coal was lifted in great baskets into the sheds which are still on the quayside. Coal was supplied to houses in the Dalkey area. W. O. MacCormick, the Dun Laoghaire coal merchants, were also based in Bullock at one time.

Bullock Harbour, with its outstanding stonework and picturesque collection of small boats, is now used mainly for pleasure purposes, though some fishermen make a living by catching crabs and lobsters, and by hiring out boats.

CHAPTER 7

Sandycove

An engraving by George Petrie showing the coastline between Glasthule and Sandycove, c. 1820

A small and rather attractive engraving of Sandycove, made from a drawing by George Petrie in about 1820, shows the rocky coastline between 'Dunleary and Bullock' with Bullock Castle in the distance. The Martello towers of Sandycove and Bullock are quite distinctly depicted and in the small harbour of Sandycove there are two quite large boats with masts. Whether these are fishing boats or vessels connected with the transport of stone is difficult to say. What is certain is that this attractive little harbour was purpose-built by the Ballast Office (later the Dublin Port and Docks Board) to facilitate the shipment of large quantities of stone to the South Wall. This stone was also used for the continuation of the North Wall and of Howth Harbour.

An engraving by John Kirkwood of the Martello tower and battery at Sandycove, c. 1845

The work began in 1735, when it was decided to replace the seventeenth-century wooden piles of the South Wall with a permanent stone structure, and to extend it a further two miles out into Dublin Bay. The top of the South Wall is constructed of long fingers of granite, some over six feet in length and about ten inches in thickness. These marvellous stones and the hewn blocks which form the sides of the South Wall were quarried at Sandycove and Bullock and shipped across the bay in barges called gabbards.

The barque Inverisk ashore at Sandycove Point in 1915

Dalkey granite, as it is generally called, earned a well-deserved reputation and was used in such prestigious building projects as the Thames embankment, the Menai Bridge in Wales, and Kylemore Abbey in Connemara. In Dublin, granite from Bullock was used to rebuild Essex Bridge (now known as Grattan Bridge) in 1874 and was extensively used for footpaths in Dun Laoghaire.

Stone, whether cut or rubble, was a most important material as these were the days before cement blocks or concrete construction existed. The quarries also presented many job opportunities for craftsmen, quarrymen and labourers, who in the early nineteenth century could earn as much as 1s. 8d. per day. As we have clearly seen, there was also much quarrying in the area all along the shore from the Forty Foot to Bullock, and close inspection of the foreshore rocks will reveal the many holes drilled by quarrymen to extract stone over 150 years ago. The Ballast Office leased a substantial parcel of land at Sandycove in the early 1800s from the Earl of Carysfort for the purpose of quarrying stone.

The construction of Sandycove Harbour is itself a fine example of the stonemason's art. The walls and the cantilevered steps are wonderfully crafted and the short pier makes clever use of the existing bedrock where a flight of steps, used by bathers, is beautifully cut into the granite. The stone wharf in front of the modern Neptune Lodge was almost certainly in use at one time for loading stone onto barges, as there was once a clear passage for carts here and there was also a greater depth of water there than inside Sandycove Harbour.

A plan by John Rennie (the designer and engineer of Dun Laoghaire Harbour), dated 1820, shows Sandycove at an interesting stage. There was no road or wall along the back of the harbour, and it was still in its natural state – a sandy cove. The south quay already existed and was served by a separate road, now Sandycove Avenue West. The Martello tower and battery were reached by means of Sandycove Avenue East and the Shore Road.

The harbour possesses a fine boat slip, and this was completed in 1864 to facilitate boating and fishing activities. There was also a water pump, which appears in a photograph of about 1860, and was provided to serve the needs of the horses used to draw the carts loaded with stone.

By the late nineteenth century the harbour was no longer in active use by Dublin Port and Docks Board and was falling into disrepair. The board received letters of complaint from time to time about the state of the harbour. During the 1960s the dangerous broken surface of the pier was repaired for the benefit of bathers, and cut granite, salvaged from the demolition of an old house called Granite Hall in Dun Laoghaire, was put to use as seats and steps around the harbour.

The lifeboat which was established at Sandycove in 1803 under the auspices of the Ballast Office, was one of three in Dublin Bay, and this is considered to be the first organised lifeboat service in the world. The lifeboat was frequently called out, and on one wild night in December 1821 it was launched at Sandycove and the crew of a ship called *The Ellen* were saved, but at the cost of the lives of four of the lifeboat men. Captain Hutchinson's report to the Ballast Board describes graphically the difficulty of the rescue and the great violence of the sea:

'I beg leave to state that on Friday evening between the hours of eight and nine o clock, I was informed by some of the pilots that a brig was ashore near Sandycove and that they would accompany me in the lifeboat to save the crew from a watery grave, their cries being most affecting. It blew a most violent gale from the South-East ... at this time, the vessel was lying nearly head to the sea which broke completely over her and while the crew were in the act of getting into the lifeboat she filled with water. While we were bailing out the water with our hats, a sea of which I shall never forget the aspect, overwhelmed the lifeboat and washed six of us out of her.

Two, fortunately, caught hold of the rope they had been holding the boat by and three then unfortunately perished. With difficulty, I regained the lifeboat and with the remainder of her crew we were drove among the breakers without oars and most providentially we got on shore having received many contusions and the loss of another of my brave companions who from exhaustion let go his hold and was washed out among the rocks.

A watercolour of Sandycove in the eighteenth century, showing fishermen's boats and cottages. The Martello tower and battery had not yet been built.

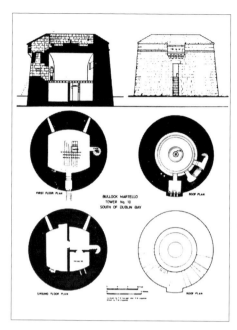

A section and plan of a typical Martello tower in Dublin Bay

Two of the unfortunate pilots have left widows and children who will be in a most desolate state without the humane grant of small pensions from your Honourable board.'

Among the crew we find several familiar local names such as Archbold, Rogan and Tallant. The extraordinary bravery and physical stamina of these men is hard for us to appreciate nowadays, given that they relied only on their oars and perhaps a small sail. The lifeboat itself must have been a heavy vessel and not easy to manoeuvre, which the crew in this case had to launch in a violent storm and row to a most dangerous position on a lee shore.

The Sandycove lifeboat was housed in a boathouse which is now part of Neptune Lodge. The engraving by John Kirkwood from about 1845 shows a boathouse with the bows of a lifeboat just visible. Beside it stands a small, two-windowed cottage, on the site of the present Neptune Lodge, a house overlooking Scotsman's Bay. During the 1830s Sandycove is described (by John D'Alton, 1838) as having a coastguard station. Perhaps the coastguard evolved out of the lifeboat service, and the cottage may have housed their personnel.

Another dramatic shipwreck occurred here in 1915, when a Scottish barque called *The Inverisk*, came in at the Forty Foot. Fortunately, all of the crew got ashore in safety and the ship was eventually towed off the rocks.

The Martello Tower and Battery

The Martello towers which dot the coastline of County Dublin are an elegant architectural curiosity of Irish history, though Weston St John Joyce did not approve of them, describing them as 'un-gainly edifices' (*The Neighbourhood of Dublin*, 1912).

Some seventy-four towers were built around Ireland, mainly concentrated in the south and east, for the purpose of resisting a much-feared attack from Napoleon's French fleet. They were erected during the period 1801 to 1804, and each took about six months to build. The average cost was £1800 per tower, and many, such as Sandycove, were attached to a battery or fort.

The stone-built towers were forty feet high, with eight-foot thick walls, and the entrance door was usually positioned ten or fifteen feet above the ground.

It is safe to say that the Martello tower at Sandycove Point is the most famous of all such towers because of the brief residence there of James Joyce. Joyce was invited to stay at the tower by his friend Oliver St John Gogarty. He arrived on 9 September 1904 and stayed only six days! But this visit, and the opening scene from *Ulysses* which takes place on the gun platform on the roof, have immortalised 'Joyce's Tower' and given Sandycove an international literary reputation.

The tower was acquired by the Eastern Regional Tourism Organisation (now Dublin Tourism) in 1964, and converted into a Joycean

The position of Sandycove Martello tower and battery marked on this early nineteenth-century map – it was one of seventy-four defensive towers strategically placed in certain parts of Ireland

museum. The museum houses all sorts of fascinating mementoes connected with the writer, such as a piano once used by him.

An early nineteenth-century painting of Sandycove Point

In more recent times it was decided to extend the tower by adding a curved reception and exhibition area. Unfortunately this new structure, concrete built, brought much criticism from those who felt that a more sensitive architectural extension might have been made.

The battery or fort, which forms the massive cut-stone bulwark between the once-sacred 'men only' territory of the Forty Foot and the general public, was erected shortly after the construction of the Martello tower. It occupies much of the rocky outcrop which comprises Sandy-cove Point, and in fact the granite bedrock rises up through the fort to form its highest point. The Kirkwood engraving shows a tall flagstaff or mast with stays rising from the centre of the battery. There must have been a similar mast at the old telegraph station on Dalkey Hill, and they were used to communicate messages by means of flags. During the Second World War an anti-aircraft gun and a searchlight were installed at Sandycove battery, and the gun was used once towards the end of the 'Emergency' in 1945.

The battery is now part of a private house which was converted in 1955 from the existing garrison buildings. These buildings included a guard room, the master gunner's store, a vaulted powder room, and the soldiers' quarters, which form the main part of the old house now known as Neptune, not to be confused with Neptune Lodge which is more modern. A privy, cess pit and three water cisterns provided for the garrison's sanitary needs. All these structures, including the semicircular walls of the battery itself, were built of the finest hewn granite, and maintain a quality of complete timelessness.

The main function of a Martello tower and battery was to resist a naval attack by means of large, swivelling guns, and a total number of thirty-six artillery men were stationed there in its heyday. As it happened, the towers and batteries had an uneventful history and never saw any military action. Some stand neglected and roofless, such as the ruined fort on Dalkey Island, but Sandycove battery has been conserved remarkably well.

The Forty Foot

It has been suggested that it was the army presence at Sandycove Point which first established the tradition of an all-male bathing place at the Forty Foot. Segregation of the sexes was the norm in Victorian times and it would have been quite natural for the men to take advantage of the excellent sea bathing when released from their duties in the fort. Equally, the nuns of the Loreto Convent in Dalkey had a private bathing place which was exclusivly female.

A sign of the past ...

The origin of the name 'Forty Foot' has attracted many theories, ranging from the presence of the fortieth foot regiment in the battery, to the forty-foot wide Marine Road in Dun Laoghaire, or that the sea is forty feet deep at this point! However, the most likely explanation relates to the fact that the place was called the Forty Foot Hole since about 1800. Many deep-water pools around the Irish coast, which were noted for their excellent fishing, received such names as the Long Hole (Ireland's Eye), Seal Hole (Hook Head) or Salmon Hole (river Suir). The Forty Foot Hole has had a long reputation as a good fishing ground for pollock, lobster and crabs. Sandycove Harbour was used not only by the stone barges but also by fishermen who made a living from the rich fishing grounds of Dublin Bay. An early member of the Sandycove Bathers' Association wrote in 1909 that he swam at the Forty Foot Hole as far back as 1851, and that, as there were no steps then, it was difficult to get in and out of the water (*The Forty Foot*, Frank Power and Peter Pearson, 1995).

Though a tradition of bathing here had been established since that time, to the extent that the Ordnance Survey of 1867 described it as a 'Men's Bathing Place', no improvements were carried out until 1880 when the Sandycove Bathers' Association was formed. In 1909, when a legal challenge was made by the local authority over the Sandycove Bathers' Association's rights, it was reported that the association had to date spent nearly £2000 in making improvements at the Forty Foot. Dangerous rocks had been removed, steps carved into the rock, ladders affixed, screen walls built and winter storm damage repaired. The Forty Foot had indeed been very well maintained.

The case was settled in favour of the association which continues to prosper, though in recent years the 'men-only' rule passed into history and today the Forty Foot is enjoyed by men and women alike.

A Forty Foot tradition which is at least a century old is the annual Christmas Day swim, when hardy types take the plunge and money is collected for charity.

Various reliable sources refer to the existence of baths at Sandycove as early as 1838. John D'Alton, for instance, tells us that 'commodious

hot and cold water baths' are located here, and according to *The Dublin Almanac and Street Directory* of 1840, a Mr John Walsh was its proprietor. Walsh's baths eventually became the Sandycove Ladies Baths, whose derelict buildings may still be seen at the head of a little inlet.

Early in the 1840s a developer named John Crosthwaite erected baths in Scotsman's Bay, close to the east pier. Crosthwaite lived in Victoria Cottage, one of several houses, now long gone, which stood close to the present Dun Laoghaire baths. It was here, on the site of a former battery, that he built his new Royal Victoria Baths, which offered open-sea bathing and hot and cold baths of salt and fresh water. The baths were eventually purchased by the Kingstown Urban District Council in 1896 and in the following year tenders were sought for the construction of new swimming baths.

By 1843 the shore of Scotsman's Bay was already well developed with terraces and houses. Windsor Terrace and Martello Terrace, which are closest to Dun Laoghaire, were built, and there was a row of houses

Bathers in the Forty Foot, c. 1890

A typical Victorian cottage-style house in Sandycove, with its stucco embellishments

and cottages at Newtownsmith. A number of detached villas, such as Fort William, Sea Bank and St Helen's also overlooked the sea.

The Proby Estate and Sandycove Houses

Before the nineteenth century the Sandycove area, situated between the two small villages of Bullock and Glasthule, was largely uninhabited. The land was rough and is often described as being scattered with rocks and water-filled, disused quarries. The first new villas or seaside residences were built here in the 1830s, not long after the construction of the Martello tower and battery.

The extension of the railway to Dalkey in 1844 and the eventual building of a station at Sandycove quickly boosted the development and popularity of the district. Simultaneously, Dun Laoghaire, with its harbour and new terraces, was rapidly growing to become an important Victorian town.

Many of the new houses were built on land which belonged to the Proby family. The Proby estate at Sandycove and Dalkey came into existence in the late eighteenth century following the marriage of a Proby to the hieress of the Allen estate in Stillorgan. The Allens were builders in Dublin during the time of Charles I and they acquired much land in south County Dublin, including that of Sandycove.

In the early years of the nineteenth century, Admiral Proby, who had the distinction of being present at the battle of the Nile, made five leases of his coastal lands between Dalkey and Dun Laoghaire, and houses were built on them by speculators. The first Proby leases in Sandycove appear to date from 1803. Many villas and terraced houses were built between 1830 and 1850 and were let to summer visitors at high rents.

A heated legal debate between the Probys and some of their tenants arose a hundred years later in the 1960s when some residents in Sandycove realised that they did not in fact own the bricks and mortar of their houses, due to the type of lease which had been made in the early years of this century. The matter was settled, though perhaps not to everyone's satisfaction, when the Proby estate offered new leases and many owners bought out the freehold and their interest in the buildings.

The first Ordnance Survey map of this area, published in 1843, marks the appearance of many new houses including Sandycove Terrace, Sandycove House, Cove Castle and houses on Sandycove Avenue West. Burdett Avenue was almost fully developed with new houses and other new buildings had appeared on Sandycove Road and Albert Road. By 1850 there were five houses on Ballygihen Avenue, two on Otranto Place, six on Brighton Terrace and four vacant houses at Mornington Cottages. The 1867 map shows over a hundred new houses, detached and terraced, in the area. Victorian Sandycove was now well established.

St Kilda's, one of Sandycove's most elegant villas, built about 1840, was occupied by one Francis Falkner, a grocer and wine merchant who owned shops in Grafton Street, Dawson Street and at 40 Charing Cross, London. This fine house, along with Rock View and Mornington, stands off Sandycove Avenue East and has open sea views and large gardens. Mornington House was built as a speculative development on a site acquired from the Ballast Office in 1844 by Robert Meekins. Under the terms of the lease he was to build a house at a cost of at least £300. Meekins himself lived at Glasthule House, a substantial Victorian residence located near Glenageary railway station. He rented more land from the Ballast Office in 1851, including a two-acre site just south of the Martello tower, where he may have built Seafort, another Victorian house which faces Sandycove Harbour, and some of the small cottage-type houses which overlook the bay on the seaward side.

Munster Terrace, Cliff Terrace and Bayswater Terrace stood on the north side of the main road to Dalkey, now called Breffni Road, and their location afforded good sea views from the rear windows. Breffni Terrace, consisting of fifteen redbrick houses, was completed by the 1880s. The impressive terrace of houses was erected by a builder named O'Rourke, and called after the old O'Rourke clan territory of Breffni. At about the same time Elton Park, which lay further inland and was probably developed by the Probys and called after their English seat at Elton Hall, already had eight houses.

The upper section of Castle Park Road remained largely undeveloped until the 1930s. In the middle of the nineteenth century, the only houses were Leslie Cottage (which stood on the site of Gosworth, a late Victorian house), a house called St Margaret's and one other cottage. Arkendale Road was also a late Victorian development, consisting of large, semi-detached, two-storey, redbrick houses raised on rustic granite basements. St Anne's, situated at the end of Arkendale Road and now demolished, was a small, double-fronted house from about 1860. It was once occupied by the British navy, and used as an admiralty house. Some older residents remember a flagstaff which stood in front and manoeuvres taking place in the fields nearby, some time before 1920.

Sandycove Road in the 1850s possessed a variety of shops and houses which stretched back to the village of Glasthule. At that time Glasthule had four dairies, three provision dealers, five vintners, three shoemakers, two car owners (a car owner was a type of taxi man, the

The entrance to St Anne's, Arkendale Road, a mid-eighteenth-century house, now demolished

Geragh, designed by Michael Scott as his own residence in 1937

owner of a small, horse-drawn cab), one private library, a physician and *accoucheur* (midwife), a fencing and dancing academy and a 'select classical school'!

Albert Road, which had eight residents in 1850, was quickly developed with small, single-storey, villa-type houses. Within twenty years this long, straight road had eighty-nine houses. Some of the 'cottage--type' houses on Albert Road were elaboratly decorated in stucco, with such devices as architraves and brackets, and in one case an unusual frieze of circular ornaments. Ornamental ridge tiles were common and decorative dwarf railings were sometimes used to enhance the low walls on the street.

Haddington House, built by 1843 and later called The Beeches, was the only residence situated above the railway on Albert Road. The house was owned by a member of the Findlater family until about 1930 when houses were built on its grounds.

Sandycove Castle In the middle of Sandycove Avenue West is a striking Victorian house with battlemented additions called Sandycove Castle. Originally called Cove Castle, it was, by the 1880s, occupied by the Misses Smith who ran a 'seminary for young ladies' there.

Sandycove was always a preferred place of residence for the genteel and the retired. Among the more colourful names to be found at that time was Horatio Nelson Wallace, who was a town commissioner.

In his books such as *The Garden* or *The Sea Wall* L. A. G. Strong evokes the life of residential Sandycove during the early years of this century. He describes, through a child's eyes, the houses and gardens with their cooks and housekeepers. He writes about a leisured way of life with much time spent fishing in rockpools, and boating and swimming at the Forty Foot.

In Strong's time, Sandycove looked much as it does today, with one notable exception – Marine Parade, the road which runs along the shore joining Sandycove and Dun Laoghaire, had not yet been constructed

*The living room at Geragh,
with its fine view over
Sandycove Harbour*

and most of the houses had gardens which ran right down to the rocks. The sea wall which Strong wrote about was swept away when Marine Parade was built in 1922. Of this Mervyn Wall, in his booklet about the Forty Foot, commented: 'When the work was completed, the local urban council erected a monument to themselves at the rate payers' expense, carefully inscribing their undistinguished names on the commemorative tablet. The monument is an ungainly one and is known locally as "the piano".'

The rocky foreshore of Scotsman's Bay has been transformed since the 1930s by the construction of a new promenade and the creation of an open space which is known as Sandycove Green. Dun Laoghaire Corporation came under fire from residents when it was recently proposed to turn this area over to parking for 180 cars. With the continued increase in car ownership and mounting pressure for parking in Dun Laoghaire, which will be even more severe if the proposed yachting marina is ever built, it is likely that these unfortunate proposals will surface again.

Geragh, architect Michael Scott's house at Sandycove Point, has become a landmark in its own right. It was designed by Scott as his own residence, something which architects of our own age seem reluctant to do, opting instead for a so-called 'period residence'. Selecting a stunning site, Scott chose the international style of the 1930s and echoed the curves of the tower in his design. Some hate it for its stark simplicity, others admire the way in which steel and concrete were used to create a ship-like elegance. Whatever one's preference, the house, built in 1937-8, is a significant building in the history of Irish architecture.

Several of the older Victorian villas have already disappeared, including Gowran Hall, St Helen's, Beaufort, Sea Bank and Ballygihen. These villas were typically two-storey houses with granite steps leading up to the hall door at first-floor level, and were ornamented with the usual classical, pillared porches and fanlights. During the 1970s and 1980s the

A Victorian print showing Ballygihen House (left) and Gowran Hall (centre)

generous-sized walled gardens made these houses attractive to developers who saw the chance to build apartments in their place. Apartment blocks were built at Sea Bank and Gowran Hall in the late 1970s, and there was much concern that we were seeing the beginning of a 'Costa del Sandycove'! The six-storey block at Sea Bank is particularly intrusive in an otherwise low skyline. Following the demolition of a very pretty villa called St Helen's, which had ornamental coved ceilings and bay windows, a three-storey block of apartments was built in 1982.

Ballygihen House was built around 1840 and is shown on early maps as Sandycove Lodge. The impressive garden front with its bay windows overlooked Scotsman's Bay, and the principal rooms had high ceilings with elegant plaster cornices. The massive chimney stacks are remarkable as they are entirely constructed of shaped granite. The house was once approached from the main road through a castellated granite gateway on which there is still a stone plaque bearing the name of the house. The arch of the pedestrian entrance survives and stands near the Londis shop. In the landscaped grounds between the house and the sea there was once an artificial mound with a statue of a sailor surrounded by seats. At the end of the eighteenth century a similar statue stood at what was then called Dunleary Pier, and it features in a print of the 1790s. When the pier was shortened, the sailor may have found a new home in Sandycove. The Ordnance Survey map of 1867 indicates that the new occupants of Ballygihen, the Sisters of Mercy, replaced the statue with a cross.

The convent had a short life and remained here only until the 1870s. A refectory was located in the basement where there was an old stone-flagged kitchen with a huge range made by Loftus A. Bryan, the noted ironmongers of Bride Street in Dublin. Ballygihen was demolished in 1984 and sheltered housing for the elderly was built there.

CHAPTER 8

Glasthule

There has been a settlement at Glasthule since the middle of the eight-eenth century, for we find 'Glosdool' marked on Rocque's map (1757) as a collection of cottages at the mouth of a tiny stream. It is from this stream that the area takes its name. Glas Tuathaill, which is generally translated as 'Toole's stream', rises in Glenageary, and in the eighteenth century would have made the short journey to the sea by crossing scrubby land full of rocks (called the scrub of Glenageary) before cross-ing the 'Road to Bullock' (now Eden Road) and on past a few cottages at Newtownsmith.

These cottages are also shown on a map from the 1790s (in the Long-field collection at the National Library) and were probably occupied by families who made a living from stone quarrying and fishing. These dwellings evolved into the 'village' of Newtownsmith, which by 1840 was connected to Kingstown by the road in front of the seafront terraces. Windsor and Martello Terraces wre erected by Samuel and George Smith who had acquired land here in 1824. By the middle of the century the whole area was well sprinkled with small villas and houses which were let.

In the mid-nineteenth century there were several groups of cottages in Glasthule, many of them probably thatched. For instance, Perrin's Row and Chalmer's Cottages stood on Eden Road while Neil's Lane and Halpin's Cottages lay off the main Glasthule Road. Many of these were replaced when the Kingstown Urban District Council set about building local authority houses in the area. At the turn of the century the three new terraces named Eden (named after the original house), Findlater and Coldwell, (named after councillors with the local Urban District Council), were erected off Eden Road while seventy-five flats were built at Glasthule Buildings in 1908. Over 220 houses were built in Glasthule between 1920 and 1934.

In 1863, with the growing population of County Dublin, three sepa-rate Catholic parishes were formed between Dalkey, Ballybrack and Glasthule, and the following year Father John Harold erected a tempo-rary wooden chapel in the grounds of Ballygihen House. There was no permanent church in Glasthule until the first stone of St Joseph's was laid in 1867. A French Gothic style was chosen, and a large church with aisles and a large rose window was completed in 1869. But the church built to the designs of Augustus W. Pugin and George Ashlin was never

This artist's impression of St Joseph's shows the church with a spire which was never built (The Irish Builder, 1867)

fully completed as an intended Gothic spire was not erected.

Father George Harold and his brother John, who was also a priest, worked with great zeal to build up the new parishes and open new Catholic schools in Dalkey and Glasthule – Father George even went to the United States on a fund-raising exercise. The schools were eventually built and were named after the two Harold brothers. The Harold National School on Eden Road is an impressive redbrick, two-storey structure with large windows to let in plenty of light and air.

The Presentation Brothers College or school is situated opposite St Joseph's Church. The college was described in 1911 as being divided into three departments: juniorate, classical, and civil service/commercial.

CHAPTER 9

Glenageary

Glenageary, or Gleann na gCaorach which means the 'glen of the sheep', describes the land around the Glasthule stream which, until the early nineteenth century, consisted of rough pasture covered in rocks and gorse.

Rocque's map of 1757 shows the land to be rough and very clearly full of rocks. A later eighteenth-century map, which covers the lands of present-day Dun Laoghaire and includes Glenageary, is covered in notes which describe the condition of the land.

This extensive survey, which appears to have been made in about 1795 for the ground landlords, Lords Longford and De Vesci, describes 'beautiful situations for building' on Upper Glenageary Road.

Later, five almost parallel roads running inland would be laid out, apparently by the landlords, in an effort to plan the development of their estates. These roads eventually included York Road, Glenageary Road, Adelaide Road, Albert Road and Castle Park Road. These were quickly developed in the nineteenth century.

All of the fields stretching from Bullock to Monkstown are carefully described and give us a picture of a rather neglected and wild country-side. Most of the fields were in pasture or meadow, but much of the land

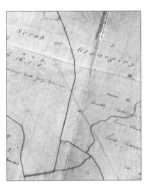

'The scrub of Glanegiry' – detail from late eighteenth-century estate map

Glenageary Road Upper, which links Monkstown and Dalkey, and was the outer limit of Victorian Dun Laoghaire

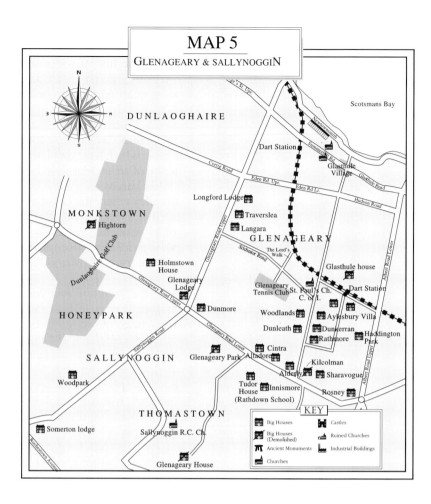

MAP 5
GLENAGEARY & SALLYNOGGIN

here was grazing land interspersed with rocks and abandoned quarries. Here and there large outcrops of granite are shown. The outcrops near the present National Maritime Museum at Moran Park and at Corrig Castle are both shown.

The 'Road to Bullock' was one of the few roads existing in the late eighteenth century, and almost certainly originated as a track which joined the two medieval properties of St Mary's Abbey: Monkstown Castle and Bullock Castle. This road, also clearly marked on Taylor's map of 1816, became Tivoli Road, and its continuations became Corrig Road and Eden Road. In the late eighteenth century the only structure in the area was a forge, which was located somewhere near the present Eden Road.

The next major period of road building was associated with the Martello towers, when the perfectly straight roads of George's Street, Park Road and Sandycove Avenue East were laid out to provide easy access for the military.

Residents of the now fashionable Glenageary might be surprised to learn that in 1795 the area was described as 'the scrub of Glanegiry'. This was a place suitable only for grazing sheep, and the fields, all of which were rented to Charles Jones, Lord Ranelagh, were full 'of rocks and stones, much interspersed with furz, briars, black thorns and rushes' and 'very much injured by the stone cutters, being quarried in deep holes and left full of water'.

Somewhere covering part of Silchester Road, Crosthwaite Park and the site of Longford Lodge (later Glengara Park School) lay a twenty-four acre parcel of land called Kilnagashaugh, a name which has completely disappeared. If the name suggests a possible site of an ancient church, it is a pity that no trace of it or reference to it has survived.

The name Swan's Hollow refers to a small valley where the Glasthule stream flows under Glenageary Road Upper, close to Rathdown School. The name, still in common usage among older residents, comes from the fact that one Timothy Swan, who was perhaps a farmer, occupied a house and garden here in the late eighteenth century. Nearby stood the bridge of Glenageary.

Among the first houses to take advantage of the 'beautiful situations for building', on Glenageary Road Upper, were Rosney, Glenageary Hall, Sion House, Minor's Hill, Glenageary Cottage, Altadore, Tudor Lodge, Tudor Cottage, Glenageary Park, Holmston, Laurel Hill and High Thorn. Among these houses, all of which appear on the first Ordnance Survey map of this area, published in 1843, Glenageary Hall, Sion House, Glenageary Park and High Thorn have disappeared and seven of the largest houses which have survived are now in institutional use. Two belong to Rathdown School, three to the Order of St John of God, one is a nursing home and another is used as a pre-school.

Each was originally built with its own spacious grounds, the perimeters of which were well planted with trees. Later, a further number of large, Victorian houses such as Dunmore, Cintra, Alderley, Kilcolman and Sharavogue were built on the remaining sites.

These houses, which formed a belt of fine residences on Glenageary Road Upper, marked the outer limits of Dun Laoghaire's Victorian development.

Top: A pair of stags' heads once graced the entrance gates to Altadore

Above: The circular room at Altadore, which is believed to have been a library

Altadore, an unusual villa with a colonial air, which is now a nursing home

Cintra, another Glenageary house of the villa type, probably built about 1850, and now used as offices

A detail of plasterwork from Sharavogue

Altadore is a large, villa-type house with a single storey of gracious rooms over a high basement. In 1844 the architect Sandham Symes exhibited drawings for this house in the Royal Hibernian Academy. It was built for John Aylmer, and has many unusual features such as a double staircase to the hall door, a transverse hallway (which runs across the front of the house) and a circular room in a projecting wing.

The entrance is covered by a canopy, which, with its decorative iron-work, creates a decidedly colonial feeling. Altadore was converted into a retirement home in 1990, and houses were built in the grounds. It once possessed a particularly fine pair of granite gate piers, surmounted by cast-iron stags with antlers.

Cintra and **Rosney** are also villa-type houses, the first having tall chimneys and a symmetrical front with a very elaborate cast-iron porch surmounted by a sphinx, while the second is in the style of the Tudor 'cottage orné' and has decorative bargeboards and mullioned windows. Cintra, a neat house, with no large rooms and quite plain inside, may have been built for letting. A nursery, where nowadays garden plants are raised and sold, gives employment to the disabled, and is run by the Order of St John of God.

Rosney, with its miniature, Gothic, vaulted hallway, dates from about 1830, and may once have been used as a summer residence by the Waldron family who were calico printers in Rathgar. It is the home of well-known writer and journalist Bruce Arnold.

High Thorn and **Laurel Hill**, both situated towards Dun Laoghaire, were also once fine villas. High Thorn, demolished in 1979, was a plain, four-bay house, while Laurel Hill has been so extended and so much altered that the original house is unrecognisable.

Dunmore and **Dunbeg** (formerly Minor's Hill), two modest houses of about 1850, are now both part of the St John of God day-care centre for mentally handicapped children. Dunmore was acquired by the order in 1964 and their work continues today.

Glenageary Hall, demolished in 1978, was a large square house of a highly ornamental character. The house appears to have been built around 1830. The interior was decorated with many plaster panels and plaques which featured classical subjects, while the exterior was also treated with many stucco embellishments, a pilastered porch, and bay windows with ironwork balconies. A rich frieze of scroll-work ornament, supported by pilasters, decorated the upper floors, while all of the windows had stucco brackets and architraves.

The subjects of the plaques included cherubs harvesting corn and goddesses riding chariots, and appear to be part of a collection of eighteenth-century plaster casts which were not probably part of the original scheme of decoration which is fairly routine. The principal drawing-room was divided by Ionic columns and had attractive but simple plaster cornices.

Sharavogue and **Kilcolman** together represented the peak of a type of high Victorian house-building. The twin houses were built around 1870

Above: The drawing room in Sharavogue.

Below: A photograph of a Victorian tennis party on the steps of Sharavogue seems to capture the confident mood of the late nineteenth century

Victorian life at Sharavogue

One of the many classical relief panels which decorated Glenageary Hall

Glenageary Hall, which was an elaborate house with an unusual collection of classical plasterwork reliefs

by a wealthy merchant named Patrick Gleeson, grocer and seed merchant of Thomas Street in Dublin who lived in Kilcolman. He came from County Offaly where the names of Kilcolman and Sharavogue originated. Of the two houses, only Sharavogue now remains and it is used as a pre-school. It exhibits both in its external stucco decoration and in its internal plasterwork the most lavish and florid style. This popular Victorian style was known as 'Italianate' because of the preponderance of decorative features such as round-arched windows, foliate scrolls and brackets, balustrades, urns, columns and other devices borrowed from the Italian Renaissance.

The house, standing two-storeys over a high basement, is square in plan, and its elaborate porch and entrance is approached by a double flight of steps.

Alderley, **Sunninghill** and **Dunluce**, standing near the corner of Adelaide Road, constitute three Tudor-style houses of asymmetrical plan. They share a pair of distinctive coach-houses which are of the same design. They are believed to have been built by Tedcastles, the coal merchants, around 1850.

Hillcourt, formerly called Innismore and now part of Rathdown School, is one of the finest remaining houses in Glenageary and has many interesting internal features including an elaborately decorated hall and a fine billiard room. The ceiling of the hall is compartmentalised by shallow arches and is ornamented with the Greek key pattern and a monochrome painted frieze. The paintings depict idealised rural scenes and Arcadian landscapes. The back panels of a study door are ornamented with embossed figures in the Art Nouveau style. In common with many rich householders of the period, the occupants of Hillcourt, probably the Siberry

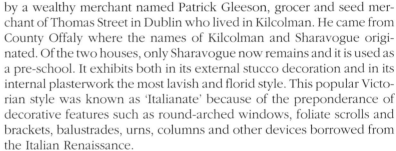

Alderley, a Tudor-style, mid-Victorian house, on Glenageary Road Upper

family whose S monogram is to be found on the newel posts of the stairs, added a billiard room in the 1890s, with a fine pitch-pine roof and an elaborate carved fireplace. It was most likely also they who added the coloured-glass window on the stairs and the elaborate tiled bathroom.

The exterior, with its four-columned Doric portico and Wyatt bow windows is completed with a strong cornice at parapet level. Two stucco lyres appear over the ground-floor windows.

Today Hillcourt has two gate-lodges, one having a miniature fluted Doric 'porch'; the other, which is Tudor in style, was once the gate-lodge to Tudor Cottage, a neighbouring house which has completely disappeared. Hillcourt was bought as a school premises in 1919 by W. P. Toone, who had earlier established Castle Park School near Dalkey. Hillcourt Girls' School was run by two sisters, the Misses Palmer.

Rathdown School eventually evolved out of three girl's schools. In 1973 Hillcourt School was amalgamated with The Hall School, Monkstown. More recently it was joined by Glengara Park School and now

Hillcourt, one of the most impressive remaining houses in Glenageary, built about 1830

Embossed panels on the back of a drawing-room door in Hillcourt

The hallway at Hillcourt

Glenageary House, with its fine symmetrical facade, which was demolished in 1978

has over four hundred pupils and eighty members of staff. Including Tudor Lodge which was acquired later, the boarding school occupies fifteen acres.

Tudor Lodge is a treble-gabled, two-storey-over-basement house, and was acquired by the Rathdown School in 1965. Though imposing in appearance, it is a deceptively small house and has only two large-sized reception rooms. Like Hillcourt, Tudor Lodge also has an elegant transverse hall which has good plasterwork. It runs across the front of the house and takes up a good deal of space. The decorated bargeboards with their long, wooden finials are very striking, and were typical of the 1840s, where the objective of the builder was to create an impressive and picturesque appearance, regardless of the arrangement of the interior.

Beside Tudor Lodge was once an entrance and gate-lodge leading to Glenageary House, an imposing Victorian mansion whose extensive grounds once covered much of present-day Sallynoggin. Another driveway connected the house with Rochestown Avenue.

Glenageary House It is difficult to say when the original Glenageary House was built, but it may have already existed by 1816. Like so many of the larger houses, it began as a modest structure, five bays wide and two storeys in height, to which gabled wings were later added. Between the projecting end-bays, at the front of the house, was added a bold colonnade with four Ionic columns which carried a balcony made of heavy, cast-iron discs. The colonnade is very similar to that of the Royal Irish Yacht Club in Dun Laoghaire, and may have been designed by the same architect, John Skipton Mulvany.

Inside, the rooms were decorated with boldly modelled plasterwork, typical of the 1840s, featuring oak leaves and other naturalistic motifs.

The house was bought by Haliday Bruce, a noted Dublin stockbroker, in 1842, and it was probably he who enlarged it by the further addition of an octagonal viewing tower. The ascent to the tower was by means of a dramatic spiral staircase, which had a decorative cast-iron hand-rail. The tower, with its cap-like roof and urn-shaped finial, had an observation room with large windows giving great views around the

surrounding countryside. Haliday Bruce died in 1857 and Glenageary House was bought by Thomas Pim of Pims in South Great George's Street. In 1903 it was acquired by Alfred J. Waller who was a keen horseman, and he may have built the elaborate brick stables to the rear of the house.

From the 1930s onwards, part of the land was acquired by Dun Laoghaire Corporation for the purpose of building houses in Sallynoggin. A strip of land was reserved for the eventual building of a new road between Glenageary Hill and Killiney shopping centre, but this has still not materialised.

The old house was converted into flats in the period between the two world wars. Then, having been left in the usual way to the mercy of vandals, Glenageary House was eventually demolished in 1978.

Silchester Road was named after Lord Silchester, the junior heir to the Longford title. The Stewarts, the land agents to Lords Longford and De Vesci, played a leading role in developing the road. It is said that the Lords' Walk, a tree-lined avenue for pedestrians which connects Silchester Road to The Metals, was once to have been developed with houses or to have become a new road. (The Metals is a right-of-way adjoining the railway once used to transport stone from Dalkey quarry to Dun Laoghaire Harbour.)

St Paul's Church, which was completed in 1868 and is the focal point of the district

Silchester Road was a late development in Glenageary, with the earliest houses being built during the 1860s. A Major Szinow Harran took a lease on the lands from the Longford and De Vesci estate for the purpose of building large houses which would be set in spacious grounds. The first new houses appeared at the Adelaide Road end, beside St Paul's Church which had recently been built.

St Paul's, a Gothic church built of rustic granite masonry with a tall spire, consists of a simple nave and chancel. It is entered by a pair of Gothic doors under the tower, and its spire, with its four pinnacles, is mostly built of limestone. The church as a whole exhibits a most successful use of three types of stone – granite, limestone and sandstone – much of which is richly carved. The limestone is used for the stringcourses, coigns and buttresses, while the sandstone is used for the window mouldings, the largest of which is the south-facing, five-light window which bears the date 1868, the year in which the building was completed.

Silchester Road, lined with its fine houses, was carefully completed with stone kerbs, and the gardens fronted with granite and brick walls. In 1887 the Glenageary and Kingstown Lawn Tennis Club was founded and grounds were leased at Silchester Road. The club had seven grass courts and a small pavilion and it was patronised by a distinguished membership of Glenageary residents.

The belvedere, or viewing tower, of Glenageary House

The stone porch and entrance at Traverslea

Apart from several detached Victorian houses there were also several pairs of semi-detached houses, mostly in red brick, such as Hughendon and Leconfield. Melrose and Stratford, with their bay windows and arched entrances, are a similar pair and are characteristically Victorian. Rossmore, situated opposite St Paul's Church, is a large Tudor-style residence, built of red brick with stone-mullioned windows.

Similar houses were constructed on Adelaide Road, including Adelaide House, Eagle Lodge, Aylesbury and Rathmore. Many high-quality, well-designed houses continued to be built until the 1930s, and examples include Tamney on Adelaide Road and Rathbarry on Silchester Road.

Marlborough Road, a quiet, L-shaped, residential development, was laid out in the 1890s with solidly built, mostly redbrick houses of spacious proportions. Life in these comfortable Victorian houses was measured and insulated from the outside world. Mary Hamilton in her book *Green and Gold* (1948) describes it well: 'In the morning my aunts would sometimes spend an hour or two sewing, in what they called the breakfast room. I can see them now, with their cream lace caps … Sitting on straight-backed chairs in that pleasant, bright room overlooking the prim little garden, where Aunt Emily grew evening primroses and carefully staked carnations.'

Glenageary Road Lower, often referred to locally as Glenageary Hill, starts in Dun Laoghaire at the People's Park and follows a straight line southward, crossing Corrig Road and eventually rising steeply to end at Sallynoggin. This road, as already suggested, appears to have been laid out at the instigation of Lords Longford and De Vesci in the early 1800s in order to facilitate the development of houses.

Glengara, a solid Victorian residence, best known as Glengara Park School

Early developments, built prior to 1843, include Longford Lodge (later Glengara Park School), Rus-in-Urbe, Ashgrove Lodge, a group of cottages known as 'the seven houses', and a variety of modest terraced and detached houses on Glenageary Hill itself.

*The elegant Regency-style porch
or loggia of Ashgrove Lodge,
demolished in 1986*

Glengara, originally a smaller house, was enlarged to the designs of Sandham Symes around 1850 for the Cooper family of Dunboden Park, County Westmeath. New rooms were added, with unusual Gothic-style cornices, and an elaborate entrance, with pilasters and recessed granite columns, which formed the new front on the seaward side of the building. Glengara was home to a girls' secondary school from the early 1900s, until the school's amalgamation with Rathdown in 1989.

Traverslea Adjoining it is Traverslea, a handsome house built of smooth red brick in 1897. It was erected by the artist Nathaniel Hone R.H.A., for Miss Hone of Ballybrack. The house was designed by Cecil Orr and has a striking entrance porch, built of Portland stone and featuring Ionic pilasters, whose capitals have interlocking volutes. There is also a fine redbrick gate-lodge and stable building. The name is said to derive from the fact that a Hone married a 'Travers-Hartley' and from that name composed the name Traverslea.

Ashgrove Lodge was demolished in 1986 and is the site of a new church. It was a very modest house to which wings were later added, and had an entrance with a delightful timber pergola or canopy in the Regency style.

Langara is a large, two-storey-over-garden-level, bay-windowed house of about 1860, which, before recent developments, had extensive grounds. It was built by the Samuels family, who later lived at Beaufort in Sandycove. Most of the older houses on Glenageary Hill were double-fronted and of modest proportions. They were mostly built during the 1850s and 1860s. Prospect House, located on the corner at the top of the hill, dated from the 1820s, and had a later redbrick extension. In its day it would certainly have commanded a fine prospect of Dublin Bay. It was well known as the home of the Ennis family and was demolished in 1996.

CHAPTER 10

Sallynoggin

Sallynoggin once consisted of this long row of thatched cottages, photographed c. 1900

Sallynoggin has one of the most interesting placenames in Dun Laoghaire, which has given rise to much speculation as to its origin. Sallynoggin is situated on high ground behind Dun Laoghaire, and is most likely a derivation of 'Saileach an Chnocáin', which means 'the willow tree of the small hill'.

A long straight road connecting Rochestown Avenue and Glenageary was laid out in the eighteenth century and in 1787 was known as Woodpark Avenue. Woodpark was the name of an old eighteenth-century house which was the Noggin Inn. The ruins of some cottages, probably built for employees of the Glenageary House estate, were still standing about ten years ago, opposite the Noggin Inn. In the open space beside the Noggin Inn are two holm-oak trees, which were once part of the grounds of Woodpark.

The name Sallynoggin does not appear before 1843, when we find on the first Ordnance Survey map of this area a long, carefully planned row of cottages, each with its own plot or garden, called 'Glenagarey or Sally Noggins'. The cottages were all thatched and whitewashed and were eventually all replaced by local authority houses. One, however, remained until 1972, becoming the pub known as The Thatch, but it was then unfortunately demolished to make way for a featureless new lounge bar. The question as to who built these cottages remains unanswered. They were built on land belonging to the Longford and De Vesci estate in an area that was undeveloped and not fashionable, and may have been erected to accommodate labourers who were working on Dun Laoghaire Harbour and on the many new buildings which were being erected.

Somerton Lodge, one of the oldest houses in the district, now divided into three residences

In 1904 the Kingstown Urban District Council sought tenders for artisans' dwellings to be built in Sallynoggin. The new houses, which were designed by the architect Caldbeck, were the first of a huge local authority building programme which eventually produced The Noggin, as it is known today. Sallynoggin Villas, a group of two-storey, terraced houses near Glenageary roundabout, are among the earliest. They are well-built, brick houses with traditional sash windows.

By 1950 the population of Sallynoggin had so increased that it was decided to build a new church. Our Lady of the Victories Church was opened in 1955 at a cost of £140,000. It was constructed in concrete in the popular style of Italian-Renaissance revival.

The Glenageary Horse Show became a regular fixture in the area and a permanent showgrounds was established in Sallynoggin in 1963. The Gold Flake Stakes sponsored by the Wills group, was the main attraction.

The Honeypark Dairy in Sallynoggin, which has a traditional shopfront, takes its name from a townland called Honeypark which now includes part of Dun Laoghaire golf course.

Somerton Lodge, standing at the top of Sallynoggin Road, is one of the oldest houses in the district, and is composed of at least three sections which date from different periods. At its centre is a long, low, two-storey house, which may once have been an inn, for in the eighteenth century the hall door opened directly onto the main Sallynoggin Road which then passed in front of it.

The road was later pushed away from the house into its present position, where at the corner with Rochestown Avenue a very fine set of entrance gates stood. The entrance consisted of four octagonal, granite

One of the impressive stone piers of the now-vanished entrance gates to Somerton Lodge

A nineteenth-century photograph of The Cedars, a Georgian house which is incorporated into Our Lady of Lourdes Hospital

gate piers, and the name Somerton Lodge was worked in wrought iron over the pedestrian gates. The gates suffered the same fate as those at Altadore and The Grange and were removed for sale as architectural salvage in 1987. No doubt they were erected elsewhere, but the locality was impoverished by their disappearance. Somerton also had an unusual circular gate-lodge, the ruins of which are still standing.

The house itself is a long one, with a Georgian, half-octagonal, bowed, two-storey addition to the northern end. At the opposite end there is another two-storey structure with a large ballroom, magnificent Regency-style windows and a canopied balcony of decorative ironwork.

Somerton, which stood on the Rochestown estate, was inhabited by the Stowell family at the end of the eighteenth century, while more recently it was the home of the noted architect Raymond McGrath, who lived here till 1978. It has since been divided into three houses, and all of the grounds were sold off for house-building.

Opposite Somerton, on Rochestown Avenue, once stood Woodpark, a small house built before 1787, but now long gone.

The Cedars Another eighteenth-century residence which does survive is The Cedars, an interesting old house which is incorporated into Our Lady of Lourdes Hospital (the Sisters of Mercy). The Cedars has an unusual plan, having projecting half-octagonal bays at both ends and at the centre. The house is two-storey-over-basement and has a most attractive oval entrance hall, with an inlaid floor. It once had a fine portico surmounted by a balcony and supported by Corinthian columns.

CHAPTER 11

Kill of the Grange

The ancient ruined church of St Fintan, which stands enclosed by a high granite wall and is now much neglected, is the focus of this once-important district. This church, which may date from the tenth century or earlier, has many similarities with St Begnet's on Dalkey Island, in particular the presence of a square-headed door, and buttresses or antae in the west gable. The chancel, with its neat, round-headed window-holes and grooves for glazing, may have been added in the twelfth century. The church once housed the sixteenth-century wall-tomb of Christopher FitzSimon and the tomb of the O'Byrnes of Cabinteely House. The graveyard has suffered severely since the 1970s from vandalism, including the smashing of headstones, and a lot of graffiti and broken glass. With the gate now closed, it seems a pity that such an important monument should remain inaccessible and neglected.

Kill of the Grange, often called Dean's Grange (or Deansgrange), once comprised extensive agricultural lands which belonged to the

The ruins of St Fintan's Church, with its chancel arch and east window

150

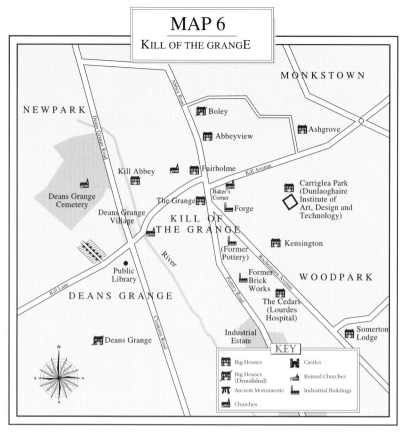

MAP 6
KILL OF THE GRANGE

MONKSTOWN

NEWPARK

Boley

Abbeyview

Ashgrove

Kill Abbey

Fairholme

Kill Avenue

Carriglea Park
(Dunlaoghaire
Institute of
Art, Design and
Technology)

Deans Grange
Cemetery

The Grange

Baker's
Corner

Forge

Deans Grange
Village

KILL OF
THE GRANGE

Kensington

(Former
Pottery)

River

WOODPARK

Public
Library

Former
Brick
Works

Kill Lane

DEANS GRANGE

The Cedars
(Lourdes
Hospital)

Industrial
Estate

Somerton
Lodge

Deans Grange

KEY

Big Houses

Castles

Big Houses
(Demolished)

Ruined Churches

Ancient Monuments

Industrial Buildings

Churches

Church since medieval times. Originally the property and farm of the Priory of the Holy Trinity, and later belonging to the Dean of Christchurch Cathedral, we learn from Ball's *History* that throughout this period great numbers of men were engaged in ploughing, weeding and harvesting crops. Unfortunately, no buildings survive from this time except for the ruins of the medieval church and an old house called Kill Abbey.

Kill Abbey, a small house with several seventeenth-century features, is said to date from 1595. It is possible that part of it is older, and some of the walls may indeed date from the sixteenth century, but it has been modernised several times since the eighteenth century. A photograph in Ball's *History* shows an old-world residence with a Gothic door and window above, and these have a definite Victorian appearance. Kill Abbey has a double-pitched roof, a central chimneystack and surprisingly few windows – perhaps a suggestion of the need for security in earlier days. High on the south wall is a heraldic stone plaque bearing what looks like a winged horse. Inside is a complete staircase, very wide, with barley-sugar balusters and a broad handrail which is certainly of late seventeenth-century date. The original roof structure may also survive, though the house has been somewhat modernised by its conversion into four apartments. During the rebellion of 1641, the wife and maid of one John Brackenbury, occupant of Kill Abbey, were both carried off and hanged by rebels at Powerscourt. This provoked a

The staircase in Kill Abbey, which may date from the late seventeenth century

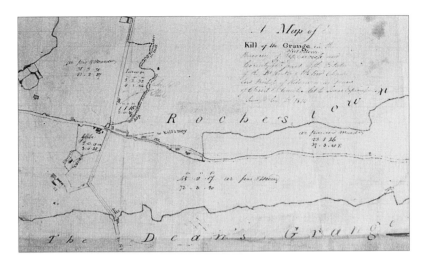

An eighteenth-century estate map showing the Dean's Grange

military response and a battle took place at Dean's Grange where about one hundred rebels were killed and another fifteen were hanged.

In the early eighteenth century the lands of Kill of the Grange passed to the Espinasses, a family of Huguenot origin, whose descendants maintained their interest in property here well into this century. It was on the Espinasse estate that Dun Laoghaire Corporation built the houses of St Fintan's Villas and St Fintan's Park sometime after 1940.

Rocque's 1757 map shows Kill and Grange as two separate places, the latter consisting of a collection of cottages and a number of gardens clustered about the bottom of Kill Lane. Taylor's 1816 map shows a group of cottages located somewhere near the present Foxrock Avenue and a 'new road' running straight as an arrow from Stradbrook Road towards Cabinteely. It seems possible that this road, now Clonkeen Road, may have been constructed to facilitate the movement of soldiers to the Loughlinstown Camp and to the Martello towers.

Taylor also marks a substantial farmhouse, known as Grange House, which once stood in the vicinity of the modern houses at Grange Park. In 1849 Henry Perry, one of two Quaker brothers who ran a successful ironwork business in Dublin, was in occupation of a house and about 121 acres at Dean's Grange. Later, in 1857, his nephew James Perry had a large new house constructed nearby.

Clonkeen House, as it was later called, was a square, two-storey-over-basement house with projecting central bay and balcony, and had many features which are characteristic of the work of architect J. S. Mulvany. Around 1920 Clonkeen was bought by Michael O'Brien, the proprietor of Lynch and O'Briens well-known grocery establishment in Dun Laoghaire – O'Brien's is said to have been the first dairy to introduce bottled milk in County Dublin, much to the annoyance of the older dairymen. When the O'Brien business ran into financial difficulties, the property was seized by the Munster and Leinster Bank (now AIB), and they developed the front-age at Clonkeen Road with new houses during the 1950s. In more recent times, Clonkeen belonged to the Smurfit family, who originated in northern England and came to Dublin to establish a box factory.

Detail from Rocque's map of 1757, showing Kill of the Grange

Clonkeen House, probably designed by J. S. Mulvany, was demolished in 1993

The drawing room in Clonkeen House

Clonkeen House, which was demolished in 1993, had once been the centre of a property which totalled some 220 acres, and extended from Foxrock to the Clonkeen Road.

Kill of the Grange parish church is a small but finely built structure. It was consecrated in 1864 and is one of the many Church of Ireland churches erected in the greater Dun Laoghaire area during the mid-nineteenth century. Built of cut stone in an early Gothic style, it has a small, gable-topped belfry and a fine rose window. The low, arched timber roof is also noteworthy.

Fairholme, situated at Baker's Corner, is an interesting old house. The three-storey section nearest to the road may date from about 1780, while the main house appears to have been added in the 1830s. Fairholme was once the glebe house or residence of the rector of Monkstown parish, and is equipped with a very substantial wine cellar!

The Grange, situated opposite Fairholme, is a large Victorian house which was built in 1864 on a site of about seventeen acres. The grounds, which once included a walled garden, an orchard and an ornamental grotto and waterfall, once stretched back to the present village of Dean's Grange. Among the many gardeners who once worked there were the Sodens, who later ran a greengrocery in Dun Laoghaire. The house, two-storey-over-basement, with striking round-headed windows, has unique carved granite urns and front steps, and is now used as a nursing home. The Grange was the home of the McComas family since 1879. William McComas, a Dublin merchant and a Methodist, founded the Kingstown Men's Christian Institute, a club somewhat like the YMCA. In the 1950s The Grange was bequeathed to the Church and in 1955 the Sisters of Our Lady of Charity, a French order, moved in. They offered help to the families of broken marriages, and after the sale of The Grange in 1985, have continued their work nearby. The grounds have since been built upon.

Close by were the potteries and brickworks from which Pottery Road takes its name. Clay suitable for making pottery had been noted here

since medieval times and the making of earthenware is recorded in the accounts of the Priory of the Holy Trinity (later Christchurch Cathedral). The potteries and clay pits are marked on the first Ordnance Survey map of this area published in 1843 and a brick-field is indicated at Sallynoggin. The pottery occupied a corner site between Rochestown Avenue and Pottery Road and in the late nineteenth century it was noted for making flower-pots and bricks, some of which bear the stamp 'Kingstown Pottery'. The business was operated by W. O. MacCormick. The manufacture of bricks ceased at Dean's Grange after the 1930s because of the arrival of mass-produced concrete blocks.

Above left: The original entrance gates to The Grange

Above right: The Grange, a typical Victorian house of the 1860s

Baker's Corner, previously known as Silkes' Corner, stands at the junction of Kill Avenue, Abbey Road and Pottery Road, and has probably been a public house since the 1830s. J. J. Silkes was a family grocer and wine and spirit merchant. Nearby stands the horseshoe-shaped entrance of a once-busy forge with its attached cottage. This was known as Larkin's forge and was still in operation in recent memory, run by the blacksmith, Billy Larkin. It is hoped that plans to demolish this unique structure will not proceed as there are so few buildings of its kind in the county.

Larkin's forge and cottage at Baker's Corner

Carriglea In the eighteenth century the road to Monkstown commenced at the point where Pottery Road joins Rochestown Avenue and passed in front of the house now known as Carriglea. The house may have been remodelled in the mid-nineteenth century, as its appearance, with its portico, stucco embellishments and plate-glass windows, is rather Victorian. However, the curved end-bays and central Wyatt window could be part of the Georgian house occupied by the family of Maunsell in 1787. Carriglea belonged to the Goff family during much of the nineteenth century, and they may have laid out Kill Avenue some time before 1840. It was known locally as Goff's Avenue and was planted with beech trees, some of which survive. Unfortunately, the terrible storm of February 1903 blew down many of these trees and damaged many buildings. The Goffs were merchants, and kin of Robert Goff, founder of Goff's Bloodstock Sales, who in the 1940s was auctioneer to the RDS and the Turf Club. They were keen yachtsmen and were early members of the Royal St George Yacht Club in Dun Laoghaire. They sold the house in 1893 to the Christian Brothers who opened the Carriglea Industrial School here.

The school was established to provide a place for homeless boys to live and to 'afford them such instruction as will fit them to grow up self-supporting and self-respecting members of society'. At its peak, in the early years of this century, up to 250 boys were taught here. Drawing and carpentry were priority subjects, but music and drama were always prominent and the Carriglea Park Band was often in demand. There was also a small school orchestra and performances were often given for charity. Before the First World War plays were put on in the old Kingstown pavilion which became the Pavilion Cinema and is now demolished. In 1900 Mrs Blake of Temple Hill, Blackrock, invited the boys from Carriglea to view the parade and royal visit of Queen Victoria from the grounds of her house, and in April 1916 about two thousand of the British forces encamped in the grounds of the school and the officers breakfasted with the Brothers. The troops were brought over to help quell the rising of 1916.

The Church of the Holy Family was erected at Baker's Corner in the early 1970s, on a site provided at a nominal cost by the Christian Brothers.

Carriglea, which now forms part of the Dun Laoghaire College of Art, Design and Technology

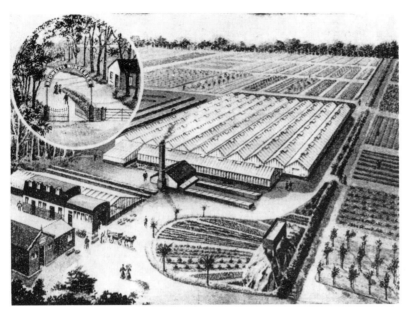

Browett's Nurseries, which once covered an extensive area near Kill of the Grange

With the decline of vocations to the Christian Brothers, and the many social changes of the last forty years, the school eventually closed and was sold, along with 30 acres, in 1982 to the Department of Education for the purpose of building a regional technical college. Part of the old schools were converted for use by the Dun Laoghaire College of Art and Design, but the plan to build a regional college here is only now coming to fruition.

Browett's Nurseries, which closed in 1960, adjoined Carriglea Park and comprised 60,000 square feet of glasshouses, and a bungalow built in 1920.

Dean's Grange cemetery was established in 1861 to answer the need for new burial grounds in south County Dublin. Many old graveyards were overcrowded and in danger of posing a threat to public health. The first burial at Dean's Grange took place in 1865 when Anastasia Carey, a servant from St Joseph's Orphanage in Kingstown, was interred. The cemetery, which was run by the 'Dean's Grange Joint Burial Board' catered for both Protestants and Catholics alike, and separate churches were erected for their convenience.

There are many notable people buried in Dean's Grange including the writer Frank O'Connor, Seán Lemass who was born in Ballybrack, and John MacCormick, the famous opera singer who died in 1945 at his home in Booterstown. There are also some very fine monuments, such as that belonging to the Talbot Power family.

The cemetery also contains many interesting, if sad, glimpses of Irish history here too, for example, in 1916 the military authorities sent a number of bodies, without coffins, to Dean's Grange for burial. Another monument records the tragic drowning of fifteen members of the Kingstown Lifeboat on Christmas Eve 1895 when they set out to rescue the crew of *The Palme*, a shipwreck driven ashore in Dublin Bay.

CHAPTER 12

Dun Laoghaire

An aquatint depicting the eighteenth-century Dunleary Coffee House, with fishermen pulling their net ashore

Dun Laoghaire was once a small fishing village located on an inlet of the rocky coast near Salthill, a small hillock once noted for the production of salt. It was called Dunleary until 1821 when a completely new town developed to the east as a result of the building of the present large harbour.

Old Dunleary, as the original village is now called, has little to show of what was, in the eighteenth century, a very complete and compact village of seventy dwellings or cottages. Some fifteen houses, including the present Purty Kitchen, comprised a row of dwellings which are all that remains of the village.

A well-known print of Dunleary in 1799 shows the eighteenth-century pier, with a sailor standing at its end as a landmark to shipping. The sailor, possibly made of stucco, may be the same figure which made its way, via Ballygihen, to Nerano in Dalkey!

A fascinating map from the 1790s reveals the presence of two piers at Dunleary. It shows the present inner coal-harbour pier, erected during the 1760s, and another, earlier pier, in the form of a curve and described as the 'old pier', which is now long buried beneath the railway line. The curved pier is also shown on Rocque's map of 1757, but the date of its construction remains unknown. The map shows the little harbour with

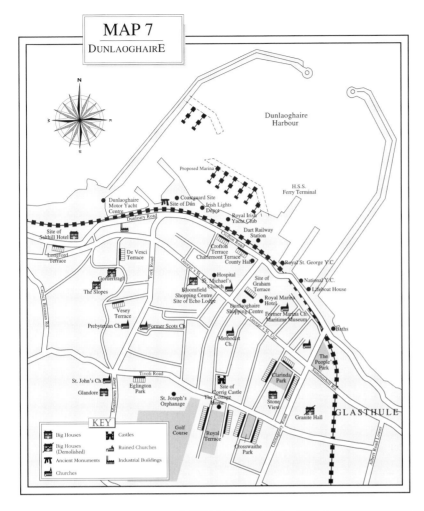

MAP 7
DUNLAOGHAIRE

Dunlaoghaire
Harbour

H.S.S.
Ferry Terminal

Proposed Marina

Dunlaoghaire
Motor Yacht
Centre

Coastguard Site
Site of Dún
Irish Lights
Depot

Royal Irish
Yacht Club

Dart Railway
Station

Dunleary Road

Site of
Salthill Hotel

Crofton
Terrace
Charlemont Terrace
County Hall

Royal St. George Y.C.

Longford
Terrace

De Vesci
Terrace

Hospital
St. Michael's
Church

National Y.C.
Lifeboat House

Gorllertragh

Bloomfield
Shopping Centre
Site of Echo Lodge

Site of
Graham
Terrace

Royal Marine
Hotel

The Slopes

Vesey
Terrace

Dunlaoghaire
Shopping Centre

Former Marina Ch.
Maritime Museum

Prebyterian Ch.

Former Scots Ch.

Baths

Methodist
Ch.

St. John's Ch.

Tivoli Road

The
People's
Park

Glandore

Eglington
Park

St. Joseph's
Orphanage

Site of
Corrig Castle
The Cottage
Monte

Clarinda
Park

Stone
View

Granite Hall

GLASTHULE

Golf
Course

Royal
Terrace

Crosswaithe
Park

KEY

🏛	Big Houses	🏰	Castles
🏚	Big Houses (Demolished)	🏚	Ruined Churches
⛩	Ancient Monuments	🏭	Industrial Buildings
⛪	Churches		

Below left: A late eighteenth-century map of Old Dunleary, showing the coffee house on the extreme right and Dunleary House (later the Salthill Hotel) on the extreme left

Below right: An estate map showing Old Dunleary with its small old pier and prominent new pier of the 1760s

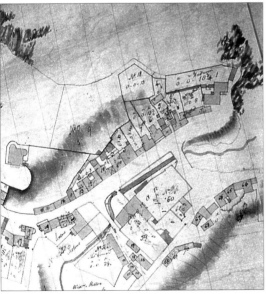

The George IV obelisk in Dun Laoghaire was erected in 1821 and is unusual as it is balanced on four granite balls

its sandy cove running in close to the site of the former Top Hat Ballroom (more recently known as The Fun Factory) where there appears to have been a small mill. Situated above the harbour on high ground and close to the site of the present petrol station, stood Dunleary's famous coffee house. A coloured print of about 1770 shows it to be a two-storey house of irregular shape, with many gables. The taking of coffee became common during the eighteenth century, and this hostelry must have been very popular with travellers and day-trippers from Dublin.

Even at this time, when the small harbour dried out at low water, Dunleary was considered to be one of the main points of departure for England. Many a traveller, arriving in Ireland for the first time in the eighteenth century, stepped ashore at Dunleary. Today's motorist who drives off the deck of the high-speed ferry should be grateful for the one-and-a-half-hour trip from Holyhead which compares favourably with the twenty-two-hour journey which the writer Arthur Young made in 1776!

Dun Laoghaire Harbour

Though Dun Laoghaire Harbour, as we know it today, was begun in 1815 at the end of the Georgian period, the first buildings of the new town started to appear only from the 1820s onwards. The new town has many fine terraces, churches, yacht clubs and other public buildings, but its overall Victorian character has been much changed by recent developments, especially near the seafront and harbour.

As we have already seen, Dublin Bay and the approaches to the river Liffey could be treacherous to the sailing ships of the early 1800s, and only after much campaigning was the building of 'a harbour of refuge' deemed necessary. The harbour, with its two splendid granite piers, took over forty years to complete, cost over one million pounds and created employment for more than six hundred men during its construction. Its embracing arms create a space of about 250 acres of water which have provided shelter to ships from most adverse weather conditions, except occasionally when north-easterly gales strike.

Postmark, 1909

After much debate about its proposed location, and after the largely futile building of Howth Harbour, it was decided to construct two long piers at Dunleary, and the foundation stone was laid in 1817 by the Lord Lieutenant. These events and the subsequent visit of King George IV to Dunleary in 1821 are recorded on the stone obelisk which stands on the harbour front near the Carlisle Pier. The obelisk, standing on four granite balls, is surmounted by a crown. To mark this royal occasion, the name Kingstown was formally adopted for the town, and it was not until 1920

Villa-type houses in Mulgrave Street, snowbound, 1981

that its original name, spelt in the Gaelic form, Dun Laoghaire, was officially adopted again. By coincidence, around 1930 two small stones bearing 'pre-Christian' decorations were dug up near the old harbour, and it was strongly suggested that these inscribed stones must have come from the original *dún* (fort) of Dun Laoghaire. The general view is that a Martello tower was built on the site of the *dún* and that the construction of the railway led to the destruction of both of these features.

A photograph from a glass plate showing the principal public buildings in Dun Laoghaire in about 1890 – the town hall, railway station and yacht clubs

Design for houses on Gresham Terrace by George Papworth

The seafront at Kingstown was the first area to be developed, with terraced houses being built from the 1830s onwards

The National Museum when consulted about the stones in 1980, did not believe that they were authentic and even suggested that they were of recent origin. It was also hinted that the stones were conveniently 'found' to give credence to the existence of a *dún* at Dun Laoghaire. It is certainly strange that when the assumed site of the *dún* was dug up in 1836 in order to extend the railway line no finds of any kind were recorded.

Shortly after 1800 the scare of a Napoleonic invasion brought about the building of Martello towers all along the coast of County Dublin. Two of these were erected at Dunleary, but unfortunately both have disappeared. One of them stood, it is claimed, within the circular site of the *dún*, and only lasted for thirty years. The other occupied a site in what later became the People's Park, and is now remembered only in the name of some houses at Martello Terrace. The long straight main street of Dun Laoghaire (George's Street Upper and Lower) has its origin in the Military Road which was constructed to provide access to the Martello towers and their accompanying batteries.

The land now covered by the centre of Dun Laoghaire was, in the eighteenth century, divided into fields which were in poor condition and partly used for pasture. The condition of all of the fields was described on the map or survey of the 1790s, and it appears that much of the land had been quarried and left with dangerous holes and stones lying about. Much of it was covered in furze, briars and blackthorn. A rocky outcrop called the Wild Cat Rock was to be found somewhere close to the bottom of the present Clarinda Park. A large plot known as the Quarry Field stood adjacent to the eighteenth-century pier (now occupied by Crofton Road) while a large, nine-acre field, which would later become the valuable harbour frontage, was leased to George Smith, stonemason.

Carrig or **Corrig Castle**, which appears as a large structure on the map, was the only eighteenth-century house of any size to have existed in this part of Dun Laoghaire. It stood in some seventeen acres of scrubby land, and was leased by James Curran.

Tivoli Road is part of a very old path which connected the castles of Monkstown and Bullock in the fourteenth century, and was probably made for the convenience of the Cistercian monks. Few buildings appeared on Tivoli Road until the 1830s when Granite Lodge, Primrose Hill and houses at Tivoli Terrace were built. York Road was one of the earlier residential areas, with such houses as Air Hill, Wellington Lodge and Fairy Hill, along with two schools and the first Presbyterian church of the new town.

George's Street was quickly developed during the two decades before 1840, as were the parallel streets of Kingstown Parade (Patrick Street), Rumley Avenue (Mulgrave Street) and Northumberland Avenue. On the seafront, lines of new terraces had been erected, including Crofton Terrace, Haddington Terrace, Victoria Terrace, Marine Terrace, Windsor Terrace and Martello Terrace. A fine hotel, the forerunner of the Royal Marine Hotel, occupied a dominant position alongside Gresham Terrace, and overlooked the harbour below.

By the 1830s it was clear that the new town of Kingstown was growing quickly, and it was decided to construct Ireland's first railway line between it and the capital. At this time the main purpose of such a railway was to carry goods unloaded from ships in Dun Laoghaire Harbour, and transport them into Dublin. However, the emphasis quickly shifted to passenger traffic. An elegant cut-stone railway station was built to accommodate travellers during the 1840s. It was designed by John Skipton Mulvany, in his favourite neo-classical style, and was constructed in flawless granite masonry. It is one of the finest buildings in the town, though it is no longer used as a station and serves as a fashionable restaurant. A new facility, well designed in its own right but with a glass and steel structure that is rather incongruous in the context of the old station,

The Slopes: Decorative ironwork from the staircase, a cast-iron lion mask, the entrance porch

Right: The Venetian Gothic garden front of Glandore House

Below: Head of Angel Gabriel from old St Michael's Church
Bottom: This photograph records the disastrous fire which destroyed St Michael's Catholic church in 1966

now spans the railway and was opened in 1998.

The arrival of the railway opened up many new development opportunities for Kingstown and the surrounding area, and quickly brought about a building boom. The newly emerging middle classes, along with some of the gentry, merchants and retired army and navy folk, found it very pleasant to live beside the sea and to commute to the city by train when necessary. Among the new terraced houses of the 1830s, Longford Terrace, Charlemont Terrace and Gresham Terrace were typical. The Gresham Terrace houses were occupied by gentry such as Earl Norbury and the Bishop of Dromore, but they were demolished in 1974 in order to make way for the present Dun Laoghaire shopping centre.

The houses were on the Georgian model, but finished in stucco rather than brick, and they were typically three-storeys-over-basement in height. Most had well-proportioned rooms, good plasterwork and attractive hallways with fanlights. Dalkey granite was widely used for window sills and steps, while decorative cast-iron was favoured for railings, gates, gas-lamp standards and sometimes balconies.

All of these houses, which include most of the seafront houses, were built to take advantage of the fine sea views. Most were finished in stucco or 'Roman cement' (a type of outdoor plaster), and were painted in a uniform colour. For instance, the building lease of De Vesci Terrace stipulated that each house was to be painted 'Portland stone colour and none other' every two years.

Many houses were let and it was common practice to rent a house for the summer months. One landlord cannot have been too pleased with the tenant who caused him to send the following bill for damages – it provides an interesting account of the furnishings of an upmarket Kingstown

House in 1871: 'one glass globe 1/6, one soap box broken 1/6, walls a good deal soiled and chipped £1, music stool moulding broken off 2/6, damask table cover missing 4/-, two plain wine coolers missing 2/-, one soup plate 7d, steel snuffers broken 1/-, three metal hooks to coach house missing 1/6, chimneys to be swept 5/-, house to be cleaned down 10/-, and gas consumed from 14th July 1870 to 8th March 1871 £7'.

Among the many Victorian terraces, mention must be made of Clarinda Park, one of the first 'squares' to be planned in the town and which was commenced in 1849. Royal Terrace and Crosthwaite Park, also laid out as squares, were begun in about 1860, while Sydenham Terrace on Corrig Road was completed by 1859. These developments were followed by Eglinton Park in 1861, Willow Bank in 1865, and Carlisle Terrace in 1866.

Most of the town's larger, detached residences have disappeared, the latest casualty being Echo Lodge, the former Dominican convent, which was demolished to make way for the new Bloomfields shopping centre. Other vanished houses include Granite Hall, The Slopes, Gortleitragh and Corrig Castle. Stone View, a large, granite-faced house like Granite Hall, was built by Samuel Smith, the stone contractor to the harbour. It stands in Clarinda Park, and has recently been converted into apartments. Samuel Smith, who lived at Granite Hall, owned all of the lands between his house and the sea at Newtownsmith. This included the area now known as Summerhill and Rosmeen Gardens.

The National Maritime Museum, most appropriately housed within the former Mariner's church

The Kingstown regatta of the 1890s and early 1900s attracted some of the largest yachts afloat

Above: The façade of the Royal St George Yacht Club, which dates from the 1840s

Exquisite stonework from the west pier at Dun Laoghaire: (top) cast-iron and (bottom) stone bollards

Glandore, another stone-built house of great quality, stands behind St John's Church in Mount Town. It was built by William Vesey, a brother of one of Kingstown's ground landlords, Lord De Vesci, and was designed by Deane and Woodward in the Venetian Gothic style. The house has many similarities with Clontra in Shankill, though it is somewhat larger. It is a large house of irregular plan with steep pitched roofs and tall stone chimney stacks. Typical pierced Venetian detail is found in the windows with their Gothic arches and sandstone balconies.

Vesey was also largely responsible for the building of St John's Church in 1858, which was built in anticipation of a growing Protestant population but, in fact, the church was rarely filled to capacity. Vesey Place, situated off York Road, is a terrace of mid-Victorian houses named after William Vesey. Nearby stood a large house called The Slopes which was built by Charles Smyth, and later became home to the well-known Findlater family who were ardent supporters of the local Presbyterian church. Both the Smyths and the Findlaters were important Dublin wine merchants.

Among the earliest places of worship to be built in Kingstown were St Michael's Catholic church, constructed in the 1820s in the town centre and, some years later, a plain Presbyterian church on York Road. These were quickly followed by the Mariner's church and Christ Church (both Church of Ireland) and a Wesleyan chapel, all of which were built by 1836.

The National Maritime Museum The Mariner's church, which closed during the 1970s became, rather appropriately, the home of the National Maritime Museum. It was a large church and accommodated over a thousand worshippers, among whom, during the nineteenth century, there was frequently a large contingent of seamen from the British naval guardship which was stationed in the harbour. The Maritime Museum contains an important collection of artifacts, paintings, maps and models which are of direct significance to Dun Laoghaire Harbour and to Dublin Bay. In this context, rumours of re-locating the museum are disturbing, not least because, apart from the new Dalkey Museum and 'Joyce's Tower', it is the only major museum in the entire region, but also because the Mariner's Church would be left without a viable use.

A silver trowel used to lay the foundation stone and a golden key used for the inauguration of the new organ – the Methodist church, Northumberland Avenue

Yachting

Dun Laoghaire can lay claim to an important position in the history of yachting, not just in Ireland, but internationally. The sport was established in Dublin Bay during the early nineteenth century, at a time when it was also becoming fashionable in Britain. The fine harbour, with its broad expanse of sheltered water, was ideal for yachting. And unlike Howth or Bullock, the harbour never dried out at low water.

Two royal yacht clubs were established during the 1840s – the Royal St George Yacht Club and the Royal Irish Yacht Club. Both acquired royal warrants which entitled them to use the term 'royal' and to fly the ensign. They quickly assembled a prestigious and élite membership, largely drawn from the titled and landed classes.

At this time, during the middle of the nineteenth century, yachts tended to be very large and required a deep pocket and a sizeable crew. It was only in the later nineteenth century that smaller boats which the 'man in the street' could afford, started to appear.

Dun Laoghaire can claim to have developed the first one-design dinghy in the world, a small racing yacht of identical design to the rest of its fleet – the Water Wag, as it is still called. The Water Wag, which looks rather like a rowing boat with sails, was first built in 1878.

Dun Laoghaire harbour, c. 1850 – the harbour was built during the period of transition from sail to steam

Eng & Pub. by Newman & Co 48 Watling St. London.

Tranquillity in Dun Laoghaire harbour, 1965 – note the almost-completed Kish Lighthouse in the background

Lavish regattas soon became a seasonal event, with bigger and bigger yachts arriving in the harbour. The naval guardship would be decked out in bunting, military bands played on the east pier and there were spectacular firework displays at night. James J. Gaskin, writing in 1869, paints a scene of elegance, wealth and privilege:

The departure of Queen Victoria from Kingstown Harbour in 1849 – shows the east pier lighthouse before the battery was built around it

'At the Royal yacht clubs the *crème de la crème* of the aristocracy and gentry assemble during the Kingstown regatta, which generally takes place in August. The usual gaiety of the place during this aquatic carnival is much increased by the appearance of the harbour, which contains an immense

assemblage of elegant pleasure vessels of every size and rig, from the ship and steamer of 500 tons burthen to the yawl of only ten.'

The architecture of the three principal yacht clubs is, in a sense, unique. As this was a new type of building, the architects were faced with the challenge of designing something both dignified and practical. The clubhouse had to reflect the social position of the members, by being grand, but it was limited to being only one-storey high so as not to spoil the view of the harbour from the new terraces of the town. The result was formal and classical, with comfortable and elegant rooms which over-looked the yachts in the harbour, while underneath there were boathouses, kitchens and stores.

The saltwater pool at Dun Laoghaire baths, 1930s

Architecturally, it is unfortunate that all of the yacht clubs have extended their 'forecourts' so much into the harbour that the historic buildings have become more and more removed from the actual water-front. However, these works of utilitarian infill are nothing to the effect that the proposed large-scale marina will have on the harbour if it is built. Two rock-armoured breakwaters with concrete walkways will straddle the main harbour and the lines of some six hundred boats will resemble a 'car park on the sea'. The attractive variety of the boats on their swinging moorings will be a thing of the past. Furthermore, the visual impact of such crude modern breakwaters on the beautiful stone-built harbour, now 180 years old and unique in Europe, may well create a jarring note. Dun Laoghaire Harbour is certainly a functional port, providing shelter to ships and yachts, but over time it has also become a monument and has the status of a special amenity, comparable to the Phoenix Park.

The 'mail packets' were at first small ships which carried important government correspondence, general mail and passengers to and from Holyhead or Liverpool. The packets used Howth until 1826 when they were transferred to the new harbour at Kingstown. These early steam-ships were for a while accommodated at the Victoria Wharf, whose cut-stone quayside now lies buried under the present car-ferry terminal. They were eventu-ally moved to the Carlisle Pier where, from 1859 onwards, the mail boats were met by waiting trains which, with great convenience, whisked passengers into Dublin in fifteen minutes.

The elegant entrance to the public baths

The most famous mail boats were probably the four sister-ships built for the City of Dublin Steam Packet Company. They were the *Lein-ster, Ulster, Munster* and *Connaught* and when they came into service in the early 1860s the journey time to Holyhead was reduced to as

The building of new, local authority houses in the early 1900s cleared many groups of small cottages, such as these, which stood near York Road

A decorative, cast-iron lamp standard

little as three hours and forty-five minutes, from anything over seven hours depending on weather conditions. They were not replaced until 1896 when four new screw-propelled ships were commissioned which bore the same names but could make the journey in under three hours. It is noteworthy that to date no conventional ship has been able to make the passage in a shorter time. One of the greatest tragedies in the history of the harbour was the sinking by German torpedo in 1918 of one of these ships, the *Leinster*. She was sunk, close to the end of the war, at the Kish bank with the loss of 501 lives.

A handsome granite obelisk on the east pier records another tragic shipwreck, and pays tribute to Captain Boyd, the commander of the guardship *H.M.S. Ajax*, who lost his life in 1861 while trying to save the crew of a coal boat which was being broken up in a storm on the back of the east pier. The Dun Laoghaire Lifeboat, whose history has been fully documented by John De Courcy Ireland (*Wreck and Rescue on the East Coast of Ireland*, 1983), can trace a long and honourable tradition of life-saving in Dublin Bay since about 1810.

The lighthouses of the east and west piers are beautifully constructed in stone, and are still fully operational. The east pier lighthouse was built as early as 1822, and a circular fort or battery was built around it in 1863, forming a powerful composition and creating a striking landmark at the entrance to the harbour.

Bathing

Since the eighteenth century, sea-bathing had been popular, not merely for relaxation but for health reasons. Two separate bathing places, one for men and one for women, are clearly shown on the 1790s map of Dunleary, but they were removed by the construction of the railway in 1836. Following several lengthy battles with the railway company, new baths were constructed at the back of the west pier. Dun Laoghaire public baths, which regrettably have been closed for some years, date from the 1840s. There was recently a proposal to demolish the baths and the attractive Edwardian entrance building which were rebuilt and modernised in 1905.

By the second half of the nineteenth century Kingstown was firmly established as 'the largest most popular watering place in Ireland' which contemporary photographs consistently show as being truly elegant and beautifully maintained. There was an air of order and spaciousness which surrounded the various elegant buildings of the harbour-front and town. Though Kingstown continued to expand and develop as 'an elegant Victorian watering place' and guidebooks extolled the splendour of the royal visits, the elegant yachts and the new town, not everything was perfect.

In some districts, particularly around York Road and Glasthule, there were 'dense hives of cabins' which were inhabited by the very poor and were without proper water supply or sanitation. These areas did not have the benefit of careful planning and sound building practice. In 1844 Charles Haliday, a distinguished resident and humanitarian, campaigned to rid the town of its many hovels, but it was not until the end of the century that new terraces of artisans' dwellings were built. Haliday found more than 144 'courts' in Kingstown, which were usually narrow yards, overcrowded with small, inadequate dwellings. Off George's Street Lower there were many such dwellings, with names like Duff's Court, Fagan's Court or Ball's Court. Several outbreaks of cholera had

Alexander Downs's coalyard at Dunleary is depicted on this billhead

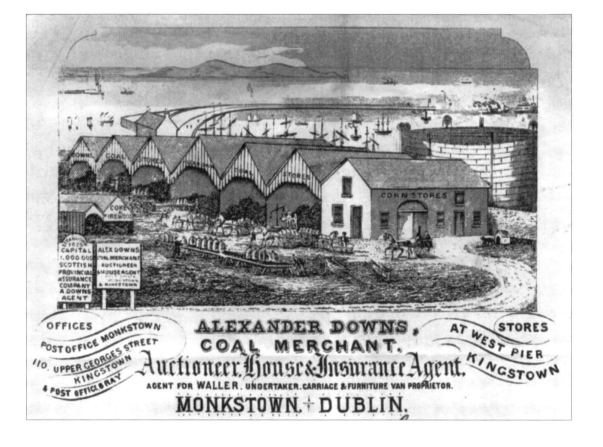

occurred and disease claimed the lives of many in the area. Haliday also made the case for a proper system of sanitation, but it was not until 1894 that a full network of sewers was connected to the sewerage works at the west pier.

Three purpose-built institutions were erected by voluntary groups to relieve the plight of orphans and under-privileged young children in Kingstown. The Bird's Nest, a tall, granite-built structure, erected in 1861 on York Road, accommodated children between the ages of five and twelve. The centenary booklet about the Cottage Home tells us that the girls were 'prepared chiefly for domestic service' while boys afterwards went on to one of the Dublin 'homes'. St Joseph's Orphanage on Tivoli Road, demolished some years ago, was built in 1860 and run by the Daughters of the Heart of Mary, who in the spirit of the nineteenth century trained its eighty orphans 'in the habits of industry and order'.

The Cottage Home was founded by Miss Rosa Barrett during the late 1870s as a day-care centre or crêche for the very young children of impoverished working parents. Later a site was found for it at Royal Terrace, and the fine Tudor-style building which fronts onto Tivoli Road was eventually erected in 1887.

Top: The Victoria Fountain, erected in 1900; it was selected from a catalogue of special ornamental features

Above: A piece of cast-iron decoration from the wrecked Victoria Fountain

Kingstown Town Commissioners

Throughout the latter part of the nineteenth century various civic improvements were made to the town by the Kingstown Town Commissioners, a body set up in 1834 to manage its public affairs. Their job was defined in a government act and included 'the paving, watching, lighting, regulating and otherwise improving the town of Kingstown'.

The most significant architectural achievement of the Town Commissioners was the erection of the Town Hall in 1880, a Venetian-style palace with a handsome clock tower. It was designed by J. L. Robinson who was also responsible for the fine granite façade of the former Post Office building which adjoined the Town Hall. Both buildings are now integrated into a new County Hall which houses the administration of the entire Dun Laoghaire-Rathdown district.

The Kingstown Town Commissioners acquired the disused quarry and site of one of the old Martello towers which they turned into the People's Park in 1890. Among the features of the park are a pair of attractive cast-iron fountains, a handsome redbrick gate-lodge, and a shelter which is now the Park Tea Rooms.

In 1899 municipal buildings were erected, a variety of utilitarian buildings which included a fire station, a store house for the Urban

District Council, a stable for their horses, and a public wash-house and baths. Many fine landmarks from Dun Laoghaire's Victorian past have vanished, such as the Victoria fountain, a wonderful cast-iron extravaganza shaped in the form of a dome and erected in 1901 as a monument to Queen Victoria. It stood opposite the railway station and was destroyed in an anti-British gesture in 1981 with sledge hammers, then pulled down with ropes – a defenceless symbol of a bygone age. The Pavilion, which stood in its own gardens and was erected in 1903, was unfortunately burnt down in 1915. It was an intricate, galleried structure with four viewing turrets, and contained a number of tea rooms, reading rooms and smoking rooms. It was used for concerts, dances and a variety of entertainments, and its festive architecture lent a lighter note to the town. The ugly rebuilding of the pavilion, which later became the cinema, during the early part of this century was the first blot on Dun Laoghaire's perfect Victorian image. Another small building of similar age, the Cabman's Shelter (built in 1912) and a relic of horse-drawn cabs, stood outside the Pavilion on Marine Road and was demolished as recently as 1997.

For a Victorian town, it is a pity that none of the elaborately carved shopfronts of the period has survived, though there were once many in Dun Laoghaire's George's Street.

By 1839 shopping in George's Street was well provided for as there

The public clock which used to hang over Findlaters' shop in George's Street

The marvellous ticket office and entrance to the Pavillion, erected 1903

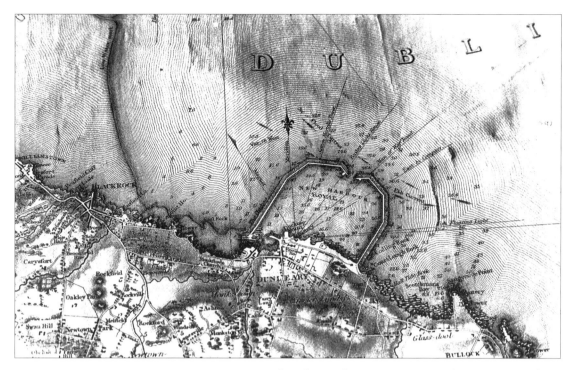

Duncan's map, 1821, showing the 'New Royal Harbour' and the old harbour at Dunleary

were nine vintners, five shoemakers, ten grocers and provisioners, three victuallers, five bakers, four dairies, two carpenters, seven drapers, one apothecary, two plumbers, two surgeons, two painters, a saddler, a stationer, a tallow chandler, a hairdresser, a cooper, a dyer, a gun maker, a bell hanger and even a painter of miniatures.

A fine public clock once hung over the premises of the town's leading grocers, Findlaters, but it was unfortunately taken down some years ago when the building was taken over by Penney's.

The Royal Marine Hotel In a town that once had many thriving hotels, only one nineteenth-century establishment remains – it seems that the presence of a busy carferry terminal in Dun Laoghaire for the last thirty years has not actually helped such hotels to survive, as owners of vehicles tend to move on to their destination as quickly as possible. The Royal Marine Hotel, which sits in a dominant position overlooking its gardens and the harbour, still retains much of its Victorian decor. The original establishment, known as Hayes's Hotel, was taken over by entrepreneur William Dargan, who in 1865 succeeded in completing only half of his planned new hotel before his company went into liquidation.

After the unfortunate rebuilding of the Pavilion, the town remained largely unaltered until the construction of the Dun Laoghaire shopping centre during the 1970s. From that time onwards, in a series of developments mainly brought about to facilitate cars, car-parking and ferry traffic, the once-elegant waterfront, with its excellent public access, was gradually eroded and its character greatly impoverished.

As Dun Laoghaire continues to change rapidly, the question must be asked: can the 'premier township' as it was once called, retain its Victorian identity? The last twenty years have seen many changes – the arrival of the DART, Ireland's first electrified railway, and the creation of ever-larger ferry terminal facilities, culminating in the present *H.S.S. Stena Explorer.* This catamaran's spacious, double car decks and the speed of the cross-channel journey are remarkable achievements, but its shopping centre-like interior and box-like appearance are not endearing features!

The new ferry terminal, however, is a modern building of style, which is appropriate to its purpose and respects the architecture of the harbour front.

Unfortunately, it is difficult to say the same of many of Dun Laoghaire's other new developments. Two large shopping centres and many new apartment blocks have made their appearance. In a very short space of time the old post office, Garda station and courthouse have been replaced. Marine Road, the principal thoroughfare to the harbour, is dominated by a petrol station.

Most notably, Dun Laoghaire, as the most important town in the district, was chosen as the site for the administrative offices and council chamber of the new Dun Laoghaire-Rathdown County Council.

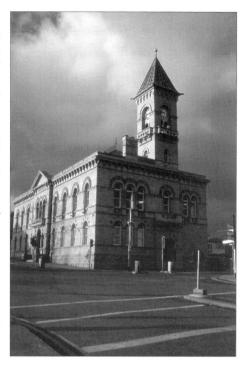

The Dun Laoghaire Town Hall, erected in 1880, now the County Hall of the Dun Laoghaire-Rathdown County Council

What is Dun Laoghaire today? It is an important yachting harbour and a ferry port, but it lacks the proper road access and car-parking for any major port development. This is perhaps a good thing as such facilities could only be provided at great cost to the residential amenities and historic character of Dun Laoghaire. Dun Laoghaire is a residential town and part of the greater suburbs of Dublin, but it has lost many of its commercial enterprises and educational establishments and has relatively few cultural attractions for a place of its size and importance.

Yet its setting is a uniquely privileged one. It has all the benefits of a town, and is situated on the shores of the splendid Dublin Bay with the city and the mountains only a short distance away. It is always a joy to walk the magnificent piers and see the terraces and church spires against the backdrop of the Dublin mountains.

CHAPTER 13

Monkstown

Postmark from Monkstown

Of the many exclusively residential areas in south County Dublin, Monkstown occupies a unique place with a definite character and architectural style. The predominant architectural style of Monkstown is largely early Victorian or sometimes Regency, although some terraces and houses were constructed after 1860 in Belgrave Square, Eaton Square and Alma Road. The abundance of trees, hedges, and gardens, along with the many stone walls and the general variety of architecture, make this a most appealing district.

Like Killiney, which as we have seen is another solely residential area, Monkstown never had anything more than its small village, which, though attractive, had only ever a handful of shops. At first all of the houses were built to enjoy the pleasant surroundings and the fine sea views and later to take advantage of the convenient railway connection with the city. Monkstown was ideally situated for development as it lay between the two growing towns of Blackrock and Kingstown, where there were excellent shops, churches and other facilities. The first Ordnance Survey map of this area shows that by 1843 Monkstown was well established.

By the 1850s the Monkstown Road had become, to use a favourite expression of Victorian writers, 'thickly studded with handsome seats and pleasing villas', while various terraces including Longford, Clifton

A typical Monkstown house; the character of the area is defined by its many fine houses of the Regency and Victorian periods

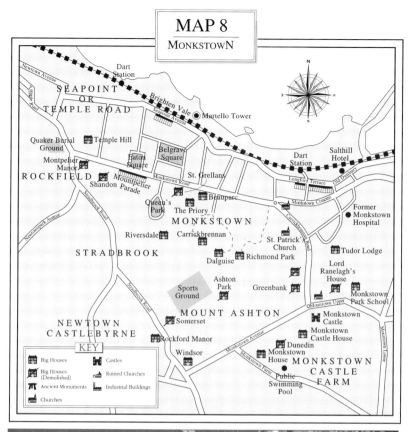

MAP 8
MONKSTOWN

Newtown Avenue

Dart Station

SEAPOINT OR TEMPLE ROAD

Brighten Vale

Seapoint Avenue

Martello Tower

N

Quaker Burial Ground

Temple Hill

Belgrave Square

Montpelier Manor

Eaton Square

Monkstown Road

St. Grellans

Dart Station

Salthill Hotel

ROCKFIELD

Mountpelier Parade

Shandon

Longford Terrace

Old Dunleary

Queen's Park

The Priory

Beauparc

Monkstown Crescent

Carrickbrennan Road

Former Monkstown Hospital

MONKSTOWN

Riversdale

Carrickbrennan

St. Patrick's Church

Tudor Lodge

STRADBROOK

Dalguise

Richmond Park

Lord Ranelagh's House

Stradbrook Road

Ashton Park

Greenbank

Monkstown Park School

Sports Ground

Mountown Upper

Monkstown Castle

MOUNT ASHTON

Somerset

Monkstown Castle House

Mountown Lower

NEWTOWN CASTLEBYRNE

Rockford Manor

Monkstown Avenue

Dunedin

Windsor

Monkstown House

Monkstown Farm

MONKSTOWN CASTLE FARM

Public Swimming Pool

KEY

Big Houses		Castles	
Big Houses (Demolished)		Ruined Churches	
Ancient Monuments		Industrial Buildings	
Churches			

An aerial view of Monkstown, c. 1980, showing the undeveloped lands of Monkstown valley and Salthill

Above right: This is probably the earliest shopfront example in the entire county, and was once the premises of Lane McCormack's pharmacy in Monkstown village

Above left: The original interior of Lane McCormack's, which has been preserved

and Brighton stood overlooking the sea near Seapoint. Monkstown Crescent, which as the name implies was a gently curving street, was already completed with a terrace of villa-type houses, and similar, very pretty, semi-detached villas had been laid out on Richmond Hill.

There were several large detached houses scattered between Kill of the Grange and Monkstown, such as Somerset, Windsor, Rockfort, Monkstown House and Ashton.

The Protestant church presided over the area, enjoying its 'centre stage' position, and was the largest major public building until the construction of St Patrick's Catholic church in 1861. Today, both churches, with their different towers and spires, are the principal landmarks of Monkstown and lend an air of dignity to the district. Nowadays, as everywhere, motor traffic dominates, to the extent that the Victorian roundabout in the centre of Monkstown, with its cut-stone plinth, circle of chains and drinking trough for horses, often goes unnoticed as a feature of interest.

Commercial developments in Monkstown Crescent have dramatically changed the character of the area

The building of the railway completely changed the appearance of the coastline at Seapoint from being rocky, with low cliffs, to being 'landscaped' into sloping ground. It also cut off access to the sea in some places, and a few residents such as Charles Haliday (the scholar and humanitarian) who saw that the poor in particular had lost their only bathing facility, campaigned to have foot-bridges built and new baths provided. A particularly elegant foot-bridge, consisting of a circular pier and spiral staircase, once stood at Salthill. Nearby, an oval 'bathing place' was constructed by the railway company, but this was eventually covered up when a dump was established beside the west pier sewage tanks. In Victorian times there was no continuous seafront road connecting old Dunleary with Blackrock at Newtown Avenue, so that the residents of Boswell Terrace, which overlooks the Martello tower at Seapoint, reached their homes by way of Seafield Avenue.

The Hampton, a coal boat wrecked on the railway embankment at Salthill, 1900

Seapoint Avenue was formed in the early 1800s when the Martello tower was built, but the road was connected through to old Dunleary only in the 1930s. The same road had been proposed, exactly a hundred years earlier, by William Dargan (the road and railway contractor) to the Earl of Rosse, then Postmaster General, presumably to improve connections with the mail packets at Dunleary.

The most dramatic changes to have taken place in Monkstown in recent years, apart from the development of 'Monkstown Valley' and Salthill during the 1980s, has been the transformation of one side of Monkstown Crescent from a row of quiet mews into a full commercial street, with all of its attendant traffic problems. It has been argued that the planning of the area would have been better served if these developments, which include a wide variety of quality restaurants and boutiques, had been confined to the town of Dun Laoghaire.

Monkstown – Its Churches

The graveyard and ruined church at Carrickbrennan is a good starting point for any study of the early history of Monkstown. An ancient church dedicated to St Mochonna, a sixth-century saint from Holm Patrick near Skerries, once stood here. In medieval times the little church fell under the control of the monks of St Mary's Abbey and later became a parish church. Indeed, until the nineteenth century the graveyard was entered by a short lane which lay directly opposite Monkstown Castle, providing easy access for the monks. There was also a collection of six or seven small houses or cottages here, most of which are long gone. By 1668 Carrickbrennan church was described as being in ruins and was completely rebuilt. It is the ruin of this church which partly survives in the graveyard today. This little church was clearly too small to meet the needs of the parish in the late eighteenth century, and in 1785 the vestry

The Church of Ireland church in Monkstown, which was remodelled to its present form in 1831

made an application to the ground landlords for a suitable site on which to build a new church. It is said that the old church was adapted as a watchhouse and provided with a chimney, to accommodate a watchman whose job was to prevent body snatching!

A dramatic site was chosen for the new Church of Ireland church, which today stands in its remodelled form, at the head of a long, straight avenue, Monkstown Road, which already existed at the time of John Rocque's map, 1757. The new church and adjoining schoolhouse were completed by 1789. Only thirty years later the parish was discussing the enlargment or possible rebuilding of the church, and two different plans were drawn up by the architect John Semple. Semple proposed to utilise the existing walls and to increase the capacity of the church to seat a congregation of about eight hundred people by adding three galleries and large transepts.

This rebuilt church was opened on Christmas Day 1831, and pews were allocated to families at £50, £25 and £20, according to position. Two pews were reserved for the Earl of Longford and Lord Viscount De Vesci in recognition of their generosity towards the parish.

The original small, rectangular church with its modest tower had been transformed into an extravaganza of 'castellated Gothic' mixed with 'Moorish' elements. Not everybody approved. In his book *In the Neighbourhood of Dublin* Weston St John Joyce described it as 'the nondescript edifice which disfigures its site' and others referred to its 'grotesque architecture, adorned with curious little pinnacles, the rounded curves of which recall the familiar pawn at chess'.

The vaults beneath the church contained some 127 interments, which were discontinued in the early 1900s. In 1940, as a precaution in case of a bomb attack, they were converted into an air-raid shelter, and later the iron gates were removed and the vaults bricked up.

The Knox Hall, a fine redbrick structure which adjoins the shops in Monkstown village, was erected in 1903 at a cost of £700 as a parish hall.

St Patrick's Catholic Church, situated in Monkstown village on Carrickbrennan Road, was begun in the early 1860s and was dedicated in 1866. This church was designed by Augustus W. Pugin and George Ashlin in the early French Gothic style and consists of a long nave with side aisles. The interior, with all of its fine stone carving and decorative detail, has been preserved intact. The capitals were carved by Early and Powell, the firm of sculptors, church decorators and stained-glass artists of Camden Street, and the builder was Michael Meade. The nave was paved with Minton tiles and the stone for the columns included Michelstown porphyry, Aberdeen granite and Ennis limestone. The elaborate rose window was carved from Caen stone.

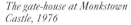

The interior of St Patrick's Catholic church, which was opened in 1866

At the dedication ceremony Haydn's *Imperial Mass* was performed, and 'large pink family tickets' were issued at £15 for seats in the upper nave while 'small white tickets' for the lower part of the aisles cost 2/6.

Monkstown Castle The ruins of Monkstown Castle stand among the trees near the roundabout at Carrickbrennan, and consist of an impressive gate-house and the remains of a tower. The arched entrance, complete with its wattle-constructed vault, was once adjoined by the tall, square tower which is depicted in an eighteenth-century painting and various drawings of Monkstown; a few steps of a spiral staircase are all that remain of this tower. Part of another vault, which supported the rooms above and beside the entrance, may also be seen.

A painting by William Ashford, probably seventeenth-century (now hanging in the offices of Guinness's), shows two other towers and a large house in the middle. As the painting shows the completed church at Monkstown, all of these impressive features must have been removed some time after 1789, but there appears to be no record of who carried out the demolition or when it was done. The painting also shows two large 'Georgian Gothic' windows which may still be seen – though blocked up – with their brick surrounds in the southern walls of the gate-house and tower.

The gate-house at Monkstown Castle, 1976

It seems, from the evidence of the artist and from the 1797 map, that the gate-house and tower were joined by a residential block, possibly of seventeenth- or even eighteenth-century date. Another tower once projected out from the castle at the south-eastern corner and can be clearly made out on the map.

A description of the castle in 1780, when it was advertised for sale, mentions a house in the Gothic style, two square 'castles' and a fine tower, 91 feet in height. The castle was three storeys in height, and 'comprised numerous apartments, including a

A painting of Monkstown Castle by William Ashford – also shows Monkstown church (extreme left) and Dunleary House (above the carriage)

The Victorian tower at Monkstown Park

saloon, library, gallery and Chapel' (Ball's *History*). Gabriel Beranger made a sketch of Monkstown at about this time and commented: 'It was at the time I drew it, inhabited, as a country house, and has since been still more mended and modernized.'

A small stream, no longer visible, once flowed to the east of the castle, and was dammed there to form an artificial pond which was, no doubt, of great importance to the twelfth-century monks, and almost certainly provided power to a cornmill, which is mentioned in the census of 1659. The pond, which became part of an ornamental garden during the occupancy of General Edmund Ludlow, was filled in during the 1960s.

The name Monkstown, of course, means 'the town or settlement of the monks' and dates back to a time in the twelfth century when the Cistercian monks of St Mary's Abbey were given all of the lands stretching from Bullock Harbour right back through Glenageary and Sallynoggin to include Monkstown and Dun Laoghaire. Monkstown Farm, or 'The Farm', is a popular residential area today and can trace its origins to that period when the lands were indeed the farm belonging to the monks – and we can imagine these lands, carefully cultivated and very productive, providing a useful income and sustenance for the abbey.

The Reformation and the dissolution of the monasteries spelt the end of the monks' occupation of Monkstown Castle and all its lands, and by the middle of the sixteenth century we find Sir Arthur Travers, a man highly regarded by King Henry VIII, in possession of the estate. Travers was made Master of the Ordnance in Ireland, and was one of the chief military adventurers of the sixteenth century, who had the advantage of being able to speak Irish (Ball's *History*). Through Travers it passed to the Cheevers family who held it until the time of Oliver Cromwell, when, being Catholics, they were dispossessed. On 19 December 1653 Cheevers with his family and many retainers were literally sent 'to hell or to Connaught'.

The next occupant was a colleague and follower of Cromwell, General Edmund Ludlow, who was appointed Commander of the Horse in Ireland and was given Monkstown Castle. Ludlow made many improvements to the castle, including the creation of pleasure grounds and gardens. However, he did not enjoy it for very long, for with the coming of the Restoration in 1660 everything was seized by the army for the Crown and returned to Walter Cheevers. Towards the close of the seventeenth century, Primate Michael Boyle, Archbishop of Armagh, bought the estate and through the marriages of his two daughters it became the joint property of the Lords Longford and De Vesci.

Monkstown Castle and Carrickbrennan graveyard are said to be haunted by the Widow Gamble, and there are many garbled stories of how her ghost originated. One suggests that she was an informer and revealed the whereabouts of some monks who were 'on the run', but regardless of the truth of the story her name lives on in the local tradition of calling the road to Mount Town The Widow Gamble's Hill. Half-way up this hill, also known as The Dark Hill, is a double-fronted, Georgian house which was once the steward's house for the Longford and De Vesci estate.

Rocque's map of 1757 and another from 1797 indicate the existence of a road which ran beside this house and along the eastern boundary of Monkstown Park, joining up with the now-disused back avenue to come out at Packenham Road near old Dunleary. Tracing this road onto later Ordnance Survey maps, one can see the logical course of a road from Dalkey passing through Glenageary and ending in old Dunleary.

Monkstown Park In the grounds of Monkstown Park, now the Christian Brothers School, there stood a house, erected in the middle of the eighteenth century by the Right Hon. Charles Jones, Viscount Ranelagh, who later became Lord Ranelagh. Lord Ranelagh is described as the tenant of much of the lands about Dun Laoghaire and Glenageary in the 1790s, and he owned a brick field, a place where brick clay is dug and bricks burnt, on the lands now known as The Hill, Monkstown. His house stood near to the present entrance of the school and was demolished in 1843 by Charles Haliday when he erected a new residence for himself.

Haliday's House, Monkstown Park, is a large, square building and is

A late eighteenth-century estate map of Monkstown Castle, showing Lord Ranelagh's house and his brick fields

One of the terraced houses in Montpelier Parade, which was built in about 1800

now incorporated into the school. It is a fine building, despite having been disfigured by the addition of concrete fire-escapes many years ago. Its long portico of Corinthian columns remains intact, and though the windows are blocked up, the house could easily be restored to its former elegant state. The house was first used as an educational establishment in the early years of this century when Monkstown Park preparatory school was run here. The school, which received boarders from seven to fourteen years of age, had a reputation for sports, including cricket and open-sea bathing. There was also a rifle club.

The Christian Brothers, who acquired the house in 1950, extended the buildings in 1953 and again in 1964 with the addition of an auditorium. More recently a new pyramid structure has added further space to the school.

An interesting and little-known feature of Monkstown Park is the tall, stone-built, viewing tower, probably erected by Haliday. The square, battlemented tower with its arrow slits is now inaccessible but was once reached by a semi-circular staircase which led to a platform.

Another attractive structure, which was demolished in 1983 following a fire, was the fine gate-lodge. It consisted of a one-storey-over-basement villa, with pediment features on three façades, a pilastered porch and pretty Regency-style windows decorated with bracketed entablatures (similar to those on the main house).

The Development of Residential Monkstown

In the eighteenth century there were few buildings between Dunleary and Blackrock, with the exception of some large houses near the small village of Newtown at Blackrock. Towards the Monkstown Road there was Neptune House and another old residence called Montpelier.

Montpelier Parade Rocque's map of 1757 shows Monkstown as open countryside, traversed only by the 'Dunlary Road', now the Monkstown Road. The first change came about with the building of a terrace of sixteen houses, in about 1800, which was called Montpelier Parade, after the French resort of that name (though with a slightly different spelling) which is famous for its hilltop position and fresh air. These houses on Monkstown Road also enjoyed an elevated location, fine views and salubrious air.

The attractive gate-lodge at Monkstown Park, demolished in 1983

The houses, three-storey-over-basement, were built in the Georgian manner as two terraces, and were a speculative development by Molesworth Greene. The houses, plain but elegantly proportioned, have many typical features of the period, such as panelled doors and shutters, chair rails, plain fireplaces and simple plasterwork. The chair rail, or dado, was a stylistic feature of eighteenth-century rooms which prevented chairs from damaging the walls. Some of the original oil-lamp holders still remain on the parade, and there is a pleasant 'green' between the houses and the road.

Montpelier Parade enjoyed full views of the sea until the second half of the nineteenth century when Belgrave Square, Eaton Square and Alma Road were developed.

Montpelier House was erected on lands adjoining Montpelier Parade, and was more recently known as Shandon. It was a five-bay two-storey house, with a prominent central gable, tall chimneys, and a viewing tower at the back. Shandon was a somewhat ungainly building by the time it was demolished, having first been altered by the addition of a large garden frontage and later by its conversion into flats. It was also rather hemmed in by the construction of bungalows in the 1950s. Still, as one of the oldest remaining houses in Monkstown, it was regrettable that it was demolished within the last five years.

The Montpelier estate included other houses on Monkstown Road such as Montpelier Manor, Montpelier Place and Row, and Mount Temple, which stands in the angle where Temple Hill meets the Monkstown Road. Montpelier Manor or Villa, now demolished, was a Tudor-style, L-shaped residence, built around 1850. It had pointed gables with elaborate bargeboards and timber finials.

Monkstown valley had been identified on a map back in 1797 as a place with 'beautiful situations for building', but it was at least twenty or thirty years later when the first houses were erected there. It is interesting that even then, well before the advent of the railway, there was a move to build in pleasant locations outside the city. The subsequent development of Monkstown took the form of middle-sized houses, most of which were detached, and generally built in the safe, classical style, being stucco-fronted and often employing Georgian motifs such as the pillared doorcase and fanlight.

Four important houses were erected on the south side of Monkstown Road not long after the completion of Montpelier Parade. Each was surrounded by attractive gardens and extensive pleasure grounds. They were Carrickbrennan, Beauparc, St Grellan's and The Priory. The first three share many features of design and neo-classical detail. Carrickbrennan and Beauparc, which are virtually identical, are both large, square houses; both have a hall with a circular ballustraded opening or gallery lit from above by a lantern or roof light, while Carrickbrennan also has a rooftop viewing platform situated between the chimney stacks.

The Priory was an exercise in the Gothic taste, and at its entrance on Monkstown Road stands a most attractive gate-lodge (but completely rebuilt in 1984). This lodge, with its

Below: Map of the Montpelier estate, which included the elegant terrace at Montpelier Parade

Bottom: Shandon, an eighteenth-century house, which was swept away within the past five years

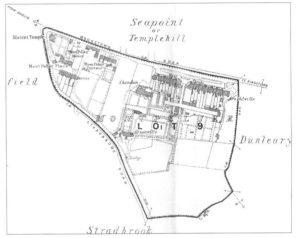

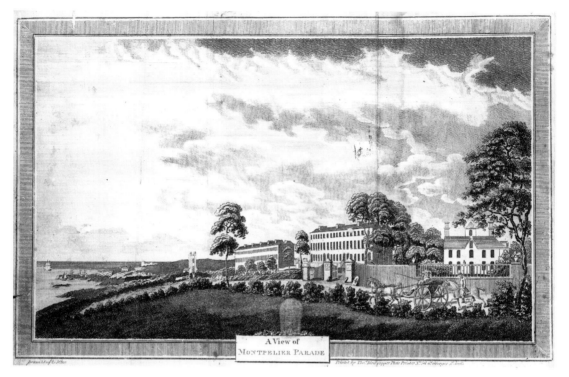

A View of
MONTPELIER PARADE

Montpelier Parade, with Shandon to the right, once had uninterrupted views of the sea (engraving of 1802)

pretty gables, bargeboards and tall chimneys, is typical of the 1830s when what is sometimes referred to as the 'Swiss cottage style' was fashionable.

St Grellan's, better known up to the 1970s as The Hall School and originally called Richview (until 1880), was situated about half-way along Monkstown Road. It was a handsome, neo-classical house from 1825, and was demolished in 1982 having lain derelict for many years. The house stood in its own grounds of about seven acres which once boasted rose and rock gardens, playing fields for hockey, rounders and netball, and tennis courts. Among the outstanding features of the house was a huge granite portico, which has been re-erected at the entrance to the new development of apartments. The mammoth Doric pillars were hewn from single blocks of granite. The portico was surmounted by a delicate ironwork balcony, and the windows were set in recessed bays. Inside, the house had typical plasterwork of the 1820 period, including an elegant plaster niche in the drawing room. The principal bathroom was fitted with unusual, embossed blue tiles of the 1890s.

The school also owned a fine Victorian house on Queen's Park called Clonmore, and this was also demolished in about 1982.

Carrickbrennan, set well back from Monkstown Road, was approached by a long avenue which it later partly shared with Dalguise (a large detached house built about 1860). The gate-lodge for Carrickbrennan was one of the earliest in Monkstown, being built around 1830. It was of symmetrical composition, featuring recessed Doric columns, pilasters and Georgian sash windows. It could be seen from the

The original gate-lodge of The Priory, with its elaborately-carved bargeboards

Monkstown Road, closing a dramatic vista through an avenue of mature trees. The design of both Carrick-brennan and its gate-lodge suggest the work of J. S. Mulvany, designer of nearby railway stations and yacht clubs.

Dalguise The avenue mentioned above is now the private drive to Dalguise, an imposing Victorian residence, which was remodelled in about 1860 around a smaller house called Richmond Cottage. Dalguise is a large house, five windows wide, with a wing added to the side and terraced gardens to the south. It is now one of the largest privately owned properties in Monkstown.

Richmond Park, another large Victorian house, stands nearby. Built about 1874 by Sydenham Davis, and originally set in secluded grounds, it was once approached by a winding avenue from Monkstown village. A second avenue, planted with lime trees, gave access to Monkstown Avenue and is now occupied by the houses of Richmond Grove. In 1987 planning permission was granted for the demolition of the house and the construction of a new housing development, but through the intervention of An Taisce (the National Trust for Ireland) the house was saved, and after restoration was later sold at a substantial profit.

St Grellan's, a fine neo-classical house, which was demolished in 1982

The whole estate, with its many fine trees and unspoilt grounds, was left in about 1980 by Mrs Mary Briscoe to the Cheshire Homes, in the hope that the house and parkland would remain unaltered. She had refused several very substantial offers from property developers because she expressly wished the whole of Richmond Park to be maintained intact.

The house, two storeys high, has many decorative features such as a bow window with a copper roof, an attractive timber porch and an Italianate tower which may have been added later. The façades are ornamented with stucco details and the roof projects onto elaborately carved timber brackets.

A tile from the bathroom at St Grellan's

In 1914 the entire Richmond Park estate was sold by the Court of the Land judges, and consisted of four other houses on Monkstown Road, including Marino and Hillsborough, the pharmacy (this was the well-known Lane MacCormack's pharmacy which had been in business in Monkstown since the 1880s), and the premises of the Royal Bank of Ireland (which was Tydall's newsagents for many years and is probably the best surviving Victorian shopfront in the county).

Quaker Meeting House The Society of Friends, or Quakers, were founded in 1647 in England and a few families came to settle in Ireland some seven years later. Quakers had a reputation for being hard-working and fair in business, particularly in industries related to agriculture, and they prospered. At first, meetings were held in the homes of prominent Quakers such as Thomas Pim's Glenageary House, or that of his son (also called Thomas) at Monkstown House. In 1832 a simple meeting house was erected at Packenham Road.

The entrance and circular landing at Carrickbrennan

Richmond Park, built around 1874

A richly-ornamented porch at Richmond Park

The Quaker Meeting House, which is still in regular use, is a plain, symmetrical building, with a rectangular hall or meeting room. This is flanked by some small classrooms and a staircase leading to a gallery. There is a minister's gallery or raised seating-area at the west end of the meeting room, and in 1867 a new classroom was added.

Richmond Hill, consisting of eight houses situated on the west side of a steep rise, was laid out around 1826, and was occupied by various Quaker families.

The families of Pim and Hutton were residents here in the 1850s and later we find George Wilkinson, architect of the Harcourt Street Station, living here. These finely built houses, one-storey-over-basement, have intimate proportions and late Georgian features such as fanlights. One of these houses has a miniature conservatory of great beauty, made by Turner, whose foundry made its name by constructing the palace of the Great Exhibition in Dublin in 1853.

In the mid-nineteenth century, this part of Monkstown was a strong-hold of Quakers, with Jonathan Pim resident at Greenbank and Thomas Hone at Yapton, two houses which stood on Carrickbrennan Road and are both now demolished. By the 1870s we find up to five Pim families resident in various large Monkstown houses.

The Sacred Heart Convent School, which was situated on Carrick-brennan Road, closed in 1977 and the two old houses which it once occupied, along with the school buildings, were subsequently demolished. The school, which was run by the nuns of the Sacred Heart Convent at Mount Anville, was founded in 1945 when the two houses, first Yapton and then Greenbank, were acquired. Yapton, the older of the two, was an attractive, double-bow fronted, Regency-style house. It was built by Thomas Hone, a stockbroker and property developer, about 1840 as his own residence. It had a particularly fine Portland stone portico with Ionic columns. Greenbank was a large mid-Victorian house, two-storey-over-basement with bay windows. The two houses were eventually linked when a new school building was completed in 1953.

The Hill Packenham Road, a quiet residential area, leads from Carrick-brennan to Old Dunleary and passes The Hill, a short crescent of houses laid out on a steep hill. The first buildings on The Hill were erected in the early 1840s when Tudor Hall and Tudor House were built. They are a pair of identical, semi-detached houses and may have been designed by the noted architect Richard Morrison. Both houses, built in a highly decorative Tudor idiom, have elaborate granite porches, and mullioned windows with small panes of glass. Uplands, built shortly afterwards, consists of two semi-detached villas which have large bow windows and elegantly proportioned rooms.

St Anne's A further eight semi-detached Victorian houses were erected on The Hill, but the most striking is without doubt St Anne's, a house which stands on a dramatically sloping site. It is a two-storey-over-basement, brick-built house with a square tower. St Anne's was designed by an architect named William Caldbeck, as his own residence. He was a versatile architect who designed many public buildings and houses during the middle of the nineteenth century. St Anne's is full of decorative detail, employing different-coloured brickwork, stucco and cast-iron, and there are plaster heads incorporated into a frieze. There is a great variety of bay windows, each of a different shape and type. The eaves of the roof are also a special feature, with their striking brackets and black-and-white colour scheme. In the garden is a most attractive turret, with yellow brick arches and an octagonal pointed roof.

Rathdown Fever Hospital Packenham Road is low-lying and partly covers the now culverted stream which flows from Monkstown Castle and once entered the sea at Dunleary Harbour. It was here, on low-lying ground, that the hospital was built, following the grant of a lease to the four trustees, Charles Lindsay (Rector of Monkstown church), William

This house, at Richmond Hill, is a fine example of the many villas in the Monkstown area

Tudor House, one of a pair of Tudor-style residences at The Hill

St Anne's, which was designed by William Caldbeck as his own residence

Disney, William Hutchinson (Harbour Master) and William Plant (surgeon), all local residents. The small sixteen-bed hospital was opened in 1834, and it was, at first, known as the Rathdown Fever Hospital, later Monkstown Hospital.

Dr Plant, who had operated a dispensary in Monkstown since about 1812, became the hospital's first doctor and surgeon. He lived in a house called Plantation, now Gortmore, on the Monkstown Road. He was succeeded by a Dr Beatty, who was said to have been very particular about the sanitary arrangements, and had a habit of flushing every lavatory he came across when doing his rounds! There were several very serious epidemics of cholera and other infectious diseases during the nineteenth century, and Monkstown Hospital was always busy. During a particularly severe epidemic in 1848 conditions were so bad that sometimes two or three patients shared the same bed!

A big building programme was planned in the late 1870s and what was practically a new hospital was opened in 1880.

The hospital continued to serve the local community throughout this century, operating at low cost, with a small budget, but giving a very personal service (as this writer experienced when, as a child, he had a serious cut treated there). Though in receipt of the smallest Government grant to any voluntary hospital in the state, as it had only thirty-three beds it did not fit in with the Department of Health's unfortunate decision to eliminate small hospitals and centralise their services. Monkstown Hospital was closed in 1990 and the buildings were demolished shortly afterwards. An apartment development called Monkstown Gate now stands on the site.

Salthill and the Seafront

Salthill Hotel Salthill takes its name from the presence of salt works here during the eighteenth century. A large house stood on this hill which overlooked Old Dunleary Harbour. The house is depicted in William Ashford's late eighteenth-century painting of Monkstown as a three-storey mansion, and I believe it was incorporated into the first Salthill Hotel which was operational in the 1830s when the Dublin to Kingstown railway was completed; the railway company had originally bought Salthill House because they required the land through which to cut the new line. In 1833 William Dargan, the railway builder and entrepreneur, employed his men to cut back the cliffs at Salthill and even still, despite the new apartments, the steep slope can be discerned.

The main entrance to Monkstown Hospital, which closed in 1990

When the railway was officially opened in 1834 a celebration dinner was held for the company directors and other guests in the Salthill Hotel. The business went well and two years later the company's architect, John S. Mulvany, was asked to design additional rooms. The early proprietors of the hotel were a Mr Marsh, followed by the Lovegrove family, but for most of the nineteenth century it was run by William Parry. In 1865 the architect John McCurdy was employed to draw up plans for the improvement and embellishment of the Salthill Hotel. The new design encased the old building in an elegant 'French chateau' envelope, with the addition of a tower over the main entrance and steep roofs, pierced by dormer windows. The façade was constructed in red brick and the windows were decorated with elaborate stucco architraves. The new hotel closely resembled the architecture of the new Royal Marine Hotel in Kingstown, also designed by McCurdy.

In 1913 it was advertised, in John Eyre's *Guide Book to Kingstown*, as 'a first class family hotel, beautifully situated, standing in its private grounds, and commanding an unrivalled view of Dublin Bay and Kingstown Harbour'. The hotel boasted electric light throughout and a motor

Drawn & Engd by Walter Dublin.

An engraved letterhead, showing the Old Dunleary House at the back of the Salthill Hotel, c. 1840

SALTHILL HOTEL, DUBLIN, FROM THE AIR

The Salthill Hotel with the coalyards and the Albright and Wilson works behind

A soup plate from the Salthill Hotel and its hotel stamp (above)

garage with an inspection pit for motor cars. It was ten minutes from Dublin by rail and an electric tram ran to the city every four minutes!

In the 1930s the Salthill Hotel was bought by the proprietors of the Royal Hibernian Hotel and was always a fashionable venue for weddings. In the early 1970s, having stood empty for a year, the hotel was burnt down and subsequently demolished in 1972. The site lay derelict for many years, a mess of builders' rubbish and weeds, while various developers juggled with planning permissions and profits, and residents complained about the debris left behind by Travellers. Eventually, the first phase of 'international luxury' apartments were built in 1980, and they were described by the auctioneers as sharing 'an entrance foyer floored in roseate marble, with velvet or leather wall panels, recesses for classical statuary, and period-style coving'.

The old Salthill House originally backed onto Tully's Row (now the site of Longford Terrace), a narrow row of old cottages which formed part of the village of Old Dunleary. Another row of cottages also ran towards the present Grosvenor Terrace, but all of these were swept away when Longford Terrace was built. Nearby stood the Salthill railway station which at one time was described as having the appearance of a Swiss chalet. It had windows glazed in the Gothic style and tall chimneys. Following its demolition, there was no station near here until 1984 when the DART service began.

Longford Terrace, one of the longest and most substantial terraces in the district, was once described as an 'aristocratic and commanding pile'. It was erected by a developer named Thomas Bradley. The first section, the terrace furthest away from Dun Laoghaire, consists of fourteen houses and was built in 1842. The second half, which is fronted by a cut-stone retaining wall, was completed within the next fourteen years. The houses, named in recognition of one of the ground landlords, were to cost at least £1000 each, and are three-storey-over-basement. The design is attributed to George Papworth, who was responsible for the very similar houses at Gresham Terrace in Dun Laoghaire.

The ground landlords stipulated, in the original lease, that the new

owners shall 'not suffer to be built or erected any house or building on the sloping or low ground between the site of the proposed dwelling house and the railway'. These lands, once called the Salthill Gardens, were also used by a tennis club, and are now in the ownership of the local authority whose original plan was to restore the gardens – but they are now under pressure to create a carpark here, to facilitate DART commuters.

A feature of Monkstown is the villa, a house-style which has all the grand reception rooms laid out above the garden level or basement where the kitchen and extra bedrooms are accommodated. There are several variations on the basic plan, but most have an attractive door-case, perhaps with a fanlight, which is approached by a flight of granite steps, that in turn leads to a well proportioned interior. Examples include Oriel Lodge on Seafield Avenue, The Albany on Albany Avenue, and Laurel Lodge on Brighton Avenue.

In 1981 the owner of Santa Maria, a High Court judge, stirred up a storm of protest when he applied for planning permission to demolish

Above left: A 1930s luggage label

Above right: The dining room at the Salthill Hotel during the Edwardian period

Longford Terrace, which has some of the largest terraced houses in the county, was begun in 1842

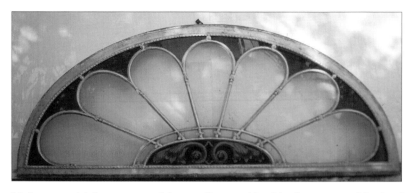

A typical fanlight from a villa of about 1830

his home, which was one of these villas, and build a four-storey block of nineteen apartments on the grounds. Permission was granted by Dun Laoghaire Corporation but on appeal to An Bord Pleanála (The Planning Appeals Board), the proposal was turned down.

The Lords Longford and De Vesci granted further leases to various developers to build on the seafront. In 1840, John Knight Boswell, a Dublin solicitor, leased lands near Seapoint to build a terrace, and he himself lived at Number 2 New Brighton. As was the fashion at this time, all such houses were rendered and painted, and the building lease stipulated that each house 'shall maintain, preserve and keep the present lines, levels and elevations' and that they shall be 'coloured in imitation of Portland stone in conformity with the adjoining buildings'.

Trafalgar Terrace, which was begun in 1844 and completed by 1855, was probably designed by the architect J. S. Mulvany. The houses were erected by a builder named Daniel Crowe, of Pearse Street, on lands leased from Harcourt Lees of Blackrock House, and Thomas Hone of Yapton. It is likely that they acquired an interest in the strip of land that had been surplus to the needs of the railway company for laying down the track. The new terrace, so named to commemorate the fiftieth jubilee of the battle of Trafalgar, was designed with clean, simple lines and ornamented by simple features such as window recesses and slightly projecting porches which are decorated with brackets and victory wreaths.

Brighton Terrace, showing that there was no continuous sea-front road here until the 1930s

Below stands Seapoint Tower, which is reached by crossing the Ordnance Bridge, so called because it had to be strong enough to carry the heavy guns of the Ordnance down to the Martello tower. Seapoint is now a popular bathing place, equipped with a variety of steps which provide access to the sea, but it was once served by only one narrow boat-slip.

There are records of bathing here and at Blackrock since the middle of the eighteenth century, and no doubt earlier inhabitants must have enjoyed the clean waters of

Dublin Bay! Seapoint baths, which is now converted to a private house, was constructed by 1840, just seaward of the railway at the end of Brighton Vale. It was probably built by the railway company, to compensate the public for lack of access to the sea. In 1911 the baths were described as the 'ladies' bathing place'.

Brighton Vale is a charming terrace of villas which was built during the 1840s on a narrow strip of land between the railway and the sea. There is great variety in the ornamentation of the fifteen houses, and they make successful use of decorative stucco details and cast-iron work. The first pair, which are slightly larger than the rest, have beautiful arched windows. Number 5, decorated in an exotic oriental style, is believed to have been the home of John Skipton Mulvany, who, as we have already seen, designed a number of houses in the area and was the architect for the Dublin and Kingstown Railway Company. He designed the local railway stations at Blackrock, Salthill and Dun Laoghaire, but his most remarkable piece of railway architecture must be the Broadstone terminus in Dublin. Through his connections with Quaker businessmen such as Jonathan Pim, he was employed to design several houses including Brighton Vale, as well as the Royal Irish Yacht Club and other features such as the massive stone wall at Longford Terrace.

Seapoint House and Martello tower – from Kirkwood's print of the railway, c. 1845

Seapoint station was opened in 1863 to accommodate the growing number of residents in the newly built areas such as Belgrave Square and Alma Road. The unusual circular openings which appear in the wall at Seapoint were once part of an underground carriageway to the stable building of Osborne House. The house, which is one of a pair, was built for William Osborne. His stables, and the extraordinary tunnels leading to them from the houses, included terraced gardens above, and were erected as part of the land deal with the railway company which included the site for Seapoint station. The large circular windows which open onto the platform at Seapoint station once lit a tunnel leading to the stables which the railway company erected in return for the site of the station.

Cast-iron railing heads such as these added greatly to the decorative quality of the houses and gardens in Monkstown

The wall at Seapoint railway station, which disguises a passageway to stables behind

A typical villa on Alma Road, built c. 1860

Ardenza and Tobernea Terraces were constructed in the 1850s, on the site of Seapoint House and Seapoint College, a rambling collection of buildings which must have been quite old at the time of their demolition. Seapoint House is shown as an enclosed courtyard on the Ordnance Survey map of 1843.

Victorian Squares and Other Developments

The Longford and De Vesci estate ended at Seafield Avenue, and all the lands to the west, which were known as the 'sea fields', were once part of the estate of Temple Hill House. These included all the land between Belgrave Square and Alma Road. Much of this property and other lands had been acquired by the railway company, along with the 'way-leaves' which were lands surplus to the needs of the railway and were eventually bought by speculators such as Thomas Hone. Hone moved into Monkstown in about 1848, when his own house, Yapton, was completed. He was a Quaker who came from a legal family, and was well experienced in property matters. Beginning in the 1850s he granted leases for building on Alma Road, Tobernea Terrace, Ardenza Terrace, Eaton Place and later, Eaton Square.

Belgrave Square The first developments at Belgrave Square took place in the 1840s with the building of eight large terraced houses on the south side. Two of these, which are now joined together, form the premises of Comhaltas Ceoltóirí Éireann, the organisation for traditional music and dance, but they were once occupied by The Hall School, before it moved to St Grellan's.

These were followed in the 1850s by the building of some detached houses on the west side and later by a long terrace of seventeen bay-windowed houses on the north side. The square was completed in the 1860s with the addition of five redbrick terraced houses on the west side. Its attractive square, with its park of shrubs and mature trees, was always in private ownership but was leased to the residents' association,

and to the surprise of many was sold in 1998 on the open market.

The noted artist, Admiral Richard Brydges Beechey, retired from the navy in 1864 and came to live at number 2 Belgrave Square. Beechey's marine paintings are of the highest quality, and some of his best work hangs in the yacht clubs in Dun Laoghaire. He painted many Irish subjects, but is best known for his beautiful paintings of the paddle steamers of the mail packet, such as the *Leinster* entering the harbour on her maiden voyage.

The square was extremely fashionable in late Victorian times and the *Lady's Pictorial* of 1890 gives us an impression of a society party: 'The house was prettily laid out, and, despite the fact that it is not extremely spacious, its dimensions proved amply accommodating to the 180 assembled guests ... the hostess wore black striped silk, with a zouave bodice abundantly trimmed with jet, and a sparkling collar of jetted lace.'

Alma Road, a steeply rising avenue which joins the Monkstown and Seapoint Roads, was laid out in the 1855, on the grounds of Temple Hill. The houses were concentrated on the west side, so that many of them had a sea view. Within ten years over twenty houses had been built, including Alma Terrace at the top, which was developed by a solicitor named Thomas Alma.

Balnootra One of the more unusual new houses was Balnootra, a brick-built, Gothic-style residence, designed in 1859 by architect Thomas N. Deane for James Sweeney, a solicitor with the Royal Bank.

An old postcard showing Belgrave Square, with its bay-windowed, terraced houses of the 1860s

The pavement of Belgrave House – many paths were decorated with limestone and quartz pebbles in this way

The large, open space at Belgrave Square, covered in snow

Deane made a feature of boldly carved timber elements, such as the brackets and bargeboards of the roof and the pierced pitch-pine staircase. He also used different-coloured brick to achieve decorative effects around doors and windows.

The same architect may also have been responsible for a pair of neo-Gothic houses, numbers 12 and 14 Alma Road, just opposite. These were built for Adam Blood, the chief brewer at the Mountjoy Brewery.

Another unusual house, built of red brick and designed in a curious baronial style, is Gortnadrew. It was designed in the 1880s by Sir Thomas Drew for himself. Drew had a wide-ranging practice, but as a church architect he worked on many Church of Ireland cathedrals and churches in Northern Ireland.

Eaton Square, with its terraced, redbrick houses, was the last major development in Monkstown, and is shown on the 1911 Ordnance

The Venetian Gothic style houses at 12 and 14 Alma Road

Survey map as being only half-completed. Thomas Dockrell lived in one of three Victorian houses, built on the south side of Eaton Square overlooking the little park. Dockrell later developed the rest of the square with redbrick terraced houses and went on to build a new house for his own family around 1890, called Camolin. The Dockrells, well-known Dublin ironmongers and suppliers of sanitary fittings, took the name from their home village of Camolin in County Wexford. It was a large, detached, redbrick house, which was demolished to make way for the Irish school, Scoil Lorcáin.

Queen's Park, another Victorian development situated off the Monkstown Road, is a cul-de-sac consisting of eight detached houses which are laid out in a semi-circular formation around the 'island site' of a fine villa called Inismaan.

The houses were developed in the late 1860s on lands which had belonged to the Pim family in an adjoining property, Stradbrook Hall. The developer was Alfred Gresham Jones, who himself lived at Inismaan. Two of these large Victorian houses, Verona and Clonmore, were demolished in the 1970s and 1980s, to be replaced by apartment blocks.

Riversdale Among the houses of Queen's Park, Riversdale is exceptional. An elaborate brick building from about 1870, with cut-stone details and a tower, it was built by the Duff Egans who were successful Dublin wine and tea merchants. Later it belonged to Sir Henry McLoughlin, and more recently to the noted decorative plasterwork specialists,

An aerial view of Queen's Park and Belgrave Square, Monkstown

Below left: Clonmore, Queen's Park, once part of The Hall School, demolished in the 1970s

Below right: The ornate, late Victorian mansion at Riversdale

A late eighteenth-century map, showing the existence of Windsor, Somerset and Ashton Park

the Creedon family, who carried out much church work, and from whom it passed into the hands of the Opus Dei Order. Though externally Riversdale is an elaborate Victorian house with a fine carved timber porch and sandstone pillars, there are no very grand rooms inside.

Stradbrook and Monkstown Avenue

The hinterland of Monkstown stretches back to Stradbrook Road and to Abbey Road which leads to Kill of the Grange. Of the remaining old houses in this area Windsor, Rockford, Stradbrook Hall, Wynberg, Monkstown House and a house called Monkstown Castle should be mentioned. As many again have been demolished, and these include Somerset, Ashton Park, Yapton, Greenbank, Dunedin and Boley.

Windsor, standing at the top of Monkstown Avenue, had been built by the 1790s on lands belonging to Charles Dunbar of Blessington, County Wicklow. Dunbar was the owner of much land about Dunleary in the late eighteenth century, and he may have acted as an agent for Archbishop Peter Boyle, whose estate eventually passed to the Lords Longford and De Vesci. Windsor may have been built by John Sproule, a builder and developer who in 1797 also owned another property on Monkstown Avenue. Philip Lecane, of Dun Laoghaire Borough Historical Society, tells us that in 1793 Patrick Bride sold his interest in the house and lands including 'part of the castle farm of Monkstown' to William Lane, whose name is now associated this area in the name Lanesville. The Lane family remained at Windsor until 1832 when it was sold to Michael Thunder, a brewer in Dublin. Within eight years he had sold Windsor to Matthew Law, a Dublin jeweller and goldsmith. The house was later occupied by other prominent Dublin merchants such as Thomas Pim, and in the early 1900s by the Millar family who owned a large wine and spirit store and bottling plant in Thomas Street.

In the eighteenth century, the original square house had its entrance facing towards the mountains. It appears that a new larger house was added, probably during the 1830s by Michael Thunder, and that the house was turned around to look towards Monkstown Castle and the

Windsor House, which was extensively remodelled during the nineteenth century

Ashton Park, a Georgian house, which until 1972 was the home of Brook House Preparatory School

sea. Thus the present front of Windsor has a rather Victorian appearance with its large, plate-glass windows and its roof with wide projecting eaves. The very handsome, cut-stone, Georgian doorcase may well have been salvaged from the older house. Further alterations made in the 1880s by a Blackrock builder named Christopher Jolley included a new billiard room. Inside, Windsor has elaborately decorated ceilings from the 1830s, with large centrepieces in the hall and principal reception rooms, coved ceilings in the bedrooms and a bow-shaped staircase.

Ashton Park By the 1830s, another member of the Thunder family was resident at a nearby house called Ashton Park. Ashton Park, which is shown as belonging to Robert Ashworth on the 1797 map, began as a modest Georgian house, but was greatly enlarged by the addition of an extra storey, a large bow, three storeys in height, and a grand porch with Tuscan columns. The house, which was demolished in 1972, is best remembered in recent times as the home of the preparatory school, Brook House.

Monkstown Castle (House) is a D-ended late Georgian-style house, consisting of two storeys and having a distinguished neo-classical porch in cut-stone. It was built in the early 1800s, possibly for Jonathan Pim, linen merchant and cotton manufacturer, of South William Street, who was living there in the 1830s. At about this time a suitable location was being sought for Dublin zoo and Pim offered his lands at Monkstown Castle. More recently the house has been associated with Dr Robert de Courcy Wheeler of Monkstown Hospital.

Monkstown Castle (House), probably erected in the early 1800s for Jonathan Pim

Monkstown Avenue was laid out in the late eighteenth century with Windsor, Ashton and two other Georgian houses, both of which have disappeared. The latter were situated on the east side of Monkstown Avenue and were marked on the 1797 National Library map. One of them was called Monkstown House and first belonged to Alderman Henry Sankey. It was later inhabited by Thomas Pim and appears to have been demolished in the late 1850s to make way for one of the finest Victorian houses of the district, the present Monkstown House. The second eighteenth-century house was once owned by John Sproule, one of the family of architects and builders. It stood to the east and was apparently replaced by Dunedin, which has also disappeared.

Monkstown House, built in 1859 for William Harvey Pim, is now used by the local community

Above: The hall and staircase at Monkstown House, where no expense was spared

Left: A beautiful cast-iron detail from the staircase

Monkstown House The present Monkstown House was built in 1859 and is a local landmark with its tall Italianate tower, built of cut granite. The house was described at the time, in *The Dublin Builder.* 'Perhaps one of the most important domestic edifices recently erected in the suburbs of this City is the mansion now nearly completed for William Harvey Pim, Esquire (one of the well-known fraternity of merchant princes bearing that surname) in the beautiful and rising locality of Monkstown. The house displays on the entrance elevation two projecting wings with large bows, in which are three handsome windows, each sash glazed with plate glass – A spacious flight of granite steps – some of the stones being 16 feet in length – from Ballyknockin quarry, and a landing of similar material – leads to this portico.'

The tower (90 feet high) is built of Dalkey granite ashlar, while the coigns and dressings are of Ballyknockin granite. The large entrance hall is elaborately decorated with Corinthian columns and coffered plasterwork ceilings.

This large, square mansion was the home of the Pim family for some twenty years and during the First World War was used, like many large houses, as a military hospital. In 1969 the house was acquired by a trust for £6000 for the purpose of providing a community centre in Monkstown.

Modern houses were erected on Monkstown Avenue during the 1950s and, later, Windsor Park and Drive were built on the lands of Windsor.

Bloomsbury, later called Boley, occupied about seventeen acres adjoining Abbey Road and included the site where the T. E. K. Dairy would eventually be established. Bloomsbury seems to have been a house of the late Georgian period as it appears on Taylor's map of 1816. The house was a large, square structure

Bloomsbury, later known as Boley, was a late Georgian house which was demolished in the 1940s

A label from a milk churn for the Tel El Kebir Dairy

An elaborate coat of arms on the wall at Rockford, with the motto of the Bruce family: 'Do well, doubt not'

Rockford, rebuilt by William Bruce in the early 1880s as an elaborate, Tudor-style house

which may have been remodelled in Victorian times but was later demolished.

When it was sold in 1944 by Sir Valentine Grace, it was advertised as 'a gentleman's handsome detached residence, containing four reception rooms, including a magnificent drawing room.' There were six cottages on the estate, all of which were let. The lands of Boley were acquired by Dun Laoghaire Corporation in the 1940s and were developed with new local authority houses.

The Tel El Kebir Dairy (T.E.K.) occupied a corner of the Boley lands and the dairy was one of the largest in south Dublin for nearly a century. It was established in the late nineteenth century by a dairyman who had been present at the battle of Tel El Kebir in Egypt. Since 1904 the dairy was managed by the Sutton family, and it gave much employment in the area. Milk was delivered throughout the district by horse and float right up until the 1970s, although electric vans were also used. The T. E. K. siren was a familiar sound in Dun Laoghaire during its latter years. The dairy was eventually taken over by Premier Dairies. The conditions of sale noted that over £1500 had been spent on additions to the house since 1865.

Rockford, an impressive granite-built mansion was, until recently, the home of the Presentation Sisters who ran the girls' school here. Called Rockford Manor, its grounds stretched from Stradbrook Road across to the Dean's Grange Road where the name is still remembered in Rockford Terrace and Rockford Cottage. Much of the lands were beautifully planted with specimen trees, and some of these are still to be seen.

The Tudor-style mansion was erected by Sir William Betham, who was Ulster King of Arms at Dublin Castle, which meant that he was responsible for collecting genealogical records and for issuing family pedigrees. During his lifetime, Betham assembled a highly important collection of rare manuscripts, heraldic documents and genealogical

'NISI DOMINUS FRUSTRA',
the stone-carved motto over
the entrance at Rockford

records, all relating to Irish families, but these were sold in London after his death in 1860. He is commemorated by a stained-glass window in Monkstown parish church.

In 1881, when Rockford was offered for sale, it was described as facing west, commanding from its elevated position a splendid view of the whole of the Dublin and Wicklow mountains: 'The house is approached from the high road by a handsome carriage drive, with an excellent two-storey gate-lodge at entrance. The dwelling house contains three reception rooms, four large and four small bedrooms, w. c., with five servants' bedrooms, kitchen, larder, pantry, dairy, wine cellar, two store and harness rooms.'

A coat of arms appears, carved in stone, on the side of Rockford, along with the motto 'NISI DOMINUS FRUSTRA', which means 'It is in vain without the Lord'.

Rockford was bought by William Bruce, who is believed to have commissioned the architect Thomas Deane to transform the house into an elaborate, Tudor-style mansion. The granite-built mansion is distinguished by its many gables, stone buttresses, diagonal chimney-stacks and mullioned windows. The drawing room has a fine plaster ceiling in the Georgian style, while the billiard room was converted for use as a chapel.

In 1881 the Rockford lands also included Stradbrook House, Brooklawn and Stradbrook Hall.

Stradbrook House was occupied by J. MacCormick, proprietor of a very large coal importing firm in Dublin's D'Olier Street. Coal was the lifeblood of Dublin's large houses, and in the 1880s it accounted for more than a quarter of all imports into Dublin port. Another successful businessman was Richard Allen, a merchant tailor who lived at Brooklawn. Stradbrook Hall was a large house built around 1830 for Richard Pim, a stockbroker.

Also included in the Betham estate were the cottages which were described as Stradbrook village, as well as Myersville, later known as Wynberg, and of course Rockford Manor itself.

Original layout of the Rockford estate at the time of its sale in 1880

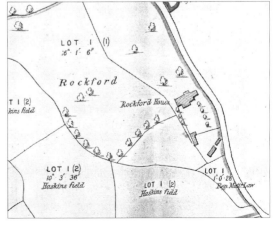

Brooklawn, an elegant villa which originally belonged to the Allen family, who established a Quaker meeting here

The staircase at Somerset, with its carved wooden brackets

Myersville had, until 1789, been the home of Christopher Myers, an architect, who according to Ball, in his *History*, worked on the chapel of Trinity College.

Brooklawn, an attractive villa, was built in 1847, and though now surrounded by houses, is still most impressive. It is a deceptively large house, with a long hallway, which runs the full depth of the house and is lit from above. The façade, with its recessed Ionic columns, massive plate-glass windows and bracketed roof and pediment, creates a striking impression. There was once a large conservatory at the back and a very pretty kitchen garden which ran back to Newtownpark Avenue.

Somerset was one of the earliest houses in the district, and was, in the 1790s, the summer 'set or seat' of Lord Mayo. It stood on Stradbrook Road opposite Rockford Manor, but unfortunately this once attractive Georgian house was allowed to deteriorate and was demolished by the Blackrock Rugby Football Club around 1987. Somerset was bow-ended, and had a particularly fine Georgian doorcase of the type found in Merrion Square. The Georgian stairs were also decorated with carved brackets.

Somerset, a bow-ended Georgian house, which was demolished in 1978

CHAPTER 14

Blackrock

Blackrock lies on the southern shore of Dublin Bay, about four miles from the city centre. Since medieval times a cross in the village has marked the limit of the jurisdiction of the Lord Mayor of Dublin. This cross, once mounted on an elaborate plinth and recently re-located close by, always seemed out of place as there are no known ancient church sites in or near Blackrock. Tradition has it that every year, the Lord Mayor would 'ride the franchises' on horseback, as far as the cross, a ritual by which the city reinforced its claim to various outlying lands.

The landscape of this part of coastal County Dublin probably changed very little between the medieval period and the eighteenth century when much new building began to take place. After the establishment in the early years of the eighteenth century of two large estates behind Blackrock, those of Mount Merrion and Stillorgan, great changes quickly followed. A century later, just after the Act of Union, Blackrock was dotted with many houses, gardens and well-planted small estates.

Detail from Rocque's map, 1757

View *of the* BLACK ROCKS, New Town Bourn, Bray Head, *&c. in* IRELAND.

A somewhat dramatic eighteenth-century engraving of the Blackrock coastline, showing the rugged nature of the shore before the construction of the railway in the 1830s

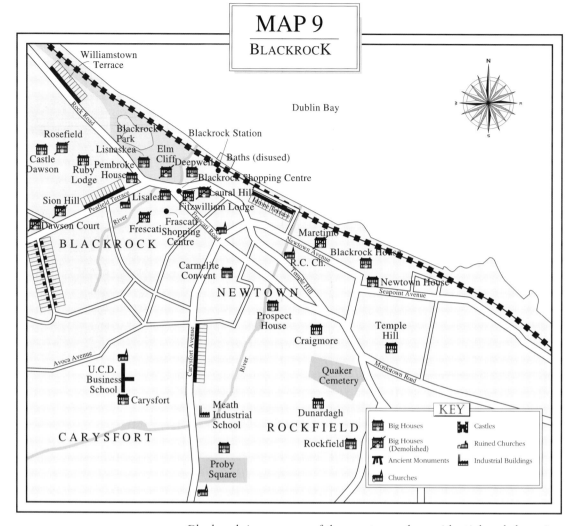

MAP 9
BLACKROCK

Williamstown Terrace

Dublin Bay

Rock Road

Rosefield
Blackrock Park
Blackrock Station
Lismaskea
Castle Dawson
Elm Cliff
Deepwell
Baths (disused)
Ruby Lodge
Pembroke House
Blackrock Shopping Centre
Sion Hill
Peafield Terrace
Lisalea
Laural Hill
Idrone Terrace
Fitzwilliam Lodge
Dawson Court
River
Frescati
Frescati Shopping Centre
Maretimo
Blackrock House
Newtown Avenue
BLACKROCK
Frescati Road
R.C. Ch.
Carmelite Convent
Temple Hill
Newtown House
Seapoint Avenue
NEWTOWN
Prospect House
Temple Hill
Craigmore
Carysfort Avenue
Avoca Avenue
U.C.D. Business School
River
Quaker Cemetery
Monkstown Road
Carysfort
Meath Industrial School
Dunardagh
ROCKFIELD
Rockfield
CARYSFORT
Proby Square

KEY
🏠	Big Houses	🏰	Castles
🏠	Big Houses (Demolished)	⛪	Ruined Churches
⛏	Ancient Monuments	🏭	Industrial Buildings
⛪	Churches		

A Blackrock postmark, 1935

Blackrock is now one of the most popular residential and shopping areas in greater Dublin. Centred on the small town or village, it is very well served with shops, schools and other facilities and, apart from the usual traffic congestion, is within easy reach of the city centre. As the name Blackrock applies to such an extensive area, the district is not an easy one to define. It stretches in several different directions and over-laps with other areas as diverse as Dean's Grange, Stillorgan and Booterstown.

Blackrock is a richly historic district, having been a much-favoured residential area since the middle of the eighteenth century. Now, in the last decades of the twentieth century, it has been subjected to many dra-matic changes. The large religious institutions have almost completely sold out their once substantial interest in Blackrock property, resulting in many new schemes of houses and apartments, while the construction of the Blackrock bypass has transformed the village, for better or worse, bringing in its wake two new shopping centres and many large office buildings.

The new order in Blackrock, where cars dominate the scene, reflects the current trend towards personal mobility at the expense of the old sense of community that might once have existed in the town. The closure of Blackrock baths, and the gradual disappearance of light industries and grocery shops from the town, are all part of the new pattern where supermarkets, with their acres of parking, and property development on every available inch, have taken full control.

However, the people of Blackrock are now vigilant and there are many residents' associations, organisations and clubs, such as the Blackrock Society, all of which take a great interest in the history and current affairs of their area.

Unfortunately, during the last thirty years, the great pressure for building land in and about Blackrock has resulted in the destruction of many interesting and historic buildings, which include Frescati House, Maretimo, Rosefield, Fitzwilliam Lodge, Laurel Hill, Elm Cliff, Dawson Court, Villa Nova, The Elms, Lisalea, Cherbury, Sans Souci, Rockville, Ardagh Park, Ardlui, Carysfort, Talbot Lodge, Hawthorn, Mount Merrion House, Clareville and the eighteenth-century stables at Newtownpark House. This list is by no means complete.

Some, such as South Hill and the old house which is the focal point of the Blackrock market, were saved from demolition through the intervention of An Taisce, even though planning permission had already been given which allowed for their destruction.

Frescati House There is little doubt that the battle over Frescati House, which ran for more than ten years, did much to highlight the problems caused by the lack of legislation for the protection of the nation's architectural heritage.

Frescati was a very large and beautiful eighteenth-century house, and was famous for its association with Lord Edward Fitzgerald. Its interior

The Blackrock cross, with a head carved in relief, which is of medieval origin

The railway is still the dominant feature of the shore at Williamstown and Blackrock

Frescati House, which was the most elegant and historic building in Blackrock

A design from one of the ceilings in Frescati House

was of great importance and contained a pillar-room, a circular room with a coffered ceiling, a book room and an eating parlour with an impressive painted ceiling. The ceiling paintings were the work of a Mr Reilly, a pupil of Joshua Reynolds, who also painted the magnificent long gallery in Castetown House. The plasterwork throughout Frescati was of the finest quality and there were many fine ceilings.

Since the early eighteenth century, Blackrock had been a fashionable resort for the gentry and well-to-do of Dublin, and the house at Frescati began on quite a modest scale as one of these elegant marine villas. It first belonged to Provost Hely-Hutchinson of Trinity College, and was sold by him to the Duchess of Leinster in the 1750s. The Duke and Duchess of Leinster had their principal residence at Carton in County Kildare, and had recently built Leinster House in Dublin as their town house. The Duchess was very fond of Frescati and greatly enlarged the house by adding wings.

Lord Edward Fitzgerald, who was one of her children, became Frescati's most famous resident. His letters reveal his love of nature, of Frescati, and of his wife Pamela and their children. They also show how, through his contact with the French revolutionaries and the other leaders of the United Irishmen, the 1798 rebellion was planned. Fitzgerald was ahead of his time – he was an enthusiast of everything Irish, was dedicated to the idea of an Irish nation, had no interest in whether people were Protestant or Catholic, and loved the whole heritage of his country.

Frescati House occupied a large tract of land behind Blackrock through which a small stream flowed and its grounds extended back as far as the present Sydney Avenue. The demise of Frescati, still then partially occupied, began in 1968 when Dun Laoghaire Corporation zoned the house and lands for commercial development and set about acquiring part of it for a new bypass road. Within two years a company called Frescati Estates had bought the property and succeeded in getting permission to demolish the house, despite recommendations from An Taisce that such an historic building should be preserved. Objections came from various groups, including the Blackrock Traders Association, who could never have imagined that within twenty years there would not be one grocer, butcher or baker left in the main street of their town.

The campaign to save Frescati, which was set up in 1971 and was championed by Marie Walker, ended in 1983 with the demolition of the ruined house by Roches Stores. The beautiful house had by then been reduced to an ugly shell – over the years it had been subjected to partial demolition, repeated vandalism and a large degree of neglect. In 1981, at a court injunction to prevent further demolition from taking place, Mr Justice O'Hanlon concluded: 'It appears to me that the developers have been completely indifferent to, or perhaps have even welcomed, this deterioration in the condition of the building and have done virtually nothing to halt it. I feel the developers have shown a complete disregard for the moral obligations which arose from their course of dealing with the Corporation on the planning application, but I feel the Corporation have also been extremely remiss in exercising whatever statutory powers are open to them to cope with the situation.'

Decorative plasterwork salvaged from the ruins of Frescati House

The sorry tale is perhaps best summarised by a letter which appeared in the *Irish Independent*: 'Softly, well before the winter dawn, the yellow monster lurched towards the grey façade. A mighty arm nudged the building, masonry fell with a rustle and hiss of dust down ivy-clad walls, to thud in moss. Within the hour, Frescati was no more. A long time later, in the dull light of the November morning, early shoppers passed along, wrapped in the world of their own concerns. They noticed nothing. Maybe our small and selfish minds, our furtive Irish ways, our ready response to the turning of a coin, could never grasp the natural nobility and great sincerity of the man [Lord Edward Fitzgerald]!' (Letter from Aidan Kelly, Blackrock, 21 November 1983.)

Eighteenth-century Blackrock

The first reasonably accurate charts of Dublin Bay, which date from the late seventeenth and early eighteenth centuries, all indicate the extent of the shallow waters and sandy shoreline which stretched from Seapoint and Blackrock back to Ringsend. Though this was a great hazard for ships and wrecks were frequent, the clear waters provided ideal bathing opportunities to the inhabitants of Dublin. A small village called Newtown lay between Blackrock and Seapoint and until the eighteenth century was known as Newtown on the Strand.

It is on this strand that a large outcrop of limestone, which is locally called calp, occurs. This stone turns black when wet and it is from this that Blackrock takes its name. The location of the outcrop has been the subject of some debate, but Rocque's map and various other descriptions seem to agree that it was slightly offshore, near the present disused public baths. Rocque shows a bath for women close to the place where he identifies 'The Black Rock from whence the town takes its name'. Further west, but now covered by Blackrock Park, there was a separate bath for men.

An old illustration of a ship-wreck scene in Dublin Bay

Seapoint Manor at Newtown Avenue, which may well have been the site of the Great Room of Castle Byrne, where huge entertainments were held during the eighteenth century

Despite the provision of these separate baths in 1757, an early eighteenth-century pamphleteer described a large bathing party at Blackrock and suggested that both men and women often swam there in the nude: 'Over the spacious strand so many were going both on foot, in coaches, on horseback and cars to bath, and bath we did, and had as many gazers of both sexes as a Mountebank has ... here you might view men and women, thinking it was Adam's days again, turn Indians' (*A Trip to Blackrock, c.* 1700).

Even in the early 1700s, Blackrock had a reputation for its 'houses of entertainment', and one of these, at Newtown Castlebyrne, was a popular rendezvous during the summer months. It was known as the Great Room of Castle Byrne, and may have been attached to an early house which stands behind the present Seapoint Manor, at Meany's corner (the corner of Newtown and Seapoint Avenues where Meany's shop stood until recently). Our eighteenth-century pamphleteer was not impressed with the events which he witnessed at Blackrock, and went on to write about the 'scabby parcel of pigmy tents' which were set up, and described the general throng of dubious individuals who were out to make a quick buck! He gives the impression that morals were loose and that strong drink was freely imbibed.

Many other writers extolled the healthy airs and attractive landscape of Booterstown and Blackrock, and John Ferrar, whose *A View of Ancient and Modern Dublin* was published in 1796, was no exception: 'The situation so near the bay is extremely healthy and pleasant, commanding one of the most expansive sea and land prospects in Europe which is viewed to great advantage from Dalkey. The principal villas at the Rock are the Duchess of Leinster [Frescati], Miss FitzMorris [Lios an Uisce], Mr Secretary Lees [Blackrock House], Lord Clonmel [Temple Hill], and the Lord Chancellor [Lord Clare who was renting Mount Merrion House].'

Mount Merrion and the Fitzwilliam Estate

The family of Fitzwilliam had been landowners in Dublin since the fourteenth century, but in 1666 we find King Charles II reaffirming the grant of the lands of 'Ringsend, Donabrok and mill, Bagattrath, Merryon, Symonscourt, Dundrum and other lands' to Oliver Fitzwilliam, whom he created Earl of Tyrconnel. Thus the Fitzwilliams, who were originally an Irish Catholic family, succeeded in holding onto their property throughout the many difficult periods of Irish history.

This was the origin of the very extensive Fitzwilliam property in south County Dublin, which was eventually to be known as the Pembroke estate. The Fitzwilliam estate, which in 1816 passed into the hands of the Earls of Pembroke, is the largest family-owned estate in County Dublin. Its control over the lands and people living there, in centuries past, was once very great, and though many of the freeholds have now been

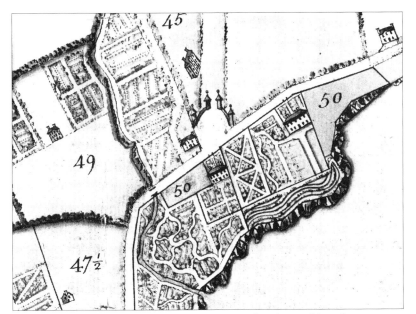

Map by Jonathan Barker, 1762, showing the entrance gates at the bottom of Merrion Avenue, Frescati House (at 49, to the left) and Lios an Uisce (at 50, to the right)

bought out, it seems extraordinary that one family could end up in possession of such a large and important tract of land after so many centuries.

The story of how the Pembroke family, who were only distantly related to the Fitzwilliams, came into possession of the estate is romantic. Some time during the eighteenth century, the son and heir of the sixth Viscount Fitzwilliam fell in love with a local girl, a barmaid whom he proposed to marry. His father objected to such a liaison and so the young Fitzwilliam was sent off on the 'grand tour' to finish his education

A drawing by William Ashford, showing the stables at Mount Merrion

*A thatched, rustic summerhouse,
which once stood in the park at
Mount Merrion*

*A detail from William Ashford's
drawing, showing horse riding
at Mount Merrion*

in Europe where it was hoped he would forget about the girl. He returned some years later to find her settled down and with her own children, and he swore never to marry. The young man did not marry and instead devoted his energies to music and art. He inherited the estates but had no heir, and legend has it that he decided to choose an heir from either the distantly connected Pembrokes or the Fitzwilliams of Yorkshire and County Wicklow, who were not related to him at all.

The Fitzwilliam candidate came to visit, perhaps at Mount Merrion, and, finding his tea too hot, poured it into the saucer and blew on it. This so annoyed his host that he is said to have exclaimed, 'No one who drinks his tea like a washerwoman shall be my heir!', and on his death in 1816 he left his estates to the Earls of Pembroke! Whether the story has any truth in it or not is hard to say, but a cup and saucer of the period is preserved in England to this day by the descendants of the Pembrokes!

In the early 1900s one of the Pembroke descendants married Sir Neville Wilkinson, who in a booklet which he produced about Mount Merrion, where they lived, wrote: 'The memory of the faithless damsel was still fresh after all these years, and the seventh Viscount bequeathed his South Sea stock, his pictures, books and prints to the University of Cambridge, to found the great museum whose pillared portico bears his name.' In this way, part of the vast fortune of the Fitzwilliams went into the building of the famous Fitzwilliam Museum in Cambridge, where two beautiful pictures of the Mount Merrion estate, painted by William Ashford, still hang today.

Sir Neville Wilkinson is perhaps best remembered for having created, in 1907, the now world-famous Titania's Palace, an extraordinary doll's house, filled with miniature furniture and everyday objects of great beauty and outstanding craftsmanship. The doll's house was widely exhibited in the early twentieth century and raised substantial funds for charity. It is now on display in Legoland in Denmark.

The Fitzwilliams abandoned their old castle at Merrion in 1710, when they built a new residence on the hill at Mount Merrion. There they erected a house which took the form of two wings, but it lacked a main block. In a letter to Horace Walpole in 1761, George Montagu writes: 'I was yesterday to see Mount Merrion, a villa of Lord Fitzwilliam. He has built fine stables, and there is to be a fine house.' It is not clear why the house was never built, but it would appear that the family preferred to live in England during the eighteenth century, and Mount Merrion was rented out. In 1789 a newspaper noted that Lord Fitzwilliam had leased Mount Merrion to John Fitzgibbon, the Lord Chancellor, who was preparing the place for a party to celebrate the birthday of the Prince of Wales. Fitzgibbon, who later became the Earl of Clare, was passionately anti-Irish and anti-Catholic and is probably one of the most loathed figures in Irish history.

The cup and saucer which decided the future ownership of the Fitzwilliam estate!

The main courtyard of the house, which consisted of three ranges of buildings, each with a central pediment, has disappeared and only the vacant northern wing survives. It could hardly have been a shortage of funds which prevented the completion of such a mansion, as vast amounts were spent on laying out the pleasure grounds, lawns, woods, avenues and farm at Mount Merrion. At the summit of the hill, a large oval-shaped wood was planted, with trees radiating out like a fan from a central enclosure, whose focus was a circular shell house constructed with columns and a dome.

A painting by William Ashford of the part of Mount Merrion House which survives today. This deserves to be fully restored, as it is one of the most historically significant buildings in the district

There was also a geometrically planted grove of ash trees, and a very organised 'elm wilderness'! The east avenue ran down from the house to

Drawing by Jonathan Barker of
Mount Merrion, 1762, showing
the stables (left) and house
(right) and (below) some of the
adjoining farm buildings

join Mount Merrion Avenue, and on either side were fields, such as the 'Pigeon Park', and another with a fish-pond.

Rocque's map of 1757 indicates that, in the mid-eighteenth century, there were two major estates in the hinterland of Blackrock and these were Mount Merrion belonging to Lord Fitzwilliam, and Stillorgan Park which belonged to the Allen family. The long, formal avenues, which we now know as Mount Merrion Avenue and Cross Avenue, were laid out by Richard Viscount Fitzwilliam as part of a hugely ambitious landscaping plan. The avenues were lined with trees and on one of many estate maps made by Jonathan Barker in 1762 we can see a large, sweeping entrance, at the bottom of Mount Merrion Avenue, with four cut-stone gate piers surmounted by balls. Another set of almost identical gates stood at the junction of Cross Avenue and Booterstown Avenue, marking a separate approach to the private parkland of Mount Merrion. One of these sets of gates was re-erected at the entrance to Willow Park School on the Rock Road.

Bishop Pococke, in his tour of Ireland (1752), describes how at that time Lord Fitzwilliam began to lease some of his fields near Blackrock for building houses. 'We came by Mirian [Mount Merrion] the seat of Lord Fitzwilliam, a most glorious situation commanding a fine view which appears very beautiful from the top of the hill through the Vistoes [vistas] cut in the grove of fir trees. Butterstown is the same kind of situation where Lord Fitzwilliam has let his land in small parcels for building country houses.' Some twenty country houses were then erected in Blackrock and Booterstown, and most were later extended or enlarged. A surprising number of them are still standing today.

Mary Pat O'Malley, in her excellent book about the house Lios an Uisce, lists some of the Blackrock houses: Castle Dawson and Clareville (both once part of Blackrock College) were built by Thomas Keating in about 1752; Sea Mount, which was incorporated into St Helen's, was

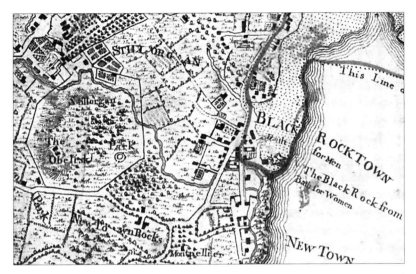

A detail from John Rocque's map, which shows the roughly octagonal layout of the Stillorgan Park demesne (left), which lay between the town of Blackrock and the village of Stillorgan

built in 1754 by Thomas Cooley; and Sans Souci was erected by Lord Lanesborough by 1760. At Newtown, James Dennis built the house which Lord Clonmel would later re-name Temple Hill, and was later again known as Neptune, and not far off Lord Cloncurry built a summer residence for himself, in 1774, which he called Maretimo. Blackrock House was also constructed at this time by John Lees, Secretary to the Post Office.

Lios an Uisce   At the bottom of Mount Merrion Avenue, William Medcalf, a merchant and brewer, leased a number of plots from Fitzwilliam with the intention of building several fine houses. The terms of the lease obliged him to spend at least £300 on each house, and plant 'on the backs or in the breasts of all the ditches oak, ash, walnutt or English elm' (Pembroke estate papers).

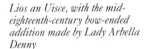

Lios an Uisce, with the mid-eighteenth-century bow-ended addition made by Lady Arbella Denny

Medcalf built the house now known as Lios an Uisce (or Lisnaskee) on high ground overlooking what is now Blackrock Park. Peafield Cliff, as the house was at first called, was a simple building, two storeys high and five windows wide. It was sold in 1754 to Lady Arbella Denny, along with two fields on the south side of the Rock Road, which would later be occupied by Sion Hill Convent and Peafield Terrace at the bottom of Mount Merrion Avenue.

As the existing house had no rooms large enough for entertaining in the Georgian manner, where large gatherings would assemble to dine and dance, Lady Arbella built a large addition with double bow ends, on the seaward side, which contained an elegant staircase and hall, a fine upstairs drawing room, and a large dining room. She also laid out and planted a beautiful garden in the

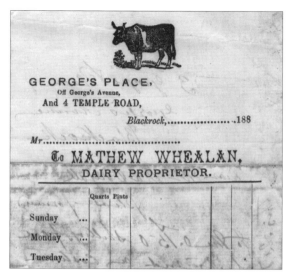

Above: Grehan's, the last butcher's shop in Blackrock, which closed during the 1980s

Above right: A weekly bill from a Blackrock dairy, Whealan's of George's Place, in the 1880s

newly fashionable romantic style of natural landscaping. This meant no formal geometric flower beds or terraces, but, rather, winding paths, shrubberies and features such as grottoes and secluded seats which offered fine views of Dublin Bay. One of her many distinguished visitors was John Wesley, the founder of the Methodist Church, who afterwards commented: 'On Tuesday sixth [April 1783] I waited on Lady Arabella [sic] Denny at the Blackrock, four miles from Dublin. It is one of the pleasantest spots I ever saw, the garden is everything in miniature; on one side is a grove, with serpentine walks; on the other is a little meadow and a greenhouse or study (which she called her Chapel) hanging over the sea; between these is a broad walk, leading down almost to the edge of the water, along which run two narrow walks commanding the quay one above the other.'

Vauxhall In 1757 Medcalf erected another seaside house called Fort Lisle between the Denny residence and Blackrock village. It was built for James Henry and his wife Mary, who was a relation of Lady Arbella. Fort Lisle, which is better known by its later name of Vauxhall, was approached by gates which stood near to the present entrance to Blackrock Park. Here was a scene of much merriment where musical entertainments were provided twice a week by military bands, and, no doubt, large amounts of alcohol were consumed! It was a modest Georgian house of five bays, and was demolished when Blackrock Park was laid out in the 1870s.

An engraving of Vauxhall was published in 1793 as part of an advertisement for a hotel and pleasure grounds which the new owners had just established. The advertisement was written in the lyrical language which even advertising editors of our day would find hard to match! 'This place, which is opened with every advantage of situation, commands a beautiful view of the sea, harbour, and shipping, from the rear. It is built upon a steep decline over the sea ... the ground is planted with taste, and divided into dark walks, with seats and alcoves for the entertainment of the company ... The house is extremely well furnished, much beyond the customary style of our public places.'

The town of Blackrock, as it is described on Rocque's map of 1757, was a small place in the eighteenth century, not much bigger than the villages at Old Dunleary or Dalkey. Few buildings of this period survive in Blackrock, with the exception of the old house which accommodates part of the Blackrock market, and the former Garda station next door, both of which date from about 1750. It is probable that both houses once had a clear view of the sea, and are typical of the type of small residences, like Vauxhall, which were built for renting out during the summer months. The 'market' house has survived with almost all its original features intact, such as the granite doorcase, panelled doors and shutters, and an unusual 'Chinese Chippendale' staircase. The scale is small, and gives us a good idea of what Vauxhall, or Peafield Cliff might have been like when they were first built.

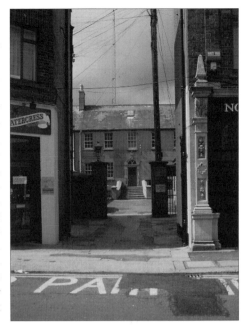

Three Blackrock Houses – Temple Hill, Maretimo and Blackrock House

Temple Hill In the second half of the eighteenth century, a number of larger houses began to appear around Blackrock. Near Newtown, on an elevated site close to Monkstown Road, James Dennis, who was chief Baron of the Exchequer, built Temple Hill, later known as Neptune. A large, square-shaped mansion with a façade of cut-granite ashlar, it was built around 1770, possibly to the designs of a well-known architect called Davis Ducart. The use of granite in the façade is unusual and, despite its being a difficult stone to carve, the house has a handsome Doric doorcase. Inside, the rooms are generously proportioned and elegantly decorated with plasterwork by Patrick Osborne. The principal reception rooms are connected by fine mahogany doors, and in the hall there are two dummy doors made of plaster and painted in perfect imitation of mahogany. This very unusual feature sometimes causes unfamiliar guests to pull the handles off the doors in frustration!

The drawing room, which was used as a chapel by the last occupants, the Sisters of Charity, has an elaborate Venetian window from which there must once have been a wonderful view across the gardens of Temple Hill towards Seapoint. The view is now gone, but in 1990 this writer was privileged to be given the job of painting a mural on the large plaster panel in this room of a contemporary panoramic view of Dublin Bay.

Most large Georgian houses had an ice house, where ice made during the winter would be stored for use during the year. Ice houses, which were built below ground level, were usually circular structures with a domed roof built of brick. The ice house for Temple Hill originally stood

Top: The former Blackrock Garda station, which occupied one of a pair of small Georgian houses, and probably once enjoyed an uninterrupted view of the sea

Above: Mid-eighteenth-century Georgian doorcase, from the house now occupied by the Blackrock market

The cut-stone façade of Temple Hill, built around 1770

An eighteenth-century plasterwork frame enhances a contemporary painting by Peter Pearson, in the drawing room of Temple Hill

on the piece of ground where the small park lies at Temple Crescent.

Following the death of James Dennis, Baron Tracton, in 1782, Temple Hill was bought by John Scott, the Earl of Clonmel. On the staircase, whose ceiling has been lowered, the nineteenth-century picture rails can still be seen. The picture rails are a relic of Victorian taste, when it was the fashion to crowd the walls with paintings, sometimes in rows right up to the ceiling!

The gardens of John Scott, later Lord Clonmel, were famous, but the well-known story of how they were wrecked in 1789 by John Magee, promoter of the *Dublin Evening Post* newspaper, in an extraordinary vengeful scheme, must be related.

Lord Clonmel, as Chief Justice, had tried a case for libel and went out of his way to find in favour of his friend Francis Higgins, otherwise known as the 'Sham squire'! Magee lost the case and was jailed, but on his release he organised a massive 'festival' on fields adjoining Temple Hill, where he invited every publican in Dublin to set up tents and arranged the most chaotic sports and wild events, which were guaranteed to cause mayhem! Everything went according to plan, and over eight thousand people assembled on the day, who, having drunk large quantities of porter which was supplied by Magee, proceeded to chase pigs dressed up in legal costumes through Lord Clonmel's beautiful gardens!

Magee published a poster to advertise the event which would begin with a boat race from the pier at Dun Laoghaire at one minute before eleven o'clock. 'At one o'clock the ball will be kicked on Fiat Hill, the grounds adjoining John Scott, Baron Earlsfort [later Lord Clonmel], premier of the Court of Kings bench ... dinner on the tented field at three o'clock ... at seven o'clock his worship, the Sham, will be coursed over the grounds ...'

Apart from his thwarted gardening activities at Temple Hill, Clonmel also took a lease on Killiney Castle and Hill, where he laid out a deer park.

Delicate plasterwork by Patrick Osborne on the dining-room ceiling at Temple Hill

In the nineteenth century, during the ownership of Robert Gray, most of the Temple Hill lands were built upon. In 1910 Miss Mary Cruess, who had founded a home for unmarried mothers in Dublin, opened St Patrick's Infant Hospital at Temple Hill as a development of this. Some twenty years later, it was taken over by the Sisters of Charity, and many of the several thousand children who were looked after here were eventually adopted.

The elegant, classically-proportioned entrance hall at Temple Hill

Following the closure of St Patrick's, it was bought in 1987 by an Irish American philanthropist, who has made the building available to Trinity College for the use of its business faculty.

Lord Clonmel's neighbours, who lived at Maretimo and Blackrock House, were colourful characters and also lived in buildings of architectural interest.

Maretimo was built as the seaside residence of Nicholas Lawless, Lord Cloncurry, whose main house was at Lyons, County Kildare – his son Valentine Lawless, also Lord Cloncurry, rebuilt Lyons in the early nineteenth century, and was a devoted admirer of all things classical. Maretimo was an attractive redbrick house, built about 1770, which had interior plasterwork by the stuccodore Robert West. The rococo-style ceiling and a room decorated with Chinese-style wallpaper were destroyed when Maretimo was demolished in about 1970. Now all that remains of the house is a block of granite with the name Maretimo carved into it. A block of apartments now occupies the site.

When the Dublin to Kingstown railway was

*The twin towers of the private
railway bridge at Maretimo*

built across the sea frontage of Maretimo, Lord Cloncurry was well compensated. He received the sum of £2000, a very large sum of money at the time, and also got the railway company to construct a small private harbour and a very fine footbridge with twin towers. The bridge, once approached from the garden of Maretimo, is composed of twin granite towers. It is now in a sadly neglected state, with blocked-up and broken windows, and an ugly, corrugated-steel walkway. An early print of the railway shows the bridge as its architect, J. S. Mulvany, had made it, complete with Georgian sash windows and ball-shaped finials. The detailing of the granite blockwork, architraves and cornices is an outstanding example of stone-cutting.

Cloncurry was a keen collector of classical antiquities, and had many consignments of Roman statues, stone urns, marble chimney pieces, mosaic tables and even pillars shipped from Italy to Dublin. Tragically, one of these ships full of antiques was wrecked in 1803 off the Wicklow coast and some of the passengers were drowned. The ship, which was called *The Aid,* had on board at least fifteen packing cases belonging to Cloncurry, which contained stone tables, a font of white marble, a statue of Venus and other treasures. However, Cloncurry's losses of over £1000 worth of antiques were small compared with the goods worth £18,000 which a very wealthy Mr Moore lost in the same shipwreck. To date, the general opinion is that this priceless collection of treasures has not yet been recovered from the bottom of the Irish sea!

Lord Cloncurry was also a generous patron of the arts. He commissioned the eminent sculptor John Hogan to create a piece entitled 'Lord

Cloncurry with Hibernia', one of Hogan's best works, which is now on loan to the National Gallery. Also, the new Catholic church of St John the Baptist in Blackrock was not only built on a site donated by Cloncurry, but he contributed to the building fund, presented a stained-glass window which bears his coat of arms, and later donated a copy of Bartolomé Murillo's 'Madonna and Child' to the parish.

Above left: An ornate, eighteenth-century ceiling in Maretimo, now destroyed

Above right and detail on opposite page: Chinese wallpaper in Maretimo

A detail from the cut-stone entrance gates of Blackrock House

Blackrock House, built in about 1774, one of the few brick-built eighteenth-century houses of the district

Cloncurry was also a nationalist, descended from the Lawless family who had once owned Shankill Castle. At the age of twenty-two, he joined Lord Edward Fitzgerald in the United Irishmen. In 1798 he was suspected of being a traitor and was imprisoned in the Tower of London.

Blackrock House John Lees, who was Cloncurry's neighbour in Blackrock House, couldn't have been more different to Cloncurry and Fitzgerald. Born in Scotland, he came to Ireland as Secretary of the newly established Irish Post Office. He later received other government appointments. John Lees, and later his son Edward, maintained a position of control over the Irish Post Office from 1774 until 1831.

Lees's job was extremely important as the Post Office was responsible for developing the postal service, improving the post roads, and introducing mail coaches and the mail packet-boats which sailed between Ireland and England. At the time, many people were unhappy

The ruin of a summerhouse, once belonging to Blackrock House, which still stands on the shores of Dublin Bay

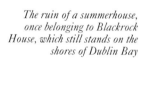

about the way in which the office was run and there were allegations of blatant corruption. Indeed, there was a question mark over Lees's accumulated wealth, which was believed to be vast, considering his relatively modest salary of £432 per annum. (The extraordinary abuse of positions of power, through which great fortunes were amassed, was documented in parliamentary reports of the time, and has been thoroughly researched by Beatrice Bayley Butler, in her article 'John and Edward Lees', published in the *Dublin Historical Record*, 1953.) The Irish Post Office was eventually closed down in 1831, when it became part of the British service.

Blackrock House was built by Lees in about 1774 at Newtown Castle-byrne, on a site overlooking the sea. Among the once numerous Georgian houses of the area, Blackrock House is unusual as it is built of brick. Such brick houses were, like Maretimo, often plastered over in later times, but in this case the original structure, with its russet-stained brickwork, can still be seen. It was also fairly common practice in the late eighteenth century to stain brickwork with a red dye, in order to achieve a uniform colour in the façade. The house, now sub-divided into many flats, has several grand reception rooms and two low wings, one of which once contained a ballroom. A two-storey, redbrick porch, which was added to the front in the late nineteenth century, has an unusual Portland stone doorcase, carved in the Renaissance style.

To the side, there is a large coach house and stableyard and also a gate-lodge. An ice house is said to stand in the garden of one of the modern houses nearby. Another remarkable feature of Blackrock

Newtown House – its elegant Victorian façade encases an older house of late Georgian date

Above: The lavishly-decorated interior of Newtown House, with its carved woodwork and murals

Above right: The redbrick, Victorian gate-lodge of Newtown House, with its striking chimney stack

House is the cut-granite wall which is partly curved and fronts onto Newtown Avenue.

Like Cloncurry, Sir Harcourt Lees, as he had become, the then occupant of Blackrock House, also objected to the building of the railway, but was handsomely compensated with £7500 and had a tunnel built through his property. On the shore, near Cloncurry's private harbour (later known as Vance's Harbour), is the ruin of a small, octagonal summer-house, which once belonged to Blackrock House.

Newtown House Next door to Blackrock House is Newtown House, with its imposing white-painted façade, portico and balustraded roofline. Although there was almost certainly a much earlier house on this site, perhaps even the castle of Newtown, the front part of the present house dates from the early 1800s, which is evidenced by its cut-stone doorcase and Regency-style joinery. This part of the house contains an elegant hall, which has an ornate plasterwork ceiling featuring a giant eagle, military trophies and musical instruments. The early house was remodelled around 1850, possibly by the architect J. S. Mulvany, when a substantial addition was made to the rear, which created a suite of lavishly decorated drawing rooms. Large plate-glass windows with rounded corners were designed to replace the older, Georgian-style windows. The principal reception rooms lie in the later part of the house, and overlook the garden. They are ornamented with richly carved Corinthian pilasters, mirrored doors and a whole series of murals which depict the Swiss and Italian Alpine landscape. There are also paintings of the Rhine, Lugano and Lago Maggiore in northern Italy. Some were damaged by fire, and new paintings of Dublin, Wicklow and Venice, carried out by this writer, were commissioned by the present owners in 1982.

There is also a very quaint gate-lodge, built about 1880, which was once the home of the Apollo art gallery.

Prospect is an attractive three-storey, six-windowed, eighteenth-century residence, with a bow to one end. The Vincentian Order bought it in 1873, and a chapel, with an exceptionally fine plasterwork ceiling, was added in 1887. Around 1978, the order sold the house and 11 acres of land on both sides of the planned Blackrock bypass. Prospect narrowly escaped demolition. A housing estate called Berkeley Court was developed on part of the Vincentian lands and a large office block was erected on Temple Road.

Stillorgan Park House Had Stillorgan Park House remained intact with its magnificent demesne, there is little doubt that it would be one of the largest and most important historic properties in the county. The house, which bore the date 1695, was built for Lord Allen, Earl of Carysfort, and was an imposing structure set in an elaborately planted parkland. Allen was descended from a family of builders and bricklayers who had come to Ireland from Holland around 1630. During the eighteenth century the family became prominent in public life – Sir Joshua Allen became Lord Mayor of Dublin and lived in an attractive house in Tallaght called Allenton.

An estate map of the Stillorgan demesne, showing the house (centre), extensive planting of trees, formal avenues and three rectangular ponds (top, right)

Stillorgan Park obelisk, built in 1727 and situated near the top of Carysfort Avenue, is one of the oldest and finest follies in Ireland

All traces of Stillorgan Park House and its demesne have vanished, leaving only the impressive obelisk and grotto. Most of the former estate has been completely built over although one or two of the very old trees of the demesne may still be standing. The old mansion was, according to Joyce's *The Neighbourhood of Dublin,* demolished in about 1887 and though it is now difficult to pinpoint its exact position, it appears to have stood on the site of the present Stillorgan House.

The Allen estate stretched from Stillorgan village across to Newtown-park Avenue, down to Blackrock, and adjoined the Fitzwilliam property at Mount Merrion Avenue. It covered all of what is now Priory Park, Grove Avenue, Avoca Avenue, Stillorgan Grove and Carysfort Avenue.

The house faced north towards Mount Merrion Avenue, and stood at the head of a long grove of trees planted three rows deep on either side.

It was close to the sides of this grove that a number of villas, such as Talbot Lodge, were built in the late eighteenth century and the name Grove Avenue came into use during the Victorian period when the area was more intensively developed.

A fine painting by Gabriele Ricciardelli and two plans of the demesne show us what Stillorgan Park looked like in the eighteenth century. The house was two storeys over a basement with an attic floor, and was seven windows wide. On the north front it was connected to single-storey wings by curved screen walls, while on the south side the house and wings presented an impressive continuous façade of twenty-one windows! This is the aspect of Stillorgan Park which was depicted in Ricciardelli's painting.

Ball's *A History of the County of Dublin* (1902) says that the original gardens were laid out in the Dutch style 'with straight avenues and alleys, with curious edgings of box, carefully clipped yew trees, knots of flowers, topiary work, and grassy slopes'. By the early eighteenth century the fashion in garden design had changed, and long, formal avenues, with architectural features such as the obelisk, were the order of the day.

The obelisk at Stillorgan, which until recently stood in the grounds of St Augustine's Park at the top of Carysfort Avenue, is the finest of its kind in Ireland. It was built in 1727 as a monument to Lady Allen, who was to have been buried there. In the end, it was probably the burial place of Lord Allen's favourite white horse! The tall, granite obelisk, some 50 feet in height, is perched on a cross-vaulted, rock-covered base, and steep steps enable the visitor to climb up and enter a small, domed chamber at the bottom of the obelisk, and admire the view. It was designed by Edward Lovett Pearce, who spent much time in Rome and would have been inspired by the very similar obelisk in the Piazza Navona which was the work of Giovanni Bernini.

Pearce also designed the extraordinary grotto at Stillorgan, which is now hidden in a private garden, and is consequently not well known. It was originally part of an elaborate formal walk which brought the visitor

Carysfort Lodge, pictured in about 1984; it was one of the first mid-eighteenth-century villas to be erected on the Stillorgan demesne

Linden was run as a convalescent home from 1864 to 1996, and its extensive buildings were formed around the eighteenth-century villa, to the left above

The entrance hall in Linden, photographed in 1985

through a line of seven large domed underground chambers, constructed of brick. Today, the whole structure is evocative of some ancient Roman ruin, and indeed this may have been the original intention. The various niches and circular openings in the brickwork were almost certainly intended to be filled with statues or busts.

The entire demesne was carefully surveyed in the mid-eighteenth century and depicted on a coloured map, which is now in the National Library. It shows the position of the obelisk, the formal avenues and various carriage drives, and of the three rectangular fish ponds which were located close to the present St John of God Hospital in Stillorgan.

The fact that a golf course briefly existed on part of these lands may seem extraordinary to recent residents of Stillorgan Grove and Stillorgan Park. In 1908 Stillorgan Park Golf Club was established here, but only lasted nine years. It was the club which filled in the artificial lakes or fish ponds which bordered Stillorgan Grove.

Obelisk Park, a large rambling house which has lately been converted into apartments, was built around 1790 for Richard Sinclair. Quaker businessmen James and Henry Perry purchased Obelisk Park in 1829. The Perrys enlarged the house as their two families were in occupation of different halves of it. The Perry brothers ran a successful ironworks at Ringsend, and also dealt in hinges, locks and large items such as boilers. They had a lot of property and many financial interests, including being one of the first investors in coal mines in the Ruhr Valley in Germany. James Perry was also a board member of the Dublin and Kingstown Railway Company.

Though they were wealthy, they did not forget their

fellow countrymen, and during the catastrophic famine of 1847 James Perry and other Quakers, such as the Bewley and Pim families, established the 'Central Famine Relief Committee of the Society of Friends in Ireland' and gave much practical help to those in need.

Talbot Lodge, which began as a small eighteenth-century villa, was then doubled in size, but was demolished in 1989

The original, square, Georgian house lies behind the elaborate main entrance, with its arched porch. This porch was one of many additions made in the 1890s by the architect, Thomas Drew, for Marcus Goodbody, whose monogram appears in the pediment of the porch. Goodbody also built the now-derelict, attractive gate-lodge in 1896, which cost the princely sum of £165. Goodbody was also a Quaker and an in-law of the Perry brothers.

The Goodbody family lived at Obelisk Park until 1923 when it was sold to the brothers of the Order of St John of God. Since then it served as a centre for the care and training of the mentally handicapped. Now the house has been sold for conversion into apartments and much of the original land has been built over.

Georgian Developments – Grove Avenue

As we have already seen, many new houses were built on the Fitzwilliam estate during the mid-eighteenth century. The Allen estate also sold off several sites at this time and about four villas were erected on the Blackrock side of the formal grove of trees which eventually gave rise to the name Stillorgan Grove. One of these villas was called Carysfort Lodge, a single-storey Georgian house, with a half-octagonal bow of two storeys projecting from the front. A large addition was made to the back of the house in the early nineteenth century. Carysfort Lodge was demolished in 1985.

Linden The oldest part of Linden, which in recent times was best known as a convalescent home, stood to the left of the main building, and was another Georgian villa. Unfortunately the house, which was elegantly fronted by a pair of half-octagonal bows, was demolished,

The attractive, bow-ended Carysfort Park, built around 1803 – now owned by UCD

A bookplate from Carysfort Park

along with a square tower of Victorian date. The name Linden derived from the grove of lime trees, sometimes known as linden trees, which is clearly shown on the eighteenth-century estate map. In 1864, the Sisters of Charity, who ran St Vincent's Hospital in St Stephen's Green, purchased Linden in order to establish a convalescent home for patients. The acquisition, which cost £2000, was made possible through the generosity of Francis Coppinger of Monkstown Castle. The following extract from the life of Mother Mary Aikenhead, founder of the Sisters of Charity, paints a peaceful picture of the place: 'Adjoining the Linden fields is a place called "the Grove" which is rented by the Sisters of Charity, and affords patients shady walks and resting places, where, "*unter den Linden*", they may spend the day without fatigue or danger. "The Grove" originally formed a part of the grand approach to the seat of the Earls of Carysfort, the whole avenue having been planted in days gone by, with six long lines of lime trees.'

Talbot Lodge A third house of contemporary date was Talbot Lodge, which also stood alongside the grove of lime trees and was eventually acquired by the Sisters of Charity. Talbot Lodge also had a Georgian bow front, but its original form was somewhat altered when the house was enlarged in Victorian times. In 1989, Talbot Lodge, once part of the Linden convalescent home, was sold by the nuns to a property developer, who promptly demolished it. The four-acre site was developed with houses.

A map dated 1793 of the Stillorgan Park estate shows another house, very similar to those already described, which was let to William Cope by its builder and owner, a Mr N. Le Favre, who it seems had developed other sites here.

Carysfort

Carysfort Park, now owned by University College Dublin, was originally built in the north-east part of the old Stillorgan demesne, and was laid out to take advantage of the existing parkland. The house was built in 1803 by Sir John Proby, and leased to Judge William Saurin, a distinguished legal figure. Proby, who became the first Baron of Carysfort, had inherited the Stillorgan estate in 1742 from his father-in-law, Joshua Allen.

Carysfort is a large, three-storey-over-basement house with a striking portico which was added later and rather unusually constructed with cast-iron columns. The elegant entrance hall, with its double niches, plasterwork eagles and swags, leads to the drawing room with its large curved bow. The drawing room is also decorated with delicate plasterwork and, rather unusually, has gently curved niches on either side of the fireplace. The room commands an excellent view across the terraced gardens to a lake which has recently been made the focus of a small park. The old house was, until the recent development, completely surrounded by open fields, but it must be said that the new apartment blocks and houses which were built here sit well in the parkland, and are well spaced out.

The estate was purchased in 1891 by the Sisters of Mercy, who added the large range of redbrick buildings four years later. For a short time they ran an 'industrial school for children' but in 1903 a teacher-training college for women was established here. It was in this college that President Éamon De Valera was professor of mathematics from 1906 until 1916.

The main college building is an impressive redbrick structure, which contained many classrooms, all connected by long, tiled corridors which the nuns kept polished every day. The chapel, with its granite belfry and windows, is an impressive building whose altar was sculpted by the father of Pádraig Pearse.

The other old buildings of Carysfort College included the novitiate, a hall of residence and the old farm buildings. Among the newer structures were the College of Education, a restaurant, a classroom block and a sports hall.

In 1989 the Sisters of Mercy decided to put their convent and teacher-training college at Carysfort on the market, and though some of the very extensive lands were built on, the main buildings were bought by UCD for £8 million and a business school was established there.

The ornate ironwork gateway to the walled garden at Carysfort Park

The elegant Newtownpark House, probably built in the 1790s

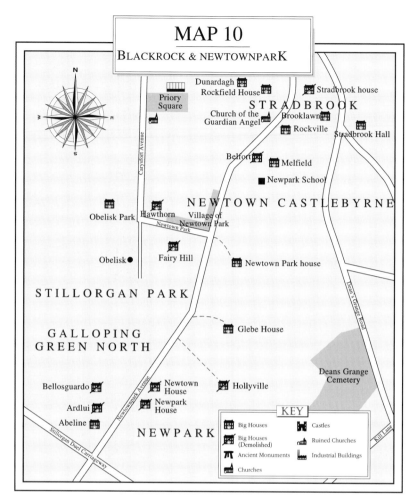

MAP 10

Bᴌᴀᴄᴋʀᴏᴄᴋ & ɴᴇᴡᴛᴏᴡɴᴘᴀʀᴋ

Dunardagh
Rockfield House
Stradbrook house
Priory Square
S T R A D B R O O K
Church of the Guardian Angel
Brooklawn
Rockville
Stradbrook Hall
Belfort
Melfield
Newpark School
N E W T O W N   C A S T L E B Y R N E
Obelisk Park
Hawthorn
Village of Newtown Park
Newtown Park
Obelisk
Fairy Hill
Newtown Park house
S T I L L O R G A N   P A R K
Glebe House
G A L L O P I N G
G R E E N   N O R T H
Deans Grange Cemetery
Bellosguardo
Newtown House
Hollyville
Ardlui
Newpark House
Abeline
N E W P A R K

KEY

Big Houses		Castles	
Big Houses (Demolished)		Ruined Churches	
Ancient Monuments		Industrial Buildings	
Churches			

Detail of one of the eighteenth-century sidelights, which was vandalised before the house was converted to use as a nursing home

Newtownpark Avenue

Newtownpark Avenue descends in a northerly direction from White's Cross on the Stillorgan Road, and runs downhill for about a mile and a quarter, curving a little to meet Stradbrook Road. The avenue, which was already in existence by 1757 when Rocque's map of County Dublin was published, has been fully developed with houses during the last fifty years. A number of important houses were built on it during the eighteenth century.

Rocque's map also shows very clearly the extent of the enclosed grounds of the Stillorgan deer park, which was almost octagonal in shape and ran up to Newtownpark Avenue, where a village later evolved.

Though several interesting houses such as Stradbrook, Rockville, Ardlui and Bellosguardo have disappeared, three houses of the eighteenth century remain on Newtownpark Avenue. They are Rockfield (now Cluain Muire), Melfield (now part of Newpark School) and Newtownpark House.

Newtownpark House is, without question, the most interesting of these remaining houses, although its fine interior has been considerably altered by its recent conversion into a nursing home as many of the larger rooms have been sub-divided into small bedsits.

However, the attractive sequence of oval entrance halls and one small sitting room remain unspoilt. Like so many old houses, Newtownpark was enlarged in the nineteenth century. The front section which contains the oval halls is the older part of the structure, while the large, bow-ended, five-bay block was probably added to the garden front around 1820. The plan and layout of the original house is very similar to that of Belfield, in UCD. In the nineteenth century the house was occupied by a banker named Samuel Close.

Newtownpark was carefully restored and beautifully decorated with eighteenth-century paintings and furniture by Senator E. A. Maguire, owner of Brown Thomas's, whose family lived there from 1946 until 1984. The present stone portico was also added by him.

In the period just before the nursing home was established, the house was left empty and was vandalised, the beautiful fanlight and many of the original windows being destroyed. Unfortunately, the original timber sash windows were not reinstated and the plastic replicas do not do justice to such a fine building.

Top: Melfield, the eighteenth-century residence of Joseph Atkinson

Above: The demolition of Strad-brook House, about 1985

An even greater loss was the demolition of the handsome brick stable buildings and cobbled yard. The old coachhouse was ornamented with a white-painted domed cupola, which now sits on the roof of a new residential building on the same site.

Below Newtownpark House is Marian Park, a development of local authority houses which was completed in 1954, the Marian year. This land had previously belonged to Jack Acres, who up until the early 1970s had managed to carry on farming in Blackrock.

Melfield, now in the grounds of Newpark School, is a much-altered Georgian house which was described by John Ferrar in 1796 as 'the villa of Joseph Atkinson' who wrote *The Comedy of Mutual Deception* and the comic opera *The Match for the Widow*. Atkinson had served in the British army in the West Indies, Africa and America. On his retirement in 1792 he settled in Melfield and was appointed High Sheriff of County Dublin.

A fragment of a screen wall suggests that Melfield probably had two curving wings, on either side of the house. The interior has been heavily remodelled at various times and little of the original fabric survives. This house was for many years occupied by the Avoca and Kingstown Junior School.

A pair of pineapple-topped gates at Rockfield which are identical to a pair that once stood at Rochestown House

Belfort Nearby is Belfort, a solid Victorian house of 1870, with redbrick bay windows. Avoca School, which was founded in 1891, moved from its original premises in Numbers 2 and 4 Sydney Avenue, off Carysfort Avenue, to Belfort in 1936. At this time, the stated aim of the school was 'To provide a sound education and also to give a cultured and tolerant outlook on life. An appreciation of such subjects as painting, music and architecture is encouraged.'

In 1968, Kingstown Grammar School and Avoca School were amalgamated and the combined schools settled into the buildings at Newtownpark Avenue. It was this establishment which four years later, under the name of Newpark, would become one of the first comprehensive schools in Ireland. The functional and rather sprawling new school building was erected on the once lovely gardens in front of Belfort. Also, during the excavation of the old grass playing fields to create the all-weather pitches, a Bronze Age ornament was discovered.

Rockville The two remaining houses which lay at the bottom of Newtownpark Avenue were Rockville and Stradbrook House, both of which have been demolished. The gardens and tropical orchard houses of Rockville were famous in horticultural circles during the nineteenth century, when Thomas Bewley lived there. The largest was 60 feet long and 22 feet high and the interior was constructed to resemble a romantic, crumbling ruin. *The Dublin Builder* described it in 1861: 'The subdued light, the agreeable and soothing temperature, and an atmosphere peculiarly quiet and still, produce a calm quite in keeping with the idea.'

The ballustraded, terraced garden at Dunardagh, laid out in the 1860s

While the accuracy of Rocque's map is not always certain, it would appear that Stradbrook House and a third house called Rockfield were already in existence by the middle of the eighteenth century. Rockfield, now owned by the Eastern Health Board and called Cluain Muire, is used as a day centre, giving help to families since 1970.

Rockfield began as a three-storey-over-basement, five-bay house. But it was somewhat institutionalised when it became a nursing home, and now retains little of its original internal features. It was once the summer retreat of Lord Townsend, the Lord Lieutenant, and Ball's *History* states that there was elaborate plasterwork on the staircase, and a display of military trophies which recorded Townsend's involvement in the capture of Quebec in Canada. A small fragment of Rococo plasterwork still ornaments the landing arch. Despite various additions, the core of the house remains, and it is possible to identify the Georgian features such as the double-bowed garden front and a Venetian window over the main entrance.

One of the old entrance gates to Rockfield, though no longer in use, may be seen at Temple Hill, where a pair of granite gate piers, surmounted by pineapples, and a fine gate-lodge still stand. The gate piers may well have come from Rochestown House, at the time of its demolition. The heavy iron gates were operated by means of a capstan, which was connected to the gate by chains. A second entrance, the one currently used on Newtownpark Avenue, is also most unusual, each of the granite piers having a Gothic pinnacle and a Gothic niche.

The garden frontage of Dunardagh, a large Italianate house erected in the 1860s for George Orr Wilson

Craigmore, with its bow ends and cut-stone porch, is a handsome Victorian house

Part of the extensive grounds of Rockfield were acquired by the Society of Friends during the nineteenth century, to establish a Quaker cemetery at Temple Hill. The graveyard, whose appearance is unusual because every memorial is of the same size and bears no ornament of any kind, is entered from Temple Hill.

Dunardagh Behind Rockfield a large house called Dunardagh was erected around 1860 in the extravagant Italianate style. It is a substantial, square house, with a multiplicity of arched and wide Venetian windows, all of which are filled with plate glass. Inside, the spaces are generous, with a spacious hall and large reception rooms with bay windows which overlook the terraced garden. Such terraces, with their long balustrades, were fashionable in the Victorian period. Formal gardens with rose beds and borders, gravel paths, statuary and urns, all interspersed with lawns,

Above: A decorative gesso plaque from Ardlui

Right: This advertisement for the sale of Ardlui in the 1940s gives some idea of the enormous size of the house

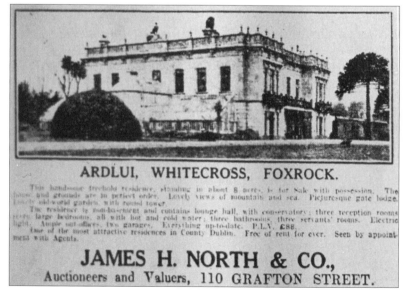

ARDLUI, WHITECROSS, FOXROCK.

This handsome freehold residence, standing in about 8 acres, is for Sale with possession. The house and grounds are in perfect order. Lovely views of mountain and sea. Picturesque gate lodge. Lovely old-world garden, with round tower.

The residence is semi-basement and contains lounge hall, with conservatory; three reception rooms, large bedrooms, all with hot and cold water; three bathrooms, three servants' rooms. Electric light. Ample out-offices, two garages. Everything up-to-date. P.L.V. £88.

One of the most attractive residences in County Dublin. Free of rent for ever. Seen by appointment with Agents.

JAMES H. NORTH & CO.,
Auctioneers and Valuers, 110 GRAFTON STREET.

were tended by a small army of gardeners.

Dunardagh once shared a magnificent pair of granite entrance gates situated on Temple Hill, but these were since re-located on the Blackrock bypass. The gate piers bear a heraldic crest, and are outstanding examples of the stonemason's craft. The house was built for a Belfast merchant named Orr Wilson; later, during the First World War period, it was owned by Lady Arnott and noted for its garden parties held in aid of wounded soldiers. St Catherine's Seminary was founded at Dunardagh in 1939, and is run by the Daughters of Charity.

Craigmore, though contemporary with Dunardagh, was designed in a more restrained Georgian style, with bow ends and a most attractive stone porch. It was built to the designs of John McCurdy, probably in the 1850s, for a wealthy Quaker tea merchant named Jonathan Hogg. It consists of two storeys over a basement and has a magnificent granite cornice at roof level. Craigmore is now called St Teresa's, and is a centre for mentally handicapped people.

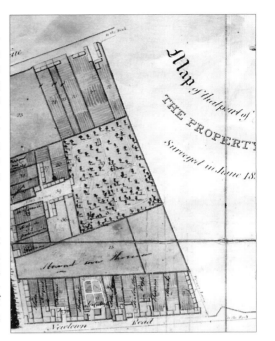

Map of 1833 showing the village of Newtown Park with its many cottages

Ardlui Of the many impressive Victorian houses built in this area, mention must be made of Ardlui, a large, two-storey, Italianate house, which had a very large curvilinear conservatory running the full length of its south front. Handsome ironwork embellished both the conservatory and the parapet of the house itself. All that remains today of Ardlui is a circular tower which stands in a small garden in Ardlui Park. The house was demolished about 1955. This fine Victorian house was featured in the fashion magazine *Irish Life* in 1913, when the gardens were the subject of particular comment. Ardlui, once called Maesgwyllyd, was once the home of William Perry, a brewer with premises at Harold's Cross, who had grown up in nearby Obelisk Park.

Bellosguardo Not far off stood Bellosguardo, more recently called Ardagh Park, which was another elegant residence of nineteenth-century date. Bellosguardo, which in Italian means 'beautiful view', began as a plain house but was later enlarged in the Italianate manner by the addition of a two-storey bow and a water tower with arched windows. The house stood on about 38 acres, all of which were developed after its demolition in the early 1950s.

In 1833 a map was made of the property of James Price, whose property adjoined that of Bellosguardo. Price's land consisted of 27 acres of the former Stillorgan Park, and lay between Carysfort Avenue and Newtownpark Avenue. His land had been heavily developed since the late eighteenth century and included two Georgian houses above the line of Cross Avenue, now called Newtown Park, and over eighty cottages and other dwellings which lay below, on the Blackrock side. There are many cottages surviving in this area today, and some may date from the early 1800s. A number of other dwellings survive in their original form, especially the cottages of Anna Ville and Orchard Lane, previously known as

The entrance to Hawthorn, ornamented by a pair of Victorian cast-iron lamps

Prince Edward Terrace, Carysfort Avenue

The Little Avenue. Below the modern thatched pub known as The Playwright, there was a continuous row of small houses which constituted the village of Newtownpark, but most of these have disappeared, including the cottages of Price's Lane.

Between the two larger houses above Cross Avenue lay Fairy Hill, another Georgian house built on the Carysfort estate, now long vanished and recorded only in the name of the house development which replaced it.

Hawthorn A Victorian house called Hawthorn was built around 1850 on a field occupying a corner site at Carysfort Avenue. It was demolished in 1987 and its grounds are now completely built over. It was a large house, whose most interesting feature was a curved projecting porch with a flight of granite steps and a pair of old gas lamps. The lamps, now erected at the entrance to the new houses, were supported by dolphins, and are identical to those on Grattan Bridge in the centre of Dublin.

Plans for Proby Square, dating from about 1840, which were never completed

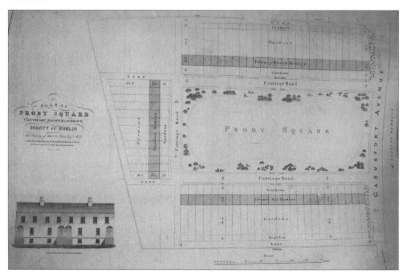

Waltram Terrace, composed of delightful, early-Victorian one- and two-storey villas

Victorian Squares and Terraces

During the eighteenth and early nineteenth centuries, most of the development of Blackrock had taken the form of detached houses of varying sizes. The first terraces to be built in the area were erected around 1800 at Montpelier Parade and at the bottom of Mount Merrion Avenue. By 1840 the lower part of Carysfort Avenue had been fully developed with houses, some of them terraced, as in the case of Prince Edward Terrace. The houses, which are rendered, all have attractive doorcases and fanlights, and are typical of the 1830s. An interesting feature here is the curved wall and railings which may be seen opposite the main entrance to Carysfort, and may have been created to facilitate the turning of horses and carriages.

Idrone Terrace, standing above the railway and the sea

Angelsea Avenue and Sydney Avenue were also laid out in about 1830 with terraced houses of a late-Georgian type. A number of detached houses were also built here, such as Herbert Lodge, built in 1831 for Michael Mortimer, and Eagle Lodge which was built in 1835 for Neville McGowan. As the names Sydney and Herbert suggest, all of these houses were built on lands which belonged to what had been the Fitzwilliam estate, which by then had become the Pembroke estate – Sydney Herbert was Earl of Pembroke in the early nineteenth century.

A proposal to build a square off Carysfort Avenue was first mooted in about 1840. The planned three-sided square would be called Proby Square, and would consist of sixty-six terraced houses. This plan, of which a published copy exists in the National Library, was drawn up by William Longfield, a map-maker and surveyor, for a Dr Robert Graves. An elevation of one of the houses shows a restrained, late-Georgian type of dwelling, brick-built and very typical of much of suburban Dublin. For some reason the square did not materialise, and by 1843 only four tall houses had been built on the north side. Rather curiously, the short cul-de-sac is still called Proby Square.

Later, in 1868, the Church of All Saints, with its vicarage, was erected on the corner of the south side. The church, which was built by the noted contractors, Beckett, cost £3044. The stone-built rectory was added in 1873.

The first Wesleyan church on George's Avenue, Blackrock

Close by are the stone buildings of the Meath Protestant Industrial School for Boys, which was established in 1875 to house homeless children and those convicted of minor criminal offences. It was set up under the patronage of the Earl of Meath, and at its height accommodated 150 boys aged between five and fifteen.

One of the most attractive streets which was laid out at this time was Waltram Terrace, situated off Mount Merrion Avenue. In about 1810 a detached house called Beaumont was built by Sir Henry Cavendish, and it stands at the head of Waltram Terrace. By 1834 Arthur Ormsby, a lawyer for the Church of Ireland, had acquired the lands and set about building the thirty-seven semi-detached villas which he mostly let out to suitable tenants. By 1900 many of the houses were in poor condition, and new leases were given with very onerous conditions for the repair and rebuilding of some of the properties. In Victorian times Waltram Terrace was – and perhaps still is today – considered to be one of the very few totally respectable addresses in Dublin! At one time a private school was run here by the Misses Lett, of Enniscorthy. One was tall and thin, the other short and fat, and they were known locally as 'Pomp and

Circumstance'. By 1911 the school had become the Ladies' Collegiate School and was located on Idrone Terrace.

Apart from Prince Edward Terrace, Idrone Terrace is Blackrock's most complete formal terrace of houses. It stands above the railway, close to the town, overlooking Dublin Bay. Dr Henry Kavanagh, the owner of Kavanagh's apothecaries in Kingstown, acquired the land and twenty-seven houses were then built over a twenty-year period, beginning in the late 1840s. One of the characteristic features of the houses is the square doorcase with its elaborate timber brackets. The name of the terrace, 'Idrone Sur Mer', is emblazoned in Roman cement above the more prominent central houses of the terrace. It is thought that Kavanagh brought the name Idrone from his family home in County Carlow. Such names, with overtones of French or Italian health resorts, were already popular, and close by we find Qui Si Sano and Montebello. Others, such as Frescati and Montpelier, have already been mentioned.

The houses of Idrone Terrace were not generally equipped with stables, which perhaps were unnecessary as they were very convenient to the railway.

An engraving, c. 1840, of the railway at Blackrock, showing how it was constructed across the strand below the rocky shore

Entrance to the new Methodist church

The Town

The town of Blackrock, as Rocque showed it in the middle of the eighteenth century, was little more than a jumble of small houses, shops and taverns. The best-known pub in Blackrock in 1764 was the Sign of the Ship while another, which had survived until recently in the town, was the Three Tun Tavern.

There does not seem to have been any dramatic growth until the first decades of the nineteenth century. J. Archer, in his *Statistical Tour of County Dublin* (1801), commented that Blackrock was 'a large, handsome and pleasant town'. The following year another publication, which was entitled *Observations on Mr Archer's Statistical Survey,* commented quite differently, and probably more accurately: 'The Black Rock is capable and worthy of great improvements: the leading one seems to be an increase of the supply of fresh water … the next improvement that presents itself, would be paving the streets, and preventing the inhabitants from throwing dirt on the road or footpath.'

By 1843 Blackrock had a well-developed town structure, with many buildings on George's Place, Carysfort Avenue, Sweetman's Avenue and Temple Road, then called the Back Road. The main street, which was called Rock Street, was built up on the south side only, giving those premises a clear view of the sea. Similarly, the houses on Newtown Avenue, near the present Carraig Books, had an uninterrupted view of the sea. One of these, with its fine Georgian bow front, was clearly designed to take advantage of the view, which was first blocked with the building of Idrone Terrace in the 1850s, and later by the Methodist church in 1861, the town hall in 1866 and finally by the library and technical schools in 1905.

Other Georgian houses which enjoyed a full sea view until quite recently were Idrone House, Montebello and Qui Si Sano. These houses, although terraced, were completely different from one another, although two of them have bow-fronted rooms which overlooked long gardens and the sea.

John D'Alton, writing in 1838, described Blackrock as 'One of the most ruinous suburbs of the Metropolis, a collection of deserted lodging-houses and bathing villas', which suggests that many of the larger houses were vacant and that the new railway had not yet benefited the town. He went on: 'it has a neat Methodist church without a grave yard, and a small Roman Catholic chapel adjoining a nunnery of the order of St Clare'. The early Methodist church was located in George's Avenue. The Catholic church, which was attached to the order of St Clare in Sweetman's Avenue, was built shortly after the Carmelite nuns acquired an old house called Elmfield in 1823 – Elmfield was another seaside villa which had been erected during the middle of the eighteenth century. The Carmelites were an enclosed order, who helped the deprived population of the area by running a 'poor school' at Sweetman's Avenue. The nuns were devoted to prayer and meditation, and in about 1900 a fine stone-built chapel, designed by H. W. Byrne, replaced the earlier church. The chapel, entered by a gate on Sweetman's

A mocked-up polling card used in campaigning for Blackrock Urban District Council

Avenue, was used by the Catholics of Blackrock until the parish church of St John the Baptist was erected in 1845. The nuns attended chapel every day, as often as seven times a day, starting with mass at 7.30 in the morning.

Lewis reported in 1839 that the railway company had provided baths on the side of the railway embankment, close to the site of the present baths. In 1887 these baths were completely rebuilt in concrete, with the provision of a large 'gentlemen's bath' and a slightly smaller 'ladies' bath'. The Blackrock baths were purchased by the Urban District Council in 1928 for £2000 and were made ready for the Tailteann Games, a major national sporting event. The baths, which contained a 50-metre pool and could accommodate up to a thousand spectators, became very well known for swimming galas up to the 1960s, when indoor, heated pools began to make their appearance. Blackrock baths were closed down by Dun Laoghaire Corporation in the 1980s and in 1992 parts of it were dismantled because they

The Carnegie Library, with its ornate Edwardian façade

were becoming dangerous due to lack of maintenance. These baths, along with Dun Laoghaire baths, are now closed and their future is still uncertain. There can be no doubt that with substantial financial resources and some imagination, both could again become great assets to the area. At the very least they deserve to be reopened without frills or gimmicks, as sea-water baths.

The Blackrock Town Commissioners came into existence in 1863, and lost no time in setting about building a town hall. The building, with its elaborately decorated cement façade, was completed by 1866 and extended some fifteen years later. The Blackrock Urban District Council, as the body soon became, was one of the first local authorities in Ireland to elect a woman, Lady Margaret Dockrell, as its 'chairman', in 1926.

The three cement-rendered, highly decorated buildings, of which the town hall is a part, are in need of some repairs, as some of the decorative detail has fallen off. The entrance hall of the library is decorated with a mosaic which features an old cross, the symbol of the Blackrock Urban District Council, and the date 1889, and it reminds us of the library's generous benefactor, Andrew Carnegie, with the inscription 'Carnegie Library'.

Blackrock fire station, erected by the Urban District Council

Nearby stands a small but very interesting building which bears more resemblance to a boathouse than anything else, but was in fact the Blackrock fire station. It is now used as a store by the Order of Malta and Dun Laoghaire Corporation.

In the 1890s Blackrock had a postal telegraph service at its post office in the main street. The present post office was built in 1909 to the designs of Howard Pentland, and is a rather striking building with its strong horizontal lines of granite.

At this time, in the late 1890s, trams ran to and from Dublin every fifteen minutes. The tram depot and sheds were located on Newtown Avenue on the site of the Europa Garage.

The Ulster bank in Blackrock's main street was built in 1892 to the designs of W. M. Mitchell.

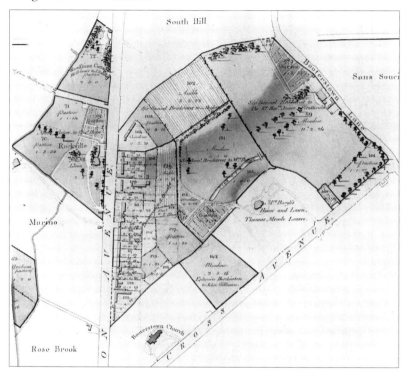

Map of the Mount Merrion Avenue area c.1830, showing the Elms (left), Chesterfield on Cross Avenue and Cherbury on Booterstown Avenue

The Elms, a Victorian residence on Merrion Avenue set in spacious grounds; it was demolished in 1982

As already mentioned, the building of the Blackrock bypass involved the demolition of several old buildings and, in 1973, a judge and a barrister sold their respective houses, Frescati Lodge and Fitzwilliam Lodge, to a property developer for what was then the very large sum of £200,000 for both. The old houses, which were plain in character and were of early nineteenth-century date, had very large gardens. It was the combined sites of these houses, and that of Laurel Hill, which eventually became the Blackrock shopping centre, with Superquinn as its 'anchor tenant'.

Another Blackrock House, which has somehow survived intact, is Deepwell, which stands overlooking Blackrock baths and Merrion Strand. Deepwell is a large, square house with bay windows and a very grand garden staircase. In 1986, Dun Laoghaire Corporation rezoned the lands of Deepwell for office development, but so far the handsome Victorian house has remained in residential use, and is a landmark easily viewed from the DART trains.

Mount Merrion Avenue

Mount Merrion Avenue, as we have already seen, was once a stately approach to the Fitzwilliam residence at Mount Merrion. The first intrusion into this eighteenth-century landscape occurred in about 1800, with the building of seven very plain, double-fronted houses at Pembroke Terrace. This early development at the bottom of Mount Merrion Avenue was quickly followed by the building of Peafield Terrace, almost opposite. Later, other terraces, single houses and cottages were built along the length of the avenue, giving it the great variety of house-type and period which it has today. St Andrew's Presbyterian Church was erected in 1886 and is octagonal in plan, which recalls the layout of the Early Christian Byzantine churches. The development of Sion Hill School and Convent took place in the 1830s, and took its name from the house which once stood on the site. The convent, with its imposing, three-storey façade, consisted of a central block with pedimented wings on either side. The main feature of these wings was a large, arched

South Hill
Top: Wooden finial from the conservatory
Above: Cast-iron gas lamp
Below: South Hill, a late-Georgian house to which several additions were later made

*Right: Mount Merrion,
a large, nineteenth-century house
now replaced by the Stillorgan
Park Hotel*

*Below: The finely-chiselled stone
portico*

recess, containing a window and statues. This building was demolished in 1993, but an attractive Gothic-style oratory, dedicated to the Sacred Heart of Jesus and erected in 1872, may still be seen.

The Elms, a large, detached house which was earlier known as Rockville (not to be confused with the Rockville already discussed), was built in about 1830 for John Vance, and later belonged to the Hope family. It was sold in 1973 for £412,000, a huge sum at that time. The old house, which was two-storeyed and had an attractive bow, was demolished in 1982 and the six-acre site was later developed with apartments. Another house which almost adjoined The Elms was Villa Nova, which vanished from Mount Merrion Avenue during the 1970s and was a single-storey villa with a decidedly colonial aspect.

South Hill is an eighteenth-century house which was considerably altered and enlarged by the family Apjohn during the 1890s. An elaborate new porch which conceals the original Georgian doorcase was

*The committee for Watering the
Rock Road, c.1830, to keep the
dust down!*

WATERING THE BLACK ROCK ROAD.

COMMITTEE.

EARL of ERROLL,	HICKMAN KEARNEY, Esq.
LORD WILLIAM PAGET,	JAMES SAURIN, Esq.
HON. JOHN JONES,	SIR HARCOURT LEES, Bart.
SIR WILLIAM BETHAM,	JAMES PRICE, Esq.
JAMES FERRIER, Esq.	W. H. CARTER, Esq.
SAMUEL BEWLEY, Esq.	COLONEL GREY,
THOMAS PIM, Esq.	COLONEL KINGSMILL,
THOMAS LYSTER, Esq.	JONATHAN PIM, Esq.
HENRY ROE, Esq.	PATRICK JAMES HART, Esq.
J. M. CHAYTOR, Esq.	JOHN ARMIT, Esq. *Treasurer.*
JAMES PIM, Jun. Esq.	
	PHILIP MOLLOY, Esq. } *Secretaries.*
	FRANCIS LOW, Esq. }

added, along with a large billiard room and a conservatory. South Hill was occupied by the Du Gros family, the one-time owners of the Dunlop rubber tyre company, and also by the Huets, who had a motor business in Dublin. The house was also the home of the well-known author Nevil Shute, who lived there during his youth.

Mount Merrion By far the greatest loss in this area was a substantial Victorian house called Mount Merrion, which is not to be confused with the old Fitzwilliam residence. This house stood close to the Stillorgan Road, beside the old South County Hotel. A routine early nineteenth-century house, it was greatly enlarged by the addition of gabled wings and a fine portico, fashioned in granite. The façade was further embellished with granite coigns and roundels with festoons. The result was an elaborate Victorian mansion which also possessed a fine garden front composed of a pair of half-octagonal bows, giving fine views over Blackrock and Dublin Bay. These costly mid-nineteenth-century alterations were made by the Brudenell Murphy family who were wealthy salesmasters in Dublin's Smithfield market. The interior was lavishly decorated with gilded plasterwork, fine woodwork and stained glass. The house incorporated a private oratory, and a library with false doors and murals.

Early in this century a builder named M. P. Kennedy owned Mount Merrion and erected a number of fine houses in its grounds at the top of Merrion Avenue.

The Oratory at the Sion Hill Convent

The Rock Road

The Rock Road is, apart from the Stillorgan dual carriageway, probably the busiest road in south County Dublin. It has been busy since the eighteenth century, and was probably so for many centuries before that too. The residents of Blackrock were always concerned about the condition of this road, especially when they had to travel by horse. A committee was established during the 1820s to administer a fund for

Above: Mr Kelly and grandson standing at the door of Rosefield Left: Rosefield, built around 1750, was an untouched miniature estate until its demolition in 1983

Rosefield
Above: Head of a fawn
plasterwork from the hall
Right: The hall in 1982

'Watering The Black Rock Road' in order to keep the dust down! The committee was composed of many of the wealthy residents of the area, including the Earl of Errol, Sir William Betham, Samuel Bewley, Thomas Pim, James Saurin, Sir Harcourt Lees, and many more. The committee paid William Dargan, the road and railway contractor, a substantial £80 a month for the four summer months, just to control the dust.

A number of important houses were built during the eighteenth century on the lands between Blackrock and Booterstown, and they enjoyed the best views of Dublin Bay. Nearly all of these properties have been owned by different religious or educational institutions, with the exception of Rosefield House.

Pembroke House, at the bottom of Mount Merrion Avenue, is now in use as the Benin Casa school, and is a plain house, built about 1830 and enlarged by Jonathan Goodbody, a Dublin stockbroker, who came to live here in the 1880s. He added a two-storey, bow-fronted extension and an elaborate granite doorcase. The drawing room in the new wing

The old houses of Williamstown
village in 1889 – note the
horse-drawn omnibus in the
distance

contains a handsome plaster ceiling with an unusual palmette pattern.

The Sion Hill Convent or residence was formerly known as Ruby Lodge and dates from the late eighteenth century, but it can no longer be seen from the Rock Road due to the building of new apartments.

Rosefield, which was previously called Belleville, was built in about 1750 as one of the first seaside villas on the Fitzwilliam estate. It was demolished in 1983 to make way for the Blackrock Clinic. Jonathan Barker's map of 1762 shows the house and formal kitchen garden behind. It was a two-storey-over-basement, five-bay, Georgian house, to which a wing containing a ballroom was later added. Rosefield had a timber portico, surmounted by a delicate ironwork balcony which partly disguised the original Georgian doorcase and hall door. Right up until its sale in 1981, the house and five-acre grounds had remained as an example of an untouched miniature estate since the eighteenth century, where the winding drive, with its daffodils in spring, skirted around a field whose sole occupant was a pony! It had been the home of the Kelly family since the 1850s. It was sold for just under £1 million to a consortium of leading medical practitioners, who in 1983 announced their plans for the new Blackrock Clinic. A private hospital was also constructed behind the octagonal-shaped clinic, in the former garden of Rosefield.

The main entrance gates, with their curved walls and two pedestrian gates, all constructed of cut granite, stood on the Rock Road at Williamstown, until the demolition of the house.

Williamstown

Williamstown lies about halfway between Blackrock and Booterstown and was once a significant village, with many houses and cottages on either side of the main road. A narrow lane, which still separates the Blackrock Clinic from Blackrock College, was called Castle Dawson Avenue and on it there were about twenty houses and cottages, which were cleared away by the college when the leases from the Pembroke estate expired in 1903. There was another street here too of fourteen now-vanished houses, called Williamstown Avenue. These two-storeyed, whitewashed terraces had the appearance of estate houses and once occupied the land beside the main driveway into Blackrock College. All of these dwellings, including those on the Rock Road, were cleared away when the leases ended and were replaced by the present wall and railings in about 1904. Many of the older houses on the seaward side of Williamstown were also demolished but were later rebuilt, and the local authority also erected new houses and flats at Emmet Square in 1908 to accommodate some of the families who had previously lived in the Blackrock College houses.

There was a slight inlet on the coast between Williamstown and Blackrock before the construction of the railway, and there were ponds here from which salt was collected. An early engraving of Blackrock (*c.* 1744) shows a salt tower near here, which presumably was used for drying and storing salt. The railway embankment created an area which was flooded at high tide, and which was described by W. F. Wakeman in his *Tourist's Guide through Dublin and its Interesting Suburbs* (1865) as 'a dismal, foul smelling swamp'. But in 1873 the Blackrock Town Commissioners spent £3000 in works to reclaim the land and create what is now Blackrock Park. The park, which was laid out around the hill at Vauxhall and contains an artificial lake, was furnished with a shelter at the main gate, a bandstand and many seats.

Blackrock College

One of the greatest expanses of unspoilt open space left in this area is the land belonging to Blackrock College. The perfectly maintained grounds are not marred by any unsightly intrusions. The college is run by the Holy Ghost Fathers, who originated in Paris and were more commonly called the French Fathers by the people of Blackrock. The order later expanded and acquired Kimmage Manor in 1911, which they also still own.

The lands of the college were assembled through the acquisition of four large houses with their grounds over a long period of time: first Castle Dawson in 1860, then Williamstown Castle in 1875, Clareville in 1899 and Willow Park in 1924.

The school, which today accommodates over one thousand pupils, had more modest beginnings. The first school prospectus announced that the course of instruction would include 'the Latin, Greek, English, French, German and Italian languages, ancient and modern history, and geography, cosmography, mathematics, book-keeping, and commercial correspondence, zoology, mineralogy, music, drawing and the various other branches of a liberal education'. Furthermore, the students 'will be taught to write and to speak the French language with ease and correctness'.

Castle Dawson, the first home of the French Fathers, had been built for James Massy Dawson in 1762, one of the family of Massy who owned Killakee House in Rathfarnham. All of the mid-eighteenth century features may still be seen in the house, such as the fine plasterwork ceilings and cornices, chair-rails and original doors and staircase, all of which give it an authentic character. On the seaward elevation there is a wide bow which gives the principal reception rooms a magnificent view of Dublin Bay.

Blackrock College was established at Williamstown in 1860, and forms a remarkable collection of mainly nineteenth-century buildings

In the 1870s a covered gallery was formed to link the house to the chapel and to St Patrick's Hall. The chapel was completed in 1868, and its interior was decorated by a member of the French order. These buildings, originating with the old house, form a nearly perfect quadrangle or square. It was also at this time that Williamstown Castle was purchased and a large dining hall was built.

The original Williamstown Castle stood two-storeys-over-basement and had two half-octagonal, projecting bays. It had flanking turrets and a viewing tower on the roof. The

1905-6 enlargement of the castle, which was drawn up by Father Eben-recht, involved the addition of great three-storey-over-basement wings, corner towers and battlements, all carried out exactly in the style of the original castle or house. The Gothic sash windows were also faithfully reproduced.

The imposing façade of Williamstown Castle which now accommodates school boarders

The demolition of Clareville, another old Georgian residence situated within the grounds of Blackrock College, was unfortunate as it represented the passing of yet another link with Blackrock's eighteenth-century history. Though various extensions had been made, the original house, built shortly after 1752, remained essentially unaltered. It was a two-storey house, with a projecting central bay which its builder Thomas Keatinge described as a gazebo window. The principal rooms were decorated with delicate plasterwork and the staircase was ornamented with an unusual fluted pilaster. Keatinge, the builder of a number of Georgian houses in Blackrock, was descended from a long-established family of Dublin builders, some of whom were carpenters and bricklayers in the sixteenth century and were made Freemen of the City of Dublin (Hazel Smyth, *The Town of the Road*).

Blackrock extends towards Booterstown, almost merging with it and making it difficult to decide which is which, especially at Cross Avenue. There is no absolute dividing line, and thus we move to discuss Booterstown in the next chapter.

Classical detail from the attractive staircase in Clareville

CHAPTER 15

Booterstown

In the eighteenth century Booterstown was an important village on the shores of Dublin Bay

Booterstown, which means 'town of the road' from 'Baile an Bhóthair', lies on the gently sloping lands between Dublin and Blackrock and on the route of an ancient road once known as the Slíghe Chualann. The Slíghe Chualann once connected the residence of the High King of Ireland at Tara with his outlying lands in Cualann, which is the ancient name for the area of land stretching towards Bray, which in Irish is Brí Chualann. Today's traffic at Booterstown, whether speeding past or stuck in a long queue, thus follows a route that is nearly two thousand years old. As we have already seen, the Fitzwilliam family were, by the fourteenth century, firmly in possession of all of the lands of Booterstown and much more besides.

Booterstown Avenue was called Booterstown Lane in the eighteenth century and, like Blackrock, was the scene of much house-building. Jonathan Barker's estate map of 1762 shows quite a number of significant houses such as Sans Souci, Rosemount, Cherbury, Booterstown

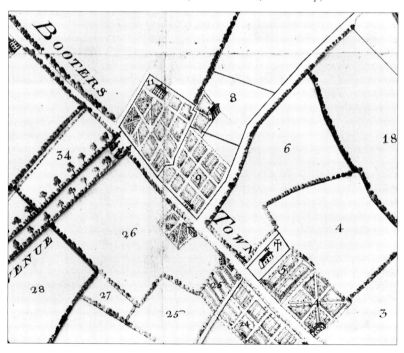

Jonathan Barker's map of the Fitzwilliam Estate, 1762, shows Booterstown Avenue with its Catholic chapel, Booterstown Castle almost opposite, Sans Souci (at 11), Rosemount (at 8) and Booterstown House (at 26)

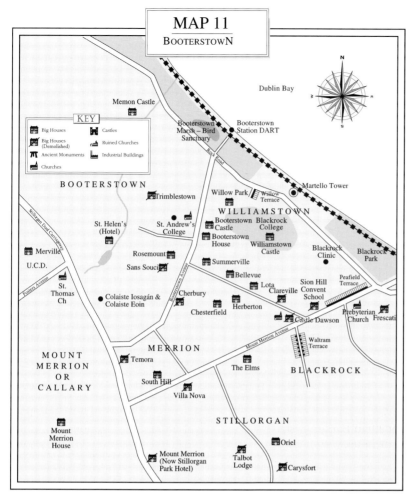

MAP 11
BOOTERSTOWN

KEY

- Big Houses
- Big Houses (Demolished)
- Ancient Monuments
- Churches
- Castles
- Ruined Churches
- Industrial Buildings

Dublin Bay

Memon Castle

Booterstown Marsh – Bird Sanctuary

Booterstown Station DART

Martello Tower

BOOTERSTOWN

Trimblestown

Willow Park / Willow Terrace

WILLIAMSTOWN

St. Helen's (Hotel)

St. Andrew's College

Booterstown Castle

Blackrock College

Booterstown House

Williamstown Castle

Blackrock Clinic

Blackrock Park

Merville

Rosemount

Summerville

U.C.D.

Sans Souci

Bellevue

St. Thomas Ch

Colaiste Iosagán & Colaiste Eoin

Cherbury

Lota

Clareville

Sion Hill Convent School

Peafield Terrace

Chesterfield

Herberton

Castle Dawson

Presbyterian Church

Frescati

Waltram Terrace

MERRION

Temora

The Elms

BLACKROCK

MOUNT MERRION OR CALLARY

South Hill

Villa Nova

STILLORGAN

Oriel

Mount Merrion House

Mount Merrion (Now Stillorgan Park Hotel)

Talbot Lodge

Carysfort

House and Booterstown Castle, now St Mary's. There was also a Catholic chapel and a number of smaller houses and cottages. Sans Souci and Seamount, later called St Helen's, were two of the most important houses built on the Fitzwilliam estate in the Booterstown area during the mid-eighteenth century.

A plan of Sans Souci

Sans Souci originated as a small, double-fronted house, built by the Earl of Lanesborough around 1760. It was a modest house of five bays, to which a large wing was added about 1802. This addition, designed by Richard Morrison, provided a new entrance and pillared hallway, on either side of which were two gracious reception rooms, one oval and the other with a shallow bow. There were extensive outbuildings to the back of the house, including stables and an octagonal dairy. The work was carried out for William Digges La Touche who lived here in the early 1800s. The La Touches were a Huguenot family who had been very successful in business and had founded their

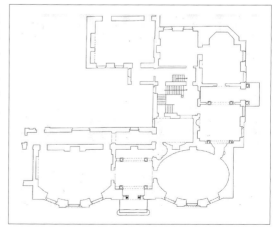

Top: St Helen's, originally built in 1754, was the headquarters of the Christian Brothers in Ireland from 1925 until 1988

Above: A recent photograph of St Helen's, now reincarnated as a luxury hotel

own bank, whose premises were located in Castle Street, Dublin. Their principal residence was a magnificent house on St Stephen's Green, and Sans Souci was a country retreat, where they maintained fine gardens. Sans Souci was demolished in 1948.

St Helen's is without question the finest house in Booterstown, and one of the grandest residences in the county. Until its sale in 1988 by the Christian Brothers, its lands represented the single most important undeveloped and unspoilt property in Booterstown. It has recently been refurbished as a luxury hotel, following a lengthy planning wrangle during which great concern was expressed about its future and that of its grounds with their fine trees, open space and terraced gardens. Though ideally one might have preferred to see no development close to St Helen's, the outcome is ultimately a happy one, with the road plan dropped, for the moment at any rate, and the house given a new lease of life. As Professor Kevin B. Nowlan pointed out when making the case for its preservation: 'It has an almost princely quality about it. The view from the terraces across Dublin Bay to Howth, unencumbered by any intrusive structures, must be one of the finest in the Dublin area.'

The original house was begun in 1754 and was built for Thomas Cooley, a Dublin barrister and MP. It later belonged to Robert Alexander, who was one of the early patrons and church wardens of St Philip and James Church in nearby Cross Avenue. In the late nineteenth century it was greatly enlarged and improved by Viscount Lord Henry Gough, who employed the architect John McCurdy to design and oversee the work. In 1898 another wealthy owner, Sir John Nutting, further remodelled and embellished the house by facing the original brick façade with

Portland stone. The centre block is flanked by single-storey, bow-fronted wings on the garden side. The stone façade and balustrade unites the overall composition and creates a harmony between the eighteenth- and nineteenth-century sections of the house.

Nutting also completely re-ordered the interior in the most lavish style, making great use of Italian marble and decorative plasterwork. The hall and stairs are beautifully finished in a veined grey-and-white marble, the floor being paved in black-and-white squares while the walls are decorated with elaborate plasterwork panels in the classical style. The large ballroom, with its elegant, fluted columns and gallery which once housed an organ, became the chapel during its occupation by the Christian Brothers. There is also a very unusually decorated dining room, with a *repoussé* copper frieze made in about 1900 and depicting ships and galleons. It is signed by James Smithies of Manchester, a craftsman who specialised in this sort of ornamental work. Upstairs, over the hall door, there is a study or smoking room, which is panelled and decorated with a strapwork plaster frieze in the Jacobean style.

The terraced gardens, which were laid out by Ninian Niven, were a feature of interest during the nineteenth century. In 1870 the gardeners had to raise 12,000 plants for the beds of the formal gardens. A line of vases in front of the house were always filled with scarlet pelargoniums.

In 1925 St Helen's was bought by the Christian Brothers as their Provincial Residence and Novitiate. It remained the headquarters of the order until 1988. The house and 71 acres were then sold and Dun Laoghaire Corporation bought nine acres for a road reservation. Many new houses and apartments were built around the house which itself was declared a National Monument in 1994, following the demolition of a nineteenth-century wing and arising out of general concern for the future of the house. Many feared a repeat of the Frescati story.

When it was sold in 1988 the estate consisted of much agricultural land which the brothers had farmed. Their property ran from Booterstown Avenue across to the houses of Seafield Road. Two large tracts of land fronting onto the Stillorgan Road had previously been sold off in order to build two schools, Coláiste Eoin and Coláiste Íosagáin. During the 1920s surplus land was sold for building, and the houses of St Helen's Road were erected by Cramptons, the well-known builders.

Booterstown House appears on Barker's map of 1762, and was then a relatively small house, facing the wide lane which led to Rosemount and the back entrance of St Helen's, where a blocked-up gateway still exists. The impressive, wide front of Booterstown

Top: Book plate from the library at St Helen's

Above: A calling card of Sir John Nutting

Booterstown House, which was built before 1762

An eighteenth-century staircase window in Booterstown Castle, now St Mary's

House, with its symmetrical wings, disguises the fact that the house is only one room deep, and that many additions were made to the original building. It is a neat and elegant house with several interesting features. To one side, upstairs, there is a spacious drawing room with a generous bow and a coved ceiling. A feature of this room is its fine curved iron-work balcony and canopy, of late Georgian date, which overlooks the garden. At the bottom of the garden is an unusual feature where a short spiral stairs leads to a culverted stream. Booterstown House was once the home of Francis Elrington Ball, whose book *A History of County Dublin*, published in 1903, remains the most authoritative work on the early history of the area.

Ball noted that Booterstown Castle, which stands next door, was built in 1449 and that 'the vaults are said to be incorporated in the house which stands upon its site, as indicated on the Ordnance Survey map.'

Booterstown Castle is indeed to be found incorporated into the northern half of a Georgian house called St Mary's. The eighteenth-century house was cleverly added to the old structure, and a new façade, which was centred on a beautiful stone doorcase, was created by making large windows in the thick walls of the castle in order to make an almost symmetrical new front.

The Georgian doorcase and fanlight is delicate, and is similar to those found on the best town houses in Dublin. Inside, the hall and stairs are elegantly proportioned and there is a drawing room with a half-octagonal bow, overlooking the garden. The principal room in the castle is now used for restoring pianos, and the extremely thick walls are very evident.

The lower half of Booterstown Avenue is comprised of many terraces and houses, mainly dating from the early nineteenth century. Here, at Number 3 Vernon Terrace, the historian Dr Richard Robert Madden lived until 1886. He is best remembered for his *History of the United Irishmen.*

Booterstown Castle (on the right) was incorporated into the house now known as St Mary's

Cherbury, owned by Sir Samuel Bradstreet in the eighteenth century, was demolished during the 1970s to make way for a development of apartments

St Andrew's College occupies the site of an old house called Collegnes. It was originally another eighteenth-century villa, a plain house just three windows wide. It was later enlarged with extra rooms at each end, a new Ionic portico and windows with stucco architraves. In 1795 it belonged to the D'Olier family, who remained there for at least seventy years.

Mulcaire The large office building of the First National Building Society also stands on the site of an old house. A Victorian residence called Mulcaire occupied the land adjoining Willow Park and was eventually demolished following its sale in 1971.

Rosemount, the headquarters of the Medical Missionaries of Mary, is another fine eighteenth-century house, five windows wide, square in plan, with a large central chimney stack. The house was built around 1760 and, though several extensions have been made which have altered the original external appearance, many original features survive such as the staircase, plaster cornices and the two very attractive fanlights of the hall.

Cherbury, was yet another of the fine eighteenth-century villas which were built on the Fitzwilliam estate, and was shown on Barker's map (1762). In 1840 it was called Herbert House and was often described as the dower house of the Pembroke estate, and was unfortunately demolished during the mid-1970s. Like Sans Souci, the original house was greatly enlarged to produce a long frontage of twelve windows, which overlooked the garden. The entrance front, which stood close to Booterstown Avenue, was some six bays wide, with a treble arched window over the hall door.

Sir Samuel Bradstreet, who was a noted lawyer and an MP for Dublin in 1776, lived in Cherbury during the eighteenth century. In 1802, following the death of his widow, Lady Bradstreet, a notice appeared in *Saunder's Newsletter:* 'The late Lady Bradstreet's delightful villa, situated in Booterstown Lane, and subject to the final rent of £30 per annum. The house is in every respect commodious and in perfect repair, was painted

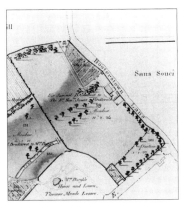

Detail of map, c.1830, showing
Cherbury with its miniature
parkland and formal gardens

and papered within this fortnight and contains 13 rooms, four of which are thirty feet long; with dressing rooms and servants' rooms over its doorcase 40 by 25: coach houses, wash and bake houses, dairy, larders, cellars, coal vaults, hen and pig houses, etc. with an extensive yard and ice house. There are six gardens, cropped with the greatest taste containing hot houses upwards of 400 feet in length, and some hundred pine, peach, apricot, nectarine and orange trees, the fruit of which alone, it is well known, would sell at market for a considerable sum etc. ... These concerns were laid out and improved by the late Sir Samuel Bradstreet, whose knowledge and taste for gardening are well known.'

The parish of Booterstown, as it existed in the eighteenth century, was a large one, including much of Blackrock, Dundrum, Ballinteer, Roebuck and Stillorgan.

The present Church of the Assumption, with its Italianate façade, was built in 1812, largely at the expense of Lord Fitzwilliam who also gave the site. It was built on the site of the earlier church, a plain rectangular structure which is shown on Rocque's map of 1757. It has often been pointed out that there were almost no Catholic churches built in Ireland during the eighteenth century, but there were a number of exceptions such as Booterstown. Taylor's map of 1816 shows that there were other chapels at Rathfarnham, Dundrum, Sandyford, Glencullen, Cabinteely, Crinken and Blackrock. These were the days before Catholic emancipation, and the building of churches, when tolerated at all, was kept simple as funds were almost non-existent in Catholic parishes. As these chapels or mass houses were very basic, the new church at Booterstown must have seemed quite grand by comparison. Even so, the architecture of the new church was restrained and the building, which was discreetly sited off Booterstown Avenue, was clearly not intended to make a loud statement.

The church consisted of a nave and aisles and was modestly decorated externally with stucco mouldings in the classical manner. It has been suggested that Lord Fitzwilliam instructed the architect to avoid any ostentatious churchlike appearance so as not to offend his Protestant tenants and friends.

A plaque inside the church commemorates Lord Fitzwilliam's generosity, arranged through his land agents, the Verschoyles, while outside there is a fine high cross, carved in sandstone, which was erected as a result of a bequest from one of Fitzwilliam's employees. Behind the church stands a convent of the Sisters of Mercy which incorporates an eighteenth-century house.

Lord Fitzwilliam died in 1833, and was succeeded by Sydney Herbert, the Earl of Pembroke. Mrs Verschoyle, who became the agent to the Pembroke estate after the death of her husband, was a Catholic, and she persuaded the Earl to give ground and money towards the erection of a convent adjoining the church. The foundation stone was laid in 1838.

The early Catholic church at
Booterstown, discreetly placed
off Booterstown Avenue

Mrs Verschoyle had, no doubt, also been instrumental in having two parochial schools erected here in 1821, largely at the expense of Lord Fitzwilliam. *The Catholic Directory* commented: 'In one school 100 boys are educated and twenty clothed, in the other 100 girls receive daily instruction and almost all are clothed.'

Collegnes House, now the site of St Andrew's College

Willow Park The lands of Willow Park were leased from Lord Fitzwilliam by John Grainger in 1751, but it was some fifteen years later that Christopher Deey, a public notary, actually erected a house there. Deey built Willow Park, a large, three-storey, five-windowed house. The back of the house is massive, consisting of large, bow-shaped projections and three-storey additions to either side. An elegant Doric portico was added in the nineteenth century, and behind it an exquisite cut-stone Georgian doorcase may still be seen. In 1766 Deey was presented with a cup which bore the following inscription: 'The gift of several eminent master builders of the City of Dublin to Mr Christopher Deey, public notary, with the Freedom of the Corporation of carpenters for his great care and attention and good services on behalf of the building trade.'

Some twenty years later we find the house leased to Hugh Viscount Carlton, whose town house lay in St Stephen's Green. Carlton became Solicitor General for Ireland in 1779, and eight years later was Lord Chief Justice 'of the common pleas'. In 1798 he presided over the trial of the Sheares brothers, whom we have already met in connection with the Loughlinstown Camp. Carlton seems to have left Ireland after the Act of

The imposing rear elevation of Willow Park, which is still in use as a preparatory school

These impressive gates, relocated at Willow Park, once graced the avenue to the Fitzwilliams' Mount Merrion House

Union, for Archer, writing in 1801, says that Willow Park is the seat of Alderman Alexander and describes it as 'a good house, [with] a demesne of about 18 acres well planted and improved, [with] fine gardens with a good deal of glass and all enclosed with a stone wall'.

Willow Park was home to many prominent families such as that of James Ferrier of Ferrier Pollock, the noted clothing company, in about 1823, and the Bewleys, of Bewleys' cafés, who lived there from 1859 until 1924.

In 1925 the house was purchased by Blackrock College and opened as a preparatory school. The magnificent entrance gates with their ball-topped stone piers came from the Mount Merrion estate, and were erected here at that time.

Willow Terrace, a short terrace of four Georgian-style houses, was developed in about 1830 between Willow Park and Blackrock College. The three-storey, brick-built houses are semi-detached and have single-storey wings with interesting semi-circular relieving arches.

Cross Avenue

Cross Avenue, as already mentioned, was originally laid out as a formal drive in Lord Fitzwilliam's estate. In 1824 Fitzwilliam gave a site for the building of a new Church of Ireland church, at the Blackrock end of Cross Avenue. Here, the Church of St Philip and St James was built at a cost of £4615. Designed by John Bowden in the English Gothic style of the fifteenth century, it has a tall, slender spire and battlemented appearance. By the mid-nineteenth century the existing church was too small and in 1868 it was decided to add a new chancel, transepts, and a robing room. This work was carried out in rusticated granite, and was carefully matched with the older section with its granite buttresses and pinnacles. A staunch supporter of this church was James Digges La Touche who lived in Sans Souci, one of the largest houses in Booterstown.

The residential development on Cross Avenue began in the late eighteenth century with houses such as Clareville, Dawson Court and

A print of the Church of St Philip and St James, Cross Avenue (from Blacker's Brief Sketches of Booterstown and Donnybrook)

Bellevue. By the early 1800s a number of houses had been built and it was clearly considered a very attractive area.

Dawson Court, a three-storey Georgian house, is said to have been a 'dower' house of Castle Dawson, which was situated not far off in what are now the grounds of Blackrock College. Dawson Court stood close to the corner at Merrion Avenue, and had, to the front, a striking three-storey bow and a Gibbsian-style arched stone doorcase. The interior possessed a handsome staircase and good mantelpieces of late Georgian style. Following its sale in 1971, the house was vandalised and subsequently demolished.

Dunamase, which has two Regency-style, bow-shaped projections, is a much-altered late eighteenth-century house which backs onto Cross Avenue.

Bellevue, nearby, which retains many of its Georgian features including a large, oval ballroom; it was cleverly converted into a private house in the 1970s. The eighteenth-century house appears to have been occupied by the Countess of Brandon and later in the nineteenth century by John Gillman MD, who was a church warden in the nearby St Philip and James Church. During the 1930s Éamon De Valera lived in Bellevue before moving across the road to a fine stone-built house called Herberton. Herberton, with its granite stonework and Gothic porch, has a rather ecclesiastical air about it.

Bellevue, Cross Avenue, an eighteenth-century house with an elegant, oval ballroom

Glenvar is one of the most unusual and distinctive houses on Cross Avenue, with its concave roofs which give it a somewhat oriental look. It

Summerville, Cross Avenue, with its elaborate Victorian ironwork

Glenvar, with its unusual, almost oriental-style roofs, designed by John S. Mulvany

was designed by John Mulvany in 1856 and bears many hallmarks of his style, such as rounded corners of doors and windows, and bracketed eaves. It is boldly modelled and a short tower is incorporated into the design. Glenvar was occupied by John Barrington, a Quaker, who in 1864 became Lord Mayor of Dublin.

Chesterfield, a large, early nineteenth-century house, has been substantially altered from its original appearance. It was probably built by Thomas Meade, a builder, who leased the land from the Fitzwilliam estate in 1803. Some thirty years later it had become the 'country' residence of Nathaniel Sneyd, who was an MP. Sneyd was a partner in the well-known firm of Sneyd, French and Barton, wine merchants in Dublin. In 1833 Sneyd met with an untimely death when he was shot, apparently by mistake, in Westmoreland Street. The culprit was a young man named John Mason who had business connections with the firm, and had mistaken Sneyd for Barton.

Summerville is an appealing Victorian house, built around 1858, which stands at the corner of Cross Avenue and Booterstown Avenue. The ground-floor windows and entrance are ornamented with elaborate ironwork canopies and there is also a fancy ironwork weather-vane on the roof.

The Rock Road

The Rock Road at Booterstown presents a variety of houses of all styles and periods, which once bore names such as Bayview or Howth View. At the corner of Booterstown Avenue is The Punch Bowl, where there may well have been an inn since the eighteenth century. Rocque shows a substantial village at Booterstown in 1757, clustered about the bottom of Booterstown Avenue. Not far off is the Booterstown Boys' National School, a granite building with three arched windows in its gable. It was erected in 1852 and originally consisted of one large room, 40 feet long, in which children of all ages were taught together.

Baymount Further along is Baymount, a small, eighteenth-century house which was originally situated on fifteen acres of land. It was bounded on the south by Collegnes and Seamount (now St Helen's).

Francis Perry obtained a lease for Baymount in 1786 from the Fitzwilliam estate, and his rent included two sugar loaves or 15 shillings in lieu. Much of the road frontage here was developed on the lands of Baymount.

A steam train crossing the strand at Booterstown (from Kirkwood, c.1845)

Glena, an attractive granite and redbrick house of the 1890s, was the home of the famous tenor, Count John MacCormack. Glena is a villa-type house, one-storey-over-basement, with its principal rooms enjoying fine sea views, and it has a most striking feature of a corner tower with a conical roof. The name of the house is a playful version of the name of its builder, a Mr Glennan.

Glena, a magnificent mansion of the 1890s, with its elaborate, redbrick ornament and cut-stone detail

Across the road, and easily missed in a speeding car, is a granite milestone of early nineteenth century date. It is one of very few which now survive in the county and is inscribed on one side: 'From Kingstown 3 miles'. A similar milestone, which stood on Merrion Road at the bottom of Ailesbury Road, was lost during roadworks around 1970.

Booterstown Marsh is an artificial creation, which was formed in 1834 following the construction of the railway. The marsh, which is the only unreclaimed section of original coastline, has become a sanctuary to many birds, some of them rare. In winter at high tide, occasional visitors include the red shank, lapwing and oystercatcher. Teal and snipe also visit Booterstown, and reed buntings, linnets and sometimes kingfishers may also be sighted.

Booterstown National School for Boys

The IMCO building once stood close to Booterstown Marsh and was a well-known landmark in the area. It was a purpose-built laundry and office headquarters, and its concrete structure, with its staircase tower, balcony and clock, was a monument to the 1930s. It was demolished to make way for a new office building called Merrion House.

Merrion graveyard was once the site of an ancient church which has long since disappeared. The graveyard, which lies behind the petrol station and is adjacent to the Tara Tower

The strand at Booterstown marsh

The IMCO laundry, an interesting modern building of the 1930s

The old graveyard at Merrion in 1762

hotel, is of great interest. Many inhabitants of the city were buried here prior to 1866, when all burials ceased. The most significant memorial is that which records the tragic drowning of hundreds of passengers in Dublin Bay in November 1807. Two ships, *The Prince of Wales* and *The Rochdale*, were driven ashore in a violent snowstorm. Some 385 bodies were recovered from the shore and some of them were buried in the graveyard at Merrion. The graveyard, though it was neglected for many years, is now very well cared for.

A major road, which, if it is ever built, will have a dramatic effect on the Booterstown area, is the eastern bypass. This road, which has been under construction since the early 1970s, would link the Port of Dublin and the northern city with the Stillorgan dual carriageway and the N11, which takes traffic to Wexford and Rosslare. Leaving the Stillorgan dual carriageway, the proposed road would swing round St Helen's on its western side, proceed through the fields below the terraced gardens and cut a narrow passage between the houses of St Helen's Road and Booterstown, to emerge at the marsh. Here a spaghetti junction, which would link up with local roads, would take its route across Merrion strand. Following great opposition from the residents of Sandymount and Booterstown, the road plan has remained 'on ice' since about 1989. The proposed siting of the spaghetti junction on the Booterstown bird sanctuary provoked great opposition from An Taisce, the National Trust for Ireland, which owns it.

With the current building of the last leg of the M50, the ring road around Dublin city, which will ultimately link the N11 at Shankill to Swords in north County Dublin, it could be argued that the so-called eastern bypass is unnecessary.

CHAPTER 16

Merrion

The lands which stretch from Booterstown to Merrion are low-lying and close to the sea, and were once dominated by the castle of the Fitzwilliams. The castle was situated near a shallow stream, which must once have fed its defensive moat.

A carved stone plaque bearing the Fitzwilliam coat of arms and a stone head, both of medieval date and believed to have come from the Fitzwilliam castle, are now incorporated into the wall of a new community building here. The eighteenth-century house has been the residence of the Sisters of Charity since 1866, when they acquired the land in order to establish St Mary's Blind Asylum. The sisters built a convent, a school and a large granite chapel on to the old house. Now, over 140 years later, the order continues its work with the blind, for whom it has provided sheltered housing and a new swimming pool.

Merrion Castle with its stream – the eighteenth-century house has been occupied by the nuns since 1866

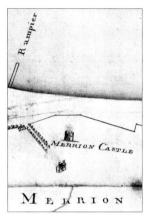

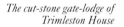

Merrion Castle controlled the shore and lands near Dublin Bay, as shown on Barker's map of 1762

As today's hectic life goes spinning past on the Merrion Road, it is hard to believe that there are cattle still quietly grazing in the fields beside the stream on the farmlands belonging to the nuns. It is the last glimpse of the old County Dublin, and a rare sight so close to the city.

In the eighteenth century the Fitzwilliams owned all of Merrion and Booterstown, which included part of Blackrock, and all of Sandymount and Ringsend. At Merrion they developed vast brick fields where clay was dug and bricks were burnt. They were the owners and developers of Merrion Square, Fitzwilliam Square and most of what is now called Dublin 4. This included prestigious developments such as Wellington and Waterloo Roads, Shrewsbury Road and Ailesbury Road. Their property extended up to Dundrum, over Taney and Ballinteer and beyond to include Ticknock in the Dublin mountains, where they owned granite quarries.

With granite quarries in Ticknock and brick fields at Merrion Gates, the Fitzwilliams were in a strong position to supply building materials to the many eighteenth-century house builders in Dublin city and county. By the middle of the eighteenth century, the Fitzwilliams were also sitting on a 'gold mine' of sites for house building, and they were not slow to exploit their good fortune. Wealthy people wanted terraced houses of quality in the city, in Merrion Square for example, and they wanted seaside villas in places like Blackrock.

The Fitzwilliam estate received ground rents from all kinds of properties, from many fine houses to numerous humbler dwellings. For instance, in 1750 Ringsend and Irishtown were quite densely populated with the houses and cottages of fishermen, seafarers and boat builders, all of whom paid rent to the Fitzwilliams.

In earlier times the family controlled their interests along the coast, and maintained fishing rights from their castle at Merrion. The middle of the river Liffey marked the limit of their property, and in many early

The cut-stone gate-lodge of Trimleston House

*Trimleston House, which was
demolished in 1974*

leases they recited their claim to the strand at Merrion which consisted of 'all the sands to the furthest reflux of the sea as far as Blindhaven'! There is evidence to show that they looked after the foreshore by building '*rampiers*', a kind of breakwater which would prevent erosion, and even stone walls, as was the case at Lady Arbella Denny's house at Blackrock. In 1807 the Fitzwilliams were involved in a dispute with Dublin Corporation over the removal of stones and sand from the strand and were able to produce their 'title' to the shore at Irishtown and Merrion.

For many centuries, the Fitzwilliams lived in their castle at Merrion Gates, which stood on the lands where an Asylum for Blind Catholic Females was built in 1866. A Georgian house and the later asylum buildings are still there, but the castle disappeared around 1780.

The townland of Trimleston or Owenstown once extended from Roebuck and Foster's Avenue as far as the sea at Merrion. There was once a Trimleston Castle which was owned by the Barnewall family, but no trace or record of it remains. Trimleston House, a Regency structure which was remodelled around 1870, has also completely vanished, and only its attractive stone-built gate-lodge survives on the Merrion Road.

Trimleston, mentioned in J. N. Brewer's *Beauties of Ireland* in 1825, was a five-bay house with a granite porch and a stucco-embellished façade. It was demolished in 1974.

In 1983 the arrival of the DART brought about the end of the manually operated level-crossing gates at Merrion. Merrion Gates, as they are still known, were once operated by a signalman from a brick-and-timber signal box. A quick turn of the large capstan or wheel effortlessly opened the gates.

CHAPTER 17

Stillorgan

There are few traces left today of the old village of Stillorgan which was located on the important main road between Dublin and Bray. Stillorgan is now a rather characterless busy suburban district, which is noted for having the first shopping centre ever built in Ireland, a large indoor bowling alley, and a cinema. Over seventy years ago it was described by Sir Neville Wilkinson, who lived at Mount Merrion, as 'the pretty village of Stillorgan', words which sadly could not be used today. Indeed, few villages in County Dublin have been so roughly treated by the twentieth century, or have lost so much of their identity in recent decades. Stillorgan is so changed that it is difficult to imagine what the village, which once had many cottages, can have looked like.

The original settlement was clustered along the main Bray road. At the bottom of a steep hill was a small stream which at one time almost certainly powered a mill. Not far off was an old church, rebuilt in the eighteenth century to become the present St Brigid's Church. An old stone slab, which was described by Austin Cooper in 1781 as 'a head-stone with rude circles thereon', is the only visible testimony to this early

A recent picture showing Stillorgan, once a country village, now part of the vast suburb of Dublin

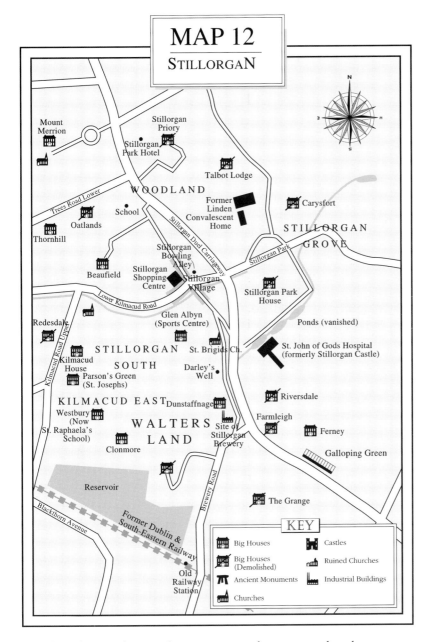

MAP 12
STILLORGAN

KEY

🏛 Big Houses	🏰 Castles
🏛 Big Houses (Demolished)	⌂ Ruined Churches
🏛 Ancient Monuments	🏭 Industrial Buildings
🏛 Churches	

church and it stands near the entrance to the present church.

In the early 1800s the road made a twisty detour around the church and its graveyard, and continued southwards to cross another stream at Stillorgan brewery, a large industrial complex whose site lies covered by the present dual carriageway.

The two streams joined to fill Lord Allen's fish ponds in Stillorgan Park and afterwards the decorative lakes at Carysfort and Prospect House, before joining the sea below the Catholic church at Blackrock.

To the north-east lay the extensive parkland of Stillorgan demesne, which Taylor's map of 1814 shows to be still quite intact. To the west lay Kilmacud and Dundrum which were dotted with houses, farms and

The Stillorgan area, as depicted by Duncan, 1821

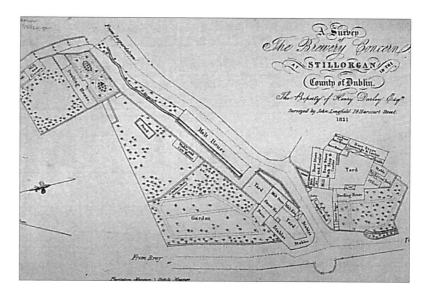

A survey of Darley's brewery in Stillorgan shows how extensive it was in 1831

small estates. The whole area was predominantly agricultural, and many of its poorer inhabitants would have found employment in the houses, gardens and farms of the ever-increasing number of wealthy property owners of the district. The road frontage of the present carpark at Stillorgan shopping centre was completely lined with cottages built during the early nineteenth century. These dwellings, which were known as Stillorgan Row and Moore's Row, were inhabited by a variety of tradesmen and labourers. Other working-class families would have occupied gate-lodges and outbuildings attached to the big houses. The general valuation of rateable property in Ireland of 1849 lists almost 120 small houses

The Stillorgan reservoir with its striking octagonal pump-house

or dwellings for the 'town of Stillorgan'. Many of these were owned and probably built by the families of Darley, Medcalf and Jolley, all of whom had strong connections with the building trade. A number of small houses remain on the hill between the traffic lights and the modern thatched public house known as the Stillorgan Orchard.

A picture of the village in 1850 is provided by the list of tradesmen given by *Thom's Directory*. This included a teacher, a shoemaker, a vintner, two dairies, two blacksmiths, a painter and glazier, a grocer, a medical attendant, a tailor, a mason, and two car owners. There was also a post mistress, and two builders, one of whom was William Medcalf, owner and builder of many of the smaller houses in Stillorgan and Galloping Green. By the 1830s Stillorgan had its own schools for girls and boys and an infant school, all of which were attached to St Brigid's parish. There was also a dispensary and a police barracks.

The stream which once powered machinery at the brewery may still be seen at Brewery Road

Henry Darley's brewery stood on land leased from the Fitzwilliam estate, close to the present Dunstaffnage House. It was described in 1850 as having been in existence for nearly a century under the ownership of the Darleys. In 1831 Stillorgan brewery was a flourishing and highly organised industry and consisted of a mill, several brew houses, a malt store, a malt kiln, a big malt house, a range of stables and a barn, a beer store, a cooperage, an office and a mill pond. There were also two dwelling houses with yards and gardens.

Nineteenth-century Stillorgan was thickly populated with fine houses and small estates, whose occupants also had the benefit of a railway connection to the city. The Harcourt Street railway line, which had been completed during the 1850s, skirted Kilmacud and the southern part of Stillorgan, and a station was erected at Brewery Road, near the Stillorgan reservoir. The route of the railway, having passed Dundrum, swung eastwards towards Galloping Green and Foxrock, following the edge of what is now the Sandyford industrial estate, where it arrived at Stillorgan. From the railway station, whose name was displayed in a neatly clipped box hedge, it was only a short ride by cab into the village or to any of the surrounding houses.

The railway lay adjacent to the deceptively large Stillorgan reservoir which was built as part of Dublin Corporation's waterworks on the lands of an eighteenth-century house called Rockland, now Clonmore. The waterworks are still very much in use and are distinguished by a handsome cut-stone entrance, a gate-lodge and a striking, octagonal pump-house, built in 1884, possibly to the designs of Parke Neville, the waterworks engineer.

Part of an ornamental gate from The Priory, Stillorgan

The course of the new Stillorgan dual carriageway takes us past many vanished houses of the area. Near Oatlands, it runs through the site of an alleged 'ruined monastery' as described on the Ordnance Survey map of 1843, the presence of which must have suggested the name for Stillorgan Priory, a large Victorian house which once stood nearby.

Oatlands and Beaufield, both of which stood between Mount Merrion and Stillorgan village, have been demolished. To the north, Mount

A forgotten village – the houses and pub of Galloping Green

Merrion, Fortwilliam, Ashhurst and Temora have also disappeared, and there is talk of demolishing the remaining section of the Fitzwilliam house at Mount Merrion. Tigh Lorcan Hall, a plain house of Victorian appearance, made way for the Stillorgan bowling alley, while Stillorgan Castle, an eighteenth-century house which formed the original part of St John of God's, was accidentally destroyed by fire.

To the south, the dual carriageway ascends past a terrace of houses and a public house which are all that remain of the 'village' of Galloping Green. The name Galloping Green is at least two hundred years old and implies that the flat lands near here were often used for horse racing – a tradition still very much alive at nearby Leopardstown today. In 1849 Galloping Green was a village consisting of twenty-nine houses, some of which survive today.

Many of the historic houses and properties which have managed to survive in this area have done so because they were taken over by various religious orders and charitable institutions. Bonny Flanagan's book, *Stately Homes around Stillorgan,* describes some eighteen houses which have found a new lease of life through their use as community centres, schools, convents or hospitals.

The St John of God Hospital is by far the largest institutional presence in Stillorgan. The hospital stands on the site of an old house called Stillorgan Castle. The castle, an eighteenth-century, three-storey house with mock battlements, may have been built close to the site of a medieval structure, the original Stillorgan Castle or manor house. This manor, of which we have no illustration, is said to have been very extensive and was occupied during the sixteenth and seventeenth centuries by the

Wolverston family. Their ownership of the lands of Stillorgan passed to the Allens in the late seventeenth century. The eighteenth-century castle, which is clearly shown on Rocque's map of 1757, was bought by the Order of St John of God in 1882 and enlarged to form a hospital, with a further wing and chapel being added in 1890. Unfortunately, all of this was destroyed by fire in 1908, and it was three years before a new hospital was officially opened. The present hospital continues to operate from these buildings, and provides a valuable psychiatric and social service.

In 1954 the hospital acquired Riversdale, an adjoining property to the south, which the order remodelled and renamed Granada, in honour of the place in Spain where their founding father established his first hospital in 1539. The house now has a distinctly Spanish appearance, with its arched windows and white-painted, battlemented walls, and it houses a museum dedicated to the history of the order.

Not far off, and lying close to Galloping Green, were the houses of Ferney and The Grange.

The Grange, demolished in the 1960s and replaced by the Esso offices and headquarters, was a Georgian house of great character. The original five-windowed house was enlarged by the addition of an extra bay and a large ballroom, which was described as being in the Adam style. It stood close to the Stillorgan brewery and was occupied by Henry Darley in the early nineteenth century.

Ferney On the opposite side of the road overlooking Dublin Bay stands Ferney, now called Beech Park, a house which was acquired in 1956 by the Daughters of the Cross of Liege for the purpose of establishing a special school for the deaf. This most attractive, single-storey-over-basement villa, with its double bows and Wyatt windows, is now part of the school. The conical, slated roofs at the front of the house are a striking feature. The low front gives no clue as to the considerable size of the house, and to the rear there are more bow-shaped projections. All of the original windows survive intact throughout the house, which appears to have been built some time after 1800, and was first occupied by the Taylor family. Later occupants included Henry Scovell, who was a noted yachtsman in Kingstown during the mid-nineteenth century. In 1880 Ferney was sold to John Henry Darley, whose family were so influential in the affairs of Stillorgan, and in particular in matters concerning St Brigid's Church.

St Brigid's Church, with its well kept graveyard, is one of the most appealing churches in the south Dublin area. The historic character of the building, with its attractive tower and

St Brigid's Church, one of the most attractive old churches in the county, with its graveyard setting of beech and cherry trees

original Georgian windows, has been perfectly maintained and there is a great sense of peace in its surroundings, where beech and cherry trees shade the various tombs and mausoleums. Among the many interesting memorials are those of the families of Darley and Guinness. Arthur Lee Guinness lived in the old mansion of the Allens before its eventual demolition in about 1860.

The small, rectangular church was built around 1712 by the Allens of Stillorgan Park on the site of an earlier church. Some hundred years later, as its date-stone records, the present tower was added along with a north aisle which enlarged the church. Inside, the asymmetrical L-shaped gallery is an unusual feature, which is almost certainly of similar date. These extensions account for the fact that the east window, with its sandstone tracery, is off-centre. Many of the 1812 Gothic-style sash windows, along with their panes of old glass, are intact.

At the entrance to the church are the St Brigid's Schools which in 1836 were described by D'Alton as 'the poor schools', and which then accommodated about forty-five boys and thirty-five girls. The two-storey schoolhouse, with its stone doorcase and pediment feature, still stands, and is joined by a tiny, single-storey structure which may have been a gate-keeper's lodge. The rectory is a plain Victorian house which was built to rehouse the rector, who had previously been required to live in the glebe house, rather inconveniently located on Newtownpark Avenue.

Two other houses which were located close to the brewery are worthy of mention – Brookvale and Farmleigh. The former was attached to the brewery, while Farmleigh, a small, three-storey Georgian house, has completely vanished.

Glen Albyn, whose lands once ran back to St Brigid's Church, has served as a community centre since 1966 and now houses a variety of social clubs. The grounds were originally bought by the GAA for playing fields and in 1973 a swimming pool was constructed. The wide-fronted, late-Georgian house has an original fanlight and Georgian doorcase,

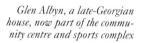

Glen Albyn, a late-Georgian house, now part of the community centre and sports complex

Redesdale, with its unusual carved return, was demolished in August 1998

which may date from the 1790s. A D-ended drawing room opens off the hall in the centre of the house. Glen Albyn, which was once called Janeville, was built on land leased from the Earl of Carysfort.

Redesdale, Parson's Green, Kilmacud House, Westbury and Clonmore form another important group of houses which, strictly speaking, are located in the townlands of Kilmacud, though today they might be considered to be part of Stillorgan.

Redesdale The first inhabitant of Redesdale was Sir Michael Smith, a lawyer who in the 1790s became Master of the Rolls. In 1799 the house was sold to an Englishman, Sir John Mitford, who had been Speaker of the House of Commons in London. Mitford came to Ireland to take up the post of Lord Chancellor, for which he was rewarded with the title Lord Redesdale. He took over the job from the much-hated Lord Clare, John Fitzgibbon, who had also lived in this district, at Mount Merrion House. Like his predecessor, Lord Redesdale was unpopular, and took a strong stand against Catholic emancipation, opposing any appointment of Catholics to positions of power or importance – the Penal Laws, first enacted in the seventeenth century, had restricted the right to worship, to build churches, to hold property, to vote, or to rise in the professions; in short, they denied all normal civil rights to those whose religion was Catholic. Mitford's unpopularity, and a sudden change of government, brought his appointment to an abrupt end in 1806, but not before he had made many improvements to Redesdale and left his title within its name.

A map of 1833 showing the Redesdale estate at Kilmacud, with its walled garden and out-buildings (courtesy National Library)

During the 1830s, we find another influential figure at Redesdale, in the form of Archbishop Richard Whateley. Sir Patrick Farrell, the sculptor, also lived there. It became a retreat house in 1903, and was called St Kevin's Park. In 1916 St Kevin's Park became the 'Irish training school of domestic economy', run by the Department of Agriculture. By 1943 it had become a convent, and was run by the Sisters of Charity as a home for 'recalcitrant girls'. The girls, many of whom worked in low-paid jobs and had limited education, were taught domestic economy. More recently, in 1975, St Anne's Day Care Centre was established by St

Kilmacud House is unusual with its cut-stone portico and large, Wyatt windows

Westbury, a Georgian house which was greatly enlarged in the Victorian style in about 1850

Michael's House, where the best of help and education is made available to the handicapped.

Originally, Redesdale was a large, three-storey-over-basement, eighteenth-century house, situated on 60 acres of land. It was approached by means of a long avenue from an entrance on the Goatstown Road. Redesdale was one of the most valuable properties in the area. The house had an unusual appearance, on account of the presence of squat top-floor windows and a bold cornice above. It was an imposing residence with a large porch containing semi-circular, *lunette* windows and there was a substantial return with an unusual quadrant bow. It is said that the house contained forty-eight rooms, which was quite possible given its height and extent. Internally it had some interesting features, including a semi-circular hall and an oval room with curved doors.

Redesdale was one of the last intact eighteenth-century houses in the whole area and, as we have seen, was of historical significance too. The house was still standing when I visited it in July 1998, and I had hoped to inspect the interior again, but most regrettably it was demolished almost as the ink was drying on this page. The demolition highlights the ongoing inadequacy of knowledge about our historic architectural heritage, even though new legislation and action is promised by the present government.

Towards Dundrum, Redesdale was joined by the lands attached to a house called Woodley, a plain, two-storey Georgian residence with an extensive farm and a walled garden. It was approached from the Goatstown Road, where the main entrance was graced by a cut-stone gate-lodge.

Parson's Green was one of the principal houses in Kilmacud before it became the convent of St Joseph at Kilmacud Manor, which the Carmelites have occupied since 1881. Like Woodley, it is a plain, eighteenth-century house, with several extensions including a stone-built chapel, which was added in 1896. The early house was occupied from 1791 until 1845 by William Snell Magee, a Dublin wine merchant.

Kilmacud House stands nearby, a three-bay, two-storey residence built about 1810. The house has five magnificent Wyatt windows and a cut-granite portico of great quality. It is ornamented with Ionic columns, wreaths and a low balustrade. During the nineteenth century it belonged to the Hoey family who gave a piece of their land on the Kilmacud Road for the building of schools and a Catholic church, which was erected in 1867. This now-deconsecrated church is partly used as a funeral parlour. Since 1949 Kilmacud House has been run as a home for the elderly by the Sisters of Our Lady of Charity, and it was they who gave the site for the present St Laurence's Church.

A hand-painted dinner plate with the crest of the Wilson family of Westbury

Westbury, now St Raphaela's Convent and Secondary School, began as a small eighteenth-century residence, evidence of which can be seen in the woodwork in the older section at the back of the house. For most of the nineteenth century, Westbury was associated with the Wilsons, a successful merchant family who, having lived there for some fifteen years, enlarged the house around 1850. Joseph Wilson had originally lived in his Dublin townhouse, which now forms part of the Temple Street Children's Hospital, and though he now lived at Westbury he maintained his townhouse up until 1870. Through marriage, Westbury passed into the ownership of the Pilkington family, whose initials may be seen in a heraldic stained-glass window on the staircase. During the mid-nineteenth century the house was substantially enlarged by the addition of a handsome portico, a dining room with elaborately carved mahogany panelling, a hall with classical figures represented in plaster panels and niches for statues, and a drawing room with superb, carved wooden over-doors with lion masks.

In 1930 Westbury was sold to the Daughters of Charity of St Vincent de Paul. Two years later they opened a home, called St Philomena's, for the children of unmarried mothers. Later a primary school was established and during the 1960s a secondary school followed to cater for the huge increase in population in the area. The school was later taken over by a Spanish order whose foundress was St Raphaela, and accordingly the name was changed in 1977.

The heraldic stained-glass window at Westbury which originally contained the Pilkington coat of arms

Clonmore, which stands close to Westbury, is another Georgian house, now much modernised but once an attractive house known as Rockland. It was situated amid a farm of eighty-eight acres and was owned by Thomas Wilson during the latter half of the nineteenth century. It was in this house that Claude Wilson, the father of Kathleen Turner (historian of Shankill and Rathmichael), lived as a child.

The original bow-ended, eighteenth-century house can be discerned behind the later Victorian additions to the façade of twin towers. A fine staircase with plaster panelling, plaster friezes and cornices in all the rooms, and old woodwork are all evidence of the eighteenth-century origins of Clonmore.

As we have already noted, the Stillorgan reservoir was constructed on the lands of Clonmore to supply water, at first only to the Rathmines township. Later it was taken over by Dublin Corporation which continues to pay a ground rent to the descendants of the Wilsons.

Merville, now only recalled in the name of a local estate, was once an

Beaufield, a plain early-nineteenth-century house, demolished in 1987

A detail of the painted ceiling in the hall of Beaufield

important farm. John Archer, in 1801, commented that it consisted of over 200 acres and that 'councillor O'Farrell of Merville uses oxen with neck yokes to plough, and to pull great wooden rollers when seeding his land'.

Two more distinguished Stillorgan houses, both close to the village, have also disappeared. They are Oatlands and Beaufield.

Oatlands was demolished in 1968 to make way for a new Christian Brothers monastery, and the site of the old house is marked by a cross. The Brothers bought the house in 1950 with the intention of establishing a secondary school in the Stillorgan area. The Christian Brothers' Educational Record of 1957 says of Oatlands: 'It was an eighteenth century mansion in a parkland of 13 acres. The house is of the old Georgian type, with ten rooms and the basement. A stair way led up to an observatory, where at one time was a valuable telescope, having lenses so powerful as to find their way to Dunsink astronomical dome.'

The house was built on lands belonging to the Allen estate although it stood almost beside the Fitzwilliam lands of Mount Merrion. Oatlands consisted of two-storeys over a basement, and was five windows wide with an Ionic portico and central Wyatt window above.

In 1840 the house was occupied by Colonel Matthew Pollock, of the noted firm of Ferrier Pollock. He was a military man, and is credited with having invented cordite, an explosive substance. Pollock had the observatory erected at Oatlands by Sir Howard Grubb, who supplied him with a six-foot telescope. This telescope was later bought by Dunsink Observatory for £50, but was unfortunately destroyed in a fire in 1977.

In 1910 the house was sold to Frederick Darley, but only six years later we find it inhabited by Sir John Ross, the last Lord Chancellor of Ireland. In his memoirs, Ross says of Oatlands: 'We were most fortunate in finding a charming house, "Oatlands" near Stillorgan. It was beautifully situated in view of the sea and mountains and there was a large and delightful old garden with abundant fruit and flowers. There was also a fine modern organ in the morning room, on which I delighted to play, making wonderful use of the stops, also an observatory on the roof, containing a splendid modern telescope constructed by Sir Howard Grubb who had the lenses made in Vienna.'

Beaufield To the south lies the well-known Beaufield Mews restaurant, the only reminder of an old house which was demolished here in 1987. Beaufield was a typical house of the 1830 period – plain, with a Georgian-type doorcase and a roof with projecting eaves. The ceiling of the hall was decorated with paintings.

In 1850 Beaufield was occupied by John Sweetman, one of two brothers who owned the long-established Sweetman's brewery in Francis Street in Dublin. His brother Patrick Sweetman lived in Stillorgan Priory, a Victorian Tudor-style house, now recalled only by the name Priory Park. Stillorgan Priory once had elaborate castellated gates on the Bray Road near Mount Merrion, which were swept away when houses were built on the lands during the 1930s.

CHAPTER 18

Leopardstown

For over a century, Leopardstown has been famous for its racecourse and has an established reputation as one of the most important racing venues in Ireland. The racecourse was opened in August 1888 and the inaugural race meeting was thronged with spectators. The opening lines from the new rule book set the scene:

'Leopardstown has been formed with the object of establishing a racecourse and a racing club in the neighbourhood of Dublin, on such a basis as to attract the attendance and support not only of the inhabitants of Dublin and its environs, but also of the residents and visitors of the fashionable resorts of Kingstown, Bray, and the thickly populated country round about. Leopardstown Park is entirely surrounded by a high stone wall of solid masonry and it is situated within ten yards of Foxrock station, of the Dublin, Wicklow and Wexford railway: it is easily accessible by rail or road from Dublin, Kingstown, Bray, from which it is between three and six miles distance respectively. The approach of the carriages is through scenery of admitted beauty. In addition to the race meetings to be held in Leopardstown it is proposed that coursing (for which the ground is admirably adapted) and polo meetings will be held, and lawn tennis courts will be constructed. The following gentlemen will form the committee of election: Lord Annaly, the Marquis of Drogheda, Colonel A. Paget, C. J. Blake Esq., W. Dunne Esq., the Earl of Clonmel, Lord Lurgan, Percy La Touche Esq., A. J. McNeil Esq., the Earl of

Rocque's map of 1757, showing Leopardstown

Leopardstown became one of the most popular and fashionable racecourses in Ireland

Above: Leopardstown's first summer meeting, 1904
Right: Theatrical winning at

The house and farm of Leopardstown House, the site of the racecourse

A chimney at Leopardstown House, adapted for use as a viewing tower

Enniskillen, the Marquis of Cholmondeley, J. Gubbins Esq., Captain Abercromby, Captain A. E. Whitaker, J. Haig Esq., W. G. Jameson Esq., M. Maher Esq., the Earl of Fingal, Colonel Forster, G. Quin Esq.'

The establishment of Leopardstown racecourse was the enterprise of Captain George Quinn and his associates. In 1888 they acquired the site of the racecourse from the Benedictine monks who had for a short time run a model farm here; the monks trained young gentlemen in the latest farming techniques at Leopardstown House which had very large farm buildings. The extensive stables were laid out around courtyards which were attached to the house, and the whole complex lay within the circuit of the new mile-and-three-quarters racecourse. The farm buildings were all eventually demolished. Long before the formation of the racecourse, horse racing had already taken place at Leopardstown when, during the 1850s, a race known as the Kingstown Stakes was held there.

The new Leopardstown racecourse was to be the ultimate in sophistication and was equipped with a special white and gold stand for the Viceroy, a members' stand which held 1200 and a grandstand which held 2000. George Quinn negotiated special arrangements with the railway company whereby inclusive tickets could be purchased at Harcourt Street station, and a ten-shilling ticket provided return travel and admission to the grandstand.

The Duke and Duchess of York (later to become King George V and Queen Mary) paid a special visit to Leopardstown in 1897 and King Edward VII, a keen yachtsman and sporting enthusiast, also made a point of attending a race meeting here in 1907. An important and interesting event took place at the racetrack in 1910 when Ireland's first aeroplane meeting took place. Several famous aviators were brought to Leopardstown for the occasion and the public paid upwards of 2s./6d. each to see the spectacle.

The elegant stands of the racecourse, with their refreshment rooms and bandstand, were located close to the neighbouring property of Leopardstown Park, the home of James Talbot Power. The Powers, who had made their fortune from the distillery in Dublin, were somewhat concerned in 1888 about the future racecourse as they felt it might be a nuisance and generally disturb their privacy. James Power specifically objected to the use of the words Leopardstown Park in the title of the racecourse as this was the name of his own house and grounds. The racecourse has since been known simply as Leopardstown.

Leopardstown Park is a very elegant Victorian house which is now in use as the administrative offices of Leopardstown Park Hospital, run by the Department of Health. The house, two-storeys-over-basement and five windows wide, has a fine portico constructed in Portland stone. There is also a cut-granite cornice and a balustrade at roof level. Though much of the lands surrounding the house were sold off to the Industrial Development Authority during the 1980s in order to establish a business park, its setting remains very pleasant and private.

A member's badge for Leopardstown racecourse

An earlier house is believed to have been built here by Charles Henry Coote, MP for Maryborough (Portlaoise), who leased the lands of Leopardstown in 1796. On his death the house was sold to Fenton Hort, who is listed as resident there in about 1830. The present house appears to date from the 1830s but was probably remodelled in the late nineteenth century when the Power family came to live there.

James Talbot Power, who purchased Leopardstown in 1877, was the grandson of the founder of the then very successful Power's Distillery in Dublin. He became a well-known philanthropist, and helped many worthy causes before his death in 1916. The following year his widow presented Leopardstown Park to the Ministry of Pensions as a hospital for disabled soldiers and sailors and other victims of World War I. The

The elegant Leopardstown Park, home of James Talbot Power, owner of Power's Distillery

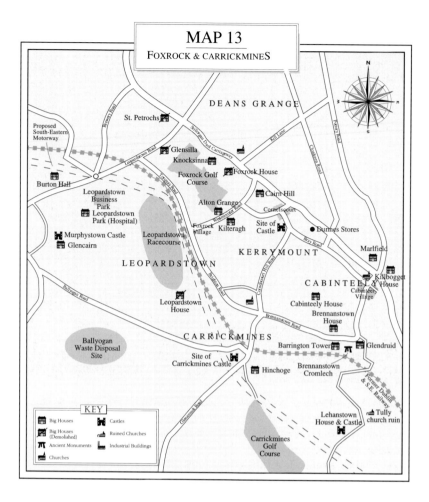

MAP 13
FOXROCK & CARRICKMINES

army and navy personnel who were looked after at Leopardstown wore a blue uniform, a white shirt and a red tie.

Burton Hall, which is now owned by the Eastern Health Board and leased to the St John of God Order, is said to have been built in 1730 by Samuel Burton. The Burtons were partners in a bank which briefly operated in Castle Street, beside Dublin Castle.

The Georgian house is distinguished by two semi-circular bows but has been substantially altered. The original position of the hall door has also been changed. During the nineteenth century it was occupied by Henry Guinness, the founder of the Guinness Mahon Bank, who made various improvements to the house, and added a large servants' wing at the back. It is said that part of the house was damaged by a fire which occurred during the 'troubles' of the 1920s. In 1939 Burton Hall was purchased by the Ryan family, who were the proprietors of the Monument Creamery in O'Connell Street. The Ryans also bought a house called Rocklands which stood across from Burton Hall on the other side of the Leopardstown Road. The last family to live in Burton Hall was that of Colonel Hume Dudgeon who had previously owned Merville, now part of UCD. Dudgeon was famous for his interest in horses and he re-established his riding school here in 1954.

Sheils Alms House Another fascinating building in Leopardstown is the former Sheils Alms House which was built in 1869 by Charles Sheils to provide housing for 'gentle ladies of slender means'. Sheils, a wealthy merchant from County Down who was widowed early in life, established other similar housing complexes in the north of Ireland. The attractive group of buildings, which stands at the junction of Brewery Road and Leopardstown Road, was laid out around a central courtyard and provided self-contained, rent-free accommodation. The elaborate clock tower, with its fine stonework, gables, arched opening and carved gargoyles, is an important local landmark. In 1986 the entire complex was sold and the old houses were renovated. New apartments, which were named The Chase, were erected nearby.

The Sheils Alms House is a magnificent, stone-built complex

The Stillorgan Convalescent Home, with its gabled front and rooftop cupola, was built some time after 1864. Later, in 1925, the Sunshine Home was built in its grounds to cater for children suffering from malnutrition.

Glencairn At the foot of the Three Rock Mountain and not far from Leopardstown is Glencairn, now the home of the British Ambassador to Ireland. In the grounds are the vaulted ruins of Murphystown Castle which gives the townland its name, Murphystown.

The first house at Glencairn was remodelled by Benjamin Woodword for a solicitor named George Gresson, and appears to have been built in about 1860. This building, of which little is known, was either completely absorbed into the later house or was demolished. The present mansion consists of a massive, battlemented, stone-built structure. This architecture gives Glencairn a feeling of baronial grandeur, while the

The palatial Glencairn, which was rebuilt on a lavish scale in about 1904 by Boss Croker

verandah, with its granite columns, creates a certain American colonial character. The whole house is constructed of locally quarried granite. The interior of Glencairn was lavishly appointed; there was a private chapel, and a morning room with a ceiling painted with birds – these were re-discovered some years ago as they had been over-painted. The saloon is richly ornamented in the Georgian style and several rooms have elaborately-carved, mahogany mantelpieces and fine, polished-oak floors. This house was owned by a Judge James Murphy who in 1904 sold it to Richard Croker, best known as Boss Croker. Croker was a wealthy American of Irish origin and, as he was also a fanatical horse owner and racer, he had an especially designed, crescent-shaped racing stable erected. He also laid out gallops for his own horses which was done by laying down thousands of tonnes of turf mould. Croker made an appearance as himself, the Old Tammany Hall Chief, in the Sidney Olcott film *The Irish Honeymoon* (1911). After Croker's death, Glencairn was offered for sale in 1939 with 375 acres, four secondary houses on the estate and the private gallops. The auctioneers described Croker's many racing successes: in one day at Leopardstown he won four races and the next day he won three, which prompted one news-paper reporter to suggest that the name of the racecourse should be changed to Croker's Town!

The railway station at Foxrock stood as a ruin until recently

The Harcourt Street Railway

It was in 1846 that the company called the Dublin, Dun-drum and Rathfarnham Railway was first incorporated to run a railway line from the city to Dundrum, with a branch to Rathfarnham. Much of this railway may still be seen, including the spectacular nine-arch viaduct at Milltown.

Even before the city to Dundrum line was completed, approval was given in 1851 for the proposed line to be extended to Bray, creating direct competition with the Dublin and Kingstown Railway Company which had already constructed a line to Bray, via the coast. Progress at Dundrum was slow as much rock-blasting was necessary and, in fact, the first section of track to be opened on the line connected Dundrum and Bray in 1853. The following year the Dublin-Wicklow Railway Company, as it had then become, opened a station at Harcourt Row, but it was only in 1859, with the completion of the beautiful station at Harcourt Street, that the line was officially declared open. Other stations were opened at Milltown, Dundrum, Stillorgan, Foxrock, Carrickmines and Shankill. All along the route the company built several fine bridges, including the viaducts at Loughlinstown and Milltown.

In 1910 the usual journey time from Stillorgan to Dublin was seventeen minutes, and the traveller had the choice of sixteen trains to the city on weekdays and fourteen to Bray on Sundays. The last train from Harcourt Street to Bray ran on 31 December 1958, following the decision of the Chairman of CIE, Todd Andrews TD, to close the line. The decision was much regretted at the time, and nowadays the utter folly of losing this valuable transport link is even more apparent. The case for reopening the route is now completely obvious when one considers the extraordinary growth of the south Dublin residential area. Furthermore, within the immediate area of Harcourt Street station there are forty new office blocks, as well as easy access to the rest of the city. The reinstatement of the nine-mile railway would involve the re-acquisition of some land, the reconstruction of a large bridge at Dundrum, and the restoration of six other bridges as well as a new station in the city.

The elegant nine-arched viaduct at Milltown once carried the trains of the Harcourt Street railway over the river Dodder

Steam power on the Harcourt Street line

CHAPTER 19

Foxrock and Carrickmines

Foxrock and Carrickmines lie between the villages of Cabinteely and Cornelscourt to the east and the area of Leopardstown to the south-west. The district is bounded by the Stillorgan dual carriageway and was once divided from Leopardstown racecourse by the presence of the Dublin and South Eastern railway.

The residential district of Foxrock is of fairly recent origin, most of it having been built between 1860 and 1920. In the early nineteenth century this area, lying between Leopardstown, Cornelscourt and Galloping Green, was all farmland and there were only two significant buildings here before 1840. These were Foxrock House and Foxrock Lodge. Foxrock House was a one-storey villa which had been added to an older, two-storey structure, possibly a farmhouse. It was demolished in about 1976. Foxrock Lodge became part of a school run by the Loreto Order sometime after 1941. These houses stood on part of the Galloping Green lands, which stretched towards Foxrock and belonged to the Lindsay family in the 1850s. It was only after the completion of the Harcourt Street railway in the 1850s that proposals for the development of Foxrock got under way. A new station was opened in Foxrock in 1862 and another was added at Carrickmines soon after, which meant that residents could commute quickly in and out of the city. Among the first areas to be developed was the Bray Road frontage where houses like Knocksinna and Shandrum were built around 1860. Others included Sefton, Kelston and Avonmore, all of which are large, two-storey houses, though the latter was demolished in 1976.

Avonmore was a typical, well-built, Victorian house with a grandiose entrance and front door. Knocksinna is a larger house with an asymmetrical front, a basement and extensive coachhouse and mews buildings. The house may well have been built for

The ruins of Avonmore, shortly before its demolition in 1976

Robert Smyth, whose famous Smyths of the Green premises on St Stephen's Green were noted as wine merchants and high-class grocers right up until the 1970s. To the front, all of these houses enjoyed views of Dublin Bay, while to the back they looked over Foxrock golf links to the mountains beyond.

Cairn Hill, one of many substantial Victorian houses in Foxrock, with members of the Lett family, c.1900

Among the spacious gardens and fine trees of Foxrock and Carrickmines one can find many houses of distinction. The most outstanding are those of the 1890s and early 1900s, while many of the earlier Victorian developments are quite dull. Westminster Road, stretching from Leopardstown racecourse and Foxrock village back to the Bray Road, is lined with neatly trimmed hedges.

Cairn Hill, which is situated at the Bray Road junction, is a substantial Victorian house of about 1860. The interior is spacious but plain and the façade has a typical Victorian appearance, with a double-arched window over the projecting porch. In the early part of this century Cairn Hill was the home of Sealy Lett, a Dublin wine merchant and great grandfather of this writer. During the 1960s it was occupied by the notorious Paul Singer who carried out the most extraordinary swindles through stamp dealing and investment, and many people lost their life's savings through his treachery. The grounds of Cairn Hill are now developed and the house has become a nursing home.

Hillside, Grasmere and Cedar Grove, also on Westminster Road, are similar to those already mentioned and are solid Victorian residences, each standing on an acre or two of grounds, and having beautiful gardens, tennis courts, and sometimes a paddock as well. Glenstall, Frankfield and Alton Grange are also to be found on Westminster Road.

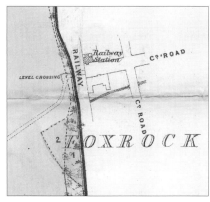

Foxrock village showing the railway station and line

Glenstall is an above-average Victorian house with good cut-stone features and Tudor-style window mullions, while Frankfield is in the old English, half-timbered idiom and has oak-beamed ceilings and a red-tiled roof. Alton Grange is also a Tudor-style residence, with similar half-timbered treatment at first-floor level. Carrickshinagh, with its fine symmetrical façade, is typical of the later taste for red roof tiles and magnificent white-painted woodwork. The same elements were used to great effect at The Chalet, which is another fine Edwardian-style house. A variety of houses was also built in the early years of this century in a style which could be described as 'the Georgian revival'. These were usually simple, two-storeyed houses with bow-shaped projections and sash windows. Belgrano on the Stillorgan Road, Priorsland in Carrickmines and Swynnerton on Brighton Road belong to this category.

The Stillorgan Road, with its central hedge, was one of the first roads of its kind ever built in Ireland. It has served its purpose well for over sixty years and is only now being upgraded and widened.

In 1859 W. W. Bentley announced that the lands of Foxrock would be developed. Bentley, who had either leased or purchased much of the Foxrock estate, planned to build many houses there and placed the fol-

Samuel Beckett's home, Cooldrinagh, is a fine example of the Edwardian style

lowing advertisement in *The Irish Times* in 1862: 'Beautiful building sites for mansions and pretty villas – Foxrock estate. The improvements recently made on this property, and still progressing, together with its natural attractions render these sites unrivalled for suburban residences. The scenery (green and mountain) from Brighton Road just finished, leading from the hotel at Foxrock station to Carrickmines, is magnificent. The land, being undulating, affords perfectly sheltered positions on Torquay Road, to the railway station at Stillorgan and Foxrock, as well as others elevated and more bracing. The rents required are exceedingly moderate: leases for 900 years are granted. Bricks, stones, lime and sand from the estate are sold at reduced prices to tenants. Stage coaches and omnibuses ply regularly between Foxrock station and Kingstown. Fare 3 pence and 4 pence. There is cheap and excellent shopping at Foxrock market. The railway subscription only £7 per annum. Apply to W. W. Bentley, Foxrock, or Bentley and Son, 110 College Green.'

Coologue, designed by Richard Caulfield Orpen for himself in the newly fashionable, Edwardian 'bungalow' style

The enterprising Mr Bentley thought of everything – bricks could be bought at twenty-five shillings per hundred, and he even organised an omnibus service to and from the railway station. He must have run into financial difficulties, however, as there is no further mention of him after about 1870 and his estate was taken over by the Royal Exchange Assurance Company. It would appear that this company continued the development of Foxrock which Bentley had so enthusiastically begun, and by 1876 *Thom's Directory* was able to state that about fifty detached villas had been erected on the Foxrock estate within the last ten years. To have an address in Foxrock quickly became a symbol of wealth and status in Victorian and Edwardian Dublin, and it is still regarded as a residential area for the rich. Foxrock was particularly favoured by the professional classes, such as solicitors, barristers and architects.

Apart from its many very well-off inhabitants, Foxrock and Carrickmines could also claim a number of residents who were either titled or famous for their artistic or creative achievements. In the early 1900s one finds the Right Hon. Viscount Ikerrin at Lissmullen, Sir Horace Plunkett, at his extraordinary house Kilteragh; the Hon. Mrs A. de Montmorency at The Grange; and The O'Morchoe (the head of the clan of O'Morchoe) at Kerrymount House – a plain, Victorian, two-storey-over-basement house with simple curved mouldings about the front door and windows. Sir Henry Robinson, KCB, who wrote two books about Ireland, lived at Lisnacerig. Lady Glenavy and Samuel Beckett are perhaps the most famous residents of the area.

Lady Glenavy, or Beatrice Elvery, came to live at Ellesmere in Carrickmines in 1888. The family were silk merchants from Spain, who came to Dublin in 1848 and changed their name from Alvarez to Elvery. The first of their well-known clothing and sports shops was established in O'Connell Street, then known as Sackville Street. Beatrice was a painter, and she illustrated a number of children's books and drew archaeological finds for the National Museum. She also designed the stained-glass windows in Tullow church.

Samuel Beckett, the world-famous playwright and novelist, was born in 1906 in Cooldrinagh, on Brighton Road. Cooldrinagh is a classic Edwardian-style house, designed by F. G. Hicks in 1903, built in the half-timbered Tudor style and set in spacious gardens. Jeremy Williams,

*The ornate furnishings of
Glen-na-Carraig*

in his invaluable book about Victorian architecture in Ireland, comments: 'A verbena clad verandah gives access to a croquet lawn shaded by a grove of larch that Samuel Beckett continuously recalled. But he never returned here. A visit was once arranged, but he did not arrive. Later the then owners were told that an elderly man had been sighted motionless at their gates!'

Beckett's father was a quantity surveyor and was connected to a well-known building family of that name. Samuel, though he had an older brother, seems to have had a lonely childhood in Foxrock. The children often accompanied their father to the Carrickmines Golf Club where he was honorary secretary. In the 1930s, when he went to live in Paris, Beckett devoted himself to writing and won the Nobel Prize for Literature in 1969. In one of his early novels, *Watt*, he makes reference to the familiar places in the Foxrock area such as Leopardstown racecourse.

Richard Millar, who came from a noted family of architects, lived at Ervillagh on Westminster Road and later at Hollywood in Carrickmines. The firm of Millar and Symes designed many Edwardian houses in this area. Glen na Carrig was built for Joseph Symes and his wife Adelaide Gibton of Gresham Terrace, Kingstown. A further member of the Millar family lived at Árdnamona, an Edwardian house on the Brennanstown Road in Carrickmines. Another Foxrock architect, Richard Caulfield Orpen, was at the height of his career in the early years of this century when *The Irish Builder* said of him: 'He may be said to be the originator of the bungalow in Ireland, and has built quite a colony of pretty, red-

The opulent interior of Glen-na-Carraig

tiled gabled houses in the fashionable residential district of Foxrock.' Richard Caulfield Orpen designed a house called Lisheens for his brother Charles St. George Orpen, and he himself lived in a house called Coologue which was built for his family. Alexander Horsburgh Porter, an artist of some note, lived at Priorsland, a large Victorian house with a fine, timber porch, which is situated close to the old Carrickmines station.

Alverstoke, an Edwardian house designed by Millar on the Bray Road

A number of distinctive Edwardian houses were built in Carrickmines, on the Brennanstown Road, and these include Glenheather, Cúil na Gréine, Árdnamona, Lisheens, Glen na Carraig, and Coologue. All were built on the Pim estate, which will be discussed later. It is interesting that a number of house-names in Carrickmines were inspired by the so-called 'druidic remains' – the cromlech at Brennan-stown – and by the fact that the lands were once owned by the Prior of Christchurch Cathedral: names such as Glen Druid, Druid Hill and Druid Lodge have an obvious origin, while others such as The Grange and Priorsland reflect the connection with the Church. Carrickmines, or Carraig-maighin, means 'the little plain of the rocks', a fairly accurate description of the landscape in some areas.

Barrington Tower in Carrickmines has also been described as 'a modern residence in the Georgian style', though its stone tower gives it an unusual aspect. The tower was built by Mr Barrington of Glendruid in 1810 as a viewing

Barrington Tower was a folly, erected in 1810, to which a large, Georgian-style house was added in 1956

One of the old embossed metal roadsigns with the distances given in miles

point and tea house in his demesne, close to the site of a medieval castle. It was described by D'Alton as 'a lofty pleasure turret erected near its [the castle's] former site by a Mr Barrington deceives the traveller'. The original castle was occupied by the Walsh family who also owned Carrickmines Castle. Near the tower is the private cemetery of the Barrington family, who were soap manufacturers in Dublin. The modern house at Barrington Tower was built onto the folly tower, and has a fifty-four foot, curved salon or dining room, which is handsomely articulated with eighteenth-century pilasters which were salvaged from Platin Hall near Drogheda. Perhaps the fan-shaped plan of this house was inspired by Kilteragh, where a similar sun-seeking layout was employed. Carrickmines House and The Grange, both on Brighton Road, were also built sometime after 1860. Neither is a very remarkable house, but the former features a large semi-circular porch and a domed, open staircase. It was until recently the home of the McInerney family who added a large extension with a bar and swimming pool.

The Bawn, situated on Kerrymount Avenue, is an interesting house which was built in 1903. Doric columns and pilasters ornament the entrance and a beautiful rectangular conservatory of timber construction makes a striking feature at the front of the house. The hall is lit by a delicate glass dome, and the whole house exhibits the finest quality joinery and plasterwork. It was built by Cramptons, the noted firm of builders, for George Panter, who was a leading figure in the decorative plasterwork business and had an important collection of paintings of Dublin interest in his home.

Carrickbyrne, which is perhaps the most out-standing Edwardian house in Carrickmines, is a large, gabled residence designed in the Tudor, half-timbered English style. It has attractive projecting leaded windows and a granite entrance porch. The house was built for William Ireland Good in about 1903.

Kilteragh Sir Horace Plunkett bought the large Kilteragh estate of in 1903 and immediately commenced building a house which was finished in 1905, the date being marked on one of the rainwater hoppers. Horace Plunkett was a Unionist MP for South Dublin, and after 1922 he

Kilteragh, one of the first truly 'modern' houses, was erected in Dublin in 1905

became a senator in the Free State. He enjoyed his new house for less than twenty years, as it was burnt down in 1923 as a political protest against his nomination as senator. It was an ironic act of vandalism as no-one had done so much for Ireland's agricultural industry or loved Ireland so much as Plunkett. In the tragic fire that destroyed his house he also lost an important art collection which included at least fifty paintings by AE (George Moore), twenty by Jack Yeats and a hundred other Irish works. Over 1500 scarce and valuable books were also destroyed in the fire. Plunkett claimed malicious damages for £28,122 for the house and £4844 for the contents, and he eventually received about half of this amount.

Kilteragh was designed by a Swedish architect named W. D. Caroe, and its plan followed the shape of a crescent, the long, curved drawing room facing out to the garden where it caught the maximum of sunshine. It was here that Plunkett used to entertain on a grand scale, and many famous political personalities came to dine and to talk about the country's problems. It was a very unusual house with its varied roofline, gables and towers. Plunkett's own bedroom, located at rooftop level, was a room which could be opened to the skies and he had a

The stone-built archway to the garage and yards at Kilteragh

The old railway station at Carrickmines, now a private house

Findlater's grocery shop at Foxrock made deliveries to the houses of the district

mechanical device installed which enabled him to turn his bed towards the sun or the moon! The magnificent oak front door in its fine granite surround and unique timber canopy are still intact. The canopy is supported from above by unusual wrought-iron brackets and has its original electric globe-light which must have seemed very futuristic in 1905. The entire house, now rebuilt as six separate residences, is not greatly changed, and the walls are still painted cream or white to reveal the finely chiselled granite coigns. Unfortunately, the original leaded windows did not survive the fire. The windows on the garden side overlook a beautiful terrace from which granite steps descend into a geometrically-planned, Italian garden with yew hedges. Near the front of the house is a magnificent arch, constructed from granite and tiles, which once gave access to the garages and a yard.

The Village

The village of Foxrock, if it could be called that, developed around the small nineteenth-century railway station which has only been demolished during the last year or two. The overgrown platforms and station house were visible until recently. The village possessed a post office and the Foxrock Tourist's Hotel which was erected around 1860. It was here that a branch of Dublin's most prestigious grocery establishment, Alexander Findlater's, was established. Findlaters specialised in supplying the wealthy merchant and professional classes with every requisite, and had a first-rate delivery service.

Tullow Church of Ireland church was completed in 1864 at a cost of £1600. It is a simple, rectangular, Gothic-style building with a small spire. The parishes of Tullow and Kill were formed in 1860 because Monkstown church was becoming too crowded and was too far from the centre of population at Foxrock. In the early 1900s a tin-built chapel

The older part of Carrickmines Croquet and Lawn Tennis Club is one of the few remaining timber sports pavilions in the country

stood in Foxrock at the top of Kill Lane, on a site given by the Royal Exchange Assurance Company, where Foxrock church now stands. This was begun in 1933 and completed the following year. Our Lady of Perpetual Succour Church is in the Italian Romanesque style, designed by Robinson, Keefe and Devane, and cost £22,000.

By the turn of the century golf and tennis had become very popular and several clubs were established in the area – Foxrock Golf Club was established in 1893 and Carrickmines was in operation by 1913, having been promoted by a stockbroker named Wilson who was living at Carrickmines House. Carrickmines Golf Club is approached by a narrow lane which in 1831 was described as 'the bridle path'. This road, on which there is an eighteenth-century farmhouse called Hinchoge, will soon be sliced in two by the construction of the South-Eastern motorway. Not far off is Carrickmines Tennis Club, which is still housed in its picturesque 'tin'-roofed pavilion.

The planned South Eastern motorway will also pass very close to the small fragment of masonry which is all that is left of Carrickmines Castle. This section of wall, with its arrow-slit opening, appears to have been part of a gate-house and substantial fortification consisting of a tower and various ditches, which have been identified by the archaeologist Paddy Healy. The remains of the castle lie in a farmyard, close to an old farmhouse. In 1642, towards the end of the rebellion, an Irish force was besieged in Carrickmines Castle, where it is claimed that over three hundred people were massacred by government forces. Though there are conflicting accounts of the siege, it is certain that the leader of the government forces, Sir Simon Harcourt, was shot and later died, and that subsequently the castle was razed to the ground.

Hinchoge and the lane, once known as 'the bridle road', which leads to Carrickmines Golf Club

The only surviving wall of Carrickmines Castle

CHAPTER 20

Cabinteely

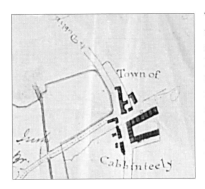

Map of Cabinteely in the early 1800s showing the village much as it is today

The village of Cabinteely, although now something of a backwater since the development of the new dual carriageway, was built around a busy crossroads on what was once the main road to Bray. Apart from the recent Bank of Ireland computer centre and the premises of John Hinde Postcards, there are no major buildings in the village, though there was a cluster of houses and cottages around the crossroads since the early 1800s. However, there has been a Catholic church in Cabinteely since the middle of the eighteenth century, if not before. The present church, which is plain and rectangular in form, was built sometime before 1838. It has a fine, exposed timber roof, a balcony and a classical-style porch which is ornamented by a small fanlight. It was erected, as John D'Alton remarked, 'with commendable economy of time and funds'. Some of the old cottages of the village survive, but only one has its original slates and windows. Cabinteely Library, which was accidentally burnt down in 1987, was carefully restored and is now a great credit to the library services. It has a tiled roof, copper cupola and leaded windows, and was built with the help of the Carnegie Trust in 1912. Further away, where the old and new roads meet, stood Cabinteely garage, an example of an early petrol filling station, built in

Cabinteely village, 1998

1929. The Horse and Hound public house occupies a prominent site and has an interesting canopied corner-entrance, which is now blocked up. The present Garda station stands on the opposite corner, but the old police barracks were situated close to the John Hinde works.

Cabinteely House and park lie to the west of the village and the demesne is entirely surrounded by a high wall, most of which is still intact. It was described by D'Alton as 'the most strongly enclosed demesne in the county'. It is said that the wall took five years to build.

The Cabinteely lands belonged to the Byrnes, one of whom married a sister of the wealthy Robert Nugent, Lord Clare, in the eighteenth century. Nugent, who was twice Lord Treasurer of Ireland, seems to have been very well disposed towards his sister and the Byrnes, and he is said to have built Cabinteely House for his own use and theirs in 1769. In that year Lady Shelbourne paid a visit to Nugent's sister, Mrs Byrne, at Cornel's Court and wrote: 'From Mr Byrne's house we saw one Lord Clare is building in the form of a castle with battlements which have a very good effect and will command, he says, a very fine view of the sea ... he has already planted a good deal about it and means to do more.' The original Georgian house which Nugent built was called Clare Hill. Its external appearance was substantially altered in Victorian times by the addition of elaborate mouldings, architraves, pediments and an Italianate frontage. However, the original doorcase remains, along with the roof-line urns and two beautiful rooms. The drawing room, which is situated on the first floor, has a coved ceiling, delicately ornamented with classical plasterwork plaques, cornices and friezes. The eighteenth-century staircase, which is also decorated with plasterwork, leads up to a long, vaulted gallery and ten bedrooms. In the hall there is a fine, eighteenth-

Cabinteely House and Park, now owned by Dun Laoghaire-Rathdown County Council

A billhead from Kennedy's Bakery in Cabinteely

The elegant drawing room of Cabinteely House

century sandstone chimneypiece which features busts and musical instruments.

The Byrnes lived at Cabinteely for most of the nineteenth century, but in 1933 it was bought by Joe McGrath, who was well known in connection with the Irish Hospital Sweepstakes and Waterford Glass. On his death in 1969 his family presented the house and part of the land to Dublin County Council as part of a deal in which planning permission was granted for a housing development on the Cornelscourt frontage. Two hundred acres were sold in 1977 for £1.6 million to McInerney's for building. The house is not yet open to the public, though it is planned to exhibit a large doll's house here along with a collection of vintage cars.

Cabinteely House and demesne are situated on high ground, from which extensive views may be had of Killiney, Rochestown and Sallynoggin. Below stand the industrial developments of Pottery Road, with Lourdes Hospital on the ridge nearby. A network of old estate roads can still be traced in Cabinteely demesne and the County Parks Department

The beautifully restored Cabinteely Library

has an extensive depot in the former yard. It is intended to completely restore the walled garden in which there was, until recently, a large range of glasshouses. At the top of the hill, looking to the south and west, are large belts of mature trees. St. Bridget's, an attractive new girls' school, has lately been built, and there is also a large housing development on the Cornelscourt side of Cabinteely demesne. The old St Bridget's school, which was located in Mart Lane behind Cornelscourt, was opened in 1912. It was designed by Richard Caulfield Orpen and is an interesting L-shaped building with granite detailing and slated roofs. An earlier school which was erected in Cornelscourt in 1844, on a site donated by the Misses Byrne of Cabinteely House, once accommodated two teachers and eighty pupils.

The stump of a medieval castle is mentioned in 1781 by Austin Cooper, who noted that it was surrounded by a couple of cabins, and its site is also marked on the early Ordnance Survey map. In 1849 all of the ten cottages in Cornelscourt were owned by Miss Clarinda Byrne of Cabinteely House. A general store, known as Foxrock Mart, was built near the village by William Bentley in about 1860.

An earlier Cabinteely House is believed to have stood on the site of Marlfield, which is located to the north of Cabinteely. Marlfield was built by John Byrne and was, until recently, occupied by St Gabriel's Hospital. The house is situated off the Johnstown Road and appears to date from the 1790s. There is an attractive square hall which contains delicate plasterwork. The façade, with its granite cornice and parapet, was once redbrick but has been rendered. The entrance is unusual as it has a semi-circular porch with Doric granite pillars and curved, sliding doors. At one time the porch was surmounted by a half-circular conservatory.

Kilbogget is a beautiful villa comprised of one grand storey over a basement, and may be attributed on stylistic grounds to John S. Mulvany, as it has many features in common with his two Dun Laoghaire yacht clubs and railway station. Kilbogget has an entrance portico with monolithic granite columns of the Doric order, and a spacious pillared hall off which one finds plain but well-proportioned rooms with high ceilings. The drawing room has elegant plasterwork of unusual design. This mid-nineteenth century house was added to an earlier farmhouse, part of which still survives to the rear. A private road joined the house to Kilbogget farm, an extensive group of buildings now swept away, along with all the remains of the old Killiney nursery, to form what is the present Watson estate. It was the home of the Broderick family in the early part of the century.

Cabinteely House

The unusual semi-circular entrance porch of Marlfield

Glendruid,
an attractive Georgian house
which remains unchanged today

Glendruid, a delightful house which has already been mentioned in connection with Barrington Tower, is situated above an unspoilt glen which stretches westward towards Carrickmines. A narrow path connected Glendruid with the tower, and passed through the valley below, where one of the finest cromlechs in Ireland is to be found. The Brennanstown cromlech, as it is known, has a massive capstone. Many have speculated as to how its builders managed to move a rock of such enormous weight and size.

A stone plaque on the front of the house records the fact that it was built in 1808 by John Barrington. It is five windows wide and has a bow end with a pretty, Ionic-pillared porch. It is said to have been built close to the ruins of a medieval castle, but this may have been a reference to the castle which once stood near Barrington Tower. Glendruid cottage, now vanished, was situated near the cromlech, and was once a pretty, two-storey, thatched house, also belonging to the Barringtons. In 1869 the cottage was occupied by the Rev. Charles Ormsby Wiley, Rector of Tullow parish.

Brennanstown House stands in a corner of the Cabinteely House demesne. It is a much-altered, late Georgian house which was adjoined by extensive stables and was occupied in 1798 by a Major Parker. In 1834 a map of the property shows that it was owned by Joshua Pim, who carried out many improvements to the grounds. Descendants of the Pim family continued to collect ground rents from all of Brennanstown until 1947, including Glendruid and most of present-day Carrickmines. It appears that the Pims had also acquired much Church property during the nineteenth century, for here at Brennanstown, as in the case of the

Killiney estate which they also owned, a tithe was payable to the Church property department of the Irish Land Commission. The Pim rents were sold by public auction in 1947.

Tully Church The high ground on which Tully church is situated is still one of the most delightful, unspoilt corners of County Dublin. But can the ancient church, with its old graveyard and the two granite crosses, keep this unique sense of place? Some years ago there was much vandalism in the graveyard, when chunks of stone were broken off tombs and a nineteenth-century Celtic cross was smashed into fragments. Tully is one of the most appealing ancient places in the county, and the preservation of its special character and peacefulness will be a challenge as development creeps ever nearer and the motorways come closer.

The two ancient crosses at Tully

As a child I was often brought here, and enjoyed the tree-lined lane, with its many twists and turns. I was attracted to the stone-built stile which led into the graveyard with its ancient ruined church. The church, situated among old trees and facing due east, commands excellent views of the surrounding countryside. The double east window and wide chancel arch suggest that Tully was once a large church, at least by twelfth-century standards. The nave has completely disappeared, and the church was described in 1630 as being neglected, with its roof collapsing, and having no parishioners.

Tully or Tullagh means 'a hillock', but Tully was known as 'Tully of the Bishops' or 'Telach-na-nun epscop'. Archbishop George Otto Simms, in his excellent study of the parish of Tullow, says that Tully of the Bishops is mentioned in the fifteenth-century Book of Lismore, which describes the life of St Brigid, the saint to whom the church at Tully is dedicated.

Simms also explains how the lands at Tully, like those of Dean's Grange and Killiney, once belonged to Christchurch Cathedral and that since its foundation in the eleventh century Christchurch controlled

The Brennanstown cromlech, as sketched by W. F. Wakeman

more than ten thousand acres in County Dublin alone – 2578 acres belonging to the parishes of Dean's Grange and Tully. We have already seen how owners of property in places like Killiney and Dean's Grange were still paying ground rents to the Church during the nineteenth century and even more recently.

The lands of Tully and Dean's Grange must have been well organised during the medieval period. It was the Normans who first brought organisation to all matters concerning Church and State. They set about dividing the country into counties and organised manors in many of the parishes. The manor was a farmhouse, and a symbol through which the prior of Christchurch Cathedral controlled lands. The prior's seneschal, who acted as a kind of steward and land agent, was in close contact with the tenants on Church lands. A parish survived on the income it received from its own produce and from its tithes. Everyone in the parish was obliged to pay a tithe, which was a tenth part of a man's total produce or income.

Two ancient crosses fashioned out of granite may be seen at Tully. The finest, which is a Celtic cross, is situated in the lane and was re-sited in 1897 on a dramatically-located, high stone plinth. The narrow steps up to the simple, undecorated cross have always been a great attraction for children, and a plaque on it records: 'Inscribed by his friends to the memory of James Grehan who saved this Celtic cross.' An old photograph of about 1890, in the Royal Society of Antiquaries of Ireland, shows the cross leaning dangerously to one side. The second cross stands in the nearby field and appears to bear a carving of a bishop or ecclesiastical figure on one side, with a head on the other.

Tully is famous for its decorated slabs or *leacs* – tombstones with fascinating pre-Christian or Early Christian marks and symbols which include concentric circles and herringbone motifs. One of these stones bears these motifs, but also incorporates a Celtic cross with narrow arms incorporated into the design in low relief. This suggests an interesting overlapping of pagan and Christian symbols.

Duncan's map, 1821, shows the demesne at Cabinteely House and the lands of Lehaunstown

The appealing ruin of Tully church will need careful protection if it is to keep its historic ambience

Lehaunstown House which has been discovered to incorporate a substantial part of a medieval castle

In July 1998 a remarkable discovery was made by archaeologists who were excavating a site near Cabinteely, when they found almost one thousand skeletons which are thought to be of Early Christian date. The site, where bones had been found before, was being prepared for a new petrol station. It seems likely that the site was some kind of cemetery, and it is interesting that the townland of Kilbogget stands close by. As the name Kill suggests, there may have been an early church here and it is clear, from the presence of the *leacs* and the later crosses, that Tully was an important religious centre.

A Gothic doorway recently discovered in Lehaunstown House

Lehaunstown has for long been well known as a large farm, with many stone outbuildings. However, recent examination of the old house has shown that it also incorporates part of a medieval castle or tower. Many of the walls are over three feet thick, and a cut-stone Gothic doorway has been discovered. The later, two-storey house is also of interest, and parts of it may date from the early eighteenth century. Unfortunately, many of the outlying stone farm buildings have already been demolished, but a fine range of Victorian stables still stands. Lehaunstown was the home of the O'Brien family, who farmed the land here until 1996. The new motorway will shortly pass very close to this historic group of buildings. Indeed, the future character of the whole area of Tully and Lehaunstown, which has a very special sense of place, may well be in jeopardy.

CHAPTER 21

Kilternan and the Dublin Mountains

Harvey's panoramic view of County Dublin, c.1850

Kilternan, or Cill Tiernán, meaning the church of Tiernán, takes its name from the ancient church which now lies ruined in a small and pictur-esque graveyard. It stands beside a little stream, close to the twisty road that leads uphill to Glencullen. The Kilternan area covers part of what could be called the 'foothills' of the Dublin mountains and stretches south towards The Scalp, and west towards Kilgobbin and Sandyford. The low hills of Carrickmines, and the slopes of the lead mines and Bal-lybetagh, have remained unchanged, and are a blaze of yellow gorse in spring. Kilternan is also, in essence, an area of unspoilt countryside, though some changes have taken place in recent times. Much of it is still farmed and it is becoming an increasingly popular residential area. The backdrop of the Dublin mountains, with Newtown Hill standing directly behind Kilternan, is mostly in its natural state, though much of it lies under a thick carpet of pine trees. Three Rock Mountain is the only exception, as it has a large collection of ugly TV transmitters and

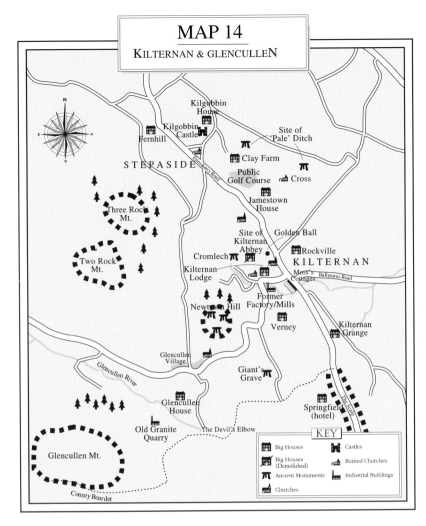

MAP 14
KILTERNAN & GLENCULLEN

Kilgobbin House
Kilgobbin Castle
Fernhill
Site of 'Pale' Ditch
STEPASIDE
Clay Farm
Public Golf Course
Cross
Jamestown House
Three Rock Mt.
Two Rock Mt.
Site of Kilternan Abbey
Golden Ball
Cromlech
Rockville
KILTERNAN
Kilternan Lodge
Moss's Cottages
Ballycorus Road
Former Factory/Mills
Newtown Hill
Verney
Kilternan Grange
Glencullen Village
Glencullen River
Giant's Grave
Glencullen House
Springfield (hotel)
Old Granite Quarry
The Devil's Elbow
The Scalp
Glencullen Mt.
County Boarder

KEY
Big Houses	Castles
Big Houses (Demolished)	Ruined Churches
Ancient Monuments	Industrial Buildings
Churches	

communications masts – like motorways, these are an unfortunate necessity of the age in which we live. The mountains were described in 1801 as 'bleak, uncultivated and in many parts barren'. J. Archer, who wrote this description in his *Statistical Survey of County Dublin*, described the difficulties which faced farmers in the mountain area. Crops were being pilfered and trees destroyed 'so that many proprietors are afraid to plant them'. This was presumably a reference to the 'wild Irish' whose descendants still inhabited parts of the Dublin and Wicklow mountains. Later, in 1838, John D'Alton commented of the Dublin mountains: 'though running within a few miles of the city it has been so greatly neglected that much of it is in the state in which the Deluge left it'.

The summits of the mountains are mostly shallow bog while ferns and gorse cover the lower slopes. Most of the coniferous forests, which were originally planted here by the State Forestry Service and are now looked after by Coillte, are easily accessible to the public. A short track winds its way up to the summit of Three Rock Mountain and provides a stunning view of the entire sweep of south Dublin.

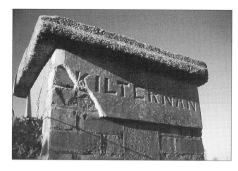

*The crumbling remains of the
entrance gate to Kilternan Abbey*

*The old millpond at the
Mill House, Kilternan*

Kilternan Village

In the early 1800s the inhabitants of Kilternan and the surrounding areas were largely occupied in dairy farming,
and made a living by supplying the needs of those living in
the city. At that time the largest farm at Kilternan was occupied by the Hoey family. The same farming activities
continue today, although some, such as the well-known
Kilternan Dairy, sold up quite recently. This dairy, which
delivered milk all over south Dublin, was run from Verney
Farm, whose lands ran up to Ballybetagh Hill. Verney
House was built in about 1820 and stood beside an eighteenth-century
farmhouse, which was in more recent times the home of the Fox family,
the proprietors of the dairy. The house has a cut-granite doorcase and a
stone-flagged hall.

All around this area one can see granite stonework, in the form of cut-stone gate piers, walls and doorcases. Loose stone walls are also a striking feature of Kilternan and Glencullen. Samuel Lewis, writing in 1837, says that the granite was quarried in many different parts of the district and that quarrying was the livelihood of many families in the area. It remains a source of employment in Glencullen valley today with the quarry of Stone Developments Limited which is situated at the Devil's Elbow.

The Keegans, once a populous and noted farming family in the area, were the original owners and builders of what became Willis's grocery and post office, which was situated on the main Enniskerry Road. A photograph from about 1890 shows Keegan's shop, then a butcher's, with sides of beef hanging up in the adjoining storeroom. Edward Willis acquired the premises in the 1890s and his descendants still own the property. It was, until its closure in 1990, one of the last 'old-world' post offices in the county, which was combined with a grocery and hardware business. The shopfront, with its carved wooden brackets and fine, cut-granite façade, has remained unaltered since the 1880s. The post office was once the focal point of Kilternan village, which, with its old schoolhouse and row of cottages, lies on the main road to Enniskerry.

The former Kilternan post office and Willis's grocery shop

The Kilternan stream passes under a bridge on the main road, and bears two plaques bearing the date 1852 and the distance from the GPO. It once powered two mills, one of which was a cotton mill founded by the Mosse family. The mills once provided considerable employment in the area and the attractive line of late nineteenth-century cottages on the main road was erected for the mill workers. These are still known as Moss's cottages. Part of a mill pond and a broad mill race still remain, but there was also a paper mill here, which has vanished.

In 1755 the proprietors of the paper mill, Messrs. Eaton and Nixon, sought a parliamentary grant to assist their 'manufacturing of paper'. The business changed hands and later D'Alton states that Mr Hely's paper mills in Kilternan were employing about thirty people for over six months of the year, but wrote disapprovingly of the way in which goods and provisions were used as settlement of wages. The Hely family later became noted stationers in Dublin and eventually settled in Rathgar. During the nineteenth century flax was grown in the surrounding fields and cotton was manufactured at Kilternan.

Kilternan Abbey The lands of Kilternan belonged to Richard Anderson in the early 1800s, and a map of 1813 shows

Kilternan Church of Ireland church was erected in 1826 in the 'late-English Gothic style'

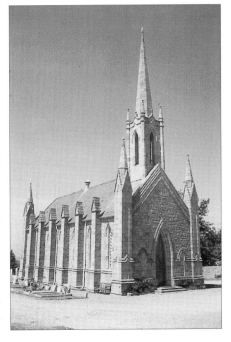

An attractive eighteenth-century, Gothic-style staircase window in Kilternan Lodge

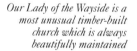

Our Lady of the Wayside is a most unusual timber-built church which is always beautifully maintained

his house at Kilternan Abbey. Kilternan Abbey and its surrounding land was originally held by the monks of St Mary's Abbey as a country residence and farm. Kilternan Abbey, which is marked on the first Ordnance Survey map of 1843, was a Georgian house which has now been in ruins for many years and is the site of the local authority water works. The old brick walls of the house and imposing entrance gates at Golden Ball suggest that it was built in the eighteenth century. The impressive gate piers were, until about ten years ago, surmounted by huge stone balls, and one wonders if the name of the locality, Golden Ball, arose from these having once been painted gold? No photographs of the abbey have yet come to light, but extensive walls of the basement and the former gardens still remain. The house was built on elevated ground and commanded a beautiful view of Killiney Hill and Dublin Bay. In the early 1900s it was the home of Count Horace Plunkett whose son, Joseph Mary Plunkett, was executed for his part in the 1916 Rising. Plunkett was one of the leaders of the Easter Rising and, like Thomas McDonagh and Pádraig Pearse, he was also a poet. Not far off is the second-largest cromlech in Ireland whose capstone measures twenty-two feet in length. Unfortunately, there is no clear public access or signage to direct the visitor to this important monument.

The old church ruins at Kilternan consist of west and east gable walls, the east wall having a good, twelfth-century, round-headed window. The original west doorway remains blocked up. An old bullaun stone, which looks like a hollowed-out grinding stone, but may have had some religious significance, may be seen inside the church.

Lewis tells us that the present Kilternan Church (Church of Ireland), which was built in the nineteenth century, was 'a handsome edifice in the later English style'. It was erected in 1826 at the cost of £1900, of

A stone buttress supports an old mill or stable building at Kilternan Lodge

which £900 was a gift from the Board of First Fruits, £500 being given by Lord Powerscourt and the remaining £500 raised by assessment from the local parishioners. It was designed by Richard Semple, and is constructed entirely in granite. The thin pinnacles and slender spire add to the graciousness of the church, which in design is not unlike Semple's Black Church in Dublin's north city centre. Until 1824 the parish of Kilternan was part of the greater parish or vicarage of Bray, but because of the distance from Bray it was decided that Kilternan and Kilgobbin should be separated from Bray and united as one parish. Besides, the old church of Kilgobbin, whose ruin still stands, was by this time too

The Scalp – a dramatic natural chasm, now dominated by speeding traffic

Rockville, an eighteenth-century house which is distinguished by its pedimented front

The ancient cross at Jamestown

small for its congregation and too much out of repair.

The new church was built on a site donated by Elizabeth and Susan Anderson, and the first vicar of Kilternan was the Reverend Henry Kearney. The schoolhouse, which stands nearby, appears to be contemporary with the church and is also marked on the first Ordnance Survey map.

There is another attractive church in Kilternan, which is completely different in style and construction. It is the unique, wooden Roman Catholic church which is dedicated to Our Lady of the Wayside. The church, standing on a spacious lawn, is constructed entirely of timber with horizontally laid, white-painted boards, and it has a plain, panelled interior.

Kilternan Lodge A study of Rocque's map of 1757 indicates that the village of Kilternan was then situated in and around the old ruined church, and close to a house called Kilternan Lodge. The map shows a cluster of buildings laid out in a rough square, perhaps as a village, but all traces of it have vanished. Kilternan Lodge is a delightful, small Georgian house, dating from about 1740. A large stable block adjoins it and the grounds are surrounded by high walls. It was once attached to the mills, and may have been the mill owner's residence.

The various maps of the district, made before 1816, show that the main road to Enniskerry did not pass through The Scalp but ran to the north of it, along the Barnaslingan Lane. Yet Archer, in 1801, states that 'there is an excellent road leading through the chasm leading to Enniskerry'. Some thirty years later Lewis describes The Scalp in romantic terms: 'a deep natural chasm in the mountain, forming a defile with lofty and shelving ramparts on each side, from which large detached masses of granite of many tons weight have fallen, on each side large masses of detached rock are heaped together in the wild confusion, apparently arrested in their descent, and threatening at every moment to crush the traveller by their fall'.

The Scalp is one of the most dramatic natural features of the Dun Laoghaire-Rathdown area and lies on its border with County Wicklow. It is perhaps not fully appreciated because of the lack of a proper pathway through it for walkers and pedestrians – the narrow road is totally dominated by speeding traffic.

Travelling from Kilternan to The Scalp one passes along a long, straight road lined with beautiful trees. To the right, overlooking The Scalp, is the extensive Kilternan Golf and Country Club, built around an early nineteenth-century house called Springfield. Springfield was the home of George Darley, a poet and mathematician, during the early part of the nineteenth century. He died in 1846. More recently it was used as a nursing home, before becoming a hotel in 1970. The attractive, five-bay house with its stone entrance porch overlooks an ornamental lake which once had a fountain. Part of the once-impressive entrance gates still stand on the main road.

To the north of this road is Kilternan Grange, a very fine, cut-stone, Tudor-style house which was added on to an earlier building. The older house was described by Lewis in 1837 as 'a handsome villa with an Ionic portico and tastefully disposed grounds'. Then it was called Kingstown Lodge, the name Kilternan Grange being adopted around 1920 when it became the home of a noted family of solicitors named Moore.

Glenamuck, which means 'the glen of the pigs', is an area which runs from Carrickmines to Golden Ball. The Glenamuck Road is bounded by agricultural land, but is becoming increasingly built up with houses. The recent erection of very large ESB pylons in the fields here has caused much controversy, and they undoubtedly spoil the views in many situations. To the west is Ballyogan tiphead, a large local authority landfill site or dump which has been in operation for nearly twenty years. The capacity of this dump will soon be exhausted and it is planned that the artificial hills that have been created will be landscaped as a park and golf course. At present methane gas is collected from the dump and used to generate electricity.

Jamestown House, now lying in the public golf course, deserves to be renovated

To the east, stretching towards Ballycorus, is a relatively unknown valley called The Dingle. This valley or escarpment is like a miniature version of The Scalp and is not visible from any nearby road. It is a fascinating rocky gorge, filled with trees and bushes, and it remains in its natural state. Nearby are the remains of an extensive granite quarry, and an old quarry road leads back to Rockville House in Kilternan.

Rockville House is situated at the head of Glenamuck Road and appears on Rocque's map of 1757. It is a medium-sized Georgian house, with a walled garden, and is similar to a group of houses which once included Allenton in Tallaght, Geraldine House in Milltown and the original house at Shankill Castle. All of these have a similar design, being five windows wide and two-storeys-over-basement, with a pediment featuring an oculous or Diocletian window – a small, either round or semi-circular window. All have fine, cut-granite doorcases with simple fanlights above, and appear to have been built in or about 1750.

Jamestown House, built in the late eighteenth century, is situated between Kilternan and Stepaside, just north of the road leading back towards Dundrum. It is unfortunately now a ruined shell, but was once an attractive house. It is late Georgian or Regency in style and some ten years ago contained the remains of a handsome, sandstone doorcase with carved rosettes, a fanlight and some internal plasterwork which featured reeded mouldings. Robin Goodbody, in his excellent study of the Kilgobbin area, *On the Borders of The Pale*, says that Jamestown House was built by Edward Rourke, a Dublin pinmaker, some time after 1780. The lands of Jamestown were eventually acquired by the former Dublin County Council, who laid out a very attractive public golf course there. To the east of the house, in a clump of trees, there is an ancient cross and the site of an old well, which are all that remain of an early medieval church.

Plasterwork from the hall of Jamestown

CHAPTER 22

Glencullen and Ballybetagh

The valley of Glencullen is the meeting point of the counties of Dublin and Wicklow and lies within the Dublin mountains. Glencullen village is situated on the slopes which first rise above The Scalp and Kilternan then become mountains extending west towards Tallaght and Brittas. The mountains themselves are covered with moorland, while below are small fields used for pasture and grazing. Above Kilternan stands the hill and wood of Ballybetagh, where in a bog or marsh over one hundred skulls of great Irish deer were found. The antlers of some of these deer or elk measured twelve feet across. It is thought that they may have drowned in a marsh or lake. There is no longer any evidence of this marsh which is marked on Taylor's map of 1816 as Killegar Lake.

There is an abundance of stone circles and evidence of very ancient habitation all over Ballybetagh and the Newtown Hill area, and this was all carefully surveyed and described in Eugene Curry's letters and sketches to the Ordnance Survey in 1837. He describes 'a giant's grave' at Ballybrack (a townland in Glencullen), which was known locally as 'The Greyhound's Bed' where a stone ten feet by seven feet lies. Curry also tells of a fascinating well which was situated a quarter of a mile west of Glencullen House near the river. He says that the peasantry call it the 'Butter Well' as they believed that 'washing dairy vessels with its waters is a certain specific against the loss of butter by witchcraft!' The well was located on Fiery Lane, which is said to be the early site of Glencullen village.

Old cottages which once formed part of Glencullen village

The Ballybetagh Road, a narrow lane which leads to Killegar, offers stunning views across Dublin Bay and in the opposite direction towards the Great Sugar Loaf mountain. In this area there is an abundance of dry stone walls which are reminiscent of Connaught and seem strange in such close proximity to Dublin city.

The mountain landscape at Glencullen, from the gates of the old Catholic church

In 1813 these lands were in the possession of George Darley, whose family had a long tradition of stonecutting and building.

Since medieval times, the lands of Glencullen belonged to the Fitzwilliams of Merrion. In the year 1240 'Glinculyn' was granted by Raymond de Carreu to Sir Geoffrey De Turville, whose rent consisted of the annual payment of six marks and a pair of white gloves or one penny at Easter!

The FitzSimon family acquired the estate in 1676. They were of Norman origin and connected with the Fitzwilliams. Both families, even though they were substantial land owners and considered to be 'Catholic gentry', were subject to the Penal Laws because of their religion. Despite this, the FitzSimons were highly respected and managed to hold onto their property. At the end of the seventeenth century, Christopher FitzSimon established, in partnership with Captain Philip Roche, an important glass factory called the Round Glass House in Mary's Lane in the city. It was one of the earliest glass factories recorded in Dublin, but was demolished in 1787 following the collapse of their business.

This statue of Daniel O'Connell once stood in Glencullen House

One of the family, who lived during the latter part of the eighteenth century and was nicknamed Racketty FitzSimon, ran up great debts through gambling. It is said that one day, when returning on his horse to Glencullen, he encountered the Protestant clergyman of Kilgobbin, who informed him that he would purchase his horse for £1. He was entitled to do this, as under the Penal Laws no Catholic could own a horse worth more than £1. Racketty rode home and had his horse put down rather than suffer such an indignity.

During the nineteenth century another FitzSimon, Christopher, married Ellen O'Connell, who came from a wealthy family. From this point onwards the family bore the name of O'Connell FitzSimon. Apart from building a fine new house called Glencullen House, Christopher was a generous landlord and built the Catholic church in 1824, along with a school and a dispensary in the new village.

The back door at Glencullen House, 1985

The original Catholic church in Glencullen, now in ruins, was erected in 1824

As already mentioned, the eighteenth century village of Glencullen was located on and around the Fiery Lane, which lies to the west of Glencullen House. The original lane which once connected Fiery Lane to the house and to the valley below has all but disappeared. Glencullen is located high on the southern slopes of Two Rock Mountain and its aspect can often be very exposed and sometimes bleak. Glencullen lies at a crossroads where the focal point today is Fox's pub.

The ruin of the 1824 St Patrick's Catholic church and its surrounding graveyard is still to be seen. The church was burnt down accidentally and replaced by the present attractive church. It is no coincidence that Glencullen became a Catholic stronghold in the nineteenth century as the native Irish, the O'Tooles and O'Byrne's, had been driven from Dublin into the mountains many centuries earlier. From here they continued to raid the well-tilled lands of County Dublin, from Norman times until the eighteenth century.

The graceful façade of Glencullen House, erected in the early 1800s

Glencullen House, beautifully situated in a tree-filled valley close to the village, is a villa which was added on to a very old farmhouse. The villa, designed in the Greek Revival style, has a handsome Doric portico of local granite. It was probably built around 1800, and may have been designed by Francis Johnson, the noted architect of the General Post Office in O'Connell Street. Looking east from the portico there is a pleasant view of the Little Sugar Loaf mountain. Glencullen House was owned by the FitzSimon family until the early years of this century, when it was sold and they moved to a house called Moreen in Sandyford. In 1953 Lieutenant Colonel Manners O'Connell FitzSimon bought back Glencullen House and lived there until his death in 1985. His ancestor Daniel O'Connell had held the first meeting of the Catholic Association there in the early nineteenth century and the dining-room table came from O'Connell's home in Derrynane, County Kerry.

The chimney of the lead mines, built in 1836, was later extended by a brick section, shown here

Glencullen valley, which is long and straight, has, as J. B. Malone writing in 1950 put it, 'an air of lonely grandeur'. The abandoned granite quarry in Glencullen must once have provided employment for many quarrymen, stonecutters and carters. Stone from Glencullen was used in many important Dublin structures, such as the GPO in O'Connell Street and the Department of Industry and Commerce building in Kildare Street. The great heaps of spoil – discarded stone and waste – can still be made out here, and pieces of shaped stone lie about, now buried by heather.

The chimney today, with its remarkable cantilevered spiral stairs

During the Emergency of 1939 to 1945 several bog roads were made on Glencullen Mountain and Prince William's Seat to provide access to the areas where turf was cut to supply the city with fuel. Many people recall that time when fires had to be lit, with great difficulty, using only the damp turf from the Dublin mountains.

Ballycorus

Not far from Kilternan is Ballycorus where extensive remains may be seen of the old lead works, especially its chimney. Mining activities began here in about 1807, sometime after lead ore was discovered, and by 1824 two veins of lead were being worked. Silver was also once found here in considerable quantities. The old mine shaft ran west from the chimney in the direction of the nearby woods, which were planted by the mining company. The picturesque granite chimney, with its external spiral staircase and viewing platform, is a noted landmark and was marked on admiralty charts as a point of reference for mariners. Photographs taken around 1900 show the chimney to have been much taller, with an extra brick section which was later dismantled. The chimney and its lengthy flue, which ran for one and a quarter miles, carried the highly poisonous fumes away from the works where the lead was being processed; the flue was periodically cleaned and

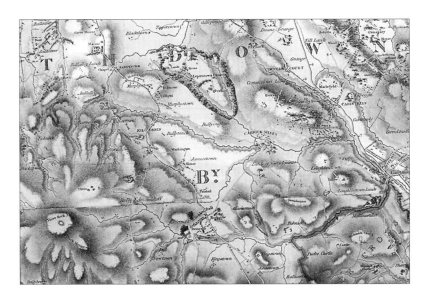

*Duncan's map gives a good
impression of the relatively
'wild' nature of the Dublin
mountains in 1821*

*Entrance to the lead-mines
chimney at Ballycorris*

valuable arsenic was collected by men who scraped the walls. It is of
stone construction with a brick roof and was sealed with a layer of earth.
Substantial parts of the flue with its inspection doors still exist and can be
explored.

A shot tower, where shot or bullets were manufactured, has survived
and has been restored along with some other old buildings. Shot was
made by pouring molten lead from a height, through a perforated tool,
into water far below where it cooled into a perfect ball.

Another, more elaborate, shot tower has vanished, but was described
by Weston St John Joyce: 'The shot tower, a conspicuous object in the
valley, is a handsome and substantial structure, having a spiral stairs
within, terminating in an artistic iron verandah on the outside, nearly
100 feet from the ground, overlooking the adjoining pond, water wheel,
machinery, shot premises, while in the immediate vicinity are a number
of cottages, built for the employees of the company.' These cottages and
other buildings still remain, comprising a very important collection of
nineteenth-century industrial buildings. All are built of granite, including the furnaces, purification tanks, lime kilns, stores, the workers'
cottages and a large house erected for the manager or superintendent,
the last of whom, when the works closed in 1913, was a man named
Roberts. As mentioned earlier, nearly all the lead ore was brought to
Shankill by train from Glendalough, and thence by horse and cart to the
works at Ballycorus. The chief use of lead in the nineteenth century was
for the manufacture of pipes and sheeting for roofs.

CHAPTER 23

Kilgobbin and Stepaside

There are no great houses or major settlements in the area of Kilgobbin and Stepaside, but there are many interesting antiquities to be found, all of which have been well described by Robin Goodbody in his book *On the Borders of The Pale*. These monuments include part of the original ditch called The Pale, the impressive cromlech at Kilternan, the ancient tower houses of Kilgobbin and Murphystown, and the ruined churches of Kilgobbin and Kilternan. The houses of the area tend to be of modest size and were mostly the homes of the bigger farmers or the well-off professional classes who began to settle here during the nineteenth century. Some of these houses remain, often in their original rural setting. The area, with its mature trees and fields, is still relatively unchanged and possesses much of the rural character that it has had for many centuries. Much of the land is still being farmed, and some of it is now used for sporting facilities, with rugby pitches and golf courses to be seen on either side of the Enniskerry Road. The Jamestown golf course, which is run by the local authority, was created on the lands of Jamestown House, the ruin of which may still be seen. During the nineteenth century most of the lands of Kilgobbin were let to John Rourke of Jamestown House and later, in the 1830s, to the family of Mowlds. Clay Farm, which appears to have been built in around 1820, and Kilgobbin Cottage stand at the top of a tree-lined laneway in an area of unspoilt farmland. Clay Farm possesses many of its original nineteenth-century

A peasant woman rests at Kilgobbin Cross, c.1890

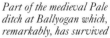

Part of the medieval Pale ditch at Ballyogan which, remarkably, has survived

stables and sheds and the land is still farmed. Goodbody describes how the lands here were farmed continuously by the Webb family since 1698 until the early nineteenth century, when they ran into financial difficulties. It was eventually sold to the Lawless family, whose descendants still farm here.

Below the fields in front of Kilgobbin Cottage lies part of The Pale ditch. The word 'Pale' is derived from the Latin for stake. The Pale was a double ditch which was stone-faced on the outside and thickly planted with

bushes. It was a defensive ditch, built in the thirteenth century by the Norman inhabitants of Leinster, principally to keep their cattle in and to keep the native Irish, such as the O'Tooles and the O'Byrnes, out. In the event of an attack, fires were probably lit on the towers or look-outs of The Pale, and all would assemble to protect their property and fight off the enemy. The Pale once ran from Dalkey across south County Dublin and out into County Kildare, but the only part to have survived is this section near Kilgobbin.

Kilgobbin Church is striking because of its elevated position. It stands on a small mound and is situated within a triangle of roads leading to Stepaside village. The church is a heavily-restored ruin, and it is curious that there are no windows or openings in the gable walls. The masonry in these walls and the belfry may be of recent date. A large Celtic cross, which is slightly damaged and stands in the lane in front of the church, bears the weather-worn image of a figure. Recently, during repairs, a decorated early grave-slab or *leac* was uncovered and this is now on view inside the church.

Top: The ruin of Kilgobbin Castle

Above: James Saunders' view of Kilgobbin Castle before its collapse in 1834

Until the nineteenth century, the main Dublin to Enniskerry road followed a winding route through Stillorgan, past Kilgobbin and Stepaside and on to Kilternan. Kilgobbin village, which has disappeared, then had some importance, and in the seventeenth century consisted of a cluster of cabins arranged around Kilgobbin Castle. The old castle today stands close to the sweeping drive and lawns of a nineteenth-century villa called Kilgobbin Castle House.

Kilgobbin Castle Though much of the castle collapsed in 1834, the ruin is quite substantial and part of its vaulted undercroft is still visible. The castle was built by the Walsh family, who also occupied other fortified houses in the Pale borderlands, such as Carrickmines and Shanganagh. In the seventeenth century we find Adam Loftus of Rathfarnham Castle in possession of Kilgobbin Castle and lands. Loftus eventually sold to Thomas Connolly of Castletown House in Celbridge, who continued to control all of the lands of Kilgobbin and much of Glencullen during the eighteenth century.

Kilgobbin Castle House This villa consists of one storey over a basement, with an unusually tall, projecting porch, and is joined on to a smaller, earlier house at the rear. It was occupied by the family of Bayly during the nineteenth century.

The Richardson family, prominent farmers and builders in the area since the middle of the nineteenth century, continue to live at Clay Farm.

Their prominently-situated mausoleum is still to be seen at the entrance to Kilgobbin graveyard. John Richardson, who was a stonemason and builder, is thought to have built the now-vanished houses of Larkfield and Elmfield which once stood near the Ballyogan Road. Richardson was also appointed to the job of building the new church at Kilternan. Elmfield was originally built in the 1820s but, following its demolition in 1914, a new house of the same name was built in its place. Larkfield was a single-storey-over-basement house, which has also completely disappeared. Greenfield, originally an early nineteenth-century house, was completely rebuilt at the end of the nineteenth century. Kilgobbin House, which stands close to the main road, is a charming, late-Georgian farmhouse with an attractive round-headed doorway and fanlight. It was probably built around 1800, and may incorporate an earlier structure.

Some of the early nineteenth-century farm buildings at Clay Farm

Robin Goodbody relates how a Catholic farmer in Kilgobbin, named Thomas Callaghan, became a victim of the Penal Laws during the middle of the eighteenth century. It would appear that there was a maximum length of time during which a Catholic could hold or rent a piece of land, and if he was discovered to have held it for too long, it could be confiscated. A Protestant could apply to the courts and have himself declared the discoverer of a so-called illegal holding and thus acquire the lands. In this instance an opportunist named Thomas Fleetwood claimed to have discovered an irregularity in Callaghan's lease and he thereby acquired the lands, which he promptly sold on. Fortunately, Callaghan was able to repossess his lands before long.

Kilgobbin House, built in the 1790s, once part of the now-vanished Kilgobbin village

Stepaside

An eighteenth-century coach in County Dublin

During the nineteenth century, Kilgobbin village fell into decline and Stepaside became the new centre of activity in the area. Stepaside lay on the busy road from Dundrum to Enniskerry, and during this period it acquired a new police station and a forge, while its inn became a well-known hostelry. The name Stepaside originated during the eighteenth century and may be a corruption of 'steepside'. It has also been suggested that Stepaside took its name from that of the inn, as this was a favourite halting place for coaches on their way to Enniskerry and County Wicklow.

Coach travel during the eighteenth century was not particularly comfortable. Roads were generally rough and often deeply rutted in wet weather, making movement difficult and travel slow – the term 'slow-coach' originated from the many complaints made about coaches that travelled at a speed of less than five miles per hour! During the eighteenth century, a heavy stagecoach might travel at eight or ten miles per hour. During heavy rains, floodwater created further risks for coaches and travellers, and where streams and rivers had to be crossed by ford there was a great danger of the horses losing their footing or being swept away altogether. Sometimes passengers crowded on to the roofs of coaches and this created even greater danger for all concerned.

The living area and fireplace of the quarryman's cottage below

Overhanging trees or bushes were further hazards for the drivers of coaches, and such trees also prevented the muddy roads from drying out in fine weather. During the eighteenth century the upkeep of many roads was the responsibility of local property owners and of the parish. Coach travel during this period was never cheap: horses had to be hired and fed; the coachman, who was well paid by the standards of the day, received perhaps eighteen shillings per week; stable boys had to be tipped, and extra luggage was charged for. Inns, such as that at Stepaside, would often have extensive stables.

The derelict, one-room, quarryman's cottage at Ticknock, which, with its yard and stone buildings, is a unique part of the history and tradition of this area

A typical coach of about 1800 was covered in dull black leather and studded with nails which traced out the panels on the sides. The names of the places of origin and destination would be carefully painted on the doors.

A disused quarry at Kellystown, Ticknock, showing one of the quarrymen's cottages

Many of the nineteenth-century Ordnance Survey maps show that the lower slopes of Three Rock Mountain were covered in small quarries. There were quarries at Barnacullia and others above Stepaside, but many have since been filled in. The granite quarries of Barnacullia provided much employment in the area and one of their principal customers was Dublin Corporation, who contracted them to supply paving stones for the city. Ticknock was the principal quarrying area and, as we have already seen, belonged at one time to the Fitzwilliam estate.

There are several ruined stone cottages which belonged to stonemasons and quarrymen on the Kellystown Road in Ticknock. Close examination of these cottages and sheds reveals many cut-stone features. There is one cottage which is probably the smallest surviving house in the county, as it has only one room!

Alderman Frederick Darley, whose family had a long tradition of stonecutting and building in Dublin, acquired the lease of a piece of land at Newtown Little, just above Kilgobbin. Here, in about 1815, he built a small house called Fernhill. The house was sold during the 1930s to the Walker family who have established a magnificent garden, which is now open to the public.

CHAPTER 24

Dundrum

A Dundrum postmark

Dundrum, or Dún Droma, means 'the fort of the ridge', and it is believed that a *dún* once existed somewhere near to the site of the present Catholic church. Dundrum, though relatively close to the city, remained a rural village until quite recent times and even today the village has retained its own distinct identity. The surrounding district, which includes Kilmacud, Goatstown, Balally, Sandyford and Churchtown, was always well known for its dairies. It is no coincidence that Hughes Dairy, now Premier Dairies, evolved from a small farm here, and established their major depot near Nutgrove where it continues its business today. Earlier this century there were up to twenty-five dairies in the Dundrum district, and one of the most famous was the jersey herd dairy at Airfield, which belonged to the Misses Overend. It was known as the Drommartin herd and was, until recently, the last surviving dairy farm in the area. The house and farm at Airfield have been left in trust to the people of Dublin and will eventually be opened as a traditional farm, using only organic methods.

John Archer, in his *Statistical Survey of County Dublin* of 1801, describes nearby Churchtown as 'a small village, three miles and a

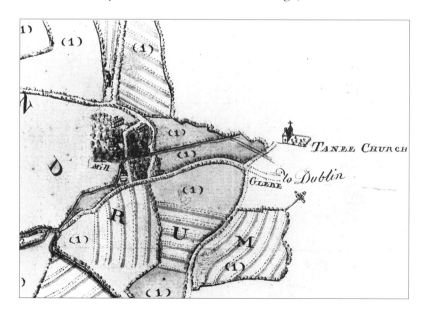

Jonathan Barker's map of the Fitzwilliam estate at Dundrum, 1762, showing the mill, with the castle and castle house above as well as St Nahi's church, which is shown as Tanee church

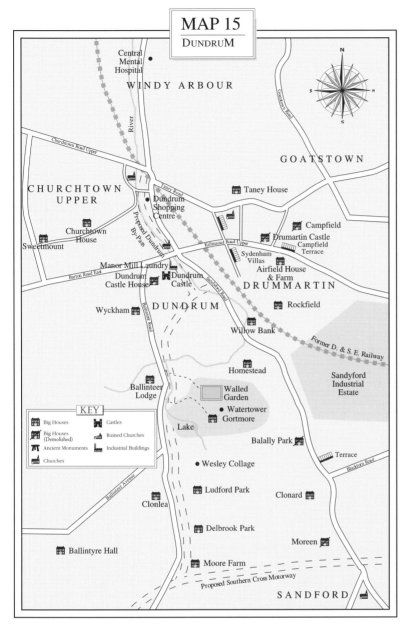

MAP 15
DUNDRUM

Central Mental Hospital

WINDY ARBOUR

River

Churchtown Road Upper

GOATSTOWN

Taney Road

CHURCHTOWN UPPER

Dundrum Shopping Centre

Taney House

Churchtown House

Sweetmount

Proposed Dundrum By-Pass

Kilmacud Road Upper

Campfield

Drumartin Castle

Campfield Terrace

Sydenham Villas

Barton Road East

Manor Mill Laundry

Dundrum Castle House

Dundrum Castle

Sandyford Road

Airfield House & Farm

DRUMMARTIN

DUNDRUM

Wyckham

Ballinteer Road

Rockfield

Willow Bank

Former D. & S. E. Railway

Homestead

Sandyford Industrial Estate

Ballinteer Lodge

Walled Garden

Watertower

Gortmore

Lake

Balally Park

KEY

🏠 Big Houses		🏰 Castles	
🏛 Big Houses (Demolished)		⛪ Ruined Churches	
🏛 Ancient Monuments		🏭 Industrial Buildings	
⛪ Churches			

Terrace

Blackfort Road

Ballinteer Avenue

Wesley Collage

Ludford Park

Clonard

Clonlea

Delbrook Park

Moreen

Ballintyre Hall

Moore Farm

Proposed Southern Cross Motorway

SANDFORD

quarter from the Castle, frequented much by invalids to drink goat's whey'. An earlier writer, John Rutty, in his *Natural History of the County of Dublin*, published in 1772, says that goat's milk is an excellent cure for consumption. The milk, which cost threepence per quart, was not drunk during August as it became very thick, but the 'whey drinking season' began again in September and the boarding houses around Dundrum were able to accommodate respectable ladies and gentlemen who went there to recuperate!

Dundrum Castle The ruin of Dundrum Castle stands on high ground above the stream and village of Dundrum. The medieval structure has

A goat herd at Kilmacud from an engraving of Dublin Bay, 1788 – the name Goatstown is a reminder of the goat-keeping activities in the area

Dundrum Castle, shown intact, with the eighteenth-century house which was recently demolished – drawing by James Saunders, 1797

Dundrum Castle today

been excavated in recent years by archaeologists, who have revealed a fascinating moat and drawbridge system. The castle was bought in 1987 by David Newman Johnson, an authority on medieval castles, who plans to restore it. The castle is thought to have been erected during the thirteenth century by the Fitzwilliams, who then owned all of Dundrum and the surrounding lands. In 1653 it became the property of a Colonel Dobson, a wealthy Dublin publisher, who restored the castle and added pleasure gardens which ran down to the stream.

An interesting sketch by Gabriel Beranger shows that it was still intact in 1780 and in the same year his contemporary Austin Cooper made the following description: 'The Castle of Dundrum, three miles south of Dublin, is inhabited and in excellent repair; at the northeast end of it are the remains of a much older building than the present castle, which is visibly a modern addition in comparison to the old mansion. There is but very little of this ancient part remaining; some of the walls are six feet thick; about the castle are several traces of old walls, avenues etc. proving it to have once been a very complete habitation. The whole is on the summit of a small hill, surrounded by ash trees, with a handsome rivulet running at its foot, but this shelter will soon be removed as they are cutting away trees.' The same description could nearly be written today, as now, over two hundred years later, the whole area is being developed with new blocks of apartments and much of its pleasant rural character is being lost.

Dundrum Castle (house) Facing the castle stood a Georgian house which had changed little since the 1790s when James Saunders made a drawing of it. The house, which was also called Dundrum Castle, was a five-windowed, mid-eighteenth-century residence with single-storey, symmetrical wings. This old house is also shown on a Fitzwilliam estate map made by Jonathan Barker in the 1760s. The wings

The long frontage of the Mill House, Dundrum

were later raised and further extensions, including a porch, were added. The house, which was used as offices in recent times, had also a cut-stone doorcase which was concealed behind the porch. Unfortunately, it was demolished without record about two years ago.

The small stream which flows in the valley below Dundrum Castle is still visible near the village and can easily be seen beside the present Dundrum library. The stream and a small mill pond once powered the mills at Dundrum, whose existence is recorded since medieval times. The mills, which stood in the valley below the castle, close to the present Mill House (a private residence), were owned by George Meyler in about 1850, and there was also an iron works in Dundrum at this time.

Later, in 1876, the Manor Mill Laundry was established here and took its name from the ancient manor mill. In 1942 the laundry closed, following a shortage of materials, rising labour costs and the introduction of domestic washing machines. James Nolan, in his book *Changing Faces*, which is a record of life in old Dundrum, describes how, in the late nineteenth century, some of the washing at the Manor Mill Laundry was done by hand, and how the washerwomen worked in their bare feet because

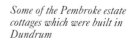

Some of the Pembroke estate cottages which were built in Dundrum

of the splashing of water on the floors. In 1917 the following advertisement appeared in *The Irish Times*: 'Manor Mill Laundry, County Dublin. Beautiful country situation, equalled only by the excellence of our work. Shirts and collars superbly finished. Washing by rail and post specially quoted for.' The former laundry buildings were recently occupied by a family called Pye, who made electrical goods, and by other light industries.

Dundrum main street has few major buildings of architectural significance, but it does possess a distinctive village atmosphere. This atmosphere is derived from the pleasant

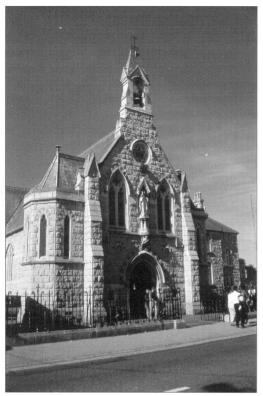

Church of the Holy Cross, Dundrum

groupings of two-storey, brick houses and shops, many of which were built at the instigation of the Pembroke estate. It is only the enormous volume of traffic which really prevents one from truly appreciating Dundrum, its pleasant corner shops and attractive estate houses. However, the traffic situation should be alleviated when the new Dundrum bypass is constructed at the back of the village. The Eagle House, an old pub with fine, carved brackets, and Ryan's Dundrum House, a tall building with unusual iron masks on its gutters, are both of interest. Most of the redbrick premises which front the main street in Dundrum appear to date from the late nineteenth century. There is a plaque on the side of Haslett's shop which bears the initials W. R. and the date 1881, suggesting that the Richardson family of builders may have been responsible for its construction. The Richardsons may also have built many of the other houses in the main street. The Pembroke estate erected the Pembroke cottages and many other terraces of small houses, some of which bear the initials H and P, which stand for Herbert or Pembroke.

The Church of the Holy Cross The Roman Catholic church in Dundrum is an attractive, Gothic-style building, erected in 1887. It is constructed of granite with sandstone dressings and has an impressive open-timber roof. The church was dedicated in 1879. It accommodates about a thousand people and was built at a cost of around £5000. Although the Catholic parish of Dundrum had existed since the eighteenth century, there was no chapel until 1813. It was some years before a church was erected near the present church site which is also thought to be the place where the *dún* of Dundrum might have stood.

Saint Nahi's, which is a very simple structure built around 1760, was the original Church of Ireland place of worship. The small, rectangular church was erected on a high mound near the Churchtown Road side of Dundrum village. It is reputed to have been the second ever Protestant church to have been built in Ireland after the Reformation, and this might account for its extreme simplicity.

St Nahi's contains several stained-glass windows by Evie Hone which she carried out in 1933 and are amongst her earliest known work. She was born in 1894 at Roebuck Grove, and some of her ancestors had lived in Dundrum during the eighteenth century – she was a direct descendant of the great eighteenth-century painter Nathaniel Hone.

The old-world graveyard of St Nahi's, which is surrounded by a granite wall, contains an attractive collection of crooked tombstones and old yew trees. There is a special plot or communal grave here for the unfortunate inmates of the Dundrum Lunatic Asylum. The Central Mental Hospital, as it has been called since 1961, was originally established in

*St Nahi's church and
graveyard, Dundrum*

1850 when it was named The Central Lunatic Asylum for the Reception of Insane Persons. The stone-built, three-storey institutional buildings cannot be seen from the road at Windy Arbour, as they are surrounded by an extremely high granite wall.

The parish of Taney originally extended from the summit of Three Rock Mountain to the shore at Dublin Bay. It embraced all of Ballinteer, Ticknock, Balally, Churchtown, Mount Anville, Mount Merrion, Roebuck, Trimleston and even parts of Milltown and Rathmines. By the early 1800s the church of St Nahi had become too small for the growing parish. Accordingly, a distinguished group of parishioners, including James Crofton of Roebuck Castle, Richard Verschoyle of Merrion, Walter Bourne of Owenstown House and Peter Digges La Touche of Belfield,

*The school house at Taney
church with its pretty, Gothic-
style windows*

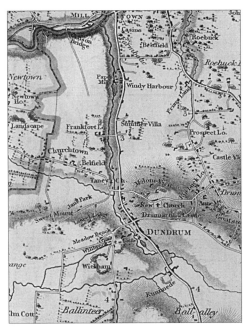

formed a committee to organise the building of a new church. A site at Taney was acquired from the Earl of Pembroke. The new building was to be 'a handsome church in a more convenient location' and was modelled closely on Monkstown church. A plan by the diocesan architect William Farrow was adopted and work got under way. The estimate of 1817 is of great interest. The work of the masons was expected to cost over £2300, and that of the carpenters more than £2138. The stonecutters' work, which would have included the finer details and mouldings, was to cost £238, while the glaziers and plasterers would receive £80. The cost of slating and roofing the church came to £136 while the architect's fees amounted to some £300. The contract for stonecutting went to Alderman Darley of Fernhill, while the masonry was done by a Mr Williams, the plastering by Mr Luke Story, and the painting and glazing by a Mr Veto. The peculiarly named Board of First Fruits gave a loan of £4300 towards the building work. The new church was opened in 1818, having cost nearly £7000.

Duncan's map, 1821, of the Dundrum district shows the profusion of large houses in the area

The location of the church on Taney Hill is outstanding and the battlemented, Gothic-style belfry can be seen from far off. In front of each side of the broad, gravel avenue are two delightful lodges, which have Georgian Gothic sash windows. One of these was the Sexton's cottage while the other housed a school for infants. In 1872 a new chancel and organ were added to the church at the expense of Henry Roe, who lived at Mount Anville Park, a fine house which was demolished in 1984 and which will be discussed shortly. The Roe family also donated the east window with its stained glass and paid off the remaining church debt. Henry Roe was the very wealthy Dublin distiller, with extensive premises at Thomas Street, and he also financed the restoration of Christchurch Cathedral.

George Kinahan of Roebuck Park, who was a partner with Edward Kinahan of Wyckham in a successful wine and spirit business in D'Olier Street where they had their own distillery, donated a carved stone pulpit to the church. The ground landlords, the Earls of Pembroke, paid for the new entrance gates, which were erected in 1884. All of these details were gleaned from the minute books of the Taney vestry by Francis Ellington Ball who co-authored an excellent history of the parish in 1885. Ball, who lived at Taney House for some time, is better known as the author of the definitive *A History of the County of Dublin*, which was completed in 1910.

Taney church, completed in 1818

Carnegie Library One of the most attractive twentieth-century buildings in Dundrum is the Carnegie Library which was built in 1910. The cement-fronted building has an attractive pillared entrance above which is an unusual oval-shaped window draped with a Renaissance-style swag. The construction of the library was funded by Andrew Carnegie, an American millionaire, who, in the last eighteen years of his life, shared his fortune with many communities by sponsoring the building of up to 2500 libraries in America, Britain and Ireland. Dun Laoghaire, Blackrock, Shankill, Cabinteely, Sandyford, Glencullen, Whitechurch and Rathfarnham libraries were all endowed by Carnegie. Carnegie, born in 1835, had come from a poor family in Scotland, but made a massive fortune in the iron and steel business in America.

Between the graveyard of St Nahi's and the Carnegie Library is Churchtown Cottage, an attractive whitewashed house with a pretty garden, a sight once so common in every part of County Dublin, but now a rarity. According to Samuel Lewis there were a number of attractive cottages in Dundrum during the 1830s.

In 1796 the church wardens of Taney employed a parish beadle who was responsible for law and order in the district and they also provided finance to erect a pair of stocks in Dundrum. We know that stocks were provided in other villages, such as Dalkey, during the eighteenth century, but there seems to be little record of their actual use, or where they stood. Such instruments of punishment may have been designed to act as a deterrent during this period of great unrest leading up to the 1798 rebellion. In 1921 during the civil war the courthouse and the police barracks, which were attractive, Gothic-style buildings designed by Deane and Woodward and erected in 1855, stood as burnt-out shells. The barracks were subsequently replaced.

The monument to Dr Isaac Usher in the main street of Dundrum

In 1792 John Sweetman, a Catholic, and James Potts, a Protestant, became Governors of the National School in Dundrum, whose master was paid £15 per annum and the Mistress £6 per annum. Coal cost £5 per annum. Clothing for the boys, of which there were about 30, came to £22 and 10 shillings. There is no account of clothes being provided for the girls. In 1897 the Church of Ireland parish of Taney erected a new parish hall adjoining the old school at Eglinton Terrace. It is a fine, cut-stone building erected in the Gothic style, also by Deane and Woodward, with prominent roofs. Another new school was opened in 1970 on a large two-acre site adjoining Sydenham Villas.

The building of the Dundrum shopping centre some thirty years ago clearly brought about one of the biggest changes in the village and, though it is no architectural beauty, it does at least form part of the village and the life there, unlike so many complexes, for example Nutgrove, which are built on green-field sites as if they were dropped out of the sky.

In front of Usher House, a small office building, is a fountain in the form of an obelisk. The monument, which once served as a drinking fountain, commemorates Dr Isaac Usher, who was killed here in 1917 by a car. Dundrum railway station, which was located at the bottom of the main street, was once the centre of activity as trains passed though with great regularity, and the large, arcaded platform was always busy with passengers. It is hard to believe now that trains once streamed across the narrow railway bridge where there is now a major traffic junction. In July

1854 when the new line was opened, *The Dublin Evening Post* wrote: 'At the Dundrum Station, although not entirely completed, the evidences of attention to the comfort of the public as well as to the details of the building are observable.'

Environs of Dundrum

The environs of Dundrum were described by Lewis in 1837 as 'abounding with pleasing and strikingly diversified scenery, and are embellished with numerous Gentlemen's Seats and elegant villas, most of which are situated in tastefully ornamented grounds and command fine views of the bay of Dublin and the land adjacent'. The route leading out of Dundrum through Sandyford to Enniskerry is pleasant and relatively unspoilt with its old road bounded by stone walls and trees. There are several fine houses on this side of Dundrum, such as Elm Lawn, one of a group of small Georgian houses which faced the Manor Mill Laundry. Further out is Herbert Hill, a bow-ended house of early eighteenth-century date, which has a cast-iron balcony running right across the front. Nearby Rockmount has been demolished. Other medium-sized houses included Clonard, Homestead (the home of Richard McCormiss in the nineteenth century) and Ballawley Park, whose lands once stretched back to the grounds of the present Wesley College. Ballawley Park (now demolished) was a one-storey, villa-type house with a two-storey and possibly older section at the back. It appears on Taylor's map of 1816 and was a late-Georgian-style house which once had an entrance in the form of a tall, Gothic gateway.

Moreen, another house which has vanished from this side of Dundrum, was also built in the late eighteenth century. The two-storey, plain house, which had a cut-stone Georgian doorcase, once boasted a beautiful avenue of beech trees. It is now occupied by the Offices of the Central Bank. Moreen was erected sometime before 1800 by William McKay, a solicitor and also a captain in the Dragoon Guards. The *Post*

Clonard, the large Victorian residence of Henry Thompson of Thompson and D'Olier, wine merchants – now part of the offices of the Irish Management Institute

Chaise Companion of 1803 states that 'with great industry and expense, is erected a neat compact house, with lawns, gardens, plantations and suitable office belonging to William McKay Esq.'

His grandson, Manners McKay, held steeple races here in the 1850s and the family were devoted to hunting and riding activities. There was a small watch-tower and guard-house beside the wall and Ball, in *The Parish of Taney*, stated that it may have been an outpost of the northern Pale; but it is fairly certain that the tower was some kind of folly or garden building of much later construction.

The colonial-style timber verandah at Homestead

The Dun Emer Guild was established in 1903 in an old eighteenth-century house called Runnimede, which was located on the Sandyford Road, just outside Dundrum. The name of Runnimede was changed to Dun Emer and a house of that name still stands there. The guild promoted the production of handmade carpets and printed books. It was set up by a number of artists, including Susan and Elizabeth Yeats (sisters of W. B. and Jack), who lived at Gurteen Dhaf in Churchtown – they are buried in St Nahi's graveyard.

The Yeats sisters went to the New York Great Exhibition in 1907 with exhibits of handwoven carpets and other handcrafted objects. The Dun Emer Guild also founded the Cuala Press, renowned for its attractive publications of Irish plays and novels.

Sandyford

A small village has existed at Sandyford since the eighteenth century where the group of small cottages, probably belonging to stonecutters, were clustered around a Catholic chapel. Lord Castlecoote of Leopardstown Park gave £500 towards the building of a Catholic church in Sandyford. The attractive church was rebuilt in the late nineteenth century and is a simple, Gothic-style church with a small tower and spire. The village was bypassed by the new main road to Enniskerry, which was constructed during the nineteenth century. This has lately been much improved through the efforts of the local people and by a new scheme of paving and planting.

Turn of the century local authority housing at Balally Terrace, Sandyford village

The name Balally, sometimes spelled Ballawley, meaning 'the townland of Olaf', is connected to an ancient church of which no trace now remains. There was also a medieval castle at Balally which is recorded in 1664 as a tower house with a thatched roof, but this has also completely disappeared. Balally Terrace, erected in about 1900, is an interesting example of early local authority housing. The terraced,

The present Roman Catholic church in Sandyford stands on the site of an eighteenth-century chapel

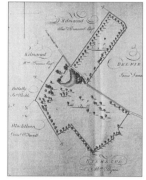

An estate map of Lakelands in Kilmacud showing the ornamental lake and gardens

two-storey houses have small dormer windows and projecting porches. Most of the new local authority houses in the area, which were built in the early twentieth century, were single-storey cottages and were usually built of rubble granite, having slated roofs and timber, sliding, sash windows – good examples may be seen at Murphystown Road, Kilgobbin and on the Ballyogan Road. The name Balally now refers to a large area of housing estates built during the 1960s and 1970s. The planned Southern Cross motorway will change the area radically as it will connect the M50 with the N11 at Shankill, cutting across the top of Marlay Park, passing by Lamb Doyle's in Sandyford, and running past the Central Bank Centre and through the Sandyford Road near Sandyford village.

Airfield, the home of the well-known Overend sisters, is a substantial Victorian house

Hazelwood The architect J. S. Mulvany, who lived in a house called Lakelands in Kilmacud during the 1850s, was responsible for the design of at least one other Victorian house in the area, Hazelwood. With its cut-granite façade, this house has many of Mulvany's characteristic design features, so reminiscent of his railway station architecture. There are full-length pilasters, strong brackets under the eaves and rounded corners to all the windows. His own house, Lakelands, was laid out as a miniature estate by Simeon Boileau in the early nineteenth century and there was an attractive U-shaped lake in the grounds.

Upper Kilmacud Road

The Upper Kilmacud Road, which joins Stillorgan with Dundrum, once boasted a number of fine houses.

Airfield, which has already been mentioned in connection with its dairy herd, began as a small, eighteenth-century farmhouse and was extended in early Victorian times. It was purchased in 1894 by Trevor Overend, a prominent Dublin solicitor, who carried out further improvements to the house by adding a large library with an elaborate, Jacobean-style ceiling. His daughters, Letitia and Naomi Overend, continued to live there until the early 1990s. The Overend sisters were well known in Dublin for their charitable work with the Red Cross, the Sunshine Homes in Leopardstown, the St John's Ambulance and the local parish in Taney. They also ran an impressive garden and kept a fine herd of Jersey cows.

The unusual façade of Dromartin Castle, demolished in 1984

But they are probably best known as the owners of a beautifully maintained 1927 Rolls Royce car, which they used until recently on a daily basis. They were often sighted in Grafton Street, prior to its pedestrianisation, in the Rolls Royce. The Overend sisters represented the end of an era, and though they had come from a

Campfield, an attractive late Georgian house, was demolished in 1985

Georgian Gothic window, Campfield

Ironwork canopy at Campfield

privileged background they had a great sense of duty towards those less fortunate than themselves. As there was no family to continue running the farm, the Overends decided to form a trust which will manage the future of the estate for the benefit of the public at large.

The name Drommartin has been associated with this part of Dundrum since the eighteenth century. In 1781 Lord Fitzwilliam granted permission to Patrick D'Arcy to burn bricks at Drommartin. Several new houses were built in the district at around this time, including Drommartin Castle and Campfield House, both of which stood between the Kilmacud and Taney roads, and were demolished in 1984 and 1985 respectively. It is possible that D'Arcy built these houses.

Drommartin Castle was an interesting house, having an unusual façade with wide, Wyatt-style windows and an exceptionally wide fanlight. The house, which was quite plain inside, was occupied by Henry Birch during the 1860s, and the adjoining Birch's Lane is called after him. The façade of Drommartin Castle, with its Georgian windows and large, blank buttresses, was impressive and its demolition is another significant loss to the architectural heritage of the district. Even more unfortunate, perhaps, was the destruction of Campfield House, which stood at the other side of Birch's Lane. It was a very attractive, small, Georgian house with delicate, Gothic-style windows and a fanlight. Unspoilt houses of this type, as we have seen, have become increasingly rare in County Dublin. The hall of Campfield was decorated with a plasterwork vault in the Gothic style and there was also a pretty, Gothic-windowed dairy incorporated into the outbuildings at the side of the house. The whole of the grounds, with their meadow and mature trees, have now been built over.

CHAPTER 25

Ballinteer

Ballinteer stretches to the south-west, back from Dundrum to Ticknock Mountain and across to Marlay Park and Rathfarnham. Among the interesting houses of this area are Dundrum House (demolished), Meadowbrook, Wyckham, Gortmore, Hilton, Ludford Park and Ballintyre Hall.

Wyckham is described by Lewis as 'The seat of W. Farren Esq., a handsome residence containing a richly stored museum of natural curiosities.' What this museum consisted of is not known, but it was the fashion of the day to collect examples of minerals, rocks, shells and fossils. Sir Robert Kane lived at Wyckham from 1853 until 1873 when the house was sold to Sir Edward Hudson Kinahan. Kinahan, as we have already noted, had a flourishing wine and spirit business at Carlisle Buildings in D'Olier Street, now the site of O'Connell Bridge House. He married in 1863 and had a large family of twelve children – not unusual in Victorian times. The house was acquired by Simpson's Hospital as a home for the elderly in 1925 and it still serves that purpose today. When it opened in 1925, up to forty-five men who were 'unable to support themselves' were looked after here. George Simpson, an eighteenth-century draper and philanthropist from Henry Street in Dublin, did much charitable work in the middle of the eighteenth century, including founding this hospital. Wyckham is an impressive, three-storey house of

Wyckham, a large, late-Georgian house of about 1800, which was enlarged during the nineteenth century

Farmhouse at Kingston, above Ballinteer, which is close to the route of the planned Southern Cross Motorway

large proportions, which was probably built in about 1800, and was subsequently enlarged and embellished in Victorian times. In one room there is a hand-painted dado or chair-rail featuring branches, twigs and garlands. An elegant, cut-stone porch with Ionic columns was a Victorian addition and the façade was modelled in the Italian style. Also noteworthy are the handsome, granite entrance gates, where the two piers of Portland stone have finely detailed pediments.

John Sweetman, who was a governor of the national school in Dundrum during the 1790s, was possibly the builder and owner of the now demolished Sweetmount House, which stands at the end of Sweetmount Avenue. Almost adjoining it are the two houses of Enderley and Orchardton. Enderley is an interesting old-world house, with many attractive Georgian features, such as the Gothic-style window at the back of the drawing room. Not far off is Churchtown House, another eighteenth-century residence now occupied by the Netherlands Embassy.

Ludford, now the residence of the Principal of Wesley College

Hilton is situated at the junction of Ballinteer Road and Ballinteer Avenue, and though its garden has been built upon, the villa-type house, which may have originated as a farmhouse, still stands.

Ludford Park lies on the lower slopes of the Dublin mountains and is a small Georgian house, built around 1820. It is now the residence of the principal of Wesley College. The attractive Georgian-style house faces west with fine views of the Dublin mountains while to the rear there are extensive outbuildings and a large walled garden. It was acquired by the Methodist Wesley College in 1963 and some of the boys at Wesley boarded there. In 1966 plans for a new college got under way and three years later a new school which catered for six hundred pupils was opened in Ballinteer.

Two new churches were added to the Catholic parish of Dundrum during the twentieth century – in 1953 the Church of Our Lady of the Miraculous Medal was constructed in Clonskeagh, while in 1974 the Church of St John the Evangelist was built in Ballinteer to cater for the rapidly-growing population of the housing estates in the area.

The lands of Ballintyre Hall in Ballinteer are one of the last undeveloped sections of the Ballinteer area. Ballintyre was occupied during the late nineteenth century by Sir Edward Grogan, a barrister and MP for Dublin.

The conservatory at Gortmore, a magnificent, cast-iron structure with coloured glass panes

Gortmore is by far the most elaborate Victorian establishment in Ballinteer. The house was probably begun during the 1850s and first belonged to Richard Atkinson, whose family are buried in St Nahi's graveyard. By the 1880s it had become the property of Edward Burke, who was yet another extremely wealthy 'wine and foreign export merchant' whose business was based at 16 Bachelor's Walk. In 1884 Burke was resident at both Ballawley Park and Gortmore – it is possible that he was renting the former while he made alterations to his new house. The magnificent interior of Gortmore was without doubt planned by Burke, and his initials E. B. appear on the newel posts of the fabulous oak staircase. Burke enlarged the house to the north by adding a new staircase, a stunning billiard room, a smoking room and a delightful, domed conservatory which is very similar to the glass canopy of the Olympia Theatre in Dublin. The conservatory, a feature of many Victorian houses, was designed to extend the space of the drawing room. In the eighteenth century glasshouses had always been situated away from the house in a walled garden where exotic fruits such as nectarines and peaches were grown. The nineteenth-century conservatory was a way of bringing the garden into the house.

Burke remodelled the principal rooms of Gortmore with fine oak panelling in every room, lavishly carved mantelpieces with onyx, marble and tile inserts, parquet flooring throughout, flamboyant panelled doors, coved ceilings which were richly compartmented and

The 'art of painting' symbolised in the Victorian tiled fireplace of the billiard room at Gortmore

The wine cellar in Gortmore, which must once have been well stocked by its owner Edward Burke

The elaborate Sham Castle at Gortmore

Brass doorknob at Gortmore

ornamented in the Jacobean style, and very delicate stained glass in the hall and staircase. The billiard room is also outstanding, with its open-work roof, its frieze of putti, embossed 1880s wallpaper and oak panelling. A very fine granite portico composed of four Ionic columns is the best feature of the exterior of the house, which is really very plain. Only the elaborate stone balcony of the staircase window gives any hint of the extravagance of the interior. A crest, probably that of Burke, is worked in plaster on the garden front of the house.

The gardens, with their fountains, artificial lake, bridges, boathouse and remarkable stone tower, were also probably laid out by Burke. A boathouse was constructed of massive rocks piled up to form a vault, which has the appearance of a grotto at first sight, and towards the walled garden there is a remarkable sham castle or tower house, which is an extremely well-built stone structure of authentic medieval appearance. Its features include a battered wall, Gothic windows and door, slits and battlements, all of which are details faithfully copied from the medieval Irish tower house. This folly was clearly built as an eyecatcher and viewing tower, but it may also have served as a water tower.

Burke did not enjoy Gortmore for very long, for by the end of the 1890s it was occupied by his relation John Nutting. In the early 1900s we find Sir Joseph Redmond, a noted surgeon, living at Gortmore, and finally in 1944 the house was purchased by the Carmelite Fathers who changed the name to Gort Mhuire. The house is now the residence of the Carmelite friars, who look after the house and grounds with great care. The lovely, buttercup-filled fields through which the avenue winds are a rare sight in today's suburbia, but sadly this may soon disappear as it is planned to build a link road through these lands to the Southern Cross motorway.

CHAPTER 26

Windy Arbour

Windy Arbour is a scattered settlement of houses and cottages located on either side of the road leading to Dundrum from Milltown. It was, without doubt, the area once inhabited by the poorer classes of Dundrum. Many of the inhabitants of Windy Arbour would have found employment in the Manor Mill Laundry in Dundrum and in the Dublin Laundry at Milltown, both of which were once very large employers. Taylor's map of 1816 indicates the existence of a proper village at Windy Arbour, and the presence of a paper mill. Later, in about 1850, there was a flour mill and a saw mill in Farrenboley, which is the townland name of the area. The village was located at the junction with Bird Avenue, which is named after Bird House. A large number of County Council houses were built in the 1930s at Farrenboley to replace the many old cottages and cabins in the district, but there are still many old cottages and terraced houses in Windy Arbour, such as Woodbine Terrace, and Rosemount Terrace which backs onto the Dundrum stream. Millmount Terrace is said to have been erected by the Dublin Laundry at Milltown for their employees.

One of the most striking features of the area is the massive, granite wall of the Dundrum Central Mental Hospital. The building can be seen from a distance and is a large, three-storey, stone structure. Built in the workhouse style, it has Tudor mullioned windows and gables. Windy

Duncan's map, 1821, showing the stream and mill at Windy Arbour

Millmount Terrace at Windy Arbour

Casino, a late-Georgian house once occupied by the Emmet family

A miniature of Robert Emmet

Arbour was also the name of a unique pair of eighteenth-century houses which were described by Maurice Craig as the earliest known examples of the semi-detached house layout in Ireland. They may have been built as early as 1780, and were perfectly symmetrical. Each had bow-ended rooms and attractive stone doorcases with matching recessed arches in the façade. The design would make a very handsome prototype for a modern semi-detached housing development.

In the 1790s Woodbine Hill, which must have stood close to Woodbine Terrace in Windy Arbour, was the home of John Giffard who held an important post as the Accountant General of His Majesty's Customs in Dublin. Giffard also became a captain in the City of Dublin Militia, a part of the Irish Volunteers, and Ball's *History* describes him as 'A strong Protestant and supporter of the English Government'. Giffard, whose son and nephew had been killed during the various troubles of the 1790s, was quick to respond to the Emmet rebellion of 1803. He raised a corps of yeomanry in the neighbourhood of Dundrum and enlisted 150 volunteers whom he marched for a review in the Phoenix Park. He was also involved in the early 1790s with the breaking up of the Back Lane Parliament, formed by the United Irishmen in Tailors' Hall.

Casino, which is located near the village of Windy Arbour, is not far from Clonskeagh Castle. It has interesting historical connections with the Emmet family, whose home it was in the late eighteenth century. A large, square house with a handsome portico of four stone columns, it once had an unusual viewing platform on the roof. The portico and windows were once ornamented with neo-classical, stucco devices, some of which have disappeared. The interior is plainly decorated, but has an attractive, semi-circular hall and a very large drawing room. The house, now belonging to the Marist Fathers and used for educational purposes, still has the spacious grounds and gardens, with a fine view of the mountains which the Emmets must once have enjoyed.

CHAPTER 27

Roebuck

The area which lies between Clonskeagh, Dundrum and Mount Merrion, and is called Roebuck, contains many interesting houses. Quite a
proportion of these are of eighteenth-century origin, while others were
enlarged during the Victorian period.

Mountanville House was erected by Henry Roe and the name was
later changed Knockrabo. Knockrabo is a corruption of the name Mount
Roebuck, from the late medieval name Rabo, hence, the 'Hill of Roe-
buck' or Knockrabo. The Baron of Trimleston, who had lived in
Roebuck Castle, married a daughter of Christopher de Brune of Rabo or
Roebuck. The attractive house of Knockrabo, which stood opposite
Mount Anville Convent, was recently owned by the Bank of Ireland who
demolished it in 1984 to make way for a new sports building.

Knockrabo was a Victorian house of exceptional quality, being
located on high ground overlooking much of south County Dublin, and
a rooftop belvedere was added in the nineteenth century to take advantage of these views. It was a long house, two-storeys-over-basement,

*A bookplate from the library
of Henry Roe, who lived at
Mountanville, and is famous
for having paid for the
restoration of Christchurch
Cathedral in Dublin*

*Mountanville House with its
extraordinary verandah or
balcony*

The mansion at Mount Anville with its tower, now the Sacred Heart Convent

The statue of William Dargan at the National Gallery of Ireland

with fine interior plasterwork. A four-pillared, Ionic porch was fronted by two elaborate cast-iron lamp standards. On the garden front an ironwork balcony ran continuously around the house and was covered by a canopy at first-floor level. The balcony, canopy and rooftop belvedere gave the house an unusual colonial character. In 1885 it became the home of Christopher Palles, Lord Chief Baron of the Court of the Exchequer. Palles was highly successful in legal circles, was widely respected as an eminent barrister and was a devout Catholic. During the nineteenth century, as we have seen elsewhere, it was the fashion for judges to live in a style which reflected their social position. Baron Deasy lived at Carysfort, Lord Plunkett at Old Connaught, Chief Justice Doherty at St Helen's and the Lord Chief Justice lived at Newlands near Clondalkin, a beautiful house which was also demolished during the 1980s. Palles kept Mountanville in an impeccable manner and had several gardeners to look after the hot-houses, greenhouses, vineries and peach houses. Two footmen, dressed in white ties and tails, served tea in the drawing room which was decorated in white and gold. Palles commuted to and from the city by train, using the station at Dundrum. He died at Mountanville in 1920.

Mount Anville One of the great supporters of the building of the so-called Harcourt Street railway line was William Dargan, who in 1851 came to live at Mount Anville, now the school of the Sisters of the Sacred Heart. Dargan, who was a Catholic and came from humble origins, was immensely successful during his lifetime. He began first as a builder of roads, but quickly moved into the construction of railways and was responsible for building many of the railways throughout Ireland. His greatest achievement was perhaps the organisation of the Great Exhibition in Dublin in 1853, to which Queen Victoria paid an official visit. She also came to Mount Anville and there she offered Dargan a baronetcy, which he declined. Sadly, Dargan lost both his health and his fortune, and died a poor man in 1865.

Mount Anville was originally known as Rowbuck Hill and appears to have been built in the late 1790s as the home of Baron Trimleston. By 1802 the house was occupied by Daniel Beare and later by John West Beattie. Mount Anville is a magnificent house which was greatly enlarged by Dargan, who also added a tower or belvedere. The mansion, with its large, Doric-style portico, is approached by a double avenue and a pair of magnificent cut-stone entrance gates. There are also fine, terraced gardens which are fronted by a long, cast-iron, decorative balustrade. Following the acquisition of the house by the Sacred Heart Order in 1865, a large new wing was built to the design of George Ashlin. The alterations and enlargements carried out by Dargan were almost certainly designed by the architect John S. Mulvany, and the gate-lodge is a magnificent example of his work.

In the area of Roebuck Road there are several eighteenth-century houses of note, and these include Owenstown, Roebuck Hill, Roebuck Hall, Ardilea and Hermitage. All that remains of Ardilea is the gate-lodge and impressive entrance, whose sweeping walls of cut granite and brick may be seen at Mount Anville Road. Roebuck Castle will be discussed later in the context of UCD and its houses. On the Goatstown Road there are other interesting houses, including Prospect Hall, Harlech, Friarsland, Roebuck Grove, and two which have been demolished, Roebuck Park and Belfield.

St Thomas's Church, situated at the bottom of Foster's Avenue, was completed in 1874. It stands on a site given by the Earls of Pembroke at the junction with the Stillorgan Road. It was built as a chapel-of-ease to Taney parish and is a small church, having only a single aisle and chancel. In 1941 the Monk Gibbon Memorial Hall was erected beside the church, and this interesting 'arts and crafts'-style building, which is buttressed and pebble dashed, contained a hall and stage, a kitchen, meeting rooms and a residence for the sexton. There is an attractive half-conical, slated roof over the main entrance.

The scroll-pattern ironwork railing on the terrace at Mount Anville

Owenstown House, a fine Georgian house, now in use as offices

Roebuck Hall

Owenstown House, standing at the top of Foster's Avenue, is now in use as offices, but much of its original interior survives intact. A late-Georgian house, it was occupied by Nathaniel Creed, a livery lace manufacturer from Great Ship Street, which lies behind Dublin Castle. During the early nineteenth century it was the home of Walter Bourne and, later, James Turbett, a wine merchant. Owenstown is a two-storey-over-basement, three-bay house, dating from about 1800. It has a wide fanlight over the hall door and the interior exhibits fine joinery and plasterwork which features reeded mouldings, rosettes and fan-shaped spandrels above the window shutters.

Roebuck Hill is a late-Georgian style house with symmetrical, single-storey wings, while its neighbour, Roebuck Hall, now demolished, was a nineteenth-century house with a recessed entrance, featuring a pair of stone Doric columns. Adjoining these was Ardilea, a handsome Victorian house, whose only remains are the magnificent set of sweeping, cut-stone entrance gates on Mount Anville Road.

Hermitage, now the convent of the Little Sisters of the Poor, backs onto the campus of UCD. It is another eighteenth-century house, somewhat modified by later additions, including a fine, granite porch composed of fluted Doric columns. An earlier Georgian doorcase may be seen behind this porch, and this belongs to the original three-storey-over-basement house.

Friarsland, a house of Victorian appearance, is situated almost opposite the junction of Goatstown Road and Roebuck Road, and is now called Glenard. The house was purchased by Opus Dei in 1964 and is used as a university residence. In 1780 the property on which Friarsland was later built, which consisted of an estate of thirty-nine acres, was leased to John Scott, the Earl of Clonmel. These lands had at one time belonged to the Dublin church of St Nicholas Within, and it was probably this connection which prompted the somewhat ecclesiastical, nineteenth-century name of Friarsland. The present house, whose composition is striking, appears to have been constructed some time after 1833, and may have been designed by J. S. Mulvany. The original entrance gates and a classical-style gate-lodge have disappeared.

Prospect Hall, the residence of Sir Robert Harty in about 1830

Prospect Hall now stands amid a modern housing estate off the Goatstown Road and is the headquarters of St Michael's House, a charitable body which is dedicated to helping the mentally and physically handicapped in the Dublin area. Prospect Hall is associated with Sir Robert Harty during the early years of the nineteenth century. Harty's career is not without interest, as he came from humble origins as a hosier in Westmoreland Street but, through a good marriage, became a man of property

A section of one of the beautiful murals in Prospect Hall

and was eventually Lord Mayor of Dublin in 1830. It was at about this time that Harty was resident in Prospect Hall.

The house is of late-Georgian date and, on the outside, has been considerably altered by the raising of the original single-storey, bow-fronted wings to the same height as the main house. The interior contains unusual treasures in the form of murals which are to be seen in the two main reception rooms and the hall. The murals, which appear to have been painted in the early 1800s, are extremely decorative and romantic in subject matter, though they also have the boldness of theatrical, painted back-drops. Italian landscapes, rocky glens and fanciful palaces

Roebuck Park, a substantial Victorian house, demolished in 1996

Detail of the fine cut-stone portico and ironwork at Roebuck Park

are peopled with soldiers and peasants in the mellow-coloured paintings which cover the walls from dado level to ceiling. The murals may have been painted by Gaspar Gabrielli or one of his followers. Gabrielli, an Italian painter, had come to Ireland to work for Lord Cloncurry at his new house, Lyons, in County Kildare. There he painted a superb series of murals in the drawing room. Sir Robert Harty was a friend of Lord Cloncurry, and Cloncurry may have inspired him to have his rooms decorated in this way. Harty's town house was at number 49 Merrion Square, where murals of similar style and age may be seen.

Roebuck Park, which was demolished in 1996, was a Victorian house of great quality. It stood to the west of the Goatstown Road and was remarkable for its fine-cut, granite portico and once-elegant interior.

To the north is a house called Roebuck Grove, whose lands also front the Goatstown Road. It is a two-storey-over-basement, Georgian house, with large, single-storey, semi-circular bows at each end. In 1912 the Ordnance Survey showed three houses in this area called Roebuck Grove!

Belfield, not to be confused with the grander house of the same name at UCD, stood to the south of Roebuck Park, and was demolished in 1984. It was another small, eighteenth-century house, which was distinguished by a Georgian-style, ironwork porch of great delicacy.

Harlech, another Georgian house of great character, was sold in 1987 with over four acres of land and permission was granted for its demolition by Dublin County Council. However, in spite of the development of about thirty new houses in its grounds, it was decided to retain the old house.

CHAPTER 28

Clonskeagh

Clonskeagh or Cluain Sceach, which means 'the meadow of the white thorns', is the name of an area which runs from the river Dodder and Milltown across to the Belfield campus of University College Dublin and south towards Roebuck.

In the eighteenth century the village of Clonskeagh consisted of a picturesque collection of thatched cottages and various mill buildings, and many of these survived until the early years of this century. A watercolour sketch by Gabriel Beranger, made during the 1770s, shows a large weir and a cluster of about eight thatched cottages close to the river.

Clonskeagh Castle, which has recently been restored as a private house, is situated off Whitebeam Road. The castle, which is said to occupy the site of a medieval structure, was built in the late Georgian

The finest cast-iron, Georgian balcony in the Dublin area is at Roebuck House

The remarkable arched entrance gates to Clonskeagh Castle, now vanished

period, later to be remodelled in a nineteenth-century, castellated idiom. A large, square house of three storeys, with two corner 'towers', it now has a distinctly Victorian appearance. The house is entered by a handsome, stone portico of Victorian date, which has six limestone columns with carved capitals. Inside, most of the original features of the 1790s house can be seen, including a curved staircase with an open, arched landing. The hall was once completely decorated with grisaille wallpaper in the Chinese style. The paper was carefully restored and was installed over thirty years ago in Leixlip Castle.

Clonskeagh Castle had extensive grounds, which were developed in the 1930s to create Whitebeam Road and Whitethorn Road. A long avenue led from Clonskeagh Road through an impressive, arched entrance gate which had mock battlements and flanking walls with niches. This gateway, now vanished, stood directly opposite the equally imposing entrance to Richview, which now houses the Scjool of Architecture of UCD.

In the eighteenth century the castle was occupied by Henry Jackson who was the proprietor of the ironworks at Clonskeagh bridge. The ironworks stood on an island site, just upstream of the bridge, and were adjoined by a large millpond.

Jackson joined the United Irishmen and became involved with the rebellion of 1798, for which he was imprisoned. On his release he went to live in America – one of his descendants, General 'Stonewall' Jackson, became president of the United States. A later resident of Clonskeagh Castle was George Thompson, who was of a very different political colour to his predecessor, and was nicknamed locally 'The Priest-hunter Thompson' because he vigorously opposed the coming of nuns to nearby Milltown House! Thompson must have carried out many improvements to the castle, and was probably responsible for building a tower in the grounds overlooking the river Dodder. Now vanished, it was known as Thompson's Tower and appeared on the Ordnance Survey map of 1840.

Clonskeagh Castle, a Georgian house which was remodelled as a 'castle' in the nineteenth century

The impressive, nineteenth-century façade of Gledswood, with its unique cast-iron porch

There are several interesting old houses on the Clonskeagh Road. St Bridget's is an unusual eighteenth-century house which has been in office use as the headquarters of the P. V. Doyle Group for many years and is now in a rather run-down state. It has an exceptionally fine, cut-stone Georgian doorcase, which is rather strangely situated in the gable end of the building.

Roebuck House, well known in recent years as the home of Sean McBride, possesses the most magnificent, antique, cast-iron canopied balcony in the county. The house began as a small block, with a large addition being made on the garden front in about 1800. This extension, with its carved limestone cornice and half-octagonal bows, was carried out in a beautiful russet-coloured brick. To this, a delicate nine-arched, covered, iron balcony was added, probably at the same time. It is possible that this balcony was produced locally at Jackson's Ironworks in Clonskeagh, but the decorative panels are of a standard type which were widely available in the late Georgian period. A further extension was made to Roebuck House when, in about 1880, a new redbrick façade was erected to the front of the house.

An early nineteenth-century engraving of cottages at Clonskeagh

The principal drawing room, which overlooks the balcony and garden, is decorated in a modest manner, with attractive, late-Georgian-style plaster cornices and frieze, a dado rail of fluted pattern, and elegant chimneypiece. Baskets of flowers and emblems with crossed spears feature in the plasterwork frieze in the dining room.

Gledswood, which was formerly called Bloomville, is situated off Bird Avenue and is a distinguished house, though it is now sandwiched between later developments. The house was built around 1830 and has a handsome, semi-circular, timber porch, stone, arched bay windows and some very fine ironwork.

Belfield, UCD, with its bow-shaped garden front

University College Dublin Campus and Its Houses

The present university campus at Belfield is principally made up of a variety of modern purpose-built structures, erected during the last twenty-five years. However, UCD has had connections with Belfield since the 1930s, when its first properties were acquired here.

To its credit, the university has maintained most of the older houses which it inherited, and they are well maintained and fully utilised today. These include Belfield House, after which the campus is called, Merville House, Roebuck Castle, Ardmore, Wood View, Richview and Roebuck Grove, now the official residence of the college president.

Three other houses owned by UCD – Belgrove, Roebuck and Rosemount – were unfortunately demolished. The latter two were interesting Georgian houses situated in their own grounds.

Belfield was erected in 1790 for Peter Digges La Touche, a member of the wealthy Dublin banking family. Other La Touche houses included Marlay in Rathfarnham, Sans Souci in Booterstown and Bellevue in County Wicklow. For most of the nineteenth century Belfield was the home of the Wallace family, followed by Sir John Lynch, a solicitor, who sold it to the university in 1930.

Belfield is a remarkably compact and elegant house. It rises two-storeys-over-basement and has a tall, narrow wing to the side. A porch with Portland stone columns leads to a hallway of outstanding beauty, its apsidal recesses all decorated with delicate plasterwork of scrolls and foliage. Beyond we find an oval drawing room, whose ceiling has the same attractive plasterwork, and where the projecting windows of the bow offer fine views over Dublin Bay.

The outstanding plasterwork decoration of the hall and rooms at Belfield House

The neat staircase, with its inlaid, mahogany handrail, its clever planning and decorative quality, is so similar to Rosemount as to suggest that they were designed and erected by the same team.

A stableyard with arched, granite openings and doorways adjoins the house, while to the west is a formal sunken garden of box hedges, which is very well maintained.

Merville, a mid-eighteenth-century house on UCD grounds, is currently used by the bio-chemistry department and several additions have been made to what was originally an extensive private house. The house was built for the Right Hon. Anthony Foster in the middle of the eighteenth century. After his death in 1778, his son, the Speaker of the Irish House of Commons, lived there for some years. The house is approached from Foster's Avenue, where the family name is still commemorated.

The main house is seven windows wide with a handsome porch composed of four stone columns. A pair of bow-shaped rooms project to the back and have balconies at first-floor level.

The porch leads through a fine Georgian door, complete

An elevation of Merville House, drawn by J. Barker for the Fitzwilliam estate

Merville, viewed from the main avenue

with its eighteenth-century lock and large, decorative, fanlight window, into a spacious hall. On the ground floor are several elegant rooms and a staircase of generous proportions. Directly off the hall is a curious narrow room with a curved end and built-in cupboards.

Part of the original stableyard remains to the right of the house, as do the very high stone walls of the original garden. The gardens at Merville were famed for their roses, an ancient magnolia tree, and mulberry and fig trees. A more recent occupant, the Right Hon. William Baron Downes, maintained a large vinery as well. In the walled garden there was a square, three-storey tower, on top of which was a viewing platform and a small cupola. The gardens are fully described in an article in *Irish Life* magazine, published in 1913.

During the early part of this century, Merville was owned by the Hume Dudgeon family whose interest in horses was well known.

Rosemount The loss of Rosemount, an attractive, late eighteenth-century house, was unfortunate. It was a rare survivor – a completely unspoilt house of the Georgian period which was hidden from the surrounding suburbia and stood among meadows and mature trees. The small demesne, which still lies at the back of the campus, was planted in the late eighteenth century in a continuous belt around the house.

Rosemount was a two-storey-over-basement house, square in plan, with projecting bows both to the rear and to the side, and it even retained its early yellow-ochre, limewashed finish on the walls.

The plasterwork of the hall featured an eighteenth-century cornice and frieze with medallions of female heads and a delicate ceiling-rose. In about 1984, the house was vandalised and set on fire, all of the plasterwork was blackened and much was destroyed. Some of the decorative pieces were later salvaged

A plan of the Merville estate, by J. Barker, 1762, showing Foster's Avenue (top), the house with its wings, and the large, walled garden

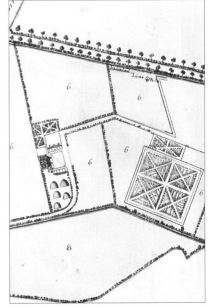

by this writer. An unusual feature of the hall was a built-in clock and two circular portraits, one of which depicted the famous lawyer John Philpot Curran – Rosemount was the home of a noted legal family, the Woolfe Flanagans, who owned it until its purchase by UCD in 1983.

The house had an elegant staircase with a coved ceiling and, at the entrance to the landing, a semi-circular, plaster plaque depicting a classical mother-and-child group. In the dining room were two arched niches, each decorated with delicate plaster swags and garlands, and made to take a pair of side-tables.

Downstairs, the high-ceilinged rooms of the kitchens and pantries were large and spacious, and had stone-flagged floors. Before demolition, all of the old Welsh slates were salvaged and re-used to restore the roof of Drimnagh Castle.

Roebuck Grove stood close to Rosemount, and was demolished in 1980 shortly after its acquisition by UCD.

It was built in 1792 and, though plain externally, was decorated internally with the most delicate plasterwork in the style of Robert Adam – the dining room with its oval ceiling featured an image of Leda being drawn on a little carriage by two swans. A fine, cut-stone, Georgian doorcase, of the type found in Merrion Square, graced the entrance. It was composed of four Ionic columns with a large fanlight and side lights.

Roebuck Castle When the Dutch artist Gabriel Beranger visited Roebuck in 1777, he found the ruins of a substantial medieval structure – a two-storey castle incorporating a gate-house, with various Gothic doorways and windows. The vaulted undercroft of this castle survives and was incorporated into a house built in the late eighteenth century by James Crofton. Crofton was one of the Kingstown Harbour Commissioners and his name is recorded on one of the seafront terraces.

Roebuck Castle is almost entirely a Victorian creation, built in an unusual Gothic style and featuring much elaborate stone carving. The hall

Rosemount: (top) the house in its rural setting; (above) a plaster medallion from the hall; (right) Rosemount shortly before its demolition in 1984

door, windows and great, treble-arched bay, with its pierced stone balcony, are all built of sandstone. The monogram of the Westby family, who rebuilt the castle in the nineteenth century, may be seen above the main entrance and their coat of arms also appears on either side of the first-floor bay. The spandrels of the Gothic windows are carved with naturalistic foliage and other decorative devices. Inside, there are several remarkable features, such as the canopied, medieval-style fireplace in the hall and a staircase made of pitch pine. The castle is now used by the faculty of law.

Roebuck Castle once possessed what could be considered to be the finest gate-lodge in County Dublin. This stone-built structure, which is possibly more appealing than the castle itself and was designed in a similar style, has recently been converted into a private house. It is a very striking building with its pointed, square tower and cut-stone work. The arched entrance gate with its wooden doors is flanked by stone buttresses, and there was accommodation for the gate-keeper in the gabled room upstairs, which bears the Westby coat of arms on its façade. Elsewhere on the gate-lodge the monogram EWP, which signifies Edward Percival Westby, and the date 1872 may be seen.

When the castle was sold in 1943, a ten-day auction took place, where everything, from an important collection of jewellery and silver down to a Ford van and an Austin Landaulette car, was sold. There was a large library of books, many carpets and quantities of antique furniture.

The imposing Roebuck Castle, which now houses the law faculty of UCD

The Westby monogram over the hall door at Roebuck Castle

Detail from the Westby coat of arms, from the gate-lodge on Roebuck Road

Masonic symbols in the mosaic floor at Richview, which are appropriate to the present occupation by the school of architecture, UCD

Richview is a late eighteenth-century house, whose Georgian features remain largely intact. The stone doorcase with its Ionic columns is unusual in having a decorative, scalloped arch above the fanlight. Inside, the rooms are bright and spacious, the drawing room having a decorated plaster ceiling, and some of the door surrounds are ornamented with gesso pilasters, typical of the 1790s.

The house was acquired by the Masonic School in 1885 and several additions were made. The school was founded to educate the sons of Freemasons, initially only those who were orphans, but the numbers quickly grew and by the 1890s there were up to a hundred pupils.

The Georgian house was quickly outgrown and many extensions were made in the latter years of the nineteenth century. New schoolrooms, a laboratory, an assembly hall and a new gymnasium were added. The main school building was of solid construction, and the date 1894 appears over the cut-stone, arched entrance and on an oak mantelpiece inside. In the keystone over the main entrance is a carving of a boy with flowing hair and wearing a Roman helmet. The mosaic hall floor bears various Masonic symbols.

In 1980 Richview was bought, along with seventeen acres, by UCD for about £2 million. The buildings were in a good state of repair and were adapted for use by the school of architecture.

CHAPTER 29

Churchtown

The area now known as Churchtown covers a densely built-up district mainly developed between 1950 and 1980. Churchtown, Baile an Team-paill, obviously derives its name from the presence of a church, most likely that of St Nahi's in Dundrum. The area covers the townlands of Churchtown Upper and Whitehall, and in 1816 there were few houses in the district with the exception of Landscape, Whitehall, Newtown, Belfield and Taney Lodge.

Whitehall, which is best known for its famous Bottle Tower, was once the site of an elegant Queen Anne-style house of the same name. An illustration of 1795 shows that it was a five-windowed house, three storeys high, with a sweeping Dutch gable and central pediment. The Bottle Tower, which may be seen to the left of the present modern house, is one of the most extraordinary structures in the county. The tower, along with a miniature companion tower, was built by Major Hall in the middle of the eighteenth century. Hall must have been inspired by Katherine Connolly's barns or follies, built during the 1740s at Castletown in County Kildare, as the design is almost identical. It is perhaps not a coincidence that the Connollys had bought Rathfarnham Castle, whose beautiful demesne was the immediate neighbour to the west of Whitehall.

An old photograph of the Bottle Tower at Whitehall

The larger tower, with its external, winding staircase, was probably used as a store for grain, while the smaller was designed as a dovecote or pigeon house. Though sometimes called Hall's Barn, it was generally known as the Bottle Tower. Some eighteenth-century bottles were slightly cone-shaped but, as James Howley points out in *The Follies and Garden Buildings of Ireland* (1993), the Bottle Tower most resembles the shape of the conical towers of old glassworks, which mostly produced bottles.

The house at Whitehall as depicted in Ball's History

Hazelbrook was the name of a farmhouse whose dairy, run by the Hughes family, gave its name to the well-known ice-cream brand HB, now taken over by Premier Dairies.

Berwick House is a small, three-storey, Georgian House with symmetrical wings. In 1895 a home established here by Henrietta

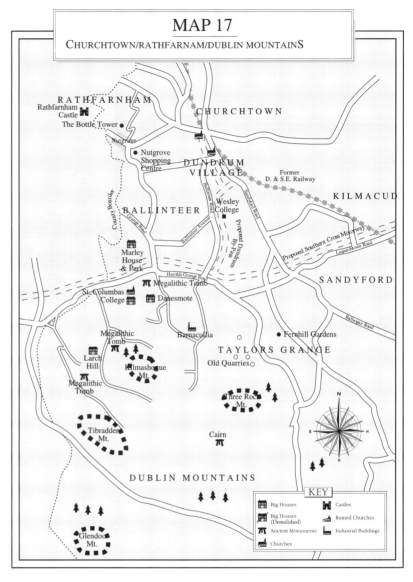

MAP 17
CHURCHTOWN/RATHFARNAM/DUBLIN MOUNTAINS

Berwick for working girls to go there for a retreat or a holiday – a inscription stone from here was later moved to the home's new premises in Dalkey.

Landscape House, surrounded by its many outbuildings and stables, was also a large dairy farm. In the middle of the nineteenth century it was occupied John Douglas, the founder of the well-known Douglas drapery firm in Wexford Street. The house, now long gone, gives its name to Landscape Park and other modern housing developments.

Nutgrove House stood at the end of Nutgrove Avenue and could be approached from the Rathfarnham side only. The house was a small, five-bay, early eighteenth-century residence with an impressive central pediment. It had an attractive bow to one side, containing rooms with extremely fine rococo plasterwork of mid-eighteenth-century date. The principal drawing room on the first floor had a heavy cornice and coved ceiling which was curved to fit the bow window. There was also fine compartmentalised plasterwork of the same date in other rooms. Nutgrove House was demolished in about 1970 and is now recalled only by Nutgrove Avenue and a modern shopping centre.

Churchtown Road was originally reached by taking the small road which passes in front of St Nahi's Church in Dundrum, as the present major junction of roads did not exist. Two Victorian houses – Woodville and Fern Bank – on the south side of the Churchtown Road, are now incorporated into the Convent and Schools of Notre Dame des Missions. Opposite

Nutgrove House, an early eighteenth-century house with exceptional plasterwork decoration

stands Wood Lawn, a large, eighteenth-century house which was re-modelled in Victorian times and was the home of the Woods family, founders of the firm Williams and Woods, makers of confectionery. Churchtown House, Churchtown Park, Ardtona and Glenshiel are worthy of mention as other large Victorian residences in the area. Belfield, a small Georgian house with an interesting interior, dating from about 1740, stands close to the present Statoil filling station. Weston House, which stood at the junction of Beaumont Avenue and Churchtown Road, was associated with the Franks family, who were involved with the once-famous Country Shop in St Stephen's Green. The Braemor Road takes its name from the builders Brady and Morton whose names were amalgamated to produce the name Braemor.

A house called Annaville in Churchtown was occupied in 1822 by Sir George Whiteford. A silk and poplin manufacturer, he was an Alderman of Dublin and was High Sheriff in 1821. He later became Lord Mayor of Dublin.

Nutgrove House interior – the drawing-room ceiling

Berwick House, a small, Georgian building once used as a place of retreat

CHAPTER 30

Rathfarnham

Duncan's map, 1821, showing the well-wooded demesne of Marlay

Part of Rathfarnham now lies within the new Dun Laoghaire-Rathdown County area, and includes a small area near Rathfarnham village, most of Marlay Park, and the two large houses, Danesmote and St Columba's College, on College Road. Kilmashogue and Larch Hill also lie within the county. This part of Rathfarnham takes in the townlands of Haroldsgrange, Taylorsgrange, Stackstown and Kilmashogue.

Just west of this artificial boundary is Rathfarnham Castle, which is one of the greatest architectural treasures of the Dublin area, and must be mentioned briefly. Though originally built as a fortified mansion in the sixteenth century, it was remodelled and lavishly redecorated in the 1760s and 1770s. Among the many fine interiors of the castle is the cold room with its gilded plasterwork and panels painted by Angelica Kauffman. The alterations to this room and to the hall and galley were designed by the architect James 'Athenian' Stuart, so called because of his love of Greek architecture. The castle, having been occupied by the Jesuit Order for almost a century, was put up for sale in 1985, and narrowly escaped having a housing estate built right up to its hall door. After considerable public pressure, the then Office of Public Works acquired the castle in 1987 for the nation and under their expert guidance Rathfarnham Castle is being slowly renovated and is open to the public.

The magnificent Marlay House, dating from the eighteenth century, is now being restored

Marlay House and Park is one of the largest eighteenth-century demesnes to remain intact in the entire county of Dublin. All of the original trees and planting survive intact and much of the original estate wall is also in place. The house, with its large stableyard and farmyards some way off, is also a perfect example of an eighteenth-century estate. A stream, known as the Little Dargle, flows into the demesne and supplies a small lake which once had a boathouse and still has a small island.

The park was opened to the public in 1975 and contains football pitches and a nine-hole golf course. It is now owned and maintained by Dun Laoghaire-Rathdown County Council. Although Marlay House and demesne were acquired by Dublin County Council in 1972 for just under £1 million for the purpose of providing a park and public playing fields, there were no immediate plans for the house – at one point during the 1970s it was proposed to demolish the magnificent building, which thankfully did not transpire. The decision to restore it was taken only five years ago and work continues with the benefit of a FÁS scheme, with most of the structural and decorative work now complete.

In about 1764 David La Touche purchased an old house on the Marlay site known as The Grange, which had been the property of Thomas Taylor, one-time Lord Mayor of Dublin. The

Interiors from Marlay House: (top) the elegant dining room; (above) the hall

Grange was an early house, possibly seventeenth-century, and parts of it may have been incorporated into the present building which La Touche rebuilt in 1794. La Touche married Elizabeth Marlay, daughter of the Bishop of Dromore, and renamed the house after her. He laid out the demesne and created Marlay House in its present form with its elegant rooms. A magnificent new ballroom facing the mountains, an oval music room and an elegant staircase were added to the house, and all of the rooms contain decorative plasterwork of high quality. Samuel Lewis, writing in 1838, states that the demesne contained about four hundred acres and that it was well stocked with extensive ranges of glasshouses. The La Touche family, who originally came from France as refugees, set up a business in High Street selling cambric and tabinet. In the early years of the eighteenth century they became involved in giving loans and investing money, which led to the establishment of the La Touche Bank, and in 1735 they acquired a business house in Castle Street, near Dublin Castle. The property remained in the La Touche family until 1864 when it was acquired by Robert Tedcastle, whose Dublin firm of coal merchants were once a household name.

There are many fine trees and woods in the Marlay demesne, and

The cottage orné in the woods at Marlay

hidden in the trees lies a small, gable-fronted house known as Laurelmere, which probably dates from the early eighteenth century. Though it has an early Georgian entrance, the house was remodelled as a Victorian 'cottage orné', with Tudor-style windows and fancy bargeboards.

The eastern fringe of Marlay, which runs along by Grange Road, was once dotted with several smaller, eighteenth-century houses, including Elm Park, Grange House, Highfield Manor, Rathfarnham Park and Eden. Eden, a mid-eighteenth-century house of some interest, has been converted into a pub, while Highfield and Grange House have both disappeared. Elm Park, a late eighteenth-century house, has been somewhat altered through its conversion into apartments, with the addition of an extra wing to the south side. The house, which has a particularly fine Portland stone portico composed of four columns, was owned by the Servite Order during the last thirty years. It was used as a residence for their students.

Highfield Manor was another late-Georgian house which once stood on about sixteen acres of land at Grange Road. It was a double bow-ended house and had a small farm, a walled garden and an orchard. It is now the site of an estate of houses.

Danesmote is a mid-eighteenth-century house, which was probably enlarged at the end of the Georgian period. The front portion, which is two-storeys-over-basement, five windows wide and has an attractive stone doorcase, contains rococo plasterwork in the principal upstairs bedroom. A particularly fine ice house, which stands quite close to the house, remains intact.

In 1838 Samuel Lewis noted the demesne of Glen Southwell (now known as Danesmote). He says it was also called Little Dargle because this small stream flows through the demesne, which was carefully planted in the eighteenth century and laid out with rustic follies, bridges and grottoes. The bridge is composed of random pieces of rock, carefully put together to create the impression of a 'natural' occurrence, and it conveys the visitor over a small rocky gorge to a woodland where there are more structures of a similar kind. Glen Southwell belonged to

Elm Park before its conversion into apartments

The rustic bridge at Danesmote

Charles Ponsonby Esq. in the early nineteenth century and Lewis informs us that the grounds were open to visitors.

Like its neighbour, Hollypark (St Columba's College), Danesmote enjoys an elevated site, and is surrounded by trees and parkland. Unfortunately the lower part of the property, which is the location of the monument, is now developed with houses and will be traversed by the new motorway. The building of houses above the line of the Southern Cross motorway is regrettable, as it allows the suburban sprawl to encroach on the Dublin mountains and slowly diminish the city's much-needed open space.

Danesmote

St Columba's College, which stands above Marlay demesne on College Road, is housed in a magnificent eighteenth-century house. Originally called Hollypark, the house was built in about 1740, and was the home of Lundy Foot, a snuff manufacturer based in Parliament Street.

It is a large, two-storey-over-basement, square house of generous proportions, with a façade seven windows wide and graced by a substantial portico. The plasterwork decoration of the ceilings in the principal reception rooms is unusual as it features eighteenth-century sailing ships, perhaps reflecting the Foot family's interest in trade. The house also contains some magnificent carved woodwork of continental origin and a series of very fine tapestries. Hollypark was acquired from Jeffrey Foot by the founders of St Columba's College who had visited it in 1848, and the house became the residence of the warden or headmaster of the school.

The school, which was founded in 1843 and operated at first in Stackallan House, County Meath, moved to Rathfarnham in 1849. The fifty-acre estate originally included a deer park which ran up on to the mountainside. In the nineteenth century the college possessed a genuine relic of St Columba, hence the name of the school. The relic consisted of a magnificent work of medieval Irish art called the Moiseach, and is now in the National Museum of Ireland. In 1849 the college set about erecting new school buildings to accommodate their students, and a chapel, of plain rectangular shape with three east windows in the Gothic style, was also added. In 1879 a new chapel was built to the design of William Butterfield.

The school today enjoys the magnificent grounds, trees and mountainside, along with three fine gardens which adjoin the house and are

The beautiful Georgian Gothic staircase window at Danesmote

St Columba's College, formerly Hollypark, built about 1740

Continental carved oak at St Columba's

A plasterwork ship from the ceiling at St Columba's

surrounded by high granite walls. Many of the old stables and farm buildings have been converted to new uses, either for classrooms, study rooms or for accommodation. There were originally two separate entrances on College Road, but, with the construction of the motorway through the grounds, a new access road has been provided at Kilmashogue Lane. The old gate-lodges on College Road will disappear as the building of the new Southern Cross motorway will mean the destruction of the original entrances and the removal of a number of trees along College Road.

The new entrance to St Columba's stands almost directly opposite an interesting pair of old mill buildings at Kilmashogue. The stone buildings, now completely roofless, were recorded by Archer in 1801 as a corn mill, but some fifty years later they were in use as a woollen-cloth mill.

The Kilmashogue Lane leads up into the valley which separates Tibradden Mountain and Kilmashogue mountain.

An eighteenth-century house called Larch Hill was built here by the Caldbeck family in an estate of about 90 acres. The old house, which appears to have been rather plain, has gone and the beautifully wooded grounds are now used by the Catholic Boy Scouts for summer camps. Here in the grounds are the massive stones of the collapsed Larch Hill cromlech. The Dublin mountains offer much evidence of pre-historic or early settlement in the area, and there is a wedge-shaped gallery grave on Kilmashogue and a passage grave on Tibradden.

In 1837 Eugene Curry noted the proliferation of stone enclosures at Ballybetagh near The Scalp on Newtown Hill at Kilternan, and he recorded a burial site which locals then called 'The Giant's Grave' near Glencullen village on Two Rock Mountain. There are also several examples of ring forts or raths at Barnacullia and Ballyedmonduff. From the earliest cromlechs of Kilternan and Danesmote to the burial sites at Tibradden and Two Rock Mountain, the Dublin mountains can trace a long history of human occupation.

Bibliography

An Act for ... Improving the Town of Kingstown (drawn up by Pierce Mahony, Solicitors), 1834.

Archer, J., *A Statistical Survey of County Dublin*, 1801.

Archer, Stella, and Pearson, Peter, *The Royal St George Yacht Club*, 1987.

Ball, F.E., *A History of County Dublin*, 1902-20.

Ball, F.E. and Hamilton, E., *The Parish of Taney*, 1895.

Ballybrack I.C.A., *The Granite Hills*, 1980.

Bayley Butler, B., *The Dublin Historical Record*, (John and Edward Lees).

Blacker, B.H., *Brief Sketches of the Parishes of Booterstown and Donnebrook*, 1860.

Blacker, B.H., *Sketches of Irish Churches*.

Blackrock Society, The, (journals) 1992-1998.

Boylan, Harry, *A Dictionary of Irish Biography*, 1979.

Bray Historical Society Journal, The, (various).

Brewer, J.N., *The Beauties of Ireland*, 1826.

Cooper, Austin, *An Eighteenth Century Antiquary*, Ed. Liam Price, 1942.

Costello, Peter, *Dublin Churches*, 1989.

Craig, Maurice, *Classic Irish Houses of the Middle Size*, 1976.

Cromwell, T., *Excursions through Ireland* (with engravings by G. Petrie), 1820.

Curran, C.P., *Dublin Decorative Plasterwork*, 1967.

Curry, W., *The Picture of Dublin*, 1835.

D'Alton, J., *The History of the County of Dublin*, 1838.

Delany, V.T.H., *Christopher Palles*, 1960.

Donnelly, Nicholas, *Short Histories of Dublin Parishes*.

Dublin and Kingstown Railway Company, *Proceedings of the Directors*, 1842.

Dublin Builder, The, 1857-1966.

Dublin Penny Journal, The, 1835.

Dun Laoghaire Historical Society Journal, The, (various) 1990-1998.

Dun Laoghaire Methodist Church, 1836-1986.

Duncan, *W., Map of County Dublin*, 1821.

Enoch, V., *Martello Towers of Ireland*, 1974.

Flanagan, Bonnie, *Stately Homes Around Stillorgan*, 1991.

Foxrock Local History Club, journals (various).

Frazer, J., *Handbook to Ireland*, 1844.

Gaskin, J.J., *Varieties of Irish History*, 1869.

Gilbert, John, *History of Dublin*, 1861.

Goodbody, Olive, *One Hundred Years of A-Growing*, 1979.

Goodbody, R., *On the Borders of the Pale*, 1993.

Griffith, R., *Survey and Valuation of the Barony of Rathdown*, 1849.

Grose, F., *The Antiquities of Ireland*, 1791.

Haliday, C., *Pamphlet on the Sanitary State of Kingstown*, 1844.

Hall, S.C. (Mrs), *Ireland, Its Scenery and Character*, 1846.

Hamilton, M., *Green and Gold*, 1948.

Harbison, Peter, *Beranger's Views of Ireland*, 1991.

Harbison, Peter, *Guide to the National Monuments of Ireland*, 1970.

Harden, R., *St. Johns, Monkstown*, 1911.

Harrison, Richard, *A Biographical Dictionary of Irish Quakers*, 1997.

Hill, *Guide to Blackrock*, 1892.

Horner, Arnold, and Simms, Anngret, Essays by, *Dublin – From Pre-history to Present,* 1992.

Ingram, John A., *The Cure of Souls,* 1997.

Irish Builder, The, 1867-1930.

Jackson, Patrick Wyse, and Falkiner, Ninian, *A Portrait of St Columba's College* 1843-1993.

Joyce, Weston St John., *The Neighbourhood of Dublin,* 1912.

Kingstown Harbour Commissioners, *Minute Books,* 1815-1836 (Public Record Office).

Knaggs, Robert, *Booterstown and Careysfort – A Parochial History,* 1984.

Lewis, S., *Topographical Dictionary of Ireland,* 1837.

Mac Cóil, Liam, *The Book of Blackrock,* 1977.

Manning, Con, (Ed.), *Dublin and Beyond the Pale, Studies in Honour of Patrick Healy,* 1998.

Monkstown Parish History, 1968.

Murray, K.A., 'Dun Laoghaire and the Railway', *Journal of Irish Railway Records Society.*

Murray, Kevin, *Ireland's First Railway,* 1981.

Nolan, J., *Changing Faces,* 1982.

O'Dwyer, Frederick, *Lost Dublin,* 1981.

O'Dwyer, Frederick, *The Architecture of Deane and Woodward,* 1997.

O'Keeffe, Peter, and Simington, Tom, *Irish Stone Bridges,* 1991.

O'Kelly, Gerard, *Titania's Palace and the Mount Merrion Connection,* 1997.

O'Malley, Mary Pat, *Lios an Uisce,* 1981.

O'Sullivan and Cannon, *The Book of Dun Laoghaire,* 1987.

Ordnance Survey, The, *Maps of County Dublin,* 1843, 1869 and 1912.

Porter, F., *Post Office Guide and Directory of Kingstown,* 1911.

Powell, G.R., *The Official Railway Handbook to Bray, Kingstown etc. ...,* 1860.

Power, Frank, and Pearson, Peter, *The Forty Foot, A Monument to Sea Bathing,* 1995.

Purcell, Mary, *A Time for Sowing,* 1979.

Riain, Ide ní, *A Short History of Mount Anville,* 1987.

Robertson, Manning, *Dun Laoghaire, Its History, Scenery and Development,* 1936.

Ronan, Myles, 'Stones from the Dún of Dún Laoghaire', *Journal of the Royal Society of Antiquaries of Ireland,* Vol. 62, 1932.

Rutty, J., *A Natural History of County Dublin,* 1772.

Ryan, Nicholas, *Sparkling Granite,* 1992.

Scott, Canon G.D., *The Stones of Bray,* 1913.

Seaman, A., *Considerations for a Harbour,* 1811.

Shepherd, Ernie, *Behind the Scenes,* 1983.

Simms, G.O., *Tullow's Story,* 1983.

Smith, Charles, *Dalkey, A Small Medieval Irish Town,*

Smith, Charles, *The Townland of Kilmacud*

Smith, Cornelius, *Stillorgan Park Golf Club,* 1982.

Smyth, Hazel, *The Town of the Road,* 1971.

St Michael's Church Dun Laoghaire, 1973.

Stratten, *Dublin and Cork, A Literary, Social and Commercial Review,* 1892.

Taylor, A., *Survey of County Dublin,* 1816.

Thom, A., *Statistics of the British Isles,* 1855.

Thom's Directory (various).

Tillyard, Stella, *Citizen Lord,* 1997.

Toutcher, R. Capt., 'Documents relating to the intended harbour ... Eastwards of Dunleary', 1807-1826 (ms. in National Library).

'Town's Survey', *The Dublin Builder,* No. 5, 1862.

Turner, Kathleen, *If You Seek Monuments.*

Turner, Kathleen, *Rathmichael, A Parish History,* 1987.

Turpin, John, *John Hogan*, 1982.
Wakeman, W.F., *Handbook of Irish Antiquities*, 1848.
Wakeman, W.F., *Tourist's Guide through Dublin and its Interesting Suburbs*, 1865.
Walker's Hibernian Magazine, 1802.
Wall, Mervyn, *The Forty Foot*, 1962.
Wilson's Directory.
Wright, G.N., *An Historical Guide to Ancient and Modern Dublin*, 1821.
Young, A., *A Tour of Ireland*, 1779.

Index